Lecture Notes in Computer Science 5063

Commenced Publication in 1973
Founding and Former Series Editors:
Gerhard Goos, Juris Hartmanis, and Jan van Leeuwen

T0223231

Antonio Vallecillo   Jeff Gray
Alfonso Pierantonio (Eds.)

Theory and Practice
of Model Transformations

First International Conference, ICMT 2008
Zürich, Switzerland, July 1-2, 2008
Proceedings

 Springer

Volume Editors

Antonio Vallecillo
University of Málaga
Bulevar Louis Pasteur 35
29071 Málaga, Spain
E-mail: av@lcc.uma.es

Jeff Gray
University of Alabama at Birmingham
126 Campbell Hall, 1300 University Blvd
Birmingham, AL 35294, USA
E-mail: gray@cis.uab.edu

Alfonso Pierantonio
Università degli Studi dell'Aquila
Via Vetoio, Loc. Coppito
67100 L'Aquila, Italia
E-mail: alfonso@di.univaq.it

Library of Congress Control Number: 2008929583

CR Subject Classification (1998): D.2, D.3, D.4.8, F.3, I.6, K.6, C.4

LNCS Sublibrary: SL 2 – Programming and Software Engineering

ISSN   0302-9743
ISBN-10   3-540-69926-0 Springer Berlin Heidelberg New York
ISBN-13   978-3-540-69926-2 Springer Berlin Heidelberg New York

Springer is a part of Springer Science+Business Media

springer.com

© Springer-Verlag Berlin Heidelberg 2008
Printed in Germany

Typesetting: Camera-ready by author, data conversion by Scientific Publishing Services, Chennai, India
Printed on acid-free paper   SPIN: 12324378   06/3180   5 4 3 2 1 0

Preface

Models have become essential for dealing with the numerous aspects involved in developing and maintaining complex IT systems. Models allow capturing of the relevant aspects of a system from a given perspective, and at a precise level of abstraction. In addition to models, the transformations between them are other key elements in model-driven engineering. Model transformations allow the definition and implementation of the operations on models, and also provide a chain that enables the automated development of a system from its corresponding models. Furthermore, model transformations may be realized using models, and are, therefore, an integral part of any model-driven approach.

There are already several proposals for model transformation specification, implementation and execution, which are beginning to be used by modeling practitioners. However, model transformations need specialized support in several aspects in order to realize their full potential. The problem goes beyond having specific languages to represent model transformations; we also need to understand their foundations, such as the key concepts and operators supporting those languages, their semantics, and their structuring mechanisms and properties (e.g., modularity, composability and parametrization). In addition, model transformations can be stored in repositories as reusable assets, where they can be managed, discovered and reused. There is also a need to chain and combine model transformations in order to produce new and more powerful transformations, and to be able to implement new operations on models. Finally, model transformations need methodology support, i.e., they need to be integrated into software development methodologies supported by appropriate tools and environments. These issues and concerns define the focus of these proceedings.

The inaugural International Conference on Model Transformations (ICMT 2008) was held in early July 2008 in Zurich, Switzerland. The conference was conducted in collaboration with the TOOLS 2008 conference. ICMT followed the success of two previous tracks on Model Transformation at the ACM Symposium on Applied Computing (SAC): MT 2006 at Dijon, France, and MT 2007 at Seoul, Korea. This first ICMT conference brought together researchers and practitioners to share experiences in using model transformations. Like its SAC predecessors, ICMT 2008 combined a strong practical focus with the theoretical approach required in any discipline that supports engineering practices.

ICMT 2008 received 54 abstract submissions of which 48 were submitted as full papers. The Program Committee suggested 17 papers for presentation and inclusion in these proceedings. This corresponds to a 35% acceptance rate, which indicates the level of competition that occurred during the selection process. All submissions were peer-reviewed by at least three members of the ICMT 2008 Program Committee, with many papers receiving four reviews. Submissions and the reviewing process were administered by EasyChair, which greatly facilitated these tasks.

The resulting program reflects the fact that the topic of model transformations encompasses many different aspects. This includes different issues related with: process and engineering of model transformations; model transformations supporting concurrency and time; matching and mapping within model transformation rules; language support for model transformation reuse and modularity; and correctness and analysis of model transformations. All of these categories of interest are included as technical sessions of the final program.

The ICMT 2008 program also included the keynote talk "Model Transformation: Sketching the Landscape" by Krzysztof Czarnecki, from the Electrical and Computer Engineering Department at the University of Waterloo. We thank him very much for accepting our invitation.

We especially devote a special thanks to the members of the Program Committee for doing an excellent job reviewing the submitted papers. Their dedicated work was instrumental in putting together a high-quality ICMT conference. Our appreciation extends to Richard Paige for his assistance in coordinating this first conference with TOOLS 2008, and to Bertrand Meyer and Jean Bézivin for helping us co-locate both events in a seamless and natural manner. The success of the conference is in great part due to them. In particular, Jean was one of the creators of this conference, and his great ideas, global view of the discipline and vision of the future have been decisive in its conception and realization. Finally, we would also like to thank the local organizers (Claudia Günthart, Manuel Oriol and Marco Piccioni) at the Swiss Federal Institute of Technology (ETH) in Zurich, for their continuous support and great help with all logistic issues.

Additional information concerning the conference (e.g., photos of the event) is available at http://www.model-transformation.org/ICMT2008/.

July 2008

Jeff Gray
Alfonso Pierantonio
Antonio Vallecillo

Organization

Conference Chair

Alfonso Pierantonio   Università degli Studi dellAquila (Italy)

Program Chairs

Jeff Gray   University of Alabama at Birmingham (USA)
Antonio Vallecillo   Universidad de Málaga (Spain)

Program Committee

Luciano Baresi   Politecnico di Milano (Italy)
Arne Berre   Sintef (Norway)
Jordi Cabot   Open University of Catalonia (Spain)
Tony Clark   Ceteva, Ltd.
Charles Consel   INRIA / LaBRI (France)
Steve Cook   Microsoft (UK)
Krzysztof Czarnecki   University of Waterloo (Canada)
Davide Di Ruscio   Università degli Studi dell'Aquila (Italy)
Gregor Engels   University of Paderborn (Germany)
Antonio Estevez   Open Canarias (Spain)
Jean-Marie Favre   University of Grenoble (France)
Robert France   Colorado State University (USA)
Jesús García-Molina   Universidad de Murcia (Spain)
Piero Fraternali   Politecnico di Milano (Italy)
Martin Gogolla   University of Bremen (Germany)
Catherine Griffin   IBM (UK)
Reiko Heckel   University of Leicester (United Kingdom)
Simon Helsen   SAP (Germany)
Howard Ho   IBM Almaden Research (USA)
Frédéric Jouault   INRIA/University of Alabama at Birmingham
Gerti Kappel   Technical University Vienna (Austria)
Gabor Karsai   Vanderbilt University (USA)
Günter Kniesel   University of Bonn (Germany)
Nora Koch   Ludwig-Maximilians-Universität München and FAST
    (Germany)
Vinay Kulkarni   Tata Research Development and Design Centre
    (India)
Ivan Kurtev   University of Twente (Netherlands)
Michael Lawley   Queensland University of Technology (Australia)

Esperanza Marcos	Universidad Rey Juan Carlos (Spain)
Tom Mens	University of Mons-Hainaut (Belgium)
Ana Moreira	Universidade Nova de Lisboa (Portugal)
Elie Najm	ENST (France)
Richard Paige	University of York (UK)
Marc Pantel	University of Toulouse (France)
Vicente Pelechano	Universidad Politécnica de Valencia (Spain)
Ivan Porres	Åbo Akademi (Finland)
Kerry Raymond	Queensland University of Technology (Australia)
Gianna Reggio	Università di Genova (Italiy)
Nicolas Rouquette	NASA/JPL (USA)
Bernhard Rumpe	TU Braunschweig (Germany)
Andy Schürr	Technische Universität Darmstadt (Germany)
Bran Selic	IBM (Canada)
Maarten Steen	Telematica Instituut (The Netherlands)
Gabriele Taentzer	Philipps-Universität Marburg (Germany)
Yasemin Topaloglu	Ege University (Turkey)
Laurence Tratt	Bournemouth University (UK)
Hans Vangheluwe	McGill University (Canada)
Dániel Varró	University of Budapest (Hungary)
Jens Weber	University of Victoria (Canada)
Jon Whittle	Lancaster University (UK)
Ed Willink	Thales Research (UK)
Andreas Winter	Johannes Gutenberg-Universität Mainz (Germany)

Local Organization

Claudia Günthart	ETH Zurich (Switzerland)
Manuel Oriol	ETH Zurich (Switzerland)
Marco Piccioni	ETH Zurich (Switzerland)

External Reviewers

Bogdan Alexe	Lex Heerink
Orlando Ávila García	Ákos Horváth
Alexej Beresnev	Maria-Eugenia Iacob
Kirsten Berkenkütter	Horst Kargl
Damien Cassou	Dimitrios Kolovos
Antonio Cicchetti	Mirco Kuhlmann
Oguz Dikenelli	Juan de Lara
Zoe Drey	Julien Mercadal
Florian Fieber	Marc Pantel
Hans Groenniger	Paolo Papotti
Ulrich Hannemann	Francesco Parisi-Presicce

Table of Contents

Process and Engineering of Model Transformations

Model Transformations Supporting Concurrency and Time

Matching and Mapping within Model Transformation Rules

Language Support for Model Transformation Reuse and Modularity

Correctness and Analysis of Model Transformations

Transformations Have to be Developed ReST Assured

Mika Siikarla[1], Markku Laitkorpi[2], Petri Selonen[2], and Tarja Systä[1]

[1] Tampere University of Technology,
Department of Software Systems
`first.last@tut.fi`
[2] Nokia Research Center
`first.last@nokia.com`

Abstract. Model transformations do not simply appear. They have to be not-so-simply developed. In early phases of development, there may exist only an intuition or an educated guess on some of the characteristics of the transformation. Instead of assuming a pre-existing complete transformation specification, we embrace change and develop transformations incrementally, gradually refining them into more complete ones as the body of knowledge of the domain grows. We present an iterative process encompassing requirements capture, design and implementation of model transformations. We describe partial transformations as so called transformational patterns and iteratively refine them. We apply the approach to developing a transformation that is used in building APIs that comply with the ReST architectural style.

1 Introduction

Model transformations are software. Developing transformations has the same inherent challenges as developing any kind of software. Transformations have to be designed, implemented and tested. But even more fundamentally, we do not always have a precise, complete or stable specification to begin with and crafting such a specification is not trivial. An application developer with proper domain knowledge can manually create a target model based on a source model. He can probably even come up with some of the most often used rules of thumb for the transformations. However, defining a complete mapping from all possible source models to target models is remarkably harder.

The amount of resources that can be used in developing a transformation is constrained by the expected gains. A transformation facilitating the application of a large-scale product line affects savings in each application project, thus the investment into transformation development can be substantial. In small single-product and one-time software projects the development resources are much tighter constrained. Fortunately, a transformation does not need to replace the application developer to produce gains, it only needs to assist him. An incomplete or partially manual transformation may be much cheaper than a complete one.

An incremental approach enables building only as much of the transformation as is understood and needed at each point, instead of trying to nail down the

A. Vallecillo, J. Gray, A. Pierantonio (Eds.): ICMT 2008, LNCS 5063, pp. 1–15, 2008.

requirements and build a complete transformation from the start. Incorporating human interaction in the transformation enables outlining a rough but useful transformation early on. Such a transformation stays usable the whole time while it is being iteratively and incrementally refined. The development can be stopped when the allocated resources have been used up or when further refining no longer yields significant gains. This may mean that even the finished transformation is incomplete or contains human interaction.

We present a systematic, iterative and incremental process for model transformation development including the process phases, artifacts, roles and communication between the roles. In particular, we propose to use what we call transformational patterns to capture the domain knowledge and to facilitate communication between the domain and transformation experts. A transformational pattern is a transformation mechanism independent description of a solution to a reoccurring sub-transformation. Our process can be used with any transformation mechanism that provides some way to incorporate human interaction in transformations. With a small industrial case, we show how our process works in practise. The case also demonstrates some practical reasons why specifying and building even a rather limited transformation requires effort.

The context for our case is developing ReSTful service APIs that follow the Representational State Transfer (ReST) [1] architectural style. API specifications have to be transformed into more detailed models for implementing the services. When gathering the transformation requirements, the ReST domain expert was able to give examples on how to transform some incomplete source models into target models. However, he was not able to define a complete transformation for generating target models for arbitrary APIs. Therefore, we captured his implicit expert knowledge into initially incomplete transformational patterns and refined them as the understanding of the problem grew along the way.

The process and the roles are described in Sec. 2 along with related work. Sec. 3 explains the ReST context and background. The story of developing one of the transformations in the ReST development is told in Sec. 4. Finally, Sec. 5 summarizes and discusses the lessons learned and future work.

2   Developing Transformations

Surprisingly little work has been done on how model transformations should be developed. In [2], Mellor and Watson examine how the roles in software development processes change when applying MDA. They focus on the development of the software product and do not look more closely on the new roles needed for developing the transformations. They extend the traditional role of a software architect with the responsibility to select the right models and mappings between them. They point out that managing future changes in an MDA process mostly deals with changing the models, rather than maintaining the code. We treat the construction of a transformation system as a software project of its own right and separate the roles of the application and transformation developers.

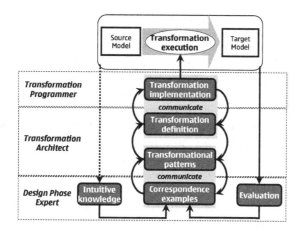

Fig. 1. Transformation development cycle and participating roles

The importance of traceability and communication among participants in the model-driven life cycle is put forward by Hailpern and Tarr in [3]. They claim that different types of models require different types of skills. They further point out that the relationships between multiple types of models, and different modeling formalisms, suggest that any single stakeholder can not understand all the impacts of a proposed change. We also suggest that different types of expertise is needed to build a transformation system. Further, we feel one can not assume that stakeholders use the same modeling notations or even that the models are at the same level of preciseness. We believe that construction of a transformation requires constant feedback from its practical applications. Thus, we adopt an iterative and incremental approach to developing model transformations.

Based on the different kinds of expertise required, we present the roles *Design Phase Expert*, *Transformation Architect*, and *Transformation Programmer*. Application development is not done in one monolithic design step, but in several consecutive design phases. Design Phase Expert has thorough—although partially implicit—knowledge related to a specific design phase and is capable of judging the work quality of other designers. He is responsible for the transformation functionality. Transformation Architect has deep understanding of transformation design and the chosen mechanisms. He is responsible for the transformation design. Transformation Programmer knows the transformation tool and can write transformation code. He is responsible for the quality of the transformation implementation. A single person can play multiple roles if they have the necessary expertise.

The cyclical transformation development process is illustrated in Fig. 1. The artifacts created and refined in the process are shown as blocks. The artifacts and the associated roles are connected with a shaded area. Naturally, there is a separate instance of the process for each design phase in application development.

In the beginning of a transformation development cycle, the Design Phase Expert provides *correspondence examples*. A correspondence example captures parts of the expert's intuitive knowledge by describing structures in well-designed target models that should result from the given source model fragment. At first, the examples are necessarily vague and do not cover all corresponding source and target model structures. Some of them might be too general or unnecessarily specific, and they can contain variation points and redundancy. A correspondence example consists of a source model fragment and a target model fragment. A model fragment is given in the notation used for the model, e.g. UML class diagrams. The notations for the source and target model fragments can be different. The correspondence examples are used for communication between people, so they do not need to be well-defined or unambiguous.

Next, the Design Phase Expert and the Transformation Architect form *transformational patterns* based on the correspondence examples. A transformational pattern is a transformation mechanism independent description of how and when one recurring partial transformation in this design phase is performed. It contains enough information for an application designer to apply it manually. Note, that transformational patterns are not related to transformation design in general (like transformation design patterns [4]), but to a single design phase.

We do not fix a format, but we follow loosely the sections Gamma *et al.* [5] suggest for design patterns. *Applicability* describes situations in which the pattern is usable, e.g. "for important superclasses". The conditions can be structural ("superclass") or non-structural ("important") and they may be informal ("important"). *Implementation* describes how the pattern is applied and it may contain variation, like "make *one* of the classes abstract". Since transformational patterns are not as general as design patterns, our Implementation covers Implementation, Structure, Participants and Collaboration in [5]. When the pattern matures, *Name, Intent, Forces* and *Consequences* may be added.

The Transformation Architect and the Transformation Programmer create a *transformation definition* from the transformational patterns. Transformation definition is transformation mechanism specific and defines the high-level structure and behaviour of the transformation code. Depending on the transformation mechanism, this precedence and default rules and sub-transformations. Possible informal parts in the transformational patterns are turned into user decisions. The transformation programmer creates the *transformation implementation* based on the transformation definition.

Once the transformation implementation is available, it is executed on selected reference source models and the execution and results are evaluated by the Design Phase Expert. In the next iteration, the correspondence examples and transformational patterns are refined and new ones are created based on the feedback. Our approach facilitates early prototyping, which can lead to fast discovery of new insight. We encourage starting with a loose transformation and modeling all unknown and/or undecided aspects as user decisions.

The use of examples for driving the transformation development brings our approach close to the model transformation by example (MTBE) approaches. Varró and Balogh [6] and, independently, Wimmer *et al.* [7] propose to use pairs of corresponding complete source and target models to semi-automatically generate a model transformation implementation. Their motivation, like ours, is for the domain expert to be able to express the transformation declaratively in the domain language (source and target models) without having to learn metamodels or transformation languages. Another similarity is their emphasis on iterative and interactive development process.

As a difference, their focus is on automatic transformations between models containing the same information in different forms. We allow interactive and even incomplete transformations. To facilitate some automation in transformation generation, MTBE examples are pairs of complete models, whereas we use pairs of partial models to represent rules of thumb. Since the transformations are (mostly) generated, there is little focus on the design and structure of the actual transformations. Although our process does not go into details about transformation design either, we do think there is need for design. Because the MTBE approaches use complete models, those models can also be used as preliminary automatic test material. In our approach, the partial models are not immediately suited for testing. We use the manual feedback and evaluation as development-time testing.

3   Transformation-Assisted Design of ReSTful Services

ReST is an architectural style for the software-driven Web, primarily considering the Web as a platform for network-based applications. The main concept is a *resource*, which serves as a key abstraction for any relevant information. In addition, ReST defines principled *constraints* that describe the possible relationships between resources and other architectural elements. ReST constraints facilitate imposing architectural properties like scalability, evolvability, visibility, and serendipity, making ReST an attractive choice when designing service APIs. For example, the *uniform interface* constraint dictates a fixed, context-independent set of operations uniformly exposed by all the resources in the system. Invoking the HTTP GET operation to browse from one site to another is a solid example of serendipity that chimes in the success of the Web as a distributed system.

Although developing ReSTful services is fundamentally simple—ReST constraints effectively limit the number of design decisions—we see that coming up with proper ReST designs is far from trivial. We believe that a major difficulty lies in the long tradition of object-orientation in software engineering. As a direct

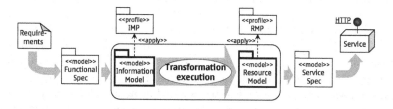

Fig. 2. A model-driven approach to ReSTful service development

opposite of hiding data with custom operations, in a resource-oriented mindset relevant information is exposed for direct manipulation. Our model-driven transformation approach aims to steer service developers to focus on the "right thing" while striving for the best possible outcome from a ReST point of view.

In our earlier work [8], we explored a similar approach on migrating legacy APIs to ReSTful services. We recognized the main phases and kinds of expertise that appear essential in developing ReSTful services. In Fig. 2, each block arrow represents a model-driven design phase that can be potentially assisted by model transformations. We focus on the step between an information model and a resource model. As a concrete service example, we take the Photo API, an experimental photo storage service prototyped at Nokia Research Center.

As we have no predefined profiles for the information and resource models, we start with guesses for these models. Our main goal is to eventually formalize our intuitive domain knowledge in the form of model transformations.

Functional specification. The requirements—typically in form of use cases—are collected and formalized into a functional specification. We begin with high-level requirements for the Photo API. A simplified version of the service is:

> The Photo API allows a user to store, retrieve and delete photos on a server. Each photo has an id. Photos can have attributes that define some predefined properties, and they can be tagged.

Information Model. The initial input from functional requirements is refined to an information model. The application domain expertise is captured in transformations that turn the problem domain knowledge into information content. The resulting operation-free, noun-centric view (see [8]) distills the key concepts and their relationships, comprising concept-level requirements derived from high level use cases.

Information model represents all relevant *nouns* and their *relationships* in the domain, so using class diagrams is an obvious choice. One specific issue is how the properties of each concept are modeled. Properties that are accessed independently should be represented as stand-alone classes. Similarly, properties should be modeled as stand-alone classes if the physical appearance is heterogeneous, e.g. some properties are binary, some are structural, and some are of simple data types. Elements that are not in the part role of a composite aggregation represent the core concepts of the domain. `Photo` and `Property` are the core concepts in the information model fragment on the left-hand side of Fig. 3.

Resource Model. The information model is transformed into a resource model. ReST expertise is captured in transformations that produce a resource-oriented view of the information content. This view enforces the structural constraints of the ReST architectural style on the target service. The resulting model represents the connected set of the resources to be exposed as a ReSTful service.

The resource model represents the *hierarchical resource structure* to be directly exposed as an HTTP-based interface following the Web Architecture [9].

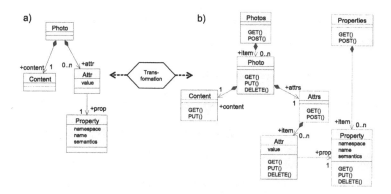

Fig. 3. Example a) information and b) resource model fragments

Again, a class diagram is an obvious choice. Our initial guess comprises two kinds of resources: *containers* and *items*. A container represents (the state of) a collection of individual resources and can be used to list the existing items or create new ones. An item represents (the state of) an individual resource that can be retrieved, rewritten, or removed. The initially allowed relationship types between resources are *subordinate* containment and navigable *reference*. The former is a strong link with a lifetime dependency, whereas the latter is a weak link for connectedness. The right-hand side of Fig. 3 shows an example fragment of the resource model with containers and available HTTP operations.

Service specification and implementation. The resource model is mapped to a concrete service specification and further refined into an implementation. As explained in [10], the key parts of the ReSTful Web service specification are: (i) a resource structure as a URI listing, (ii) available HTTP methods on each resource, (iii) links between resources, (iv) supported data formats for each resource, and (v) error conditions on each resource. With the service specification in place, expertise on the target implementation framework can be used to generate appropriate configurations and skeletons for the service implementation.

Each resource has its own URI, through which clients may access and manipulate the resource representation. In fact, we see that constructing the URI structure is probably the most important task in developing a ReSTful service. Thus, we focus on URIs in this example. The Design Phase Expert can construct a first approximation of the URI structure as shown in Tab. 1.

It is relatively easy to compare the resource model example on the right-hand side of Fig. 3 with the above URI structure. The composition relationships and association multiplicities in the resource model can be interpreted as a resource hierarchy and appropriate resource types.

Feedback for transformation evaluation. In order to support incremental development of the transformation from an information model to a resource

Table 1. Initial guess on the Photo API URI structure

Core concept	URI	Resource type
Photo	/photos	container
	/photos/{photo.id}	item
	/photos/{photo.id}/content	item
	/photos/{photo.id}/attrs	container
	/photos/{photo.id}/attrs/{attr.id}	item
	/photos/{photo.id}/tags	container
	/photos/{photo.id}/tags/{tag.id}	item
Property	/properties	container
	/properties/{property.id}	item
Tag	/tags	container
	/tags/{tag.id}	item
	/tags/{tag.id}/photos	container

model, we need a feedback loop that allows us to iterate and validate consecutive cycles. Specifically from the ReST point of view, most of the substance of validation is in assessing the unambiguity of the resulting resource model. The resource structure should satisfy all the requirements by following the 80–20 rule for "just enough data with just enough requests", i.e. find a small subset of resources with a reasonable operation sequence that implements the use case.

From the implementation point of view, it should be relatively trivial to map the resource model to implementation artifacts using the selected implementation framework. Examples of these artifacts might include URI routing tables of a web server, skeleton implementation including allowed operations for each resource, a database schema for persistent resource storage, and so on.

Both the functional requirements and the URI structure have implications on the concept-level constraints that should be reflected by the models. The information model captures the functional requirements in the noun-centric form of these constraints. As an important mechanism to ensure the fulfillment of the requirements, the resource model is also evaluated against them at the end of the transformation. The constraints of our example can be summarized as follows:

- Each Photo has exactly one Content, i.e. bits of the binary image.
- Each Photo may have n Attributes that need to be accessed separately, mainly because clients may assign new Attributes to a Photo.
- Each Attribute associates a value with a named Property that defines semantics for a name–value pair.
- Each Property can be used independently from the context of Photos.
- Each Photo may have n Tags associated with it.
- Each Tag may have n Photos associated with it.
- Photos and Tags do not have lifetime dependencies.

4 Transformation Development in Practice: The ReST Side Story

We now have a transformation development process, ReST design principles and an initial design for Photo API. We also have an idea on how to implement the Photo API. However, this information is still implicitly in the head of our Design Phase Expert. It is time to follow the transformation development cycle and see if we can capture the expert knowledge to be reused by application designers and what kinds of problems we might encounter.

4.1 Correspondence Examples

First the Design Phase Expert identified key elements (classes, composite/plain associations, generalizations, attributes) and properties (multiplicities at association ends) in the information model profile. He then created simple structures and crafted corresponding structures that could be found in well-designed resource models. These structures became source and target model fragments forming 12 correspondence examples. There were seven examples for associations, four for various inheritance configurations and one for association classes. This sounds mechanical, but there is a lot of skill behind "identified" and "crafted".

Since the information model and the resource model are both UML class diagrams, the source and target model fragments in the correspondence examples were presented as UML class diagrams as well. Fig. 4 shows one of the correspondence examples. At first it looks like a well-defined rule, however, the semantics are rather ambiguous. Is the association end attached to A restricted in some way? Can it be the container end of a composition association? Can A and B be the same class? The correspondence examples are only for the informal communication between the Design Phase Expert and Transformation Architect.

Fig. 4. A correspondence example for navigable associations with multiplicity > 1

The Design Phase Expert was confident the examples were viable, but he was not that sure whether the examples were mutually consistent, covered all important situations, contained all the necessary variations and worked independent of each other. This uncertainty emphasizes how long the jump from "can craft target model in some cases" to "can define how to craft target model in all possible cases" really is.

4.2   Transformational Patterns

The Design Phase Expert and Transformation Architect created transformational patterns by giving an interpretation to each correspondence example. We used natural language and class diagrams with OCL constraints. The correspondence example in Fig. 4 became similar to the following:

> **Applicability:** Information model classes A and B, which are connected with a non-composition association and the association end attached to B has upper multiplicity of 2 or more and the association is navigable toward B. Classes A and B can be the same class.
> **Related patterns:** (The resource model should already have classes A and B corresponding to classes A and B, respectively.)
> **Implementation:** The resource model should have class AB and associations A-B, A-AB and AB-B. Class AB has stereotype container. The name of class AB is the concatenation of the name of class A, the string "-" and the plural form of the name of class B. [...]

The first round of creating transformational patterns led to a number of discoveries. Some correspondence examples were just combinations of simpler ones. The examples regarding inheritance were just preliminary sketches. Some examples were conflicting. For example, the one in Fig. 4 implies that classes A and B have stereotype item, whereas one inheritance example implies a conflicting stereotype. In general, there are rules that cannot be captured in a single correspondence example and have to be expressed otherwise.

Due to the amount of discoveries the Design Phase Expert started refining the correspondence examples right away. We did a total of three rounds of patternizing before moving on to the transformation definition. In the second round the inheritance related correspondence examples were split to examples for abstract and concrete superclasses. In the third round the Design Phase Expert introduced a new concept called "projection". This emphasizes the incremental nature; concepts can be introduced gradually at any point in the development.

Between the second and third rounds, the resource model profile was simplified. After the change, resource models still contained the same information but in a slightly different form. We refined the correspondence examples and transformational patterns to reflect the profile changes. Since the change was syntactic and not semantic in nature, this was quite straightforward. We mention it to stress the wide range of changes that can occur during development.

4.3   Transformation Definition and Implementation

The Transformation Architect created a transformation definition based on the transformational patterns. In the transformation mechanism we used [11], a transformation definition consists of a set of task graphs and a graph rewrite system [12]. In principle, the implementation part of each transformational pattern translates into one task graph and the applicability condition into one graph rewrite system production. In practice, one transformational pattern may span several productions or several patterns may be combined into one production.

The Transformation Architect decided how the informally described variation in transformational patterns is expressed as run-time interaction. In the mechanism we used, interaction is limited to multiple choice questions and selecting model elements. The Transformation Architect also designed how to handle the rules that concern relationships between transformational patterns. There were also some extra productions for normal uninteresting technical reasons.

The transformation in our case was quite small, so there was no need for a higher level structure beyond that imposed by the transformational patterns. In a larger transformation the architecture might play a bigger role.

Transformation Programmer coded the task graph descriptions and graph rewrite system productions into the actual transformation implementation, given in a textual form proprietary to the transformation tool. The transformation implementation was finally executed on the reference information models and provided for the Design Phase Expert for evaluation.

4.4 Evaluation of the Transformation

At the end of the first transformation development cycle we evaluated the resulting resource model (Fig. 5). The main task of the Design Phase Expert was to compare the results against his mental model. We only covered a subset of the Photo API. While the functional requirements for the real-life Photo API are not considerably more complex than the ones here, the resulting resource model is larger. Our latest resource model has some 30 classes and 45 associations. Here are some of the the Design Phase Expert's observations.

Requirement coverage. We need to validate the results of each design phase against the original requirements for completeness of the transformation. In our example case, we started by interpreting the resulting resource model as a URI structure, similarly to the description in Sec. 3, and assessed how well it corresponded to the requirements. This assessment was mainly about ensuring that all the requirements were covered in terms of HTTP operation sequences based on the URIs and operations in the resource model. For example, storing and tagging a photo can be expressed as follows:

1. Create a logical photo "placeholder"
   - *Request:* `POST /photos`
   - *Response:* `Created /photos/123`
2. Upload the binary content
   - *Request:* `PUT /photos/123/content [binary content as body data]`
   - *Response:* `Created /photos/123/content`
3. Create the tag association item
   - *Request:* `PUT /photos/123/photo-tags/xyz`
   - *Response:* `Created /photos/123/photo-tags/xyz`

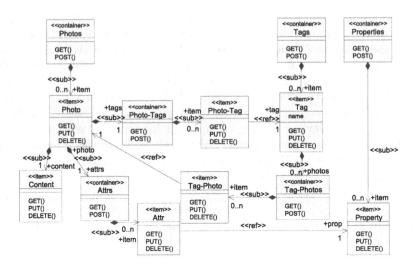

Fig. 5. Resulting resource model for the Photo API

Simplicity and intuitiveness. As we can see, a trivial-looking use case can generate a relatively long HTTP operation sequence. This is mainly due to the inherent HTTP restriction of accessing one resource at a time. Granularity and roundtrip problems are beyond the scope of this paper. We focus on expressing the requirements as HTTP operations. Nevertheless, some structural measurements of the URI structure, such as granularity and depth of the hierarchy, could be used as qualitative evaluation. This is subjective, because it measures how easy it is for a human user to grasp what different URIs really mean as resources. The first evaluation had no direct impact on patterns, but suggested adding new interpretation rules for the resource model.

Constraint compliance. Aside the service-specific requirements, the resulting URI structure should comply with the ReST constraints (unless compromises are properly justified). For example, each concept should be assigned with exactly one URI, because otherwise clients would unintentionally use different names for the same thing—an obstacle when sharing URI links among clients. In our reference case, there is one example of this: the association item between a photo and a tag, which actually appears as two resource classes (`Photo-Tag` and `Tag-Photo` in Fig. 5). Such excessive classes should be combined, based on a user decision asked and recorded during the transformation execution.

Precondition coverage. There might exist business logic rules that imply "business states" for resources. For example, adding an `Attribute` to a `Photo` may require that the referred `Property` must exist before the `Attribute` is created. These kind of referential preconditions can be hard to express with resources. Some behavioral aspects might be needed in the models. After the first iteration we considered refining the models with simple text-based rule attachments. In the future we might use statechart diagrams as part of the input.

Aesthetics for human users. Because the transformational patterns are expressed in terms of common elements independently from the vocabulary of a particular model instance, the names of generated elements may look artificial or even clumsy. For example, the `photo-tags` segment in the URI for tags of a photo (`/photos/123/photo-tags`) could be simplified into `tags`, making it easier to remember. This "prettifying" of URIs could be implemented as another design phase assisted by another transformation. Such an optimizing transformation would probably rely heavily on user decisions.

4.5   Creating Another ReSTful API

We used the Photo API as a primary tool to sketch out the transformation development process until we had a first decent transformation in place that produced some real output. Our next candidate is another experimental API developed at Nokia Research Center called the Topic API:

> Topic API allows the user to create observations—short notes—related to a particular point of interest (POI) collected under a common topic. Observations can contain an attachment like a photo or an audio clip.

Topic API implements yet another simple context-based messaging that contains `Topics`, `POIs` and `Observations`. Running the transformation on the Topic API information model produces the first attempt at a Topic API resource model. As the basic ReST expertise is already captured in the transformations, the application designer can now devise a URI structure based on the resource model and proceed to implementing his service. At the same time, the Design Phase Expert can use this second example to further evaluate the results and improve the transformation in subsequent iterations.

The evaluation of this second transformation revealed yet another type of observation, namely one related to resource granularity. The resource model turned out to have a relatively deep resource hierarchy, which may lead into efficiency problems in high-latency network environments because of the suboptimal resource granularity, especially when using the HTTP GET operation. As a solution, one might want to implement additional resource representations that effectively inline the subordinate resources across multiple hierarchy levels. This concern could be addressed in the resource model by adding derived associations down across composite hierarchies.

5   Discussion

We presented an iterative and incremental process for transformation development and applied it to a case. There was no existing set of explicit and precise rules on how the design phase should be completed. The ReST side story covered three rounds of patternization and one full iteration. The work progressed in weekly meetings over two months, mainly because of the stakeholders' other responsibilities. The Design Phase Expert (NRC) was the author of the ReST development process in Sec. 3. The Transformation Architect (TUT) was a model transformation researcher and the author of the transformation mechanism used. The Transformation Programmer (TUT) was a MSc. student. A professor (TUT) and the Topic API application developer (NRC) also participated in reviewing the correspondence examples. Because the stakeholders shared only little of each others specific expertise, there was a strong need for a neutral way to capture knowlegde. This need was emphasized because there were two organizations involved and long intervals between meetings.

Charting the resource modeling expert's tacit knowledge in an example-driven fashion proved quite fruitful. However, such examples were too vague in nature to be used even as studying material for a new developer. We defined the meaning of each correspondence example more precisely and stored the knowledge into an unambiguous but partly informal transformational pattern.

Transformational patterns were at an abstraction level where an inexperienced resource modeler could apply them, but were too informal to be automated. The patterns were completely transformation mechanism independent. This abstraction level was suited for communication between the resource modeling and transformation experts, due to their different skill sets. The resource modeler was thinking with the terminology of the design task, and did not have to learn about UML metamodel or details of the transformation mechanism.

Much of the effort went into creating patterns, because that was the biggest jump from implicit to explicit knowledge. Precisely for that reason most of the important progress in understanding the transformation happened in that phase. Humans just do not internally operate with precise and explicit rule sets. The numerous discoveries about the correspondence examples can not therefore be attributed to lack of expertise but to the nature of human brain. We think that these practical issues in mining expert knowledge are general and not specific to this case. Iterations and allowing human interactions enabled early prototyping with a full (but semi-automatic) model transformation.

Transformational patterns turned out to be a good unit for iterative refinement. Though, there were some higher level rules, such as precedence, dependencies and side-effects between rules, that could not be easily expressed with patterns. Such rules have to be recorded and analysed in a different way.

We argue that the difficulties in specifying the transformation in one go are typical, when there is no existing set of rules. We argue further, that such cases are common in software development in general, even if they are rarely used as examples in model transformation research. Although changes in target modeling notation may sound exotic and rare, we argue that they, too, are common in practice; some design phases are only restricted by the information that must be present in the models, and not by their form. Thus, the project can decide the specific form in which they want that information represented.

Crafting the transformation definition was rather uncomplicated, because the transformation at this stage was still pretty simple and because the transformation mechanism had some support for pattern-like thinking. Depending on how far the transformation is developed in the future, e.g. in terms of optimization, it could become significantly more complicated. For a large and complicated transformation there might be need to divide the transformation definition into several artifacts, or use a different kind of approach altogether. Some characteristics of a transformation engine or paradigm could possibly bring up the same problem.

Acknowledgements

This research has been financially supported by TEKES, Nokia, Nokia Siemens Networks, Plenware, Solita and grants of the ITEA project if04032 entitled SERIOUS of the Eureka Σ 2023 Programme. The authors would like to thank Heikki Suontausta for transformation implementations and Kai Koskimies for his valuable comments and feedback.

References

1. Fielding, R.T.: Architectural styles and the design of network-based software architectures. PhD thesis, University of California, Irvine (2000)
2. Mellor, S., Watson, A.: Roles in the MDA process (2006), http://www.omg.org/registration/Roles_in_MDA1.pdf
3. Hailpern, B., Tarr, P.: Model-driven development: The good, the bad, and the ugly. IBM Systems Journal 45(3), 451–461 (2006)
4. Bèzivin, J., Jouault, F., Paliés, J.: Towards model transformation design patterns. In: European Workshop on Model Transformation (EWMT) (2005), http://www.sciences.univ-nantes.fr/lina/atl/www/papers/DesignPatterns05.pdf
5. Gamma, E., Helm, R., Johnson, R., Vlissides, J.: Design patterns: elements of reusable object-oriented software. Addison-Wesley Professional (1995)
6. Varró, D., Balogh, Z.: Automating model transformation by example using inductive logic programming. In: SAC 2007: Proceedings of the 2007 ACM Symposium on Applied Computing, pp. 978–984. ACM, New York (2007)
7. Wimmer, M., Strommer, M., Kargl, H., Kramler, G.: Towards model transformation generation by-example. In: Proc. of the 40th Annual Hawaii International Conference on System Sciences, p. 285b. IEEE Computer Society (2007)
8. Laitkorpi, M., Koskinen, J., Systä, T.: A UML-based approach for abstracting application interfaces to ReST-like services. In: Proceedings of WCRE 2006 (2006)
9. Walsh, N., Jacobs, I.: Architecture of the World Wide Web. W3C recommendation, W3C, vol. 1 (December 2004), http://www.w3.org/TR/webarch/
10. Richardson, L., Ruby, S.: ReSTful Web Services, pp. 108–136. O'Reilly Media (2007)
11. Siikarla, M., Systä, T.: Transformational pattern system - some assembly required. In: Bruni, R., Varró, D. (eds.) Proceedings of GT-VMT 2006, pp. 57–68 (April 2006)
12. Rozenberg, G. (ed.): Handbook of graph grammars and computing by graph transformation: foundations, vol. 1. World Scientific Publishing Co., River Edge (1997)

Lifting Transformational Models of Product Lines:
A Case Study

Greg Freeman[1], Don Batory[2], and Greg Lavender[2]

[1]Dept. of Electrical and Computer Engineering
University of Texas at Austin
Austin, Texas 78712 U.S.A.
gfreeman@ece.utexas.edu
[2]Dept. of Computer Sciences
University of Texas at Austin
Austin, Texas 78712 U.S.A.
{batory,lavender}@cs.utexas.edu

Abstract. *Model driven development (MDD)* of *software product lines (SPLs)* merges two increasing important paradigms that synthesize programs by transformation. MDD creates programs by transforming models, and SPLs elaborate programs by applying transformations called features. In this paper, we present the design and implementation of a transformational model of a product line of scalar vector graphics and JavaScript applications. We explain how we simplified our implementation by lifting selected features and their compositions from our original product line (whose implementations were complex) to features and their compositions of another product line (whose specifications were simple). We used operators to map higher-level features and their compositions to their lower-level counterparts. Doing so exposed commuting relationships among feature compositions in both product lines that helped validate our model and implementation.

Keywords: transformation reuse, code generation, model composition, high-level transformations, features, product-lines.

1   Introduction

Model driven development (MDD) offers the potential to automate manual, error prone, and time intensive tasks and replace them with high level modeling and code generation. Modeling software has a number of advantages including strategically approaching problems top-down, documenting software structure and behavior, and reducing the time and cost of application development. *Feature oriented programming (FOP)* solves a complementary problem of building families of similar programs (a.k.a. *software product lines (SPL)*). Features are increments in program development and are transformations (i.e., functions that map a program to a more elaborate program). Both paradigms naturally invite simple descriptive models of program construction that are purely transformation-based (i.e., program designs are expressed as a composition of functions) and their integration is synergistic [32].

A. Vallecillo, J. Gray, A. Pierantonio (Eds.): ICMT 2008, LNCS 5063, pp. 16–30, 2008.

Our paper makes two contributions. First, we explain how we designed and implemented a product line of *scalar vector graphics (SVG)* and JavaScript applications. Our approach combines FOP and MDD in a way that allows us to use the language of elementary mathematics to express our approach in a straightforward and structured way, and to illustrate how transformational models of SPLs can be defined and implemented. Second, we explain how we simplified our effort by lifting selected features and their compositions from our original product line (whose implementations were complex and tedious) to features and their compositions to another product line (whose specifications were simple). Mathematical expressions define transformation paths that combine feature composition and model translation, exposing commuting relationships among transformations that helped validate our model and implementation. We begin with an overview of the domain of our case study.

2   MapStats

MapStats is an application that displays population statistics for different US states using SVG and JavaScript [26]. *Scalar vector graphics (SVG)* is a *World Wide Web Consortium (W3C)* language for describing two dimensional graphics and graphical applications. JavaScript is a scripting language that can be embedded within SVG to generate dynamic content.

MapStats displays an interactive map of the US, as shown in Fig. 1. Users can alter the map to selectively display rivers, lakes, relief, and population diagrams. A map navigator allows users to zoom and pan the primary map.

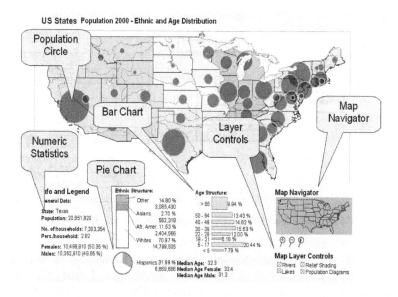

Fig. 1. MapStats SVG Case Study Application with all Features

When a user mouses over a state, various population statistics for the state are shown in text and graphical charts. Demographic attributes can be based on sex, age, and race. Statistics with charts can also be shown.

We refactored MapStats into a base application and optional features to allow a product line of variants to be created by composing the base with desired features. Fig. 2 shows a customized MapStats application that excludes statistical charts.

Fig. 2. A Customized Application

Feature diagrams are a standard way to express a product line [12][19]. A *feature diagram* is an and-or tree, where terminals represent primitive features and non-terminals are compound features. Fig. 3a shows a portion of the feature diagram for the MapStats product line; Fig. 3b lists the actual names and descriptions of the features that we created. (Not shown in Fig. 3 are the compatibility constraints among features, i.e., selecting one feature may require the selection or deselection other features [5][12]). MapStats features include: each statistic that can be displayed, each map layer, each map control, and run-time display options. For example, the Rivers feature adds rivers to the map of US states and the RiversControl feature adds a control that lets the user turn the river layer on and off at run time.

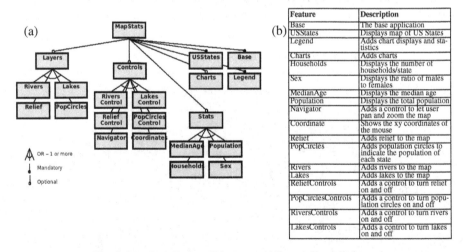

Feature	Description
Base	The base application
USStates	Displays map of US States
Legend	Adds chart displays and statistics
Charts	Adds charts
Households	Displays the number of households/state
Sex	Displays the ratio of males to females
MedianAge	Displays the median age
Population	Displays the total population
Navigator	Adds a control to let user pan and zoom the map
Coordinate	Shows the xy coordinates of the mouse
Relief	Adds relief to the map
PopCircles	Adds population circles to indicate the population of each state
Rivers	Adds rivers to the map
Lakes	Adds lakes to the map
ReliefControls	Adds a control to turn relief on and off
PopCirclesControls	Adds a control to turn population circles on and off
RiversControls	Adds a control to turn rivers on and off
LakesControls	Adds a control to turn lakes on and off

Fig. 3. MapStats Feature Diagram and Feature Descriptions

Again, Fig. 3a is a portion of the feature diagram for MapStats. We further decomposed the terminal Charts feature of Fig. 3a into a product line of charts. Fig. 4a shows its feature diagram and Fig. 4b lists the actual names and descriptions of the Charts features that we created. Charts features used three data sets: age, ethnic, and Hispanic. (The Hispanic data set was an artifact of the original application which we left intact).

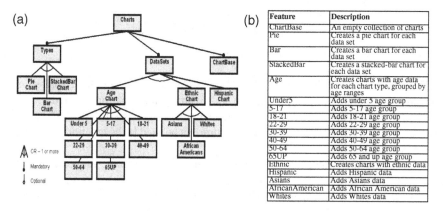

Fig. 4. Chart Feature Model and Feature Descriptions

We used features to specify chart types: bar, stacked-bar, and pie. The combination of chart types and data sets specified whole charts. So if two data sets and two chart types were specified, four charts would be created representing each combination.

Thus, we began our design in the standard way: we created a feature diagram for our product line. The next step was to implement features as transformations.

3   A Transformation-Based Model of Product Lines

GenVoca is a compositional paradigm and methodology for defining product lines solely by transformations: *it does not promote any particular implementation technology or tool*. Instead, it stresses that adding a feature to a program (however the program is represented) is a transformation that maps the original program to an extended program. There is a long history of creating and implementing GenVoca product lines in different domains (e.g. [7][8]). We review its key ideas and then explain our model of MapStats.

3.1   GenVoca

A GenVoca representation is a set of base programs and features (transformations) that extend or elaborate programs. The GenVoca representation expresses which features are used to compose a product line instance and the valid combinations of features in a product line. An example model $G=\{f,h,i,j\}$ contains the following parts: Base programs are values (0-ary functions):

```
f          // base program with feature f
h          // base program with feature h
```

and unary functions (transformations) are features:

```
i•x        // adds feature i to program x
j•x        // adds feature j to program x
```

• denotes function composition. The design of a program is expression:

```
p₁ = j•f      // program p₁ has features j and f
p₂ = j•h      // program p₂ has features j and h
p₃ = i•j•h    // program p₃ has features i, j, and h
```

The set of programs defined by a GenVoca model is its *product line*. Expression optimization is program design optimization, and expression evaluation is program synthesis [6][29]. Tools that validate feature compositions are discussed in [5][30]. Note that features (transformations) are reusable: a feature can be used in the creation of many programs in a product line.

A fundamental characteristic of features is that they "cross-cut" implementations of base programs and other features. That is, when a feature is added to a program, new classes can be added, new members can be added to existing classes, and existing methods can be modified. There is a host of technologies — including aspects, languages for object-oriented collaborations, and rewrite rules in program transformation systems — that can modularize and implement features as transformations. In MapStats, features not only refine JavaScript programs by adding new classes, methods and statements, but also new graphics elements can be added to SVG programs.

The relationship of a GenVoca model (i.e., 0-ary and unary functions) to a feature diagram is straightforward: each terminal of a feature diagram represents either a base program or a unary function. Compound features correspond to GenVoca expressions.

3.2   A Model of MapStats

A GenVoca model of MapStats has a single value (*Base* of Fig. 3); its unary functions are the remaining features of Fig. 3 and the features of the Charts feature diagram:

```
MapStats = { Base, USStates, ...    // features from Fig. 3
             ChartBase, Pie, ... }  // features from Fig. 4
```

To simplify subsequent discussions, instead of using the actual names of *MapStats* features, let us use subscripted letters. M_0 is the base program of *MapStats*, $M_1..M_n$ are the (unary function) features of the MapStats feature diagram and $C_0...C_m$ are (unary function) chart features:

```
MapStats = { M₀ ... Mₙ,      // features from Fig. 3
             C₀ ... Cₘ }     // features from Fig. 4
```

An application A in the *MapStats* product line is an expression:

$$A = (C_2•C_1•C_0)•M_1•M_0 \tag{1}$$

That is, application A is constructed by elaborating base program M_0 with a sequence of M features followed by a sequence of C features, where subexpression $(C_2•C_1•C_0)$ synthesizes the JavaScript that displays one or more charts. The original MapStats application *Orig*, which is part of our product line, is synthesized by composing all features:

```
Orig = (Cₘ•...•C₀)•Mₙ•...•M₀
```

Each *MapStats* feature can encapsulate SVG and JavaScript refinements (crosscuts) of the base application (M_0).

3.3   Implementation Overview

Our implementation of *MapStats* was straightforward. Our base program (M_0) was a pair of SVG and JavaScript programs. Each *MapStats* feature (M_i) could modify the SVG program, the JavaScript program, or both. We used the *AHEAD Tool Suite (ATS)* to implement *MapStats* features [1], and in particular, the XAK tool as the composition operator.

XAK is a language to refine XML documents and is also a tool to compose XML documents with their refinements [3]. A XAK base document is an XML file containing labeled *variation points* or *join points* to identify positions in a document where modifications can take place. A XAK refinement (unary function) is an XML file that begins with a *refine* element. Its children define a set of modifications, where each modification pairs an XPath expression with an XML fragment. The XPath expression identifies variation points or join points in an XML document, and the XML fragment is appended as a child node of the selected parent node(s). XAK can also prepend, replace, and delete nodes as well as perform operations on attributes, sibling nodes, and text nodes, however, our need was limited to child node appending.

To illustrate, Fig. 5a shows an elementary base document; Fig. 5b is a XAK refinement that appends an XML tree as another child of *<mynode>*. In *Aspect Oriented Programming (AOP)* terms, '*xr:at*' node specifies a pointcut as an XPath expression, which in this case looks for nodes called '*mynode*'. The '*xr:append*' node defines the advice action and body. The action for this example is to append '*mychildnode*' with a data attribute of '*2*'. Applying the refinement to the base yields the composite document of Fig. 5c.[1]

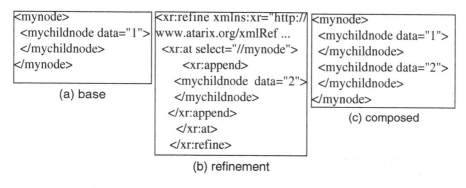

(a) base

(b) refinement

(c) composed

Fig. 5. XAK Base, Refinement, and Composition

As SVG documents are XML documents, XAK provided the language and tool for SVG document modification. However, ATS does not have a language to express JavaScript refinements, and a tool to compose refinements with a base JavaScript program. To circumvent this, we used XML to encode both JavaScript and JavaScript refinements,

---

[1] Aspects can be implemented by transformations; aspect compilers transform an input program to a "woven" program where additional code has been appropriately inserted [23].

and used XAK to compose them. The resulting JavaScript program was produced by stripping XML tags.

4 Lifting

It quickly became evident that $MapStat$ chart features $c_0 \ldots c_m$ were extremely tedious to write. We applied a key principle of MDD to save us effort: we created a high level DSL to specify charts and their features. Fig. 6 shows a fragment of a chart spec. A chart XML element defines a chart and an item defines an element in the chart. XML attributes can change the type of chart (pie, bar, or stacked-bar) as well as the names, colors, and field attribute codes for chart items.

```
<chart data-type="age-population" type="pieChart" ...
   <item attr="AGE_30_39" color="lightgreen" name= ...
   <item attr="AGE_22_29" color="lightcyan" name=...
</chart>
```

Fig. 6. A Chart Spec Fragment

Given chart specs, it is easy to write chart features (transformations). For example, a XAK refinement of Fig. 6 that appends the age data item for 18-21 is shown in Fig. 7. The underlined node defines a pointcut (XPath expression) that identifies all charts with the attribute $@datatype='age-population'$; such a chart would have the item AGE_18_21 appended to it. (In AOP-speak, this advice is homogenous [11]).

```
<xr:refine xmlns:xr="http://www.atarix.org/xmlRef ...
   <xr:at select="//chart[@data-type='age-population' ...
     <xr:append>
       <item attr="AGE_18_21" color="cyan" ...
     </xr:append>
   </xr:at>
</xr:refine>
```

Fig. 7. Example Chart Feature

We wrote XSLT transformations to map a chart spec (or chart spec refinement) to its corresponding $MapStat$ chart feature implementation (i.e., a JavaScript refinement). XSLT was chosen for the translation step since our models were XML-based. The image that is represented by the composite chart (Fig. 6 composed with Fig. 7) is shown in Fig. 8 where all three age groups are displayed. In general, we found a chart DSL specifications to be 4-10 times shorter than their generated JavaScript counterparts.

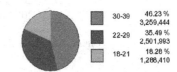

Fig. 8. Pie Chart with Three Age Categories

By *lifting* (raising) the level of abstraction of chart feature implementations, in effect what we did was create another product line — a product line of charts. That is, we lifted the chart features $c_0 \ldots c_m$ of `MapStats` into a separate GenVoca model called `Charts`:

```
Charts = { S₀ ... Sₘ }
```

where S_0 was the base chart spec, and each `Charts` feature S_i was a chart spec refinement. `Charts` features are in 1-to-1 correspondence with their `MapStats` chart features. XSLT transformations τ and τ' defined this correspondence:

$$C_0 = \tau(S_0) \tag{2}$$

$$C_i = \tau'(S_i) \quad // \text{ for all } i=1..m \tag{3}$$

τ and τ' have very similar implementations: their difference is due to the type of their argument: τ maps a `Charts` *value* to a `MapStats` function (i.e., JavaScript refinement); τ' maps a `Charts` *function* to a `MapStats` function.

Note that an *operator* maps an input function to an output function. τ' is an operator that maps a `Charts` refinement transformation to a `MapStats` refinement transformation. τ maps a `Charts` 0-ary function S_0 to the `MapStats` unary function C_0. Operators τ and τ' have a basic commuting relationship which we explain in Sect. 6.

Even though we now used lifted features, the way we specified a target `MapStats` application changed minimally. We still used the original feature diagram of MapStats to specify a `MapStats` application and to create its GenVoca expression (which starts with the base program M_0 and applies `MapStats` features to elaborate it). But instead of implementing chart features $c_0 \ldots c_m$ directly in terms of JavaScript refinements, we used chart specs and chart refinements $S_0 \ldots S_m$. To synthesize a `MapStats` application A (equation (1)), we rewrote its expression using (2) and (3):

$$
\begin{aligned}
A &= (C_2 \bullet C_1 \bullet C_0) \bullet M_1 \bullet M_0 && // \text{ original MapStats expr} \\
&= \tau'(S_2) \bullet \tau'(S_1) \bullet \tau(S_0) \bullet M_1 \bullet M_0 && // \text{ rewrite} \tag{4}
\end{aligned}
$$

and evaluated (4) to synthesize A. We call the raising of features and their compositions from one product line to another *lifting*. Lifting can be applied to any GenVoca product line. Transformations (like τ and τ') are used to define maps between unlifted features and their lifted counterparts. Constraints that govern the composition of original `MapStats` features remain unchanged.

5   Implementation Details

In this section, we illustrate some of the features and mappings discussed earlier, in order to make our discussions concrete.

A chart spec defines one or more charts. Each chart is implemented by a unique Java-Script class. For example, a pie chart that displays age information that includes the range of 18-21 is defined as a JavaScript class (below named `agePie`) that has a method (`buildData`) that populates this particular data set:

```
function agePie() {                    // JavaScript class definition
   ...

   this.buildData = function() {       // buildData method
      ...
```

```
    this.chartAttrArray.push("AGE_18_21");
    this.chartNameArray.push("18-21");
    this.chartColorArray.push("cyan");
    ...
  }
}
```

At run-time, a JavaScript object is created for each chart, populated with data, and then displayed:

```
var agepie = new agePie();      // instantiate object
agepie.buildData();             // populate data
agepie.showData();              // display
```

To see how this JavaScript class was synthesized, let's look at a *Charts* feature expression that could generate it:

```
AGE_18_21•Age•Pie•ChartBase
```

That is, the chart spec begins with *ChartBase*, it is refined to a pie chart that displays age information (Age•Pie), and then the age category 18-21 is added. Internally, our tools generate unique names for each chart. The manufactured name given to the chart of our example is "*agePie*".

Let's now focus on the AGE_18_21 feature. The XAK refinement that defines it was depicted in Fig. 7, which we reproduce below:

```
<xr:refine xmlns:xr="http://www.atarix.org/xmlRef ...
  <xr:at select="//chart[@data-type='age-population' ...
    <xr:append>
      <item attr="AGE_18_21" color="cyan" ...
    </xr:append>
  </xr:at>
</xr:refine>
```

This transformation adds the age category 18-21 to all charts of a charts spec that display age information. In our example, there is only one chart, *agePie*. Note that the underlined code denotes the pointcut (XPath expression) that captures the relevant charts to modify.

Let's see the result of transforming the AGE_18_21 *Charts* feature into its corresponding *MapStats* feature (denoted $AGE\_18\_21_{mapstats}$). The τ' operator maps AGE_18_21 to $AGE\_18\_21_{mapstats}$, where a fragment of $AGE\_18\_21_{mapstats}$ is:

```
<xr:refine ... >
  <xr:at select="//function[@data-type='age-population']
      [@parentId='ChartArea2'][@name='buildData']"...>
    <xr:append>
      <statement>
    this.chartAttrArray.push("AGE_18_21");
    this.chartNameArray.push("18-21");
    this.chartColorArray.push("cyan");
      </statement>
    </xr:append>
  </xr:at>
</xr:refine>
```

$$(5)$$

That is, the above XAK refinement adds the JavaScript code in *italic red* to the *buildData* method of each JavaScript class of a chart that displays age information. Note that the underlined code denotes the pointcut (XPath expression) that captures the relevant *buildData* methods. So the translation of AGE_18_21 to AGE_18_21$_{mapstats}$ maps a pointcut (XPath expression) whose joinpoints are in chart specs to a pointcut whose joinpoints are in JavaScript programs. Also, the addition of a chart element is mapped to the addition of statements in the JavaScript method *buildData*.

As mentioned earlier, operators τ and τ' are implemented in XSLT. They look for patterns in charts specifications and instantiate JavaScript code templates. For example, when a 'chart' element is encountered in a chart spec, a corresponding JavaScript class is added with the methods *buildData* and *showData*. When an 'item' element is found in a chart spec, statements are added to an appropriate JavaScript method. As an example, a fragment of the XSLT definition of τ' is shown below:

```
<xsl:template match="xr:at/xr:append/c:item">
    ... map Charts pointcut to MapStats pointcut...
    <xr:at select="{$path}">
     <xr:append>
       <xsl:variable name="attr" select="@attr"/>
       <xsl:variable name="color" select="@color"/>
       <xsl:variable name="name" select="@name"/>
       <statement>
        this.chartAttrArray.push("<xsl:value-of select="$attr"/>");
        this.chartNameArray.push("<xsl:value-of select="$name"/>");
        this.chartColorArray.push("<xsl:value-of select="$color"/>");
       </statement>
     </xr:append>
    </xr:at>
</xsl:template>                                                        (6)
```

Note that the code in *italic red* is a template whose parameters are provided by the input to τ'. In our example, the AGE_18_21 input to τ' assigns the value AGE_18_21 to attr, 18-21 to name, and cyan to color. The *italic red* code of (5) is generated by instantiating the τ' template with these parameters. By writing a general transformation τ' once and reusing it (to translate other *Charts* features that were differentiated only by their parameters), saved us considerable effort as mentioned earlier. Notice also that part of τ' is to map the pointcut of a charts spec to a corresponding pointcut that captures the corresponding JavaScript methods. This mapping is done via string manipulation, which we elide the details, and indicate by underlined code in (6).

6 Commuting Relationships

Lifting defines a commuting relationship between *Charts* features and *MapStats* features that relate τ and τ' and that offers us yet another way to synthesize *MapStats* applications. Instead of separately translating each *Charts* feature S_i to its C_i counterpart as we did in (4), we could synthesize a composite chart spec S (e.g., $S=S_2 \bullet S_1 \bullet S_0$) by starting with a base spec S_0, and add features S_1 and S_2, and *then* transform S into its corresponding JavaScript implementation. That is, another way to synthesize application A is:

$$A = \tau(S_2 \bullet S_1 \bullet S_0) \bullet M_1 \bullet M_0 \tag{7}$$

The equivalence of (4) and (7) is due to the commuting relationship:

$$\tau(S_i \bullet S) = \tau'(S_i) \bullet \tau(S) \tag{8}$$

where S is a Charts expression and S_i is a Charts feature. (8) says composing Charts features and translating to a MapStats representation equals translating each Chart feature separately and composing. *The value of commuting relationships is that they define properties of valid implementations of transformational models of product lines. The correctness of a model and tools is demonstrated when its commuting relationships are demonstrated. Commuting relationships provide a simple means to express and compare different methods of applying transformations and transformation of transformations (i.e., operators).*

Note: a general name for (8) is a homomorphism: given two sets X and Y and a single binary operation on them, a *homomorphism* is a map $\Phi : X \rightarrow Y$ such that:

$$\Phi(u \otimes v) = \Phi(u) \oplus \Phi(v) \tag{9}$$

where $\otimes$ is the operation on X and $\oplus$ is the operation on Y. In MapStats, X is the Charts model and Y is the MapStats model; $\otimes$ and $\oplus$ both are $\bullet$. Homomorphisms define how expressions in one algebra are translated to expressions in another, i.e., (8) defines how Charts expressions are mapped to MapStats expressions.

Note: what is the justification for (8)? Experimentally we have observed that compositions of features and derivations commute: when they do not, we find bugs in our transformation or tool chains. The commuting of features and derivations is an axiom of *Feature-Oriented MDD (FOMDD)* [31][32], which our work on MapStats is an example case study.

As we do not have formal models of Charts and MapStats, we do not have a proof of (8) for all Charts and MapStats features. Instead, we tested the correctness of (8). We synthesized multiple applications in two different ways (i.e., (4) and (7)) and then visually compared and executed both programs since (4) and (7) did not produce syntactically equivalent code. Graphical SVG applications with multiple transformation outputs allowed side-by-side visual comparison of many test cases. Other tests were performed with randomly selected features to ensure that each properly transformed the appropriately selected features. Although more sophisticated and thorough testing was possible (e.g., [24]), manual comparisons were sufficient for our goals.

Commuting relationships not only define properties that can be used to prove or test model and implementation correctness, but sometime they have additional benefits. We have observed in other domains that program synthesis can be substantially more efficient using one synthesis path (e.g., (4) or (7)) than another. For example, exploiting commuting relationships led to a 2-fold speed-up in synthesizing portlets [32], and over a factor of 10 in synthesizing test programs using Alloy [22]. Although we did observe trade-offs in building MapStats applications, they were not particularly significant. The utility of commuting relationships in MapStats was restricted to model and transformation validation.

7   Related Work

FOP and MDD paradigms have their historic roots in Lisp, which promoted the idea that programs are values (or "programs as data") and transformations are functions that map values to values.

Combining MDD and product line transformations is not new [2][4][13][17][18] [28][31][32]. Trujillo et al. used XAK and AHEAD to build web portlets from state chart models [32]. Our work builds upon theirs and provides further evidence that transformation-based models of product lines (that represent both features and model translations as transformations) expresses a general approach to software development. Also, our use of lifting illustrates how basic concepts in elementary mathematics (e.g., operators and homomorphisms) lie at the core of program-development-by-transformations. The use of elementary mathematics as a language to express our design allows us to make this connection directly.

Trujillo et al. also apply model transformations that aid in the building of FOMDD (Feature Oriented Model Driven Development) applications, which include multiple transformation steps and different paths to generate an application [31].

Avila-García and others used transformations to apply features to models [4]. Their work focused on transformations of transformations that composed features for families of UML diagrams. Our work instead focuses on transforming high level models into executable applications.

Gonzalez-Baixauli and others have proposed using MDD to help product line engineers determine application variation points, and to assess the feasibility of automating software product line development with MDD [17]. Work by Deelstra and others have also used MDD as a means of identifying variations points within a product line [15]. Both papers infer that a feature could use *Platform Independent Model (PIM)* to *Platform Specific Model (PSM)* transformations to implement features that specify different platforms and implementation technologies.

Czarnecki and Helsen combined features and MDD in a different way by surveying different types of transformation methods and analyzing the various features of these methods [14]. Other prior work defined a taxonomy of different types of transformations and classified them as endogenous and exogenous [25]. Feature composition is an endogenous transformation, which uses the same source and target model representations. The τ and τ' transformations are exogenous, which use different source and target model (XML schema) representations.

Czarnecki and Antkiewicz connect features and behavioral models using model templates [13]. Model elements are tagged with predicates that reference features; the elements appear in a model instance when selected features satisfy the predicate. This is an alternative approach to artifact development in product lines; our approach stresses the modularization of features and their connection to transformations.

Kurtev uses XML transformations to develop XML applications [21]. The design of web applications includes functionality, content, navigation and presentation components.

Many results in MDD have laid a foundation for model transformations [9][10][20]. Even though this case study covers a specific domain and does not use UML model representations, model representations serve the same purpose of abstracting representations at different levels of detail. The *Charts* model representation is a type of PIM and the SVG and JavaScript model representations are types of PSMs.

8   Conclusions

We presented a product line of SVG+JavaScript applications that was defined and implemented solely in terms of transformations. Features of a product line were implemented as transformations, and programs were specified as compositions of transformations. When we discovered that certain features were tedious to implement, we applied a basic principle of MDD to "lift" low-level implementations to DSL specifications and wrote transformations (operators) to map DSL specs (and their refinements) back to their SVG+JavaScript counterparts, ultimately saving effort.

What makes lifting interesting is its product line setting: we lifted selected features and their compositions from our original product line (*MapStats*) to features and compositions of another product line (*Charts*). We defined how features (transformations) in one product line could be transformed into features (transformations) of another via operators (τ and τ'). Doing so exposed commuting relationships between compositions of functions (i.e., tool chains and features). Such commuting relationships define properties of transformational models of program development; proving or validating (via testing) that these properties hold helps demonstrate model correctness. Our case study illustrated these ideas.

A primary reason why we were able to recognize commuting relationships and explain how features of one product line were related to another is that we used the language of elementary mathematics to express transformation-based designs of programs. Doing so enabled us to express our ideas in a straightforward and structured way and at the same time compactly illustrate how transformational models of software product lines can be defined, implemented, and explained.

Acknowledgements. We thank Prof. Hartmut Ehrig (University of Berlin), and Salvador Trujillo (University of the Basque Country) for their helpful comments on an earlier draft. We also thank the anonymous referees for their helpful insights. We gratefully acknowledge the support of the National Science Foundation under Science of Design Grants #CCF-0438786 and #CCF-0724979 to accomplish this work.

References

[1] AHEAD Tool Suite,
     http://www.cs.utexas.edu/users/schwartz/index.html
[2] Anastaspoulos, M., et al.: Optimizing Model Driven Development by Deriving Code Generation Patterns from Product Line Architectures. NetObject Days (2005)

[3] Anfurrutia, F.I., Diaz, O., Trujillo, S.: On the Refinement of XML. In: Baresi, L., Fraternali, P., Houben, G.-J. (eds.) ICWE 2007. LNCS, vol. 4607, pp. 473–478. Springer, Heidelberg (2007)

[4] Avila-García, O., García, A.E., Redbull, E.V.S.: Using Software Product Lines to Manage Model Families in Model-Driven Engineering. In: SAC (2007)

[5] Batory, D.: Feature Models, Grammars, and Propositional Formulas. In: Obbink, H., Pohl, K. (eds.) SPLC 2005. LNCS, vol. 3714, pp. 7–20. Springer, Heidelberg (2005)

[6] Batory, D., Robertson, E., Chen, G., Wang, T.: Design Wizards and Visual Programming Environments for Genvoca Generators. In: IEEE TSE (2000)

[7] Batory, D., O'Malley, S.: The Design and Implementation of Hierarchical Software Systems with Reusable Components. In: ACM TOSEM (1992)

[8] Batory, D., Sarvela, J.N., Rauschmayer, A.: Scaling Step Wise Refinement. In: IEEE TSE (2004)

[9] Bezivin, J.: Model Driven Engineering: Principles, Scope, Deployment, and Applicability. In: GTTSE (2005)

[10] Booch, G., Brown, A., Iyengar, S., Rumbaugh, J., Selic, B.: The IBM MDA Manifesto. The MDA Journal (2004)

[11] Colyer, A., Rashid, A., Blair, G.: On the Separation of Concerns in Program Families. Technical Report COMP-001-2004, Computing Department, Lancaster University (2004)

[12] Czarnecki, K., Eisenecker, U.: Generative Programming Methods, Tools, and Applications. Addison-Wesley, Boston (2000)

[13] Czarnecki, K., Antkiewicz, M.: Mapping Features to Models: A Template Approach Based on Superimposed Variants. In: Glück, R., Lowry, M. (eds.) GPCE 2005. LNCS, vol. 3676, pp. 422–437. Springer, Heidelberg (2005)

[14] Czarnecki, K., Helsen, S.: Feature-based Survey of Model Transformation Approaches. IBM Systems Journal, 45(3) (2006)

[15] Deelstra, S., Sinnema, M., van Gurp, J., Bosch, J.: Model Driven Architecture as Approach to Manage Variability in Software Product Families. In: Aßmann, U., Aksit, M., Rensink, A. (eds.) MDAFA 2003. LNCS, vol. 3599. Springer, Heidelberg (2005)

[16] Ehrig, H., Ehrig, K., Ermel, C., Hermann, F., Taentzer, G.: Information Preserving Bidirectional Model Transformations. In: Dwyer, M.B., Lopes, A. (eds.) FASE 2007. LNCS, vol. 4422, Springer, Heidelberg (2007)

[17] Gonzlez-Baixauli, B., Laguna, M.A., Crespo, Y.: Product Lines, Features, and MDD. In: EWMT Workshop (2005)

[18] Wu, H., Neema, S., Bapty, T., Gray, J., Gokhale, A., Zhang, J., Shi, F., Lin, Y., Roychoudhury, S., Sudarsan, R.: Model-Driven Program Transformation of a Large Avionics Framework. In: Karsai, G., Visser, E. (eds.) GPCE 2004. LNCS, vol. 3286, pp. 361–378. Springer, Heidelberg (2004)

[19] Kang, K., Cohen, S., Hess, J., Nowak, W., Peterson, S.: Feature-Oriented Domain Analysis (FODA) Feasibility Study. Technical Report, CMU/SEI-90TR-21 (1990)

[20] Kleppe, A., Warmer, J., Bast, W.: MDA Explained: The Model Driven Architecture: Practice and Promise. Addison-Wesley (2003)

[21] Kurtev, I., van den Berg, K.: Building Adaptable and Reusable XML Applications with Model Transformations. WWW (2005)

[22] Khurshid, S., Uzuncaova, E., Garcia, D., Batory, D.: Testing Software Product Lines Using Incremental Test Generation (submitted)

[23] Lopez-Herrejon, R., Batory, D., Lengauer, C.: A Disciplined Approach to Aspect Composition. In: PEPM (2006)

[24] Memon, A.M., Pollack, M.E., Soffa, M.L.: Using a Goal-driven Approach to Generate Test Cases for GUIs. In: ICSE (1999)
[25] Mens, T., Czarnecki, K., van Gorp, P.: A Taxonomy of Model Transformations. In: GraMoT (2005)
[26] Neuman, A.: US Population: Ethnic Structure and Age Distribution (2000),
     http://www.carto.net/papers/svg/samples
[27] Sabetzadeh, M., Easterbrook, S.M.: Analysis of Inconsistency in Graph-Based Viewpoints: A Category-Theoretic Approach. In: ASE (2003)
[28] Schmidt, D., Nechypurenko, A., Wuchner, E.: MDD for Software Product Lines: Fact or Fiction. In: Models, Workshop 8 at MODELS (2005)
[29] Selinger, P., et al.: Access Path Selection in a Relational Database System. In: ACM SIG-MOD (1979)
[30] Thaker, S., Batory, D., Kitchin, D., Cook, W.: Safe Composition of Product Lines. In: GPCE (2007)
[31] Trujillo, S., Azanza, W., Diaz, O.: Generative Metaprogramming. In: GPCE (2007)
[32] Trujillo, S., Batory, D., Diaz, O.: Feature Oriented Model Driven Development: A Case Study for Portlets. In: ICSE (2007)

Model Synchronisation: Definitions for Round-Trip Engineering

Thomas Hettel[1,2], Michael Lawley[1], and Kerry Raymond[1]

[1] Faculty of Information Technology,
Queensland University of Technology, Brisbane, Australia
t.hettel@student.qut.edu.au
[2] SAP Research, Brisbane, Australia
t.hettel@sap.com

Abstract. In a model-centric software development environment, a multitude of different models are used to describe a software system on different abstraction layers and from different perspectives. Following the MDA vision, model transformation is used to support the gradual refinement from abstract models into more concrete models. However, target models do not stay untouched but may be changed due to maintenance work or evolution of the software. Therefore, in order to preserve a coherent description of the whole system, it is necessary to propagate certain changes to a target model back to the source model. However, as transformations in general are partial and not injective, they cannot be easily reversed to propagate changes. This paper presents a formal definition of round-trip engineering and the semantics of target changes in the context of partial and non-injective transformations.

1 Introduction

In a model-centric software-development environment, such as the one described by OMG's MDA vision [9], models become first class citizens in the development process. In this environment a multitude of different models and modelling languages are used to describe a software system on different abstraction layers and from different perspectives. Ideally, all these different models are connected by model transformation. Allowing the generation of new models from existing ones, transformation forms one of the corner stones in this vision.

Due to necessary maintenance work or changing requirements, target models are altered or extended. Consequently, the modified target may no longer be the result of the transformation. To avoid inconsistencies changes to target models have to be reflected back to the source model as depicted in Fig. 1. This process is known as Round-Trip Engineering (RTE).

A motivating scenario that heavily relies on RTE can be found in the business process management community, an area where MDA-like modelling is increasingly important. Barros et al [2] propose a layered and view-point based approach to choreography modelling, which specifies and describes protocols between two or more parties interacting to achieve a common business goal. To capture potentially very complex systems, different abstraction layers and different view-points

A. Vallecillo, J. Gray, A. Pierantonio (Eds.): ICMT 2008, LNCS 5063, pp. 31–45, 2008.

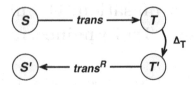

Fig. 1. Changes to the target T must be reflected back to the source S. Therefore, some kind of reverse transformation $trans^R$ is needed.

were proposed. Making changes to one model may require consequential changes in other models. As the presented approach also supports bottom-up, RTE is of vital interest with respect to a future implementation.

The difficulty faced with RTE is the often neglected fact that transformations in general are neither total nor injective. In other words, there are concepts in the source model that do not have a correspondence in the target model and vice versa. Also, there may be several source models being mapped to one and the same target model.

The contribution of this paper is a formal definition of RTE accounting for non-injective, partial transformations found in practice. Furthermore, the semantics of a target change with respect to the transformation and the source model is given. Source changes have to exactly perform a target change, i.e., without any side-effects, in order to be a viable translation of a target change. This definition will serve as a foundation for our ongoing implementation.

The remainder of this paper is structured as follows. Section 2 will provide an outline of related work. An example, which will be used throughout this paper, will be introduced in Sec. 3. The subsequent three sections contain the main contribution consisting of the definition of model synchronisation in Sec. 4, which is a prerequisite for the RTE definition presented in Sec. 5. This is followed by Sec. 6 where the semantics of target model changes is specified. The last section provides a conclusion and an outlook on further research.

2   Related Work

2.1   Definitions of Model Round-Trip Engineering

To the best of our knowledge, there is only one general formal definition of RTE by Aßman [1]. However, this definition neglects partial and non-injective transformations and is too high a level in order to be useful in practice. Giesse and Wagner [7], Foster et al [6] and Stevens [11] provide formal definitions, which, however, are limited to their approaches and will be discussed in the next section.

More insights into possible definitions and the semantics of target changes can be obtained by investigating the view-update problem in relational databases. Essentially, views can be thought of as stored database queries using relational algebra expressions, which are in general unidirectional, partial and non-injective functions; very similar to model transformations. Given the similarities between views and model transformations, some parallels can be established between the *view-update* problem and that of RTE.

An interesting approach to describing the semantics of view updates was put forward by Dayal and Bernstein [4], which translates changes to the view into changes to the underlying database. These changes are required to exactly perform the change made to the view. Applying the view definition to the changed database again must yield the changed view. This approach will be adopted in the specification of semantics of target model changes in Sec. 6.

2.2 Approaches to Round-Trip Engineering

Current approaches to model synchronisation and RTE[1] differ mainly in the restrictions placed on the transformation. These restrictions range from total, injective, bi-directional transformations [12] to partial, non-injective, bi-directional transformations [3], as summarised in Table 1.

The approach presented by van Paesschen and d'Hondt [12] is based on the idea that an element in the source model and an element in the target model are just different views of exactly the same thing, which is an instance of a third "common" model. This makes synchronisation trivial as regardless of whether the source or the target is manipulated this will instantly be reflected in the other model as source and target element are one and the same entity in the common model. However, this assumes that the source and the target model are isomorphic to each other, i.e., each source element has exactly one corresponding target element. No two different source elements are allowed to be mapped onto the same target element.

Using triple graph grammars, which are by nature bi-directional, Giese and Wagner [7] outline a model synchronisation approach. Changes are confined to the domain and range of the transformation, effectively limiting the synchronisation to the semantic overlap of the source and target model. Elements that do not have a corresponding representation in the other model cannot be added. When invalidating a target pattern, the corresponding source pattern gets invalidated by deleting all its constituting elements. Smaller changes, such as changing an attribute in order to annul the source pattern are not considered. Transformations are not required to be bijective in order to be usable for this synchronisation approach, as shown by Ehrig et al [5]. However, there must be a bijection between source and target patterns.

A different approach to reversing functions, not primarily targeting MDA, is presented by Mu et al [10] where a functional, injective language is defined. This is done by defining primitive injective functions and their also injective converse. With that, more complex functions can be constructed, which are guaranteed to be injective as well. These functions, however, are not very useful as even simple arithmetic operations are not injective. They cannot be easily reversed as there is a potentially infinite number of possibilities to arrive at a given value. To

---

[1] In the literature, model synchronisation and round-trip engineering are often used interchangeably.

overcome this problem, a log is kept recording the relationship between source and target elements. Using this log, only elements that have been produced by the function can be reversed. New elements cannot be reversed as there is no information about them in the log.

Foster et al [6] present a model synchronisation approach based on so-called lenses, pairs of functions defining the forward and the reverse transformation. The forward function solely works on the source structure. Conversely, the reverse uses the old source structure and the new target structure to produce a new source. Assuming that target models are transient, no changes are allowed that cannot be reflected back, effectively confining synchronisation to the semantic overlap. Both functions of a lens have to be total and injective, such that every change to the target structure can be reflected back to the source. With a basic set of lenses and combinators more complex transformations of tree structures can be constructed and automatically reversed.

To provide reasonable bi-directional semantics for QVT, Stevens [11] proposes a set of basic properties. These properties are shown to be equivalent to the properties for lenses proposed by Foster et al [6].

Xoing et al [13] present an approach for reversing model transformations specified using the ATL model transformation language. The transformation does not have to be total on the source or target model, i.e., elements that have no corresponding entity in the respective other model can be added, removed or changed without violating the synchronisation. Similar to the triple graph grammar approach, when invalidating a target pattern, the elements constituting the corresponding source pattern are deleted.

Fewer restrictions on the nature of the transformation are imposed by the approach presented by Cicchetti et al [3]. It allows for non-injective partial transformations. Elements that do not have a correspondence in the other model can be added, deleted and changed. Modelling is not restricted to the semantic overlap of both models. Allowing for non-injective transformations, the reverse transformation, as specified by the user, may not be a function and hence there may be several source models for a given target model. To compute all these source models, a logic programming variant supporting non-monotonic reasoning is used. However, there is no way to ensure that the provided reverse is reasonable in the sense that when brought forward again all sources result in the changed target model. Moreover, round-trips without any changes produce all source models rather than just the original one.

In summary, there is no generally applicable definition of automatic RTE that takes *partial* and *non-injective* transformations into account. Most approaches are total, restricting modelling to the semantic overlap of two languages. All but one approach require some kind of injective property of either the transformation as a whole or its rules or lenses. Only Cicchetti et al [3] do not impose this restriction. However, there is no formal definition and the semantic of changes is a by-product of whatever the user defines as the reverse transformation. Therefore, the contribution of this paper is to put forward a *formal definition* for automatic

Table 1. Comparison of model synchronisation approaches

Approach	Synchronisation	Relationship	Reverse
van Paesschen et al [12]	total	bijective trans.	given
Giese and Wagner [7]	total	bijection btwn. patterns	computed
Mu et al [10]	total	injective trans.	computed
Foster et al [6]	total	injective lenses	computed
Xiong et al [13]	partial	bijection btwn. patterns	computed
Cicchetti et al [3]	partial	not injective	given

RTE with respect to *partial* and *non-injective* transformations together with a formal specification of the semantics of target model changes.

3   Running Example

To illustrate definitions, the popular UML to relational database transformation will serve as the running example throughout this paper. It is made up of three parts: (1) A simplified version of the UML and relational database schema meta-models (cf. Fig. 2), (2) a model transformation (cf. Fig. 3) defined on both meta-models and (3) an instance of the UML meta-model and the corresponding relational database schema with respect to the transformation (cf. Fig. 4).

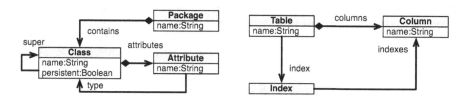

Fig. 2. A simple UML and relational database schema meta-model

Translating class diagrams into database schemes, the transformation, depicted in Fig. 3, creates one `Table` per `Class` and one `Column` for each `Attribute` of a `Class`, including inherited attributes.

This mapping is an example of a practical, partial and non-injective transformation. It is partial, because it does not map `Package`s and cannot reach `Index`es in the target and it is non-injective as there are two source models being mapped to the same target model: One is depicted in Fig. 4. The other one can be derived by deleting the inheritance relation and introducing another attribute `attr1` in `Class2`.

Moreover, when deleting a table, it is not clear whether to delete the corresponding class or to simply mark it not persistent.

```
1 RULE    class2table          1 RULE    attribute2column
2 FORALL  Class c              2 FORALL  Class c, Attribute a
3 WHERE   c.persistent         3 WHERE   c.attributes = a
4 MAKE    Table t FROM t(c)    4         AND c.persistent
5 SET     t.name = c.name;     5 MAKE    Table t FROM t(c),
                               6         Column col FROM col(c,a)
                               7 SET     t.cols = col,
                               8         col.name = a.name;
```

Fig. 3. Model transformation rules given in Tefkat [8] for mapping UML class diagrams onto relational database schema. For sake of conciseness, it is assumed that c.attributes also contains inherited attributes.

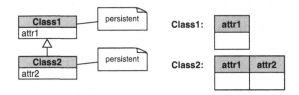

Fig. 4. A simple UML class diagram and the corresponding relational database schema with respect to the transformation depicted in Fig. 3

4   Model Synchronisation Definition

Intuitively, on a high level, two models are synchronised with respect to a transformation if applying the transformation to the source model yields the target model. Formally speaking, two models S and T conforming to their respective meta-models $\mathcal{M}_S$ and $\mathcal{M}_T$, are synchronised with respect to a transformation $trans : \mathcal{M}_S \to \mathcal{M}_T$ if $trans(S) = T$.

However, as shown by the running example in Sec. 3, transformations in general are only partially defined on the source and/or target model and are not injective. The definition of model synchronisation proposed in this section takes those properties into consideration and hence synchronisation is more complex than sketched above.

4.1   Preliminaries

A simple definition of a meta-model is used in this paper, which consists of a set of types $\mathcal{T}$ and the usual type hierarchy $\preceq$ defined on them. Furthermore, models contain a set of named relations $\mathcal{R}$, relating two types to each other. Types can also have attributes, contained in $\mathcal{A}$, which have a name and a type.

Definition 1. *A **(meta) model** $\mathcal{M}$ is defined as the tuple $(\mathcal{T}, \preceq, \mathcal{R}, \mathcal{A})$, where*

- *$\mathcal{T}$ is the finite set of types,*
- *$\preceq$ is the type hierarchy on $\mathcal{T}$, such that $t_1 \preceq t_2$ if t_1 is a super-type of t_2.*

- $\mathcal{R} \subset (Name \times \mathcal{T} \times \mathcal{T})$ *is the finite set of named relations,*
- $\mathcal{A} \subset (\mathcal{T} \times Name \times \mathcal{T})$ *is the finite set of attributes*

Comparing the UML meta-model in Fig. 2 to the transformation in Fig. 3, it becomes obvious that the transformation is only concerned with (some) Classes and (some) Attributes and is ignorant of the fact that UML class diagrams can also contain Packages. Therefore, obviously, any source model can be divided into two parts: one part that is relevant to the transformation, containing Classes and Attributes, which may or may not be mapped, depending on some conditions, and another part, containing Packages, which are completely irrelevant with respect to the transformation. The relevant part is called *relevant source model* and is illustrated by Fig. 5. Analogous to the source model, the target model can also be divided in the same way. The transformation cannot possibly create Indexes, which are used to optimise access to the database by indexing certain columns. Therefore, all instances of Index are in the irrelevant part, leaving Tables and Columns in the *relevant target model.*

Definition 2. *Let* $trans$ *be a model transformation from* $\mathcal{M}_S$ *to* $\mathcal{M}_T$. *The* **relevant source model** $\bar{\mathcal{M}}_S$ *and* **relevant target model** $\bar{\mathcal{M}}_T$ *with respect to* $trans$ *can be determined as follows:*

1. *Each explicitly mentioned exact type in the source part (target part) of* $trans$ *is in* $\bar{\mathcal{M}}_S$ *(* $\bar{\mathcal{M}}_T$ *).*
2. *Each explicitly mentioned non-exact type in the source part (target part) of* $trans$ *and all its subtypes are in* $\bar{\mathcal{M}}_S$ *(* $\bar{\mathcal{M}}_T$ *).*
3. *Each attribute or relation mentioned in the source part (target part) of* $trans$ *and their corresponding types according to (1) or (2) are in* $\bar{\mathcal{M}}_S$ *(* $\bar{\mathcal{M}}_T$ *).*

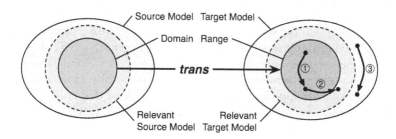

Fig. 5. Instance diagram illustrating the relevant source and target model of a transformation *trans*, as well as different kinds of changes: (1) *valid change*, (2) *invalid change* and (3) *irrelevant change*

The function *strip* is used to map models to their strip-down relevant source or target model:

Definition 3 (Strip for Models). *Let* $strip : \mathcal{M} \times (t : \mathcal{M}_S \rightarrow \mathcal{M}_T) \rightarrow \bar{\mathcal{M}}$ *be the function that maps models to their stripped down versions in* $\bar{\mathcal{M}}$ *where either* $\mathcal{M} = \mathcal{M}_S$ *or* $\mathcal{M} = \mathcal{M}_T$.

Note: Instead of *strip(M, trans)*, *strip(M)* will be used for sake of brevity if it is clear which transformation is used. Nevertheless, *strip* is always with respect to a transformation.

4.2   Synchronisation

Having defined the *relevant source/target model* it is now possible to define synchronisation between two models. Informally, two models are synchronised if the relevant part of the target can be created by applying the transformation to the source model.

Definition 4. *Two models S, T, instances of their respective meta-models $\mathcal{M}_S$, $\mathcal{M}_T$, are **synchronised** with respect to a transformation trans : $\mathcal{M}_S \to \mathcal{M}_T$ if*

$$trans(S) = strip(T).$$

Example: The two models depicted in Fig. 4 are synchronised with respect to the transformation listed in Fig. 3. Neither adding packages nor adding index information to any of the tables will impact on the synchronisation between both models.

5   Round-Trip Transformation

After having defined when two models are in sync with respect to a transformation, the question arises as to how they can be synchronised again if the target model changes. Depending on the nature of the transformation, there are several ways, which are discussed below.

Assuming that model transformations are total and bijective, the mathematical inverse $trans^{-1}$ can be used to recover a lost or otherwise unavailable source model. By applying the inverse to the target model $trans(S) = T$, the original source model can be recovered: $trans^{-1}(T) = S$.

As model transformations may not necessarily be total – there may be elements that cannot be mapped – a relaxed version is needed that only requires the inverse to be defined on the domain and range of the source and target model.

$$trans^{inv}(T) = strip(S).$$

Unfortunately, as shown in Sec. 3, transformations used in practice are not necessarily bijective and total. The concept of a reverse transformation $trans^R$ does not require the forward transformation to have these properties. All source models $S_1, \ldots, S_n$ that produce the same target T are considered equivalent and the reverse transformation is only required to return any one of them:

$$trans(trans^R(T)) = strip(T).$$

In contrast to reverse engineering, round-trip engineering does not aim at recovering lost or otherwise unavailable source models, but is rather concerned with propagating changes from target to the source model. Therefore, it assumes the availability of the source and target model, the forward transformation and the change to the target model, which all are input to the round-trip transformation $trans^{RT}$. The goal is to produce a new source model that when transformed produces the changed target model again.

Definition 5. *A function* $trans^{RT} : \mathcal{M}_S \times \mathcal{M}_T \times (\mathcal{M}_T \rightarrow \mathcal{M}_T) \rightarrow \mathcal{M}_S$ *is a* **round-trip transformation** *if it maps the source model S, the target model T and a target model change* Δ_T *to a new source model S' such that:*

$$trans^{RT}(S, T, \Delta_T) = S'$$

where S' and $\Delta_T T$ *are synchronised.*

6   Semantics of Target Changes

6.1   Changes

With models being first class citizens in the development processes, it cannot be assumed that they stay as they are and are not changed during the course of the development project. Sooner or later changes will be made to the source or the target model, which may or may not have to be reflected in the respective source or target model.

There is a number of atomic changes that can be made to models, i.e., inserting or deleting instances, inserting or deleting relations between instances and setting or unsetting attribute values of a certain instance.

Definition 6. *An* **atomic change** δ *is defined as a function:*

$$\delta : \mathcal{M} \rightarrow \mathcal{M}$$

There are six different atomic changes:

1. δ_t^+ *creating an instance of type t,*
2. δ_t^- *deleting an instance of type t,*
3. δ_{r,o_1,o_2}^+ *creating a relation r between instances* o_1, o_2,
4. δ_{r,o_1,o_2}^- *deleting a relation r between instances* o_1, o_2,
5. $\delta_{o,a,v}^s$ *setting attribute a of instance o to value v.*
6. $\delta_{o,a}^u$ *unsetting attribute a of instance o.*

Let C_S *be the set of all possible changes to the source and* C_T *be the set of all possible changes to the target.*

Most often, however, a whole sequence of atomic changes will be necessary to reach a consistent state of the model, with respect to a set of constraints, which are not considered here.

Definition 7. *A (complex) change Δ is defined as a function:*

$$\Delta : \mathcal{M} \to \mathcal{M}$$

Each change Δ is composed of a sequence of atomic changes $\delta_1, \ldots, \delta_n$ such that

$$\Delta M = \delta_1 \circ \cdots \circ \delta_n M = M'$$

As complex changes are composed of a number of atomic changes, a complex change can perform several smaller changes in different parts of the model. Some atomic changes may affect the relevant model, others may affect elements in the irrelevant part. As changes to the irrelevant part are not of interest, the function *strip* filters out those changes, leaving the complex change with only those atomic changes that actually affect the relevant source or target model.

Definition 8 (Strip for Changes).
*Let M be a model and an instance of its respective meta-model $\mathcal{M}$ and
$strip : (\Delta : \mathcal{M} \to \mathcal{M}) \times \bar{M} \to (\Delta' : \mathcal{M} \to \mathcal{M})$ the function that maps a change Δ to a change Δ' such that the change only affects elements in the relevant source or target model $\bar{M}$. Let $\Delta = \delta_1 \circ \cdots \circ \delta_n$ and $\Delta' = \delta_{i_1} \circ \cdots \circ \delta_{i_m}$, then δ_j is in Δ' if*

- δ_j *deletes/inserts instances of type $t \in \bar{\mathcal{M}}$*
- δ_j *deletes/inserts relations of type $r \in \bar{\mathcal{M}}$*
- δ_j *sets/unsets values v of attribute $a \in \bar{\mathcal{M}}$*

For a stripped-down complex change, which only affects the relevant target model, a corresponding change in the source is sought. However, not all source changes are equally desirable. Some may have side-effects and hence have a larger impact on the target, when transformed back, than it was desired by the original target change.

Example: Consider the deletion of table `Class1` in Fig. 4. This could be performed by deleting `Class1` in the class diagram. However, this change has an unwanted side-effect, as `Class2` will no longer inherit attribute `attr1` and hence the existence of column `attr1` in table `Class2` can no longer be supported. Therefore, as a result of applying the transformation to the changed source, column `attr1` will be removed as well, which is much more than what was originally requested when only deleting table `Class1`.

To avoid these kind of side-effects, a source change that performs a target change has to be exact:

Definition 9. *A change Δ_S in the source **exactly performs** a target change Δ_T if $\Delta_S = strip(\Delta_S)$, $\Delta_T = strip(\Delta_T)$ and*

$$trans(\Delta_S S) = strip(\Delta_T T).$$

Δ_S *is also called an **exact** change.*

Note: This definition corresponds to the PUTGET law in Foster et al [6].

6.2   Change Translation

Finally to translate target changes into exact source changes, a function $\phi_{S,T,trans}$ is used, which depends on the source model S and the target model T, as well as the transformation $trans$. As transformations in general are not injective, i.e., there are several source models that correspond to the same target model, ϕ returns a set of changes to the source model for a given change to the target model. These changes must be such that when applied to the source, the transformation produces the desired range in the target model again, as illustrated in Fig. 6.

However, not all target changes can be translated into an exact source change:

- *Relevant changes* modify elements in the relevant target model, which could have been the result of the transformation, and therefore need to be reflected back to the source model. Relevant changes can be further subdivided into:
  - *Valid changes* (cf. (1) in Fig. 5) that can be translated into a corresponding exact change to the source; and
  - *Invalid changes* (cf. (2) in Fig. 5) that *cannot* be translated into a corresponding exact change to the source.
- *Irrelevant changes* (cf. (3) in Fig. 5), which are all other changes.

Definition 10. *Let S, T be models conforming to their respective meta-models $\mathcal{M}_S$, $\mathcal{M}_T$, trans be a model transformation from $\mathcal{M}_S$ to $\mathcal{M}_T$ and Δ_S, Δ_T be changes.*

1. *Δ_T is a **relevant change** if $strip(\Delta_T T) \neq strip(T)$.*
2. *Δ_T is a **purely relevant change** if Δ_T is a relevant change and $\Delta_T = strip(\Delta_T)$.*
3. *Δ_T is a **valid change** if Δ_T is a purely relevant change and $\exists \Delta_S$ such that $trans(\Delta_s S) = strip(\Delta_T T)$.*
4. *Δ_T is an **invalid change** if Δ_T is a purely relevant but not a valid change.*

Irrelevant, i.e., not relevant changes, and valid changes can be translated to the source model. For irrelevant changes, no change to the source has to be performed to keep both models synchronised as the target change cannot possibly impact the transformation. The change translation therefore returns the identical change denoted by Δ_{id}. For valid changes, a set of exact changes to the source model is returned, whereas for invalid changes the invalid change denoted by $\Delta_\perp$ is returned. In this case, the corresponding target change must be rejected to guarantee a synchronised state.

Definition 11. *A function $\phi_{S,T,trans} : C_T \rightarrow \mathscr{P}(C_S) \cup \{\Delta_\perp, \Delta_{id}\}$ is a **change translation function**, mapping changes to the target model to sets of changes to the source model*

$$\phi_{S,T,trans}(\Delta_T) = \begin{cases} \{\Delta_{id}\} \text{ if } \Delta'_T \text{ is not a relevant change,} \\ \quad C \quad \text{ if } \Delta'_T \text{ is a valid change and} \\ \qquad \forall \Delta_S \in C \subseteq C_S : \Delta_S \text{ exactly performs } \Delta_T, \\ \{\Delta_\perp\} \text{ if } \Delta'_T \text{ is an invalid change.} \end{cases}$$

Where $\Delta'_T = strip(\Delta_T)$ and C_T is the set of all possible target changes and respectively, C_S the set of all possible source changes.   □

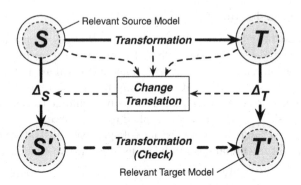

Fig. 6. Transformations are "round-tripped" by translating target changes into source changes, such that applying the transformation to the changed source exactly yields the changed target model

Note: Definition 11 for irrelevant changes corresponds to the GETPUT law in Foster et al [6].

To prove consistency of the proposed definition, the following theorem shows that no matter what the change to the target is, source and target model are always in sync.

Theorem 1. *Given source model S, transformation trans $: \mathcal{M}_S \rightarrow \mathcal{M}_T$ and target model $T = trans(S)$. For any given change Δ_T and $\Delta_S \in \phi_{S,T,trans}(\Delta_T)$:*

$$trans(\alpha(\Delta_S)S) = strip(\beta(\Delta_T)T),$$

where α is a function that returns Δ_{id} if $\Delta_S = \Delta_\perp$ else it returns Δ_S and β is a function that returns Δ_{id} if $\phi_{S,T,trans}(\Delta_T) = \Delta_\perp$ else it returns Δ_T.

Proof.

1. If Δ_T is not a relevant change

   $\overset{\text{Def. 11}}{\Rightarrow} \{\Delta_S\} = \phi_{S,T,trans}(\Delta_T) = \{\Delta_{id}\}$ and therefore $\Delta_S S = S$

   $\overset{\text{Def. 10}}{\Rightarrow} strip(\Delta_T T) = T \overset{\text{pre-cond.}}{\Rightarrow} trans(\alpha(\Delta_S)S) = strip(\beta(\Delta_T)T)$

2. If Δ_T is a purely relevant change:

   (a) Δ_T is an invalid change:

   $\overset{\text{Def. 11}}{\Rightarrow} \Delta_S = \Delta_\perp$ and therefore Δ_T has to be rejected $\Rightarrow \beta(\Delta_T) = \Delta_{id}$

   $\overset{\text{as per 1.)}}{\Rightarrow} trans(\alpha(\Delta_S)S) = strip(\beta(\Delta_T)T)$

   (b) Δ_T is a valid change:

   $\overset{\text{Def. 10}}{\Rightarrow} \exists \Delta_S$ such that $trans(\Delta_S S) = strip(\Delta_T T)$

   $\overset{\text{Def. 11}}{\Rightarrow} \phi_{S,T,trans}(\Delta_T) = \{\Delta_S^1, \ldots, \Delta_S^n\} = C$

   $\overset{\text{Def. 9}}{\Rightarrow} \forall \Delta_S \in C : trans(\alpha(\Delta_S)S) = strip(\beta(\Delta)_T T)$

3. If Δ_T is a relevant but not a purely relevant change

$\Rightarrow$ $\quad \exists \Delta_T', \Delta_T'' : \Delta_T = \Delta_T' \circ \Delta_T''$ such that Δ_T' is a not relevant change: $strip(T) = strip(\Delta_T' T)$ and Δ_T'' is a purely relevant change: $\Delta_T' = strip(\Delta_T'')$

$\overset{\text{Def. 11}}{\Rightarrow}$ $\quad \Delta_S' = \Delta_{id} \in \phi_{S,T,trans}(\Delta_T')$

$\overset{\text{as per 1.)}}{\Rightarrow}$ $\quad trans(S') = T'$ where $S' = \Delta_S' S$ and $T' = strip(\Delta_T' T)$

$\overset{\text{Def. 11}}{\Rightarrow}$ $\quad \Delta_S'' \in \phi_{S,T,trans}(\Delta_T'') \overset{\text{as per 2.)}}{\Rightarrow} trans(\Delta_S'' S') = strip(\Delta_T'' T')$

$\Leftrightarrow$ $\quad trans(\Delta_S'' \Delta_S' S) = strip(\Delta_T' strip(\Delta_T' T))$

$\Leftrightarrow$ $\quad trans(\Delta_S S) = strip(strip(\Delta_T T))$

$\Leftrightarrow$ $\quad trans(\alpha(\Delta_S) S) = strip(\beta(\Delta_T) T)$

$\qquad\qquad\qquad\qquad\qquad\qquad\qquad\qquad\qquad\qquad\qquad\qquad$ $\square$

6.3 Round-Trip Transformation

Looking at Fig. 6 one suspects that the change translation function ϕ is equivalent to a round-trip transformation (cf. Def. 5), except that it returns a set of possible changes of which only one can be applied. Used in conjunction with a function π that picks one change based on some metric or user interaction it is indeed equivalent. This is expressed by the following theorem.

Theorem 2. *Given source model S, transformation $trans : \mathcal{M}_S \rightarrow \mathcal{M}_T$ and target model $T = trans(S)$. For any given change Δ_T*

$$\pi(\phi_{S,T,trans}(\Delta_T))(S)$$

is a round-trip transformation where $\pi : \mathscr{P}(C_S) \rightarrow C_S$ picks the most appropriate source change such that $\pi(C) \in C$.

Proof. Directly results from Theorem 1.

6.4 Example

To illustrate the semantics of exact changes, consider the following example. Given two models as depicted in Fig. 4: A simple UML class diagram and the corresponding relational database schema with respect to the model transformation as shown in Fig. 3. The transformation basically creates one table per class and one column per attribute and class[2].

Now consider the deletion of column `attr1` in table `Class1`. One simple solution seems to be to delete the corresponding attribute, i.e. `attr1` in class `Class1`. This would certainly eliminate column `attr1` of table `Class1`, which is what was requested. However, as attribute `attr1` is deleted, it can no longer be inherited by `Class2` and hence the existence of column `attr1` in table `Class2` can no

---

[2] Note: This includes inherited attributes as well. So an attribute in a super-class will result in a column in the table corresponding to the super-class and each of its subclasses.

longer be supported. Therefore, simply deleting attribute `attr1` is not a viable solution with respect to the exact changes semantics.

To give an example of an exact change, consider the deletion of column `attr1` in table `Class2`. One possible solution is to remove the inheritance between `Class1` and `Class2`. Therefore, attribute `attr1` will no longer be inherited, hence removing column `attr1` in table `Class2`.

For another example where there is a choice between two exact changes, consider the deletion of table `class2`. Now there is a choice between deleting the corresponding class `class2`, or marking it as transient. Either change will be an exact change.

7   Discussion and Conclusion

The original contribution of this paper is the formal definition of round-trip engineering in the context of model transformation. The definition put forward goes beyond any existing approaches as it embraces partial and non-injective transformations, which were shown to be more realistic than the injective transformations required for existing approaches to RTE or model synchronisation.

In order to implement RTE a round-trip transformation is needed, which transforms changed target models back to a corresponding source model. To do so, it relies on the availability of the original source model, the original target model and the change that lead to the new target model. It is also required that the new source and the changed target are in sync, i.e., the forward transformation applied to the new source model has to produce the changed target model. Furthermore, the semantics of target changes were specified and the properties of a function translating target changes to source changes were defined. For this function it was shown that it is equivalent to a round-trip transformation and, that no matter the target change, source and target are always synchronised.

Ongoing research is being conducted as to how source changes can be computed from a given target change satisfying the presented definitions of a change translation function and thus implementing a round-trip transformation.

Over 25 years of research on the view-update problem suggests that there may not be a perfect solution and therefore, any approach to round-trip engineering must acknowledge this. An approach should rather aim at providing a sensible list of legal options to a modeller who then has to decide, which of the changes are most appropriate.

Due to the highly complex nature inherent to the problem, the size of changes may have to be restricted to "small" changes in order to make the problem tractable.

References

1. Aßmann, U.: Automatic Roundtrip Engineering. Electronic Notes in Theoretical Computer Science 82(5) (April 2003)
2. Barros, A., Decker, G., Dumas, M.: Multi-staged and Multi-viewpoint Service Choreography Modelling. In: Proceedings of the Workshop on Software Engineering Methods for Service Oriented Architecture (SEMSOA), Hannover, Germany. CEUR Workshop Proceedings, vol. 244 (May 2007)

3. Cicchetti, A., Ruscio, D.D., Eramo, R.: Towards Propagation of Changes by Model Approximations. In: Proceedings of the 10th International Enterprise Distributed Object Computing Conference Workshops, p. 24. IEEE Computer Society, Los Alamitos (2006)

4. Dayal, U., Bernstein, P.A.: On the correct translation of update operations on relational views. ACM Trans. Database Syst. 7(3), 381–416 (1982)

5. Ehrig, H., Ehrig, K., Ermel, C., Hermann, F., Taentzer, G.: Information Preserving Bidirectional Model Transformations. In: Dwyer, M.B., Lopes, A. (eds.) FASE 2007. LNCS, vol. 4422, pp. 72–86. Springer, Heidelberg (2007)

6. Foster, J.N., Greenwald, M.B., Moore, J.T., Pierce, B.C., Schmitt, A.: Combinators for Bi-Directional Tree Transformations: A Linguistic Approach to the View Update Problem. ACM Transactions on Programming Languages and Systems (2007)

7. Giese, H., Wagner, R.: Incremental Model Synchronization with Triple Graph Grammars. In: Nierstrasz, O., Whittle, J., Harel, D., Reggio, G. (eds.) MoDELS 2006. LNCS, vol. 4199, pp. 543–557. Springer, Heidelberg (2006)

8. Lawley, M., Steel, J.: Practical Declarative Model Transformation with Tefkat. In: Bruel, J.-M. (ed.) MoDELS 2005. LNCS, vol. 3844, pp. 139–150. Springer, Heidelberg (2006)

9. Miller, J., Mukerji, J.: MDA Guide. Technical Report omg/03-06-01, OMG (June 2003)

10. Mu, S.-C., Hu, Z., Takeichi, M.: An Injective Language for Reversible Computation. In: Kozen, D. (ed.) MPC 2004. LNCS, vol. 3125, pp. 289–313. Springer, Heidelberg (2004)

11. Stevens, P.: Bidirectional Model Transformations in QVT: Semantic Issues and Open Questions. In: Engels, G., Opdyke, B., Schmidt, D.C., Weil, F. (eds.) MODELS 2007. LNCS, vol. 4735, pp. 1–15. Springer, Heidelberg (2007)

12. Van Paesschen, E., D'Hondt, M.: SelfSync: A Dynamic Round-Trip Engineering Environment. In: Bruel, J.-M. (ed.) MoDELS 2005. LNCS, vol. 3844, pp. 347–352. Springer, Heidelberg (2006)

13. Xiong, Y., Liu, D., Hu, Z., Zhao, H., Takeichi, M., Mei, H.: Towards automatic model synchronization from model transformations. In: ASE 2007: Proceedings of the twenty-second IEEE/ACM international conference on Automated software engineering, pp. 164–173. ACM, New York (2007)

The Epsilon Transformation Language

Dimitrios S. Kolovos, Richard F. Paige, and Fiona A.C. Polack

Department of Computer Science, University of York,
Heslington, York, YO10 5DD, UK
{dkolovos,paige,fiona}@cs.york.ac.uk

Abstract. Support for automated model transformation is essential for realizing a Model Driven Development (MDD) process. However, model transformation is only one of the many tools in a model engineering toolkit. To apply MDD in the large, automated support for a number of additional tasks such as model comparison, merging, validation and model-to-text transformation, is essential. While a number of successful model transformation languages have been currently proposed, the majority of them have been developed in isolation and as a result, they face consistency and integration difficulties with languages that support other model management tasks. We present the Epsilon Transformation Language (ETL), a hybrid model transformation language that has been developed atop the infrastructure provided by the Epsilon model management platform. By building atop Epsilon, ETL is seamlessly integrated with a number of other task-specific languages to help to realize composite model management workflows.

1 Introduction

The ability to automatically transform between models expressed in different languages (metamodels), technical spaces [1], or levels of abstraction is of paramount importance to the wide-spread adoption of Model-Driven Development (MDD). Although various approaches to automated model transformation have been proposed, the current consensus is that specialized languages, such as QVT [2] and ATL [3], which provide a mixture of declarative and imperative constructs, are most suitable for specifying model transformations.

While model transformation has been characterized as *the heart and soul of MDD* [4], it constitutes only one of the tools in the model engineering toolkit; automating other tasks such as model-to-text transformation, model comparison, validation and merging is of significant, if not of equal, importance. Moreover, it is essential that task-specific languages used in a model engineering environment are consistent and interoperable, so that the users can compose complex workflows of model management operations with enhanced reuse and minimal (unintentional) diversity.

While a number of successful hybrid model transformation languages have been currently proposed, most of them appear to be *isolated* in the sense that they have been developed from the ground up, in most cases only building conceptually on a subset of OCL for model navigation and querying. This introduces unnecessary diversity to the model engineering toolkit and requires a potential user to learn and use similar – but inconsistent – languages to automate different model management tasks.

A. Vallecillo, J. Gray, A. Pierantonio (Eds.): ICMT 2008, LNCS 5063, pp. 46–60, 2008.

Motivated by this, we present the Epsilon Transformation Language (ETL), a hybrid model transformation language that has been built atop the infrastructure provided by the Epsilon Eclipse GMT component [5]. By building on Epsilon, ETL achieves syntactic and semantic consistency and enhanced interoperability with a number of additional languages, also been built atop Epsilon, and which target tasks such as model-to-text transformation, model comparison, validation, merging and unit testing.

The rest of the paper is organized as follows. In Section 2 we provide a detailed discussion on our motivation for designing and implementing a new model transformation language. Section 3 briefly discusses Epsilon and the advantages of building new model management languages atop it. In Section 4 we present the abstract and concrete syntax of ETL as well as an informal discussion of its execution semantics. In Section 5 we demonstrate how ETL can be used together with other languages that build atop Epsilon to realize composite model management operations. Finally, in Section 6 we conclude.

2   Background and Motivation

To date, a large number of languages have been proposed for specifying and executing transformations between models conforming to (potentially) different metamodels. In this section we provide an overview of the different *styles* of transformation adopted by transformation languages, and discuss issues of *integrating* transformation languages with other languages used to perform tasks such as model-to-text transformation, model validation, comparison and merging. Finally, we examine four of the most widely used and actively developed transformation languages in terms of the styles that they offer, and their integrability.

2.1   Styles

Three styles are generally recognized in model transformation languages: declarative, imperative and hybrid, each one demonstrating particular advantages and shortcomings [6]. Purely declarative transformation languages are generally considered to more suitable for scenarios where the source and target metamodels are similar to each other in terms of structure and organization. However, such languages are challenging to use in cases where significant sequential processing and complex mappings are involved. By contrast, purely imperative transformation languages are capable of addressing a wider range of transformation scenarios. Nevertheless, they typically operate at a low level of abstraction which means that users need to manually address issues such as tracing, resolving target elements with their source counterparts, and orchestrating the transformation execution. To address those shortcomings, hybrid languages provide a declarative rule-based execution scheme as well as imperative features for handling complex transformation scenarios.

2.2   Integration with Other Model Management Languages

While model transformation is a very important component in the model engineering toolkit, it is not the only one. A model management workflow typically involves other tasks such as model validation, comparison, merging and code generation, each of which may be supported by a different language. As an example, consider the steps required to generate a data-intensive application from a UML model:

1. Validate the UML model
2. Transform the UML model into a DB model
3. Generate Java code from the UML model
4. Generate SQL code from the DB model

This simple workflow involves three different model-management languages: a validation language for step 1, a model-to-model transformation language for step 2 and a model-to-text transformation language for steps 3 and 4.

2.2.1   Model Format and Runtime Interoperability

The simplest way in which two model management languages can interoperate is by being able to access the same type of models. However, in this case, in every step of the workflow, each language runtime has to load the models from their physical location and store them (if necessary) afterwards. Thus, if Mv, Mt, Mg are (respectively) languages for validation, model-to-text and model-to-model transformation, and if they can only be integrated by accessing the same type of models, the workflow above would involve the following steps:

1. Load the UML model in Mv
2. Validate the UML model
3. Load the UML model in Mt
4. Transform the UML model
5. Store the DB model
6. Load the UML model in Mg
7. Generate the Java code
8. Load the DB model in Mg
9. Generate the SQL code

On the other hand, if Mv, Mt and Mg shared a common internal model representation scheme, the workflow could be simplified to the following:

1. Load the UML model
2. Validate the UML model
3. Transform the UML model into an in-memory DB model
4. Generate the Java code
5. Generate the SQL code from the in-memory DB model
6. (optionally) Store the DB model

Loading and storing big models is a resource- and time-consuming activity, and even this simple example demonstrates that using languages that interoperate only at the model format level introduces a number of (potentially expensive) model loading and storing steps which could otherwise be unnecessary.

2.2.2   Code Consistency and Reuse

Another significant issue when using many languages to implement the steps of a work-flow is reuse and consistency of code. Consider, once again, a worfklow in which we want to carry out validation, transformation, and model-to-text generation tasks, as above. When managing UML2 models, a typical activity in all three tasks is to examine model elements to check if they have certain *stereotypes* attached. If the three languages selected for these tasks were OCL, ATL and MOFScript, respectively, then the user would need to specify the same *helper* operation (which checks whether a specified stereotype is attached) three times, using similar but inconsistent syntaxes, as illustrated in Listings 1.2, 1.1 and 1.3 respectively.

Listing 1.1. The hasStereotype() helper expressed in ATL

```
1  helper context UML2!Element def:hasStereotype(s:String):Boolean
2  self.getAppliedStereotypes()->exists(st | st.name = s);
```

Listing 1.2. The hasStereotype() helper expressed in OCL

```
1  package uml
2     context Element
3     def Operations:
4        let hasStereotype(s : String) : Boolean =
5           getAppliedStereotypes()->exists(st | st.name = s)
6  endpackage
```

Listing 1.3. The hasStereotype() helper expressed in MOFScript

```
1  uml.Element::hasStereotype(s : String): Boolean {
2     result = self.getAppliedStereotypes()->exists(st | st.name = s);
3  }
```

Duplication of code in different languages introduces a maintenance problem and is also a potential source of coding errors as it requires the user to work concurrently with similar but inconsistent syntaxes.

2.3   Overview of the Most Widely-Used Transformation Languages

Due to the large number of transformation languages, and the imposed space limitations, in this section we only concentrate on those transformation languages which, to our knowledge, are most widely-used and actively developed. These languages are: QVT [7] which is the currently adopted OMG standard, ATL [3] that is probably the most widely-used transformation language today, Kermeta [8], and XTend, which is the transformation language of the popular openArchitectureWare framework [9].

With respect to integration, only XTend is integrated with additional model management languages of the openArchitectureWare framework that target other tasks such as code generation (XPand) and model validation (Check). Nevertheless, XTend is a purely imperative language and as discussed in Section 2.1, imperative languages require the user to implement transformation rules, scheduling and support for traceability almost from scratch for each transformation.

Kermeta adopts a different approach to model management by providing a general-purpose imperative language which can be used to perform all model management tasks. However, being purely imperative, the language also suffers from the aforementioned shortcomings.

ATL is the most successful hybrid model transformation language to date. It integrates with the TCS tool [10] which provides support for model-to-text and text-to-model transformations. Moreover, it has been shown that ATL can be used to perform other tasks, such as model validation [11] and merging[1], for which however the language is, to our view, not particularly suitable as it is not tailored to the specific requirements of these tasks.

Finally, QVT – the current OMG standard for model transformation – adopts a hybrid style by providing both declarative and imperative constructs. With regards to integration, the OMG has also standardized a model-to-text transformation language (MOF2Text) [12] which reuses parts of QVT, and both QVT and MOF2Text are aligned with OCL. Nevertheless, the OMG has not (yet) proposed languages for tasks such as model comparison and merging nor a solution for specifying and orchestrating multi-step model management workflows.

Table 1. Feature Matrix of Model Transformation Languages

Language	Style	Integrations?
XTend	Imperative	XPand, Check
Kermeta	Imperative	General-purpose language
ATL	Hybrid	TCS, Can also perform model validation, merging
QVT	Hybrid	MOF2Text, OCL

2.4 Motivation

Throughout this section we have argued that existing hybrid model transformation languages suffer from integration problems with languages that support other tasks. On the other hand, languages such as Kermeta and XTend, which can be used in the context of a framework that supports other model management tasks as well, are purely imperative and thus suffer from the problems discussed in Section 2.3. Driven by this motivation, in Section 4 we present the Epsilon Transformation Language (ETL), a hybrid model transformation language that integrates seamlessly with a number of other model management languages developed atop the Epsilon model management platform.

3   Epsilon

Epsilon is a component of the Eclipse GMT project [13] that provides infrastructure for implementing uniform and interoperable model management languages. It can be used to manage models of diverse metamodels and technologies. At the core of Epsilon is the Epsilon Object Language (EOL) [14], an OCL-based imperative language that

---

[1] http://ssel.vub.ac.be/ssel/research:mdd:casestudies#mergemodel_modelmerge

provides features such as model modification, multiple model access, conventional programming constructs (variables, loops, branches etc.), user interaction, profiling, and support for transactions. Although EOL can be used as a general-purpose model management language, its primary aim is to be reused in task-specific languages. Thus, a number of task-specific languages have been implemented atop EOL, including those for model comparison (ECL) [15], model merging (EML) [16], model validation (EVL) [17], model refactoring (EWL) [18] and model-to-text transformation (EGL) [19].

With regard to the types of models supported, Epsilon provides the Epsilon Model Connectivity (EMC) layer that is used to provide a uniform interface for models of different modelling technologies. Currently, EMC drivers have been implemented to support EMF [20] (XMI 2.x), MDR [21] (XMI 1.x), Z [22] and XML. Also, to enable users to compose workflows that involve a number of individual model management tasks, Epsilon provides ANT [23] tasks and an inter-task communication framework discussed in detail in [24].

4   The Epsilon Transformation Language

The aim of ETL is to contribute model-to-model transformation capabilities to Epsilon. More specifically, ETL needs to be able to capture and execute specifications of transformation scenarios that involve an arbitrary number of input and output models of different modelling languages and technologies at a high level of abstraction.

4.1   Style

As discussed in Section 2.1, hybrid transformation languages are very appropriate for constructing flexible, expressive, and abstract model transformations. Therefore, ETL has been designed as a hybrid language that implements a task-specific rule definition and execution scheme, but which also inherits the imperative features of EOL to handle complex transformations where necessary.

4.2   Source and Target Models

The majority of model-to-model transformation languages assume that only two models participate in each transformation: the source model and the target model. Nevertheless, it is often essential to be able to access/update additional models during a transformation (such as trace or configuration models). Building on the facilities provided by EMC and EOL, ETL enables specification of transformations that can transform an arbitrary number of source models into an arbitrary number of target models.

Another common assumption is that the contents of the target models are insignificant and thus a transformation can safely overwrite its contents. By contrast, ETL - like all Epsilon languages - enables users to specify for each involved model separately if its contents need to be preserved or not.

4.3   Abstract Syntax

As illustrated in Figure 1, ETL transformations are organized in modules (*ETLModule*). A module can contain any number of transformation rules (*TransformationRule*) and

EOL operations [14]. Each rule has a unique name (in the context of the module) and also specifies one *source*[2] and one or more *target* parameters. A transformation rule can also *extend* a number of other transformation rules and be declared as *abstract*, *primary* and/or *lazy*. To limit its applicability to a subset of elements that conform to the type of the *source* parameter, a rule can optionally define a guard which is either an EOL expression or a block of EOL statements. Finally, each rule defines a block of EOL statements (*body*) where the logic for populating the property values of the target model elements is specified.

Besides transformation rules, an ETL module can also optionally contain a number of *pre* and *post* named blocks of EOL statements which, as discussed later, are executed before and after the transformation rules respectively.

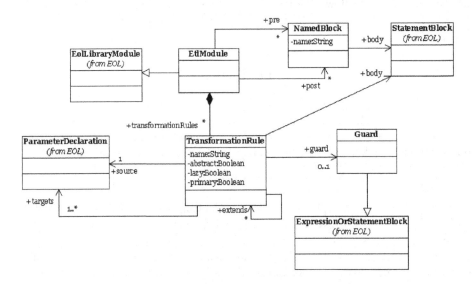

Fig. 1. ETL Abstract Syntax

4.4   Concrete Syntax

The concrete syntax of a transformation rule is displayed in Listing 1.4. The optional *abstract*, *lazy* and *primary* attributes of the rule are specified using respective annotations. The name of the rule follows the *rule* keyword and the *source* and *target* parameters are defined after the *transform* and *to* keywords. Also, the rule can define an optional comma-separated list of rules it extends after the *extends* keyword. Inside the curly braces (), the rule can optionally specify its *guard* either as an EOL expression following a column (:) (for simple guards) or as a block of statements in curly braces (for more complex guards). Finally, the *body* of the rule is specified as a sequence of EOL statements.

---

[2] While an ETL module can transform multiple input models, each rule can transform only one type of model elements.

Listing 1.4. Concrete Syntax of a TransformationRule

```
1  (@abstract)?
2  (@lazy)?
3  (@primary)?
4  rule <name>
5    transform <sourceParameterName>:<sourceParameterType>
6    to (<rightParameterName>:<rightParameterType>
7    (, <rightParameterName>:<rightParameterType>)*
8    (extends (<ruleName>,)*<ruleName>)? {
9
10   (guard (:expression)|({statement+}))?
11
12   statement+
13 }
```

Pre and *post* blocks have a quite simple syntax that, as presented in Listing 1.5, consists of the identifier (pre or post), an optional name and the set of statements to be executed enclosed in curly braces.

Listing 1.5. Concrete Syntax of Pre and Post blocks

```
1  (pre|post) <name> {
2    statement+
3  }
```

4.5 Execution Semantics

Having discussed the abstract and concrete syntax of the language, in this section we provide an informal discussion on its execution semantics.

4.5.1 Rule and Block Overriding

An ETL module can import a number of other ETL modules. In this case, the importing ETL module inherits all the rules and pre/post blocks specified in the modules it imports (recursively). If the module specifies a rule or a pre/post block with the same name, the local rule/block overrides the imported one respectively.

4.5.2 Rule Execution Scheduling

When an ETL module is executed, the *pre* blocks of the module are executed first in the order in which they have been specified.

Following that, each *non-abstract* and *non-lazy* rule is executed for all the elements on which it is applicable[3]. To be applicable to a particular element, the element must have a kind-of relationship with the type defined in the rule's *sourceParameter* and must also satisfy the *guard* of the rule (and all the rules it extends). When a rule is executed on an applicable element, the target elements are initially created by instantiating the *targetParameters* of the rules, and then their contents are populated using the EOL statements of the *body* of the rule.

---

[3] As discussed in the sequel, lazy rules are invoked explicitly using the equivalents() operation.

Finally, when all rules have been executed, the *post* blocks of the module are executed in the order in which they have been declared.

4.5.3   Resolution of Source Elements in the Target Models

Finding the target elements that have been (or can be) transformed from particular source elements by other rules is a recurring task in the body of a transformation rule. To automate this task and reduce coupling between rules, ETL provides the *equivalents()* and *equivalent()* built-in operations that automatically resolve source elements to their transformed counterparts in the target models.

When the *equivalents()* operation is applied on a single source element (as opposed to a collection of them), it inspects the established transformation trace and invokes the applicable rules (if necessary) to calculate the counterparts of the element in the target model. When applied to a collection it returns a *Bag* containing *Bags* that in turn contain the counterparts of the source elements contained in the collection. The *equivalents()* operation can be also invoked with an arbitrary number of rule names as parameters to invoke and return only the equivalents created by specific rules. Unlike the main execution scheduling scheme discussed above, the *equivalents()* operation invokes both *lazy* and *non-lazy* rules.

With regard to the ordering of the results of the *equivalents()* operations, the returned elements appear in the respective order of the rules that have created them. An exception to this occurs when one of the rules is declared as *primary*, in which case its results precede the results of all other rules.

ETL also provides the convenience *equivalent()* operation which, when applied to a single element, returns only the first element of the respective result that would have been returned by the *equivalents()* operation discussed above. Also, when applied to a collection the *equivalent()* operation returns a flattened collection (as opposed to the result of *equivalents()* which is a *Bag* of *Bags* in this case). As with the *equivalents()* operation, the *equivalent()* operation can also be invoked with or without parameters.

The semantics of the *equivalent()* operation are further illustrated through a simple example. In this example, we need to transform a model that conforms to the Tree metamodel displayed in Figure 2 into a model that conforms to the Graph metamodel of Figure 3. More specifically, we need to transform each *Tree* element to a *Node*, and an *Edge* that connects it with the *Node* that is equivalent to the tree's *parent*. This is achieved using the rule of Listing 1.6.

In lines 1-3, the *Tree2Node* rule specifies that it can transform elements of the *Tree* type in the *Tree* model into elements of the *Node* type in the *Graph* model. In line 4 it specifies that the name of the created Node should be the same as the name of the source Tree. If the parent of the source *Tree* is defined (line 7), the rule creates a new *Edge* (line 8) and sets its *source* property to the created *Node* (line 9) and its *target* property to the *equivalent Node* of the source *Tree*'s *parent* (line 10).

Listing 1.6. Exemplar ETL rule demonstrating the *equivalent()* operation

```
1  rule Tree2Node
2     transform t : Tree!Tree
3     to n : Graph!Node {
4
```

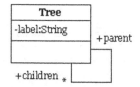

Fig. 2. A Simple Tree Metamodel

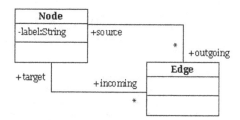

Fig. 3. A Simple Graph Metamodel

```
5        n.label := t.label;
6
7    if (t.parent.isDefined()) {
8        var edge := new Graph!Edge;
9        edge.source := n;
10       edge.target := t.parent.equivalent();
11   }
12 }
```

4.5.4   Overriding the Semantics of the EOL SpecialAssignment Operator

As discussed above, resolving the equivalent(s) or source model elements in the target model is a recurring task in model transformation. Furthermore, in most cases resolving the equivalent of a model element is immediately followed by assigning/adding the obtained target model elements to the value(s) of a property of another target model element. For example, in line 10 of Listing 1.6 the *equivalent* obtained is immediately assigned to the *target* property of the generated *Edge*. To make transformation specifications more readable, ETL overrides the semantics of the *SpecialAssignment* (*::=* in terms of concrete syntax) operator that EOL provides to set its left-hand side, not to the element its right-hand side evaluates to, but to its *equivalent* as calculated using the *equivalent()* operation discussed above. Using this feature, line 10 of the *Tree2Node* rule can be rewritten as shown in Listing 1.7

Listing 1.7. Rewritten Line 10 of the *Tree2Node* Rule Demonstrated in Listing 1.6

```
1  edge.target ::= t.parent;
```

4.6   Interactive Transformations

Using the user interaction facilities of EOL discussed in [25], an ETL transformation can be made interactive by prompting the user for input during its execution. For example in Listing 1.8, we modify the *Tree2Node* rule originally presented in Listing 1.6 by adding a *guard* part that uses the user-input facilities of EOL (more specifically the *UserInput.confirm(String,Boolean)* operation) to enable the user select manually at runtime which of the Tree elements need to be transformed to respective Node elements in the target model and which not.

Listing 1.8. Exemplar Interactive ETL Transformation

```
1   rule Tree2Node
2       transform t : Tree!Tree
3       to n : Graph!Node {
4
5       guard : UserInput.confirm
6           ('Transform tree ' + t.label + '?', true)
7
8       n.label := t.label;
9       var target : Graph!Node ::= t.parent;
10      if (target.isDefined()) {
11          var edge := new Graph!Edge;
12          edge.source := n;
13          edge.target := target;
14      }
15  }
```

4.7   Summary

This section has provided a detailed discussion on the Epsilon Transformation Language (ETL). Unlike most contemporary model transformation languages, ETL is capable of transforming an arbitrary number of source models into an arbitrary number of target models. ETL adopts a hybrid style and features declarative rule specification using advanced concepts such as *guards*, *abstract*, *lazy* and *primary* rules, and automatic resolution of target elements from their source counterparts. Also, as ETL is based on EOL reuses its imperative features to enable users to specify particularly complex, and even interactive, transformations.

5   Integration with Other Model Management Languages

Integration of ETL with other model management languages of the Epsilon platform is achieved in two ways. First, since all languages of the Epsilon platform build atop EOL, they can all import and use libraries of operations specified in EOL. Therefore, with regard to the example of Section 2.2.1, if *Mv*, *Mt* and *Mg* are EVL, ETL and EGL respectively, the *hasStereotype(s : String)* operation will only need to be defined once in an EOL library which can then be imported by the different model management programs.

Besides reuse of code, ETL is integrated with other Epsilon languages at runtime through the workflow mechanism discussed in [24]. More specifically, the worfklow supports the *epsilon.etl* task for executing ETL transformations. Listing 1.9 demonstrates using the *epsilon.etl* task in the context of the worfklow outlined in Section 2.2.1.

In line 7 the *loadModels* target loads the UML and DB model (without reading the existing contents of the DB model due to the *readOnLoad=false* property in line 14). Once the models have been loaded, they are made accessible to any subsequent Epsilon tasks in the workflow. In line 18, the *validate* target uses EVL to validate the UML model. In line 24, the *transform* target uses ETL to transform between the two models. The ETL task also specifies that it exports its internal trace as a variable named *transTrace* which the *storeTransformationTrace* EOL task in Line 33 can then read and store in the form of a trace model. Finally, the *uml2java* and *db2sql* code generation targets in lines 41 and 47 use EGL to generate the Java and SQL source code from the UML and DB models respectively.

Listing 1.9. Implementation of the Workflow of Section 2.2.1 using the Epsilon ANT workflow

```
1    <project default="main">
2
3      <target name="main"
4        depends="uml2java,db2sql,storeTransformationTrace">
5      </target>
6
7      <target name="loadModels">
8        <epsilon.loadModel name="UML" type="MDR">
9          ...
10          <property name="readOnLoad" value="true"/>
11        </epsilon.loadModel>
12        <epsilon.loadModel name="DB" type="EMF">
13          ...
14          <property name="readOnLoad" value="false"/>
15        </epsilon.loadModel>
16      </target>
17
18      <target name="validate" depends="loadModels">
19        <epsilon.evl src="UMLConstraints.evl">
20          <model ref="UML"/>
21        </epsilon.evl>
22      </target>
23
24      <target name="transform" depends="validate">
25        <epsilon.etl src="UML2DB.etl"
26          exporttransformationtrace="transTrace">
27
28          <model ref="UML"/>
29          <model ref="DB"/>
30        </epsilon.etl>
31      </target>
32
```

```
33    <target name="storeTransformationTrace" depends="transform,storeDBmodel">
34        <epsilon.eol src="StoreTransformationTrace.eol">
35            <uses ref="transTrace"/>
36            <model ref="UML"/>
37            <model ref="DB"/>
38        </epsilon.eol>
39    </target>
40
41    <target name="uml2java" depends="validate">
42        <epsilon.egl src="Uml2Java.egl">
43            <model ref="UML"/>
44        </epsilon.egl>
45    </target>
46
47    <target name="db2sql" depends="transform">
48        <epsilon.egl src="DB2Sql.egl">
49            <model ref="DB"/>
50        </epsilon.egl>
51    </target>
52
53    <target name="storeDBmodel">
54        <epsilon.storeModel model="DB"/>
55    </target>
56
57 </project>
```

A more complex and detailed case study that demonstrates using ETL together with other languages provided by the Epsilon platform is available in [26].

6 Conclusions

In this paper we have raised the issue of consistency and integration between model transformation languages and languages that target other model management tasks such as code generation, model comparison, merging and validation. We have presented the Epsilon Transformation Language (ETL), a hybrid model transformation language that has been built atop the infrastructure provided by the Epsilon model management platform. We have also shown that ETL can be seamlessly integrated with existing languages of the Epsilon platform that target a wide range of model management tasks using a workflow mechanism built atop ANT.

Acknowledgements

The work in this paper was supported by the European Commission via the MOD-ELPLEX project, co-funded by the European Commission under the "Information Society Technologies" Sixth Framework Programme (2006-2009).

References

1. Kurtev, I., Bezivin, J., Aksit, M.: Technical spaces: An initial appraisal. In: Proc. Tenth International Conference on Cooperative Information Systems (CoopIS), Federated Conferences Industrial Track, California (2002)
2. Object Management Group. MOF QVT Final Adopted Specification, http://www.omg.org/cgi-bin/doc?ptc/05-11-01.pdf
3. Jouault, F., Kurtev, I.: Transforming Models with ATL. In: Bruel, J.-M. (ed.) MoDELS 2005. LNCS, vol. 3844, pp. 128–138. Springer, Heidelberg (2006)
4. Sendall, S., Kozaczynski, W.: Model Transformation the Heart and Soul of Model-Driven Software Development. IEEE Software 20(5), 42–45 (2003)
5. Extensible Platform for Specification of Integrated Languages for mOdel maNagement (Epsilon), http://www.eclipse.org/gmt/epsilon
6. Czarnecki, K., Helsen, S.: Classification of Model Transformation Approaches. In: OOPSLA 2003 Workshop on Generative Techniques in the Context of Model-Driven Architecture (2003)
7. QVT Partners Official Web-Site, http://qvtp.org/
8. Chauvel, F., Fleurey, F.: Kermeta Language Overview, http://www.kermeta.org
9. OpenArchitectureWare, Official Web-Site, http://www.openarchitectureware.org/
10. Jouault, F., Bézivin, J., Kurtev, I.: TCS: a DSL for the Specification of Textual Concrete Syntaxes in Model Engineering. In: Proc GPCE 2006: Proceedings of the fifth international conference on Generative programming and Component Engineering (2006)
11. Jouault, F., Bezívin, J.: Using ATL for Checking Models. In: Proc. International Workshop on Graph and Model Transformation (GraMoT), Tallinn, Estonia (September 2005)
12. Object Management Group. MOF Model to Text Transformation Language Language Final Adopted Specification, http://www.omg.org/docs/ptc/06-11-01.pdf
13. Eclipse GMT - Generative Modeling Technology, Official Web-Site, http://www.eclipse.org/gmt
14. Kolovos, D.S., Paige, R.F., Polack, F.A.C.: The Epsilon Object Language (EOL). In: Rensink, A., Warmer, J. (eds.) ECMDA-FA 2006. LNCS, vol. 4066, pp. 128–142. Springer, Heidelberg (2006)
15. Kolovos, D.S., Paige, R.F., Polack, F.A.C.: Model Comparison: A Foundation for Model Composition and Model Transformation Testing. In: Proc. 1st International Workshop on Global Integrated Model Management (GaMMa), ACM/IEEE ICSE 2006, Shanghai, China, pp. 13–20. ACM Press (2006)
16. Kolovos, D.S., Paige, R.F., Polack, F.A.C.: Merging Models with the Epsilon Merging Language (EML). In: Proc. ACM/IEEE 9th International Conference on Model Driven Engineering Languages and Systems (Models/UML 2006), Genova, Italy. LNCS (October 2006)
17. Kolovos, D.S., Paige, R.F., Polack, F.A.C.: On the Evolution of OCL for Capturing Structural Constraints in Modelling Languages. In: Proc. Dagstuhl Workshop on Rigorous Methods for Software Construction and Analysis (2007)
18. Kolovos, D.S., Paige, R.F., Rose, L.M., Polack, F.A.C.: Update Transformations in the Small with the Epsilon Wizard Language. Journal of Object Technology (JOT), Special Issue for TOOLS Europe 2007 (2007)
19. Rose, L.M.: The Epsilon Generation Language (EGL). MEng Thesis, Department of Computer Science, The University of York (2008)
20. Eclipse.org. Eclipse Modelling Framework, http://www.eclipse.org/emf
21. Sun Microsystems. Meta Data Repository, http://mdr.netbeans.org

22. Woodcock, J., Davies, J.: Using Z: Specification, Refinement, and Proof. Prentice Hall, Englewood Cliffs (1996)
23. The Apache Ant Project, http://ant.apache.org
24. Kolovos, D.S., Paige, R.F., Polack, F.A.C.: A Framework for Composing Modular and Interoperable Model Management Tasks. Under review (2008), http://www.cs.york.ac.uk/~dkolovos/publications/AntWorkflow.pdf
25. Kolovos, D.S., Paige, R.F., Polack, F.A.C.: Novel Features in Languages of the Epsilon Model Management Platform. In: Proc. 2nd Workshop on Modeling in Software Engineering, 30th International Conference on Software Engineering (ICSE), Leipzig, Germany (May 2008)
26. Kolovos, D.S., Paige, R.F., Rose, L.M., Polack, F.A.C.: Implementing the Interactive Applications Case Study using Epsilon. In: Proc. Model-Driven Development Tool Implementers Forum (MDD-TIF), Tools Europe (2007), http://www.dsmforum.org/events/MDD-TIF07/Epsilon.2.pdf

Transforming Process Algebra Models into UML State Machines: Bridging a Semantic Gap?

M.F. van Amstel, M.G.J. van den Brand, Z. Protić, and T. Verhoeff

Department of Mathematics and Computer Science
Technische Universiteit Eindhoven
Den Dolech 2, P.O. Box 513, 5600 MB Eindhoven, The Netherlands
{M.F.v.Amstel,M.G.J.v.d.Brand,Z.Protic,T.Verhoeff}@tue.nl

Abstract. There exist many formalisms for modeling the behavior of (software) systems. These formalisms serve different purposes. Process algebras are used for algebraic and axiomatic reasoning about the behavior of distributed systems. UML state machines are suitable for automatic software generation. We have developed a transformation from the process algebra ACP into UML state machines to enable automatic software generation from process algebra models. This transformation needs to preserve both behavioral and structural properties. The combination of these preservation requirements gives rise to a *semantic gap*. It implies that we cannot transform ACP models into UML state machines on a syntactic level only.

We address this semantic gap and propose a way of bridging it. To validate our proposal, we have implemented a tool for automatic transformation of ACP process algebra models into UML state machines.

1 Introduction

In this paper we address the semantic gap that arises when transforming models specified in one formalism into models in another formalism. A transformation between models in different formalisms needs to bridge a syntactic gap. This is a well-known problem. However, in many applications one also needs to preserve semantic properties. This is not trivial since the semantic domains of the source and target formalism may differ, or a formal semantics may be lacking. Moreover, additional requirements on semantical properties can affect a transformation.

The goal within the FALCON project [1] is to model embedded systems in a warehousing environment and use these models initially for simulation, but later for, amongst others, automatic software generation. These systems are being modeled using a process algebra [2]. Process algebra is a formalism used for algebraic and axiomatic reasoning about the behavior of systems, in particular those involving concurrency [3]. However, little is known about automatic code generation from process algebra models. We use UML state machines as an intermediate step because multiple techniques are available for automatic code

A. Vallecillo, J. Gray, A. Pierantonio (Eds.): ICMT 2008, LNCS 5063, pp. 61–75, 2008.

generation from them. Therefore we propose a transformation from process algebra models to UML state machines [4]. We start with plain process algebra in order to understand the basics of software generation from, and model transformations based on process algebras. In this paper we use the well-known process algebra ACP (Algebra of Communicating Processes) [5,6] without encapsulation. In the transformation of this small process algebra we already encounter a semantic gap. The obtained results will be used when translating process algebra based formalisms like timed χ [7] or mCRL2 [8].

Processes in distributed systems are allocated to different machines that run in parallel. Therefore we have to ensure that the automatically generated code can also be deployed on different machines. This requires that the ACP models and the obtained state machines are structurally equivalent with respect to parallel behavior. The ACP models and the state machines obtained from this transformation obviously need to exhibit the same behavior. It is this combination of requirements, i.e., preserving structural and behavioral properties, that confronted us with the problems of bridging a semantic gap. In ACP, constructs are available for modeling synchronous communication between parallel processes. UML state machines are inherently asynchronous, hence no primitives exist for modeling synchronous communication. This means that the transformation from ACP to UML state machines encompasses more than translating syntax. Special care is needed to ensure that the semantic gap is bridged in order to preserve both behavioral and structural properties.

The remainder of this paper is structured as follows. Section 2 describes related work. In Section 3 our approach to transform ACP models into UML state machines is explained. In this section also the semantic gap is explained in depth and we propose and evaluate some solutions for bridging this gap. Section 4 describes the implementation of our transformation. An illustration using our implementation can be found in Section 5. Section 6 contains the conclusions of our work and gives some directions for further research.

2   Related Work

Many papers have been published on the subject of transforming process algebras into various formalisms. In one of the first papers in this area a transformation from the Algebra of Timed Processes (ATP) into a variant of timed graphs is presented [9]. The authors aim at unifying behavioral description formalisms for timed systems. In [10], a transformation of a timed process algebra based on LOTOS operators to Dynamic State Graphs is presented. The main purpose of that mapping is to visualize and simulate process algebra models. In [11] three different process algebras are analyzed and compared. The results of that analysis are used to propose a framework for visualizing process algebras. In a recent technical report [12], a transformation from timed χ into UPPAAL timed automata is presented. The main purpose of that mapping is to enable model checking and verification of process algebra models. Our approach, however, focuses on automatic software generation.

Research has also been performed in the field of software generation from UML state machines. In [13] an overview is given of different approaches for generating code from UML state machines. The authors identify the weaknesses in these approaches and also propose their own technique. The approach described in [14] generates object-oriented code from UML state machines. In our work we use the tool Telelogic Rhapsody to generate simulation code from state machines. The semantics of Rhapsody state machines differs slightly from UML state machines [15], but this does not affect our approach.

3 Transforming ACP Models into UML State Machines

In this section first a short introduction is given to the relevant parts of ACP. Next, our transformation from ACP to UML state machines is described. In Section 3.3 the semantic gap is discussed in more detail. Section 3.4 presents our solution to bridge this gap.

3.1 Algebra of Communicating Processes

In this paper, we consider basic ACP without the encapsulation operator (∂) to illustrate one of the main issues in bridging a semantic gap. It suffices to leave out the encapsulation operator because a semantic gap already emerges without it. An *ACP model* consists of a *process term* (P) and a *communication function* (γ). A process term is built from *atoms* and *operators*.

In ACP there are three types of atoms. First, there is the deadlock constant (δ) that denotes inaction. When this constant is encountered in a process it deadlocks. Second, there is the empty process constant (ϵ) that denotes doing nothing. Third, there are the actions that can be performed by a process term.

In ACP there are six operators. First, there is the sequential composition $(\cdot)$. The sequential composition of n process terms, $P_1 \cdot P_2 \cdot \ldots \cdot P_n$, denotes that the execution of P_1 precedes the execution of P_2 and so on. Second there is the action prefix operator (.). This operator is similar to the sequential composition, therefore we consider it as such. Third, there is the alternative composition $(+)$. The alternative composition of n process terms, $P_1 + P_2 + \ldots + P_n$, denotes that only one of these process terms is executed. This choice is made non-deterministically. Fourth, there is the parallel composition $(\|)$. The parallel composition of n process terms, $P_1\|P_2\| \ldots \|P_n$, denotes that these process terms are executed quasi-parallel. This means that the process terms are arbitrarily interleaved whilst maintaining their internal ordering. Consider for example the parallel composition $(a \cdot b)\|(c \cdot d)$. The arbitrary interleaving may not result in a situation where the execution of b precedes the execution of a, or where the execution of d precedes the execution of c. There is, however, more to the parallel composition which will be explained in Section 3.3. Fifth, there is the left merge operator $(\|\!\|)$ which is closely related to the parallel composition. It denotes that the first action to the left of the operator is executed first whereafter the remaining process term continues as a parallel composition. Consider for example the process term $(a \cdot x) \| y$. This means that first action a is executed whereafter the process term behaves as $x \| y$. This operator occurs for technical reasons [16] in the reduction of ACP process terms and is seldomly used in modeling directly. Last, there is the communication merge operator ($|$). This operator is used together with the communication function (γ) to express communication (or interaction) between two actions. The communication function expresses which actions can communicate and what the result of this communication is. For example $\gamma(a, b) = c$ expresses that in the process term $a|b$ actions a and b communicate, resulting in action c. If this communication function does not exist, actions a and b cannot communicate. This means that the process term $a|b$ results in a deadlock (δ). The communication merge operator also occurs for technical reasons [16] in the reduction of ACP process terms and is seldomly used in modeling directly.

3.2   Transformation

Our transformation f from ACP models to UML state machines takes an ACP model, which consists of a process term and a communication function, as an argument and returns a UML state machine.

$$f : \text{ACP model} \rightarrow \text{UML state machine}$$

Every non-atomic process term is built from smaller process terms, resulting in an implicit tree structure. Our transformation traverses this tree and transforms every subtree into a partial state machine that is structurally equivalent to the process term in the node. ACP has axiomatic rewrite rules. This means that an ACP process term can be rewritten (transformed) into a different-but-equivalent process term using these rules. An example of this rewriting process is given in Figure 1. In order to ensure the required structural equivalence with respect to parallel behavior, the original ACP model should not be rewritten such as to remove parallel composition operators. In general it is not required to maintain structure. However, we will maximize structure preservation for the other ACP constructs as well, since we want to preserve designer's choices as closely as possible. Therefore the ACP axioms for rewriting a process term are used as little as possible by our transformation.

We use the formal semantics of ACP described in [17] and the semantics description of UML presented in [4] to explain informally the behavioral equivalence of ACP constructs and the resulting UML state machines. With behavioral equivalence we mean that the the state machines need to define exactly the same traces as the original ACP models.

The state machine constructs for the sequential, alternative, and parallel composition are straightforward, i.e., the semantics is clear from the syntax. The sequential composition maps to the state machine depicted in Figure 2(a). This construct enforces that the execution of P_1 precedes the execution of P_2 and so on. The dotted state labeled $f(P_i)$ represent the partial state machine acquired after applying f to process term P_i. The state machine to which the alternative composition maps is depicted in Figure 2(b). The choice state ensures that

$$a.x + (b.y + a.x)$$
$$= \{\text{Axiom A1}: \ x + y = y + x\}$$
$$a.x + (a.x + b.y)$$
$$= \{\text{Axiom A2}: \ (x + y) + z = x + (y + z)\}$$
$$(a.x + a.x) + b.y$$
$$= \{\text{Axiom A3}: \ (x + x) = x\}$$
$$a.x + b.y$$

Fig. 1. Example of rewriting using the ACP axioms

only one of the paths will (non-deterministically) be selected for execution. Figure 2(c) depicts the state machine for the parallel composition. The fork and join states are used to ensure that all parallel branches start and end simultaneously. The transformation of the atoms is explained in Section 3.4.

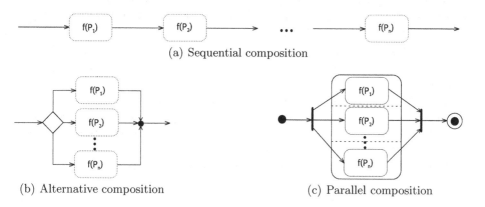

(a) Sequential composition

(b) Alternative composition   (c) Parallel composition

Fig. 2. Transformation

The left merge operator cannot be expressed in a natural way in a state machine. It is impossible to express that a specific action in one branch of a parallel composition should be performed first. Therefore, the left merge operator is eliminated by rewriting according to the axioms of ACP. Also the communication merge operator cannot be expressed in a natural way in a state machine. Therefore, when communication of two actions is encountered the communication function (γ) is consulted whether this communication should be rewritten into an action or the deadlock constant. These are the only two cases in which structure is not preserved, but since these two constructs are seldomly used in modeling this is acceptable.

3.3   Semantic Gap

In ACP the parallel composition of two or more process terms represents not just the interleaving of these terms. It also involves communication of the actions inside them. Consider for example the ACP process term $a\|b$. This will rewrite using the ACP axioms to $a \cdot b + b \cdot a + a|b$. Suppose now the communication function $\gamma(a, b) = c$ exists for some action c. In this case actions a and b can be executed simultaneously $(a|b)$ and communicate. The result of this communication is action c. So the traces allowed by this parallel composition are $a \cdot b$, $b \cdot a$, and c. In UML state machines the parallel composition, created by transitions that fork into orthogonal regions, represents interleaving or concurrent execution of the traces in the orthogonal regions. There is no communication between the actions in these traces like in ACP. This gap between the semantics of ACP and UML state machines needs to be bridged.

One possibility to bridge this gap is to use the ACP axioms to rewrite an ACP model such that all parallel composition operators are removed. In this way all communication is made explicit. The state machine acquired after rewriting is sketched in Figure 3(a). This is not a valid solution since one of the requirements is that the UML state machines need to preserve the structure of the ACP models, at least with respect to the parallel composition. In fact, the combination of the requirements of preserving both behavioral and structural properties gives rise to the semantic gap.

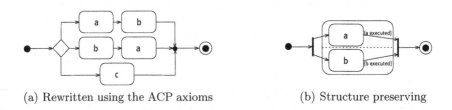

(a) Rewritten using the ACP axioms   (b) Structure preserving

Fig. 3. State machine representations of $a\|b$

Another possible solution is to exploit the semantic openness of UML state machines. Therefore we propose an action dispatcher that takes care of executing all actions. Actions are not executed in the state machine itself. Instead, an action is announced to the action dispatcher and the branch of the state machine that contains the action is blocked. After the action dispatcher executes the action, it enables the appropriate branch again such that the state machine can continue. If multiple actions that can communicate have been announced, the action dispatcher ensures that communication can occur in accordance with the communication function. Suppose for example that actions a and b are announced and that $\gamma(a, b) = c$, i.e., actions a and b can communicate resulting in action c. The action dispatcher now also allows action c to be executed. Using the action dispatcher, we succeed in preserving most of the structure of the ACP model. Figure 3(b) sketches the resulting state machine.

It can be argued whether having a global action dispatcher that exploits the semantic openness of UML state machines is a proper solution. The disadvantage of having this global action dispatcher is that communication behavior is invisible in the state machine. In the case of ACP this is not a problem. Communication in ACP models is also invisible because it is expressed by a global communication function (γ) and not in a process term itself. The effect on the semantics is also limited since the action dispatcher can be modeled using the UML as well. We generate a state machine from an ACP model and add an implementation of the action dispatcher in the form of a UML class and state machine to it.

3.4 Action Dispatcher

Figure 4 depicts the class diagram representing the (single) action dispatcher. This action dispatcher object has an *action pool* of zero or more action objects. The action pool consists of all action objects ready for execution. The γ attribute of the class is the communication function γ. It is, like in ACP, used to determine whether a pair of actions can communicate. The methods of the class handle adding actions to, executing actions in, and removing actions from the action pool. The functionality of the methods is explained below. The action dispatcher is generic. This means that the same action dispatcher is generated for all ACP models. Only the γ attribute is generated from the model.

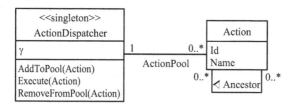

Fig. 4. Action dispatcher class diagram

An action object has two attributes: an identifier to uniquely identify the syntactic occurrence of the action and the name of the action. This name is the same name as the one occurring in the ACP process term. An action can be related to other actions, its *ancestors*. If an action x is the result of communication, e.g. $\gamma(a, b) = x$, actions a and b are considered to be its *parents*. The set of ancestors of x can be found by taking the transitive closure of the '*is parent of*' x relation. Note that an action that is the result of communication can communicate with other actions, e.g. $\gamma(a, b) = c$ and $\gamma(c, d) = e$. Because an action cannot communicate with its ancestors, the ancestors of an action need to be known to correctly handle communication. If an action is not the result of a communication it does not have any ancestors.

The life cycle of an action object is such that it will first be added to the action pool. After some time, it may be executed whereafter it is removed from the action pool. In case of communication, action objects can also be removed from the action pool without having been executed themselves. Action objects can even stay in the action pool forever in case of a deadlock.

Fig. 5. Transformation of atoms

Transformation of Atoms. The transformation of all constructs except for the atoms has already been explained in Section 3.2. The atom a maps to the state machine depicted in Figure 5. The entry activity on the simple state creates an action object from atom a and invokes the *AddToPool* method of the action dispatcher. This puts the newly created action object in the action pool. In order to ensure that the state machine does not continue until the action has been executed, a guard is present on the outgoing transition. This guard is *true* when the action object is not in the action pool. This is the case when the action has been executed or has communicated.

Addition. The method *AddToPool(x)* is invoked by the entry activity on the simple state an atom is mapped to (cf. Figure 5). Its purpose is to extend the action pool with x and to maintain closure of the action pool under γ. If an action object x is added to the action pool, and it can communicate with another action object a already in the pool that is not one of its ancestors, then a new action object for the communication result given by γ is recursively added to the action pool (lines 3–6 in Figure 6). On line 5 a new action object is created with a new identifier and as name the result of the communication function γ. Also, the set of all ancestors of x is assigned to this action object.

Execution. An action object x in the action pool that does not represent a deadlock constant will non-deterministically be selected at an arbitrary moment for execution. The purpose of method *Execute(x)* is to find all actions that execute along with x, i.e., all actions that, directly or indirectly, gave rise to x through communication, and to clean up the action pool. If the state machine cannot proceed and there are only action objects in the action pool that represent a deadlock constant, it is in a deadlock state.

Removal. The purpose of method *RemoveFromPool(x)* is to remove action object x from the action pool. To maintain closure of the action pool under γ, also all action objects that are the result, directly or indirectly, of communication involving x are removed. Note that these resulting action objects do not occur in the conditions of outgoing transitions (cf. Figure 5), because they are the result of communication.

Correctness Considerations. Interference between methods of the action dispatcher can be avoided by executing them under mutual exclusion. The action dispatcher controls the state machine through conditions of the form $a \notin ActionPool$ only. Note that a is added to the action pool, falsifying the condition, upon entry into the immediately preceding simple state, and is removed upon its execution, making the condition true. During execution of each method, the action pool changes monotonically to avoid glitches (undesired condition changes).

1. $AddToPool(x: Action)$:
2.   ActionPool := ActionPool $\cup$ $\{x\}$;
3. $\forall_a : \gamma(a.\text{Name}, x.\text{Name}) = y$
4. $\rightarrow$ if $a \in$ ActionPool $\land$ $a.\text{Id} \notin x.\text{Ancestor}$
5. $\rightarrow$ NewAction := Action(NewId(), y, $a.\text{Ancestor} \cup x.\text{Ancestor} \cup \{a, x\}$);
6. $AddToPool(\text{NewAction})$

7. $Execute(x: Action)$:
8. $\forall_a : a.\text{Id} \in x.\text{Ancestor}$
9. $\rightarrow Execute(a)$
10. $RemoveFromPool(x)$

11. $RemoveFromPool(x: Action)$:
12.   ActionPool := ActionPool $-$ $\{x\}$;
13. $\forall_a : a \in$ ActionPool
14. $\rightarrow$ if $x.\text{Id} \in a.\text{Ancestor}$
15. $\rightarrow RemoveFromPool(a)$

Fig. 6. Pseudo code for the action dispatcher methods

4   Implementation

The transformation from ACP models into UML state machines expressed in the XMI format is too complex to implement in a single step. Therefore we split the transformation into four independent steps. This modular approach makes the transformation more transparent, which benefits extensibility, maintainability, and testability. Moreover, every step is (re)usable in isolation.

In the first step of the transformation the ACP model is rewritten using the ACP axioms to remove all instances of the left merge and communication merge operator. Consider for example the ACP process term $a \| (b|c)$ and suppose $\gamma(b, c) = d$. This rewrites to $a.d$. This step has as in- and output an ACP model expressed in the ACP metamodel[1] we have defined. After this step the ACP model will only consist of constructs that have a state machine equivalent. With a few extensions the transformation used in this step can also be used for rewriting ACP models to their normal form.

In the second step the implicit tree structure of an ACP model is made explicit. For the representation of this tree structure we use an intermediate language for which we defined a metamodel. This language uses a prefix format. Consider for example the alternative composition $P_1 + P_2 + \ldots + P_n$. The transformation function finds all the alternatives and represents them as $alt(P_1, P_2, \ldots, P_n)$.

These first two steps are mere preparation for the actual transformation. In the third step the tree representation of an ACP model is transformed into a state machine. This state machine is defined in a state machine language for which we have also defined a metamodel. This language closely resembles UML

---

[1] Our metamodels are in fact context-free grammars.

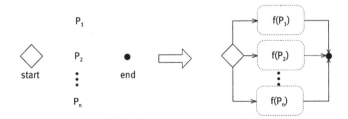

Fig. 7. Transformation of the alternative composition

state machines. The only difference is that it does not support the history mechanism. We chose to use this intermediate format to avoid having to transform into complex XMI constructs directly. Moreover, it enables the transformation of any UML state machine defined in our state machine language into XMI. This third transformation step is similar to Thompson's algorithm for transforming regular expressions into non-deterministic finite automata [18]. The transformation function has as arguments an ACP process term represented as a tree and a start and an end state. For the alternative and parallel composition these start state and end state are respectively the choice and junction state, and the fork and join state. In Figure 7 an example is depicted in which the partial state machines for n alternatives are generated and connected to the choice and junction states. For the sequential composition it is more difficult because the end state of the first partial state machine in the sequence is the start state for the next. These states are not known in advance. To overcome this problem, dummy states are inserted such that the start and end states are known in advance. These dummy states are removed afterwards.

In the last step a state machine is transformed into its XMI [19] representation. This back-end part is isolated, because the XMI standard is actually not so standard. Most UML tools use a different dialect of XMI requiring different backends. Currently our implementation is able to generate XMI files for the UML tools ArgoUML [20] and Telelogic Rhapsody [21]. Our state machine language closely resembles UML state machines and there is a one-to-one mapping from UML state machine constructs to XMI. Therefore, this final transformation step is straightforward.

The Telelogic Rhapsody tool allows for execution of state machines. We use this feature to simulate the execution of ACP models. To ensure a correct handling of communication, an implementation of the action dispatcher presented in Section 3.4 is added to the XMI file.

We use the term rewriting system ASF+SDF [22,23] for the development of our metamodels and for the implementation of our transformation. Transformations between languages is one of the main applications of ASF+SDF. These transformations are performed between languages specified in the Syntax Definition Formalism (SDF) using conditional equations specified in the Algebraic Specification Formalism (ASF). Because the concrete syntax of the source and target language of a transformation are formally defined in SDF, syntax-safety of the input and output of a transformation is guaranteed. This implies that every syntactically correct ACP model is transformed into a syntactically correct XMI document representing a state machine that preserves structural and behavioral properties. Syntax-safety also implies that every ACP model that is syntactically incorrect is not transformed at all.

5 Illustration

We have used our implementation on multiple ACP models to verify the correctness of our transformation. This section describes the transformation of an ACP model of a conveyor system into a UML state machine that preserves structural and behavioral properties.

The conveyor system is schematically depicted in Figure 8. Machines M_1 and M_2 put products on a conveyor belt. The products from machine M_1 can go to machines M_3 or M_4 for further processing and the products from machine M_2 can go to machines M_4 or M_5. When products are sent to machine M_4 by both machines M_1 and M_2 at the same time a collision will occur and an operator should ensure that both products can still enter the machine for processing.

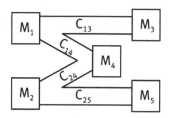

Fig. 8. Conveyor system

The ACP model representing this system is depicted in Figure 9. The process term expresses that a product is produced by machine M_1 which is then sent to machine M_3 or M_4 for further processing and that another product is produced by machine M_2 which is then sent to machine M_5 or M_4 for further processing, possibly at the same time. The communication function (γ) expresses that an operator rearranges products that collide if two products go from machines M_1 and M_2 to machine M_4 at the same time. Note that only one iteration is modeled.

$$\gamma(C_{14}, C_{24}) = operator$$

$$(M_1 \cdot (C_{13} \cdot M_3 + C_{14} \cdot M_4)) \parallel (M_2 \cdot (C_{25} \cdot M_5 + C_{24} \cdot M_4))$$

Fig. 9. ACP model of the conveyor system

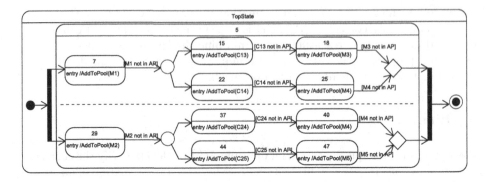

Fig. 10. ArgoUML screen shot depicting the acquired state machine diagram

Fig. 11. Three Telelogic Rhapsody execution results

The state machine resulting from the transformation should exhibit the same behavior. A screen shot of the state machine acquired from the transformation imported in ArgoUML can be found in Figure 10. Note that ArgoUML uses circles for choice states and diamonds for junction states.

We also transformed this ACP model into an XMI file for Telelogic Rhapsody, enabling simulation of the state machine. Three screen shots showing the results of three different executions of the simulation are depicted in Figure 11. In trace 1 and 3 both products go to different machines. In trace 2 the operator is needed to rearrange collided products.

6   Conclusion and Further Research

6.1   Conclusions

We have addressed the semantic gap that arises in the transformation from the process algebra ACP without encapsulation into UML state machines. Transforming a model specified in one formalism into a model in another formalism involves more than transforming syntax. Differences in the characteristics of semantics need to be handled meticulously to ensure a correct transformation. In our case a semantic gap emerged as a result of the requirements on the transformation. The transformation should preserve both structural and behavioral properties. Our transformation preserves structure for all operators except for the seldomly used left merge and communication merge operators. It also preserves behavior by exploiting the semantic openness of UML state machines. We have extended UML state machines with an action dispatcher to ensure that they can generate the same execution traces as the ACP model.

Note that trace equivalence is in general only one aspect of semantic equivalence. Without providing a formal semantics for the UML we cannot guarantee that we have bridged the semantic gap completely. Since there are many formalisms with different (or without) formal semantics, there are probably many model transformations that are not proven to be semantics preserving. Proving that a model transformation preserves semantics requires different expertise.

In general, to bridge a semantic gap when transforming models from one formalism into another, it first has to be identified. Therefore, two steps should be taken. First, the semantics of the source and the target formalism should be well understood. Second, additional requirements on the (static) semantics should be made explicit. When bridging the semantic gap is not a straightforward affair, it is advisable to address a simplified version of the source metamodel first. Another possibility is first to relax the semantic requirements on the transformation. It can also be that the semantic gap is simply too large to be bridged at all.

We have used the term rewriting system ASF+SDF to implement a transformation from ACP without encapsulation to UML state machines. This required us to define metamodels for both ACP and UML state machines. We have created a metamodel for ACP and for UML state machines without history mechanism. The modular implementation of our transformation has proven to be useful for decreasing the complexity. Moreover this benefits reuse, extensibility, maintainability, and testability of the implementation.

Using the CASE tool Telelogic Rhapsody we can generate code to execute the acquired UML state machine and action dispatcher. In this way the execution of an ACP model can be simulated. Since our transformation preserves most structure of ACP models, UML tools can be used for visualizing this structure.

We performed several case studies using our implementation to illustrate our transformation of ACP models into UML state machines.

6.2 Directions for Further Research

We have considered ACP without the encapsulation operator (∂). The next thing to consider is the transformation of the encapsulation operator. This makes the semantic gap even larger. The encapsulation operator prevents certain actions from being executed, which cannot be expressed in a state machine. This requires an extension of the action dispatcher such that it forbids the execution of encapsulated actions. Moreover, the alternative composition is no longer nondeterministic. In ACP the alternative composition of an encapsulated and a non-encapsulated action, e.g. $\partial_{\{a\}}(a) + b$, rewrites to the non-encapsulated action (b) only. In a structure preserving state machine, care has to be taken that the selection of a branch with an encapsulated action is prevented to avoid unwanted deadlocks. This gets even more delicate when an action cannot be executed itself but can communicate with another action.

Acknowledgements. This work has been carried out as part of the FALCON project under the responsibility of the Embedded Systems Institute. This project is partially supported by the Netherlands Ministry of Economic Affairs under the Embedded Systems Institute (BSIK03021) program.

We would like to thank the anonymous reviewers for their comments which helped us improving an earlier version of this paper.

References

1. FALCON, http://www.esi.nl/falcon/
2. van Amstel, M.F., van de Plassche, E., Hamberg, R., van den Brand, M.G.J., Rooda, J.E.: Performance analysis of a palletizing system. SE Report 2007-09, Department of Mechanical Engineering, Eindhoven University of Technology (2007)
3. Baeten, J.C.M.: A brief history of process algebra. Theoretical Computer Science 335(2–3), 131–146 (2005)
4. Object Management Group: Unified Modeling Language: Superstructure specification, version 2.1.1. Document – formal/2007-02-05, OMG (2007)
5. Bergstra, J.A., Klop, J.W.: Algebra of communicating processes. In: de Bakker, J.W., Hazewinkel, M., Lenstra, J.K. (eds.) Proceedings of the CWI Symposium. CWI Monographs, vol. 1, pp. 89–138. Centre for Mathematics and Computer Science, North-Holland (1986)
6. Baeten, J.C.M., Weijland, W.P.: Process Algebra. Cambridge Tracts in Theoretical Computer Science, vol. (18). Cambridge University Press, Cambridge (1990)
7. van Beek, D.A., Man, K.L., Reniers, M.A., Rooda, J.E., Schiffelers, R.R.H.: Syntax and semantics of timed Chi. CS-Report 05–09, Department of Computer Science, Eindhoven University of Technology (2005)
8. Groote, J.F., Mathijssen, A., Reniers, M., Usenko, Y., van Weerdenburg, M.: The formal specification language mCRL2. In: Brinksma, E., Harel, D., Mader, A., Stevens, P., Wieringa, R. (eds.) Methods for Modelling Software Systems (MMOSS). Number 06351 in Dagstuhl Seminar Proceedings, Internationales Begegnungs- und Forschungszentrum fuer Informatik (2007)
9. Nicollin, X., Sifakis, J., Yovine, S.: From ATP to timed graphs and hybrid systems. Acta Informatica 30(2), 181–202 (1993)
10. Pardo, J.J., Valero, V., Cuartero, F., Cazorla, D.: Automatic translation of a timed process algebra into dynamic state graphs. In: Proceedings of the 8th Asia-Pacific Conference on Software Engineering, pp. 63–70. IEEE Computer Society, Los Alamitos (2001)
11. Cerone, A.: From process algebra to visual language. In: Lakos, C., Esser, R., Kristensen, L.M., Billington, J. (eds.) Proceedings of the 23rd Conference on Application and Theory of Petri Nets. Conferences in Research and Practice in Information Technology, vol. 12, pp. 27–36. Australian Computer Society (2002)
12. Bortnik, E.M., Mortel-Fronczak, J.M., Rooda, J.E.: Translating χ models to UP-PAAL timed automata. SE Report 2007-06, Department of Mechanical Engineering, Eindhoven University of Technology (2007)
13. Pintér, G., Majzik, I.: Program code generation based on UML statechart models. Periodica Polytechnica 47(3–4), 187–204 (2003)
14. Niaz, I.A., Tanaka, J.: Code generation from UML statecharts. In: Hamza, M.H. (ed.) Proceedings of the 7th IASTED International Conference on Software Engineering and Applications, pp. 315–321. ACTA Press (2003)

15. Crane, M.L., Dingel, J.: UML vs. classical vs. Rhapsody statecharts: Not all models are created equal. In: Briand, L.C., Williams, C. (eds.) MoDELS 2005. LNCS, vol. 3713, pp. 97–112. Springer, Heidelberg (2005)
16. Bergstra, J.A., Klop, J.W.: Process algebra for synchronous communication. Information and Control 60(1–3), 109–137 (1984)
17. Baeten, J.C.M., Basten, T., Reniers, M.A.: Algebra of communicating processes. Lecture notes (DRAFT) (2005)
18. Thompson, K.: Regular expression search algorithm. Communications of the ACM 11(6), 419–422 (1968)
19. Object Management Group: Meta Object Facility MOF 2.0/XMI mapping specification, version 2.1. Document – formal/05-09-01, OMG (2005)
20. ArgoUML v0.24 (Viewed January 2008), http://argouml.tigris.org/
21. Telelogic Rhapsody 7.1.1 (Viewed January 2008), http://modeling.telelogic.com/products/rhapsody/index.cfm
22. van den Brand, M.G.J., van Deursen, A., Heering, J., de Jong, H.A., de Jonge, M., Kuipers, T., Klint, P., Moonen, L., Olivier, P.A., Scheerder, J., Vinju, J.J., Visser, E., Visser, J.: The ASF+SDF meta-environment: A component-based language development environment. In: Wilhelm, R. (ed.) CC 2001 and ETAPS 2001. LNCS, vol. 2027, pp. 365–370. Springer, Heidelberg (2001)
23. van Deursen, A.: An overview of ASF+SDF. In: van Deursen, A., Heering, J., Klint, P. (eds.) Language Prototyping: An Algebraic Specification Approach. AMAST Series in Computing, vol. 5, pp. 1–29. World Scientific, Singapore (1996)

On Specifying and Visualising Long-Running Empirical Studies

Peter Y.H. Wong and Jeremy Gibbons

Computing Laboratory, University of Oxford, United Kingdom
{peter.wong,jeremy.gibbons}@comlab.ox.ac.uk

Abstract. We describe a graphical approach to formally specifying temporally ordered activity routines designed for calendar scheduling. We introduce a workflow model *OWorkflow*, for constructing specifications of long running empirical studies such as clinical trials in which observations for gathering data are performed at strict specific times. These observations, either manually performed or automated, are often interleaved with scientific procedures, and their descriptions are recorded in a calendar for scheduling and monitoring to ensure each observation is carried out correctly at a specific time. We also describe a bidirectional transformation between *OWorkflow* and a subset of Business Process Modelling Notation (BPMN), by which graphical specification, simulation, automation and formalisation are made possible.

1   Introduction

A typical long-running empirical study consists of a series of scientific procedures interleaved with a set of observations performed over a period of time; these observations may be manually performed or automated, and are usually recorded in a calendar schedule. An example of a long-running empirical study is a clinical trial, where observations, specifically case report form submissions, are performed at specific points in the trial. In such examples, observations are interleaved with clinical interventions on patients; precise descriptions of these observations are then recorded in a *patient study calendar* similar to the one shown in Figure 1(a). Currently study planners such as trial designers supply information about observations either textually or by inputting textual information and selecting options on XML-based data entry forms [2], similar to the one shown in Figure 1(b). However, the ordering constraints on observations and scientific procedures are complex, and a precise specification of this information is time consuming and prone to error. We believe the method of specification may be simplified and improved by allowing specifications to be *built formally and graphically, and visualised* as workflow instances.

Workflow instances are descriptions of a composition of activities, each of which describes either a manual task or an application of a program. One of the prominent applications of workflow technology is business processes modelling, for which the Business Process Modelling Notation (BPMN) [8] has been used as a modelling language. Recent research [9] has also allowed business processes

A. Vallecillo, J. Gray, A. Pierantonio (Eds.): ICMT 2008, LNCS 5063, pp. 76–90, 2008.
© Springer-Verlag Berlin Heidelberg 2008

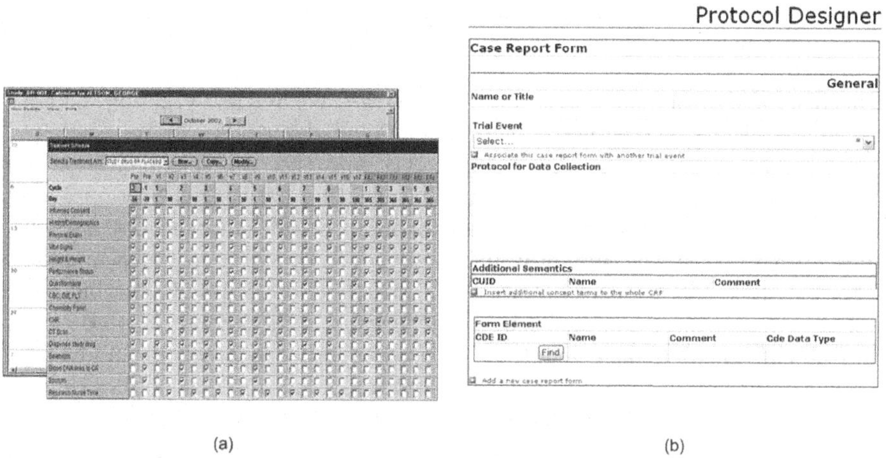

(a)   (b)

Fig. 1. (a) A screen shot of the patient study calendar [3], (b) XML-based data entry forms [2]

modelled as BPMN diagrams to be translated into executable processes in the Business Process Execution Language (WS-BPEL) [1], the "de facto" standard for web service compositions. Furthermore, BPMN has been given formal relative timed semantics [10]; these allow BPMN diagrams to be interpreted without ambiguity. BPMN, being a graphical language, lends itself to being used by domain specialists without computing expertise.

For example, we consider part of a cancer clinical trial, where there is a choice over two *case report form* submissions. The two reports are on tumour measurement or toxicity level. Both which to choice and when to report depend on the blood pressure of the patient concerned. Trial descriptions such as this could be specified as BPMN process and simulated as BPEL process for validation; in this paper, we present a customised workflow model *OWorkflow*, which is an extension to the CancerGrid trial model. Our notation allows empirical studies to be easily viewed and monitored through *study calendars*, while it is not intuitive to translate BPMN diagrams for calendar scheduling. We will revisit this example in Section 5.

This paper has two main contributions. Firstly, we introduce a generic observation workflow model *OWorkflow*, an extension of the workflow model implemented in the CancerGrid trial model [4], customised for modelling empirical studies declaratively. Secondly, we describe bidirectional transformation functions between *OWorkflow* and a subset of BPMN. While the transformation from BPMN to *OWorkflow* provides a medium for empirical studies to be specified graphically as workflows, transforming *OWorkflow* to BPMN allows graphical visualisation. Moreover, the BPMN descriptions of empirical studies may be translated into BPEL processes, whereby manual and automated observations may be simulated and executed respectively, and both of which can be monitored during the enactment of studies. Furthermore, BPMN has a formal semantics and the transformation induces such behavioural semantics to *OWorkflow*. This means empirical study plans can now be formally specified, and interpreted without ambiguity.

The rest of this paper is structured as follows. We begin by giving a brief overview of BPMN in Section 2; a more detailed description of its abstract syntax may be found in our longer paper [11], and the complete definition of its relative timed semantics may be found in our other paper [10]. Section 3 describes the abstract syntax and the semantics of our workflow model *OWorkflow*. Here we only describe the semantics informally, even though a formal semantics has been defined via transformation to BPMN. Section 4 details the bidirectional transformation function between *OWorkflow* and the subset of BPMN by introducing BPMN constructs that are used as building blocks for modelling *OWorkflow*. We have implemented both the syntax of our observational workflow model and BPMN and the transformation functions in the functional programming language Haskell (see: `http://www.haskell.org`). Section 5 discusses how this transformation allows simulation and automation of empirical studies, and how formalisation has assisted the transformation process. Section 6 discusses related work and concludes this paper.

2   BPMN

In this section we give an overview of BPMN. For the purpose of specifying and simulating observational workflow *OWorkflow*, our implementation of BPMN states captures only a subset of BPMN, shown in Figure 2. This is a strict subset of the subset of BPMN formalised in our other paper [10]. We have implemented the corresponding syntax in Haskell. A fuller description of the syntax of this subset can be found in our longer paper [11].

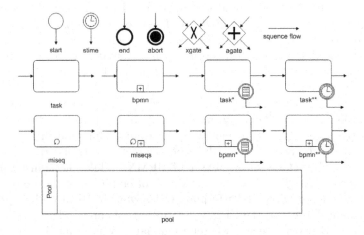

Fig. 2. States of BPMN diagram

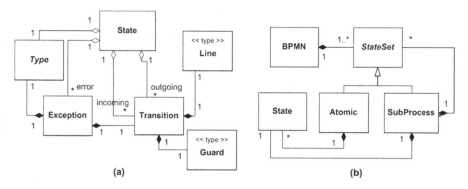

Fig. 3. Abstract syntax of (a) BPMN state and (b) BPMN diagram

States in our subset of BPMN [8] can either be events, tasks, subprocesses, multiple instances or control gateways, each linked by a normal sequence or an exception sequence flow. A normal sequence flow can be either incoming to or outgoing from a state and have associated guards; an exception sequence flow, depicted by the state labelled *task**, *bpmn**, *task*** and *bpmn***, represents an occurrence of error within the state. A sequence of flows represents a specific control flow instance of the business process. Figure 3(a) shows the abstract syntax of a BPMN state, where each state records its type, its lists of incoming and outgoing transitions, and its exception sequence flows as a list of pairs of exceptions types and corresponding transitions. Figure 3(b) shows the abstract syntax of a BPMN diagram, where each diagram is a collection of StateSets. Each StateSet defines either a list of non-subprocess states (Atomic), or a subprocess state (SubProcess), which records the type and sequence flows of the subprocess states, and a list of StateSets representing the subprocess's constituent states.

3   Abstract Syntax of Observational Workflow

In this section we describe the observation workflow model *OWorkflow*. This model generalises the clinical trial workflow model defined in the CancerGrid project [4]. Each workflow is a list of parameterised *generic* activity interdependence sequence rules, where each rule models the dependency between the prerequisite and the dependent observations. Figure 4(a) shows the abstract syntax of *OWorkflow*. Each sequence rule is implemented using the Haskell tuple type EventSequencing, which contains a single constructor Event and each observational workflow hence is a collection of sequence rules.

```
type OWorkflow = [EventSequencing]
data EventSequencing = Event ActId PreAct Condition Condition
                           (Maybe Obv) [RepeatExp] (Maybe Works)
```

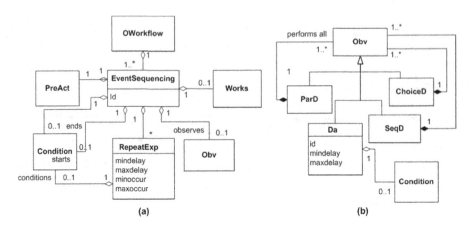

Fig. 4. Abstract syntax of (a) *OWorkflow* and (b) *observation group*

Each sequence rule is identified by a unique name of type `ActId` from the first argument of the constructor `Event`, and contains zero or more dependent observations. There are four reserved names of type `ActId` for identifying a start, a generic termination, a successful termination and an unsuccessful termination of a workflow execution. Each rule defines a structural composition of dependent observations of type `Maybe Obv`, in the fifth argument of the sequence rule. (A value of type `Maybe a` either contains a value of type `a`, or is empty.)

```
data Obv = ChoiceD [Obv] | ParD [Obv] | SeqD [Obv] | Da Act
type Act = (ActId,Duration,Duration,Condition,ActType)
```

We define a single dependent observation by the tuple type `Act`, whose first component is a unique name from a set of names `ActId` distinct from those which identify sequence rules. When performing dependent observations specified by each sequence rule, there exists a delay: a range with a minimum and a maximum duration, specified by the second and third component of `Act` of type `Duration`. Each duration records a string value in accordance with XML schema datatypes. For example in a clinical trial, the follow-up observation should be made between two and three months after all observations associated with the end of the treatment have been carried out. Each observation may either be a manual or an automated observation, denoted by the fifth component `ActType` of `Act`.

Each composition of observations defines an *observation group*, as shown in Figure 4. Figure 4(b) shows the abstract syntax of an *observation group*. Each observation group structurally conforms to Kiepuszewski's *structure workflow model* [5, Section 4.1.3]. The following inductive definition of compositional rules of an observation group follows from the definition of `Obv`:

1. If `obv :: Act` is a single observation, then `Da obv :: Obv` defines an observation group that yields to completion when the observation identified by `obv` has been made. We write `e :: T` to denote the expression `e` has type T.

2. Let `obv1,...,obvN :: Obv` be observation groups; their sequential composition `SeqD [obv1,...,obvN] :: Obv` also defines an observation group.
   Given an observation group `SeqD obvs`, observations are made sequentially
   starting at the head of `obvs`.

3. Similarly, let `obv1,...,obvN :: Obv` be n observations groups. An application of the choice operation over them `ChoiceD [obv1,...,obvN] ::`
   `Obv` defines an observation group, which structurally conforms the structure workflow model; it yields to completion when observations from one of
   the observation groups from the given list have been made. Likewise, `ParD`
   `[obv1,...,obvN]` yields to completion when observations from all of the
   observation groups have been made.

4. Nothing else defines an observation group.

Dependent observations are performed after the observations associated with
the *prerequisite* sequence rules, identified by the data type `PreAct`, are completed. For example in a clinical trial the follow-up observation should be made
after all observations associated with the end of the treatment have been carried
out. A prerequisite is a collection of names that identifies preceding sequence
rules, recorded in the second argument of `Event`. It is defined using the data
type `PreAct`; we call each collection a *prerequisite rule group*.

```
data PreAct = All [PreAct] | OneOf [PreAct] | Pa ActId
```

The constructor `Pa` defines a single prerequisite rule by its argument, which
yields to completion when all observations associated with the rule identified
by the argument are made. The branching constructor `All` denotes synchronisation over its given list of prerequisite rule groups; this yields to completion
when observations from all of the prerequisite rules groups from the given list
have been made. The branching constructor `OneOf` denotes an exclusive merge
over its given list of prerequisite rules groups; this yields to completion when
observations from one of the prerequisite rules groups from the given list have
been made.

Each sequence rule also defines a list, possibly empty, of *repeat* clauses described by the sixth argument, typed `[RepeatEx]`, of `Event`. Each clause specifies
the condition, the minimum and the maximum numbers of iterations and the
delay between iterations for the dependent observations of the sequence rule.
These clauses are evaluated sequentially over the list after one default iteration
of performing the rule's dependent observations.

```
type RepeatExp = (Duration,Duration,Int,Int,Condition)
```

Each clause, of type `RepeatExp`, contains a condition specified by the fifth component of type `Condition`. Our definition of `Condition` extends the *skip logic*
used in the CancerGrid Workflow Model [4]. Specifically, its syntax captures
expressions in conjunctive normal form.

```
data Condition = None | Nondeter | And [Alter]
data Alter = Alt [SCondition]
type SCondition = (Range,Property)
data Range = Bound RangeBound RangeBound | Emu [String]
data RangeBound = Abdate Duration | Abdec Float | Abint Int |
                 Rldate Property Duration | Rldec Property Float |
                 Rlint Property Int
```

Each condition c :: Condition yields a boolean value and is either empty (true), denoted by the nullary constructor None, nondeterministic denoted by the nullary constructor Nondeter, or defined as the conjunction of clauses, each of which is a disjunction of boolean conditions, of type SCondition. The type SCondition is satisfied if the value of specified property (typed Property) falls into the specified range (typed Range) at the time of evaluation. The specified property is a name that identifies a particular property in the domain of the empirical study and this corresponds the local property to the whole BPMN process [8, Section 8.6.1]. Note while our formal semantics of BPMN [10] allows behavioural process-based specifications and corresponding verifications for *OWorkflow*, it is at a level of abstraction in which we do not directly model the value of each properties.

The range may be an enumeration of values via the constructor Emu, or a closed interval of two numeric values via the constructor Range over two arguments of type RangeBound, which may be absolute or relative to a property.

Given a list of repeat clauses res defined in some sequence rule, evaluation begins at the head of the list. Each clause res!!n, where n ranges over [1..(length res - 1)], it may be evaluated after the evaluation of the clause res!!(n-1) terminates. res terminates when last res terminates. (The operator !! denotes list indexing in Haskell.)

For example, the follow up sequence rule of a clinical trial might specify that follow up observations should be made every three months for three times after the default observations have been made, after which observations should be performed every six months for four times.

Each sequence rule might also include work units, recorded by the last argument of the constructor Event. Each work unit represents an empirical procedure such as administering a medical treatment on a patient in a clinical trial. In each sequence rule, the procedure defined by work units are interleaved with the rule's observations. Each collection of work units is defined by the data type Works and is called *work group*.

```
data Works = ChoiceW [Works] | ParW [Works] | SeqW [Works] | Wk Work
```

The type Work records a unique name that identifies a particular empirical procedure. Our definition of work group also structurally conforms to Kiepuszewski's structure workflow model, and both its abstract syntax and compositional rules are similar to those of observation groups.

Finally the third and fourth arguments of a sequence rule are two conditional statements, each of type Condition. While the third argument defines the condition for enacting the sequence rule, the fourth argument defines the condition for interrupting the enactment of the sequence rule.

4   Transformation

In this section we describe the bidirectional transformation between observation workflows of type OWorkflow and their corresponding subset of BPMN diagrams. Specifically we have implemented a total function transforming OWorkflow to BPMN and its inverse, a partial function transforming a subset of BPMN to OWorkflow.

```
w2b :: OWorkflow -> BPMN
b2w :: BPMN -> OWorkflow
```

For reasons of space we only informally describe the transformation of a single sequence rule to its corresponding BPMN subprocess state by explaining the transformation over each of the components that make up the 7-tuple of a sequence rule. We describe the transformation of individual components by introducing some building blocks in BPMN, which may be mapped to those components. A fuller description of the transformation may be found in our longer paper [11]. We stress that these transformation are completely automated.

4.1   Observation

Figure 5 shows an *expanded* BPMN subprocess state depicting a single dependent observation, of type Act. An observation may be performed after a delay ranging from the minimum to the maximum duration, provided that its associated condition is satisfied. The delay range is graphically modelled by first modelling minimum duration as the *stime* state (timer start event), and then modelling the duration ranges from the elapse of the minimum duration to the maximum duration using a task state which halts for an unknown duration, with an expiration exception flow, of which the expiry duration is the difference between maximum and minimum durations of the delay. We use a *xgate* (exclusive choice) decision gateway state for accepting either the task state's outgoing transition or its expiration exception flow.

The decision gateway is then followed by a task state, which models the actual observation itself and is identified by applying the function idToTName to the identifier of the observation being mapped.

```
idToTName :: ActId -> TaskName
```

An *end* state follows immediately for terminating the execution of the subprocess. The subprocess itself has one incoming and one outgoing transition,

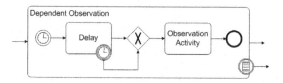

Fig. 5. A BPMN subprocess state depicting a single observation

denoted as the *outermost* incoming and outgoing transitions respectively. We have implemented the function mkAct to transform the subprocess state modelling an observation of type Obv, encapsulating a tuple Act describing a single observation via the constructor function Da. We have also implemented the function mkDpt to transform the tuple Act describing a single observation to a BPMN subprocess modelling that observation.

```
mkAct :: StateSet -> Obv
mkDpt :: Act -> Line -> ([StateSet],Line)
```

4.2 Groups

Each sequence rule contains zero or more observations and work units. Whereas the transformation of a single observation has been described in Section 4.1, each work unit is modelled as a task state, of which the name that identifies the task is obtained by applying the function workToTask on the unique identifier of the work unit. Conversely, the function taskToWork is defined to map a task state name to the unique name of the work unit it models. One or more observations compose into an observation group, which has been defined inductively in Section 3. Similarly one or more work units compose into a work group. Due to the conformity of both types of compositions to the structured workflow model [5] as mentioned in Section 3, we have generalised the notion of *group* and here we describe the transformation between a group and its corresponding BPMN subprocess state, which may be applied to both observation group and work group.

An example BPMN subprocess modelling a group is shown in Figure 6. It shows a BPMN subprocess state describing an observation group defined by the constructor ParD over a list of two observations, each defined by the constructor Da. A similar BPMN subprocess state may be defined to describe a work group. We describe informally the transformation rules for a group as follows:

1. Given group *go* defined by the constructor over a single activity *sa*, specifically Da applied over a single observation for an observation group and Wk applied over a single work unit for a work group respectively, we transform *sa* according the type of the activity, for an observation, the transformation rule has been described in Section 4.1, and a work unit is simply represented

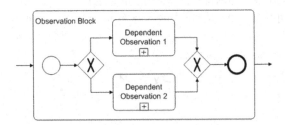

Fig. 6. A BPMN subprocess state depicting an observation group

by a task state, of which the task is identified by the name of the work unit. We use sa's outermost incoming and outgoing transitions as go's outermost incoming and outgoing transitions.

2. Given a group go defined by either a choice or a parallel constructor over a list of n groups, specifically ChoiceD and ChoiceW or ParD and ParW applied over a list of observation groups and work groups respectively, where $n \geq 1$, the corresponding BPMN states are either two *xgate* decision gateways for choice construction or two *agate* decision gateways for parallel construction. The first of these has one incoming transition, denoted as the go's outermost incoming transition, and n outgoing transitions, each matching the outermost incoming transition from one of the n groups, and the other one has n incoming transitions, each matching the outermost outgoing transition from one of the n groups, and one outgoing transitions, denoted as the go's outermost outgoing transition. The transformation of the n groups are defined recursively.

3. Given an observation group go defined by the sequential constructor over a list of n groups, specifically SeqD and SeqW over a list of observation groups and work groups respectively, where $n \geq 1$, the outermost outgoing transition of each group is matched by the outermost incoming transition of its next group. The outermost incoming transition of the first group defines the outermost incoming transition of go, and the outermost outgoing transition of the last group defines the outermost outgoing transition of go.

We have implemented the function getObv to transform the subprocess state describing an observation group to an observation group of type Obv.

```
getObv :: StateSet -> Obv
getInv :: StateSet -> Works
```

Similarly, we have implemented the function getInv to transform a work group of type Works. Conversely, we have implemented the functions extObv and extWks to transform an observation group of type Obv and a work group of type Works to a subprocess state describing that group, respectively.

```
extObv :: Line -> Obv -> ([StateSet],Line)
extWks :: Line -> Works -> ([State],Line)
```

4.3   Repeat Clauses

Figure 7 shows a BPMN subprocess modelling a single repeat clause. According to the semantics of a repeat clause, each repeat clause in a sequence rule repeats all dependent observations defined in that rule; the number of repetitions from each clause ranges between a minimum and a maximum value, and there is a delay, ranging between a minimum and a maximum duration, before each repetition can start. We model the delay range of a repeat clause graphically according to the transformation rules defined for a single observation in Section 4.1.

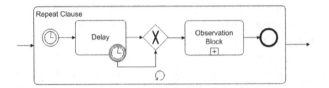

Fig. 7. A BPMN subprocess state depicting a repeat clause

We model each repeated observations as a subprocess state according the transformation of groups in Section 4.2. The subprocess, which defines the repeat clause, is a multiple instance *miseqs* state, and it has one incoming and one outgoing transition, denoted as the *outermost* incoming and outgoing transitions respectively. The multiple instance subprocess state is implemented by the Haskell type `Miseqs` which takes an integer value to specify the maximum number of repetitions and a condition to specify the conjunction of the minimum number of repetitions required and the clause's conditional statement.

A list of repeat clauses is therefore transformed iteratively over each clause starting from head of the list, similar to the transformation of a group for some sequential constructor described in the Rule 3 in Section 4.2. Figure 8 shows a BPMN subprocess state representing a list of two repeat clauses. Individual repeat clause is shown as collapsed subprocess state.

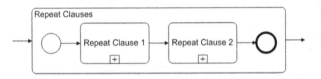

Fig. 8. A BPMN subprocess state depicting a list of two repeat clauses

4.4   Sequence Rules

Figure 9 shows a BPMN subprocess state representing a single sequence rule. The subprocess state is defined by three other subprocess states, collapsed in the figure, which model observations, work units and repeat clauses defined in the sequence rule. A sequence rule is enacted by first performing all its observations once, modelled by the subprocess *observation block*, after which the list of repeat clauses, modelled by the subprocess state *repeat clauses* is evaluated. As explained in Section 3, work units are empirical procedures and their executions are interleaved with their corresponding observations, hence we use an *agate* decision gateway state to initialise both observations and work units. We do not constrain how work units are interleaved with observations as our current workflow model focuses on the specification of observations, therefore it solely depends on the study planners. Note if no work unit is defined in the sequence rule,

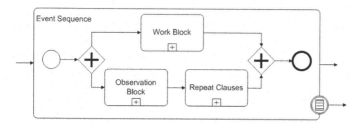

Fig. 9. A BPMN subprocess representing a single sequence rule

the corresponding subprocess will not have *agate* states and will be represented by a sequential composition of the *observation block* and *repeat clauses* states.

Finally we associate a *conditional* exception sequence flow with each subprocess state to model the enacting and the interrupting conditions of the sequence rule. A detailed description can be found in our longer paper [11].

5   On Simulation, Automation and Formalisation

In this section we discuss briefly the application of business process management technique to empirical studies. We describe informally, via a simple example, how modelling empirical studies in BPMN allows their study plans to be simulated and partially automated by translating the BPMN diagrams into executable BPEL processes. We also discuss how modelling empirical studies in BPMN has consequently induced a formal behavioural semantics upon our observation workflow model and hence removed ambiguities in both the transformations and interpretation of *OWorkflow*.

As useful as it is to visualise and formally specify a complete study plan, it is also beneficial to validate the plan before its execution phase, especially if the study has a long running duration, since it is undesirable to run into an error three months into the study! One method of validating a study is by simulation. When considering either simulating or automating a portion of a study, we assume the observations specified in that portion can be appropriately simulated or automated; an observation might define the action of recording a measurement from a display interfacing with a software application or submitting a web form to a web service for analysis. For example, the following specifies a simplified observation group, modelling a choice over two different case report form submissions in a clinical trial described briefly in Section 1.

```
ChoiceD [Da (Id "Tumour Measurement Report", Dur "P1D",Dur "P1D",
            Ands [Ors [(Emu ["low"],"blood pressure")]],Manual),
        Da (Id "Toxicity Review", Dur "P1D",Dur "P1D",
            Ands [Ors [(Emu ["high"],"blood pressure")]],Manual)]
```

While submitting a report form is a manual task, due to the transformation, it is possible to simulate this action by translating its corresponding BPMN subprocess state into the corresponding sequence of BPEL activities:

```
<switch>
 <case condition="getVariableData('blood pressure') == high">
  <wait for="PT1M"><operation name="sendToxicityReview">
   <input message="toxicityMessage" /></operation></wait></case>
 <case condition="getVariableData('blood pressure') == low">
  <wait for="PT1M"><operation name="sendTumourReport">
   <input message="tumourMessage" /></operation></wait></case>
</switch>
```

where each *wait* activity is an invocation upon the elapse of a specified duration. Since the derived BPEL process is for simulation, we scale down the specified duration of each observation. Note each invocation in a BPEL process is necessarily of a web service; if the specified observation defines an action to invoke a web service, e.g. uploading a web form, the translated BPEL operation will also be invoking that web service, and otherwise, for simulation purposes, a "dummy" web service could be used for merely receiving appropriate messages. Similarly, partial automation is also possible by translating appropriate observations into BPEL processes which may be executed during the execution phase of the study.

In recent work, BPMN has been given a formal relative timed semantics; in particular one has been defined in the process algebra CSP [10]. By defining a transformation function between `OWorkflow` and BPMN, it has automatically induced a behavioural semantics for `OWorkflow`. For example, Figure 10 shows

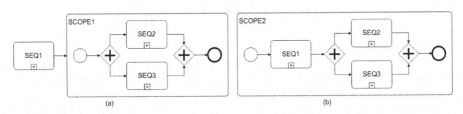

(a)   (b)

Fig. 10. Two BPMN diagrams modelling semantically equivalent observation workflow

two different BPMN diagrams partially, each modelling the same observation workflow described below, omitting description of observations and work units.

```
[Event (Id "SEQ1") (Pa START), Event (Id "SEQ2") (Pa (Id "SEQ1")),
 Event (Id "SEQ3") (Pa (Id "SEQ1")),
 Event NORMAL_STOP (All [Pa (Id "SEQ2"),Pa (Id "SEQ3")])]]
```

Although applying the function `w2b` over this *OWorkflow* definition will yield the diagram in Figure 10(a), one would like to know if applying the function `b2w` over the two diagrams will yield the same *OWorkflow* definition. The formal semantics of BPMN in CSP [10] allows us to show that these two diagrams are in fact semantically equivalent, by model checking the following failures refinement assertions: $PLAN1 \sqsubseteq_F PLAN2 \land PLAN2 \sqsubseteq_F PLAN1$ where $PLAN1$

and $PLAN2$ are CSP processes describing the semantics of the partial BPMN diagrams in Figure 10. This means both $PLAN1$ and $PLAN2$ have the same behaviour and yields the same *OWorkflow* definition. Our semantic definition also allows formal verification of observation workflow against behavioural specifications, an example of which may be found in our longer paper [11].

6   Conclusion

Specifications of long running empirical studies are complex; the production of a complete specification can be time consuming and prone to error. We have described a graphical method to assist this type of specification. We have introduced an observation workflow model *OWorkflow* suitable for specifying empirical studies, which then can be populated onto a calendar for scheduling, and described bidirectional transformations, which allow empirical studies to be constructed graphically using BPMN, and to be simulated and partially automated as BPEL processes. The transformation also induces a behavioural semantics upon *OWorkflow*, and we have described the use of the semantics to remove ambiguity in the transformation process.

To the best of our knowledge, this paper describes the first attempt to apply graphical workflow technology to empirical studies and calendar scheduling, while large amounts of research have focused on the application of workflow notations and implementations to "in silico" scientific experiments. Notable is Ludäscher et al.'s Kepler System [6], in which such experiments are specified as a workflow graphically and fully automated by interpreting the workflow descriptions on a runtime engine. On the other hand we employ BPMN as a graphical notation to specify and graphically visualise experiments and studies that are typically long-running and in which automated tasks are often interleaved with manual ones. Studies such as clinical trial would also include "in vivo" intervention. Furthermore, our approach targets studies that are usually recorded in a calendar schedule to assist administrators and managers. Similarly, research effort has been directed towards effective planning of *specific types* of long running empirical studies, namely clinical trials and guidelines. Notable is Modgil and Hammond's Design-a-Trial (DaT) [7]. DaT is a decision support tool for critiquing the data supplied specifically for randomized controlled clinical trial specification based on expert knowledge, and subsequently outputting a protocol describing the trial. DaT includes a graphical trial planner, which allows description of complex procedural contents of the trial. To ease to complexity of protocol constructions, DaT uses macros, common plan (control flow) constructs, to assist trial designers to construct trial specification.

Future work will include extending our observation workflow model for more detail specifications of work units, such as temporal and procedural information, thereby allowing study plans to be verified against specifications of the relationship between work units and observations.

Acknowledgments

This work is supported by a grant from Microsoft Research. The authors are grateful to Radu Calinescu for many insightful discussions during this work. The authors would also like to thank anonymous referees for useful suggestions and comments.

References

1. Business Process Execution Language for Web Services, Version 1.1. (May 2003), http://www.ibm.com/developerworks/library/ws-bpel
2. Calinescu, R., Harris, S., Gibbons, J., Davies, J., Toujilov, I., Nagl, S.: Model-Driven Architecture for Cancer Research. In: Software Engineering and Formal Methods (September 2007)
3. Clinical Trials Management Tools. University of Pittsburgh, http://www.dbmi.pitt.edu/services/ctma.html
4. Harris, S., Calinescu, R.: CancerGrid clinical trials model 1.0. Technical Report MRC/1.4.1.1, CancerGrid (2006), http://www.cancergrid.org/public/documents
5. Kiepuszewski, B.: Expressiveness and Suitability of Languages for Control Flow Modelling in Workflows. PhD thesis, Queensland University of Technology, Brisbane, Australia (2002)
6. Ludascher, B., Altintas, I., Berkley, C., Higgins, D., Jaeger-Frank, E., Jones, M., Lee, E., Tao, J., Zhao, Y.: Scientific Workflow Management and the Kepler System. In: Concurrency and Computation: Practice & Experience, Special Issue on Scientific Workflows (to appear, 2005)
7. Modgil, S., Hammond, P.: Decision support tools for clinical trial design. Artificial Intelligence in Medicine 27 (2003)
8. Object Management Group. BPMN Specification (February 2006), http://www.bpmn.org
9. Ouyang, C., van der Aalst, W.M.P., Dumas, M., ter Hofstede, A.H.M.: Translating BPMN to BPEL. Technical Report BPM-06-02, BPM Center (2006)
10. Wong, P.Y.H., Gibbons, J.: A Relative-Timed Semantics for BPMN, Submitted for publication. Extended version (2008), http://web.comlab.ox.ac.uk/oucl/work/peter.wong/pub/bpmntime.pdf
11. Wong, P.Y.H., Gibbons, J.: On Specifying and Visualising Long-Running Empirical Studies (extended version) (2008), http://web.comlab.ox.ac.uk/oucl/work/peter.wong/pub/transext.pdf

Programmed Graph Rewriting with Time for Simulation-Based Design

Eugene Syriani and Hans Vangheluwe

McGill University, School of Computer Science, Montréal, Canada
{esyria,hv}@cs.mcgill.ca

Abstract. The Discrete EVent system Specification (DEVS) formalism allows for highly modular, hierarchical modelling of timed, reactive systems. DEVS can be used to describe complex control structures for programmed graph transformation. A side-effect of this approach is the introduction of an explicit notion of time. In this paper we show how the explicit notion of time allows for the simulation-based design of reactive systems such as modern computer games. We use the well-known game of PacMan as an example and model its dynamics with programmed graph transformation based on DEVS. This also allows the modelling of player behaviour, incorporating data about human players' behaviour and reaction times. Thus, a model of both player and game is obtained which can be used to evaluate, through simulation, the playability of a game design. We propose a playability performance measure and vary parameters of the PacMan game. For each variant of the game thus obtained, simulation yields a value for the quality of the game. This allows us to choose an "optimal" (from a playability point of view) game configuration. The user model is subsequently replaced by a visual interface to a real player and the game model is executed using a real-time DEVS simulator.

1 Introduction

Programmed (or structured) graph transformation is one of the keys to making graph transformation scalable (and hence industrially applicable). Tools such as FUJABA [1], GReAT [2], VMTS [3], PROGReS [4], and MOFLON [5] support programmed graph transformation. These tools mostly introduce their own control flow language. In [6] we have shown the advantages of re-using a discrete-event modelling/simulation formalism to describe transformation control. In this paper, we will focus on the time aspect of modelling complex transformations, a side-effect of using a discrete-event modelling formalism. This is done by means of the well-known PacMan example, presented in Section 2. Section 3 introduces the DEVS formalism and how it is used for structured graph transformation. Section 4 describes how not only the PacMan game, but also the player can be explicitly modelled. Section 5 describes game simulation experiments in detail. Finally, Section 6 summarizes, concludes and proposes future work.

A. Vallecillo, J. Gray, A. Pierantonio (Eds.): ICMT 2008, LNCS 5063, pp. 91–106, 2008.

2   Case Study: The PacMan Game

To demonstrate the power of timed, programmed graph transformation, in particular in the context of simulation-based design, we use a simplified version

Fig. 1. PacMan Semantics: Ghost kills PacMan rule

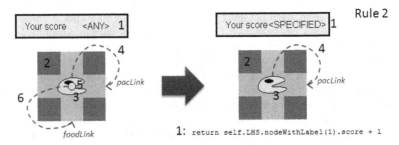

Fig. 2. PacMan Semantics: PacMan eats Food rule

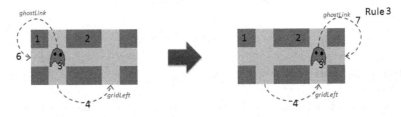

Fig. 3. PacMan Semantics: Ghost moves right rule

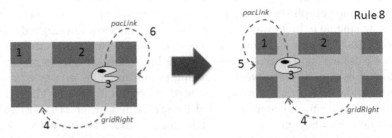

Fig. 4. PacMan Semantics: PacMan moves left rule

of the PacMan video game inspired by Heckel's tutorial introduction of graph transformation [7].

2.1   The PacMan Language (Abstract and Concrete Syntax)

The PacMan language has five distinct elements: PacMan, Ghost, Food (Pellets), GridNode and ScoreBoard. PacMan, Ghost and Food objects can be linked to GridNode objects. This means that these objects can be "on" a GridNode. GridNode objects are geometrically organized in a grid, similar to the PacMan video game. Adjacency implies that PacMan and Ghost "may move" to a connected GridNode. A ScoreBoard object holds an integer valued attribute score. Our tool AToM^3 [8] allows modelling of both abstract and visual concrete syntax (including geometric/topological constraint relations such as a PacMan being centered over a GridNode). From these models, an interactive, visual PacMan modelling environment is synthesized.

2.2   The PacMan Semantics (Graph Transformation)

The operational semantics of the PacMan formalism is defined in a Graph Transformation model which consists of a number of rules. In the rules in the following figures, concrete syntax is used. This is a useful feature for domain-specific modelling specific to AToM^3. Dashed lines were added to explicitly show the "on" links. Rule 1 in Figure 1 shows killing: when a Ghost object is on a GridNode which has a PacMan object, the PacMan is removed. Rule 2 in Figure 2 shows eating: when a PacMan object is on a GridNode which has a Food object, Food is removed and the score gets updated (using an attribute update expression). Note how in the sequel, we will focus on game playability and will ignore the score. Rule 3 in Figure 3 expresses the movement of a Ghost object to the right and rule 8 in Figure 4 the movement of a PacMan object to the left. Similar rules to move Ghosts and PacMan objects up, down, left and right are not shown. Rules 1 and 2 have priorities 1 and 2 respectively. All remaining rules have the same priority 3.

3   DEVS for Programmed Graph Transformation

We previously [6] demonstrated how the *Discrete EVent system Specification* (DEVS) formalism can be used as a semantic domain for Programmed Graph Transformation. In this section, our approach is described, elaborating on the the implementation in AToM^3 of the ideas introduced in [6]). This description will form the basis for following sections which will focus on the use of time in our models.

3.1   The Discrete Event System Specification (DEVS)

The DEVS formalism was introduced in the late seventies by Bernard Zeigler as a rigorous basis for the compositional modelling and simulation of discrete event systems [9].

A DEVS model is either *atomic* or *coupled*. An atomic model describes the behaviour of a reactive system. A coupled model is the composition of several DEVS sub-models which can be either atomic or coupled. Submodels have *ports*, which are connected by channels. Ports are either *input* or *output*. Ports and channels allow a model to send and receive signals (events) between models. A channel must go from an output port of some model to an input port of a different model, from an input port of a coupled model to an input port of one of its sub-models, or from an output port of a sub-model to an output port of its parent model.

Informally, the operational semantics of an atomic model is as follows: the model starts in its initial state. It will remain in any given state for as long as specified by the *time-advance* of that state or until input is received on some port. If no input is received, after the time-advance of the state expires, the model first (before changing state) sends output, specified by the *output function* and then instantaneously jumps to a new state specified by the *internal transition function*. If input is received before the time for the next internal transition however, then it is the *external transition function* which is applied. The external transition depends on the current state, the time elapsed since the last transition and the inputs from the input ports.

The semantics for a coupled model is, informally, the parallel composition of all the sub-models. A priori, each sub-model in a coupled model is assumed to be an independent process, concurrent to the rest. There is no explicit method of synchronization between processes. Blocking does not occur except if it is explicitly modelled by the output function of a sender, and the external transition function of a receiver. There is however a *serialization* whenever there are multiple sub-models that have an internal transition scheduled to be performed at the same time. The modeller controls which of the conflicting sub-models undergoes its transition first by means of *select* function.

For this paper, we use our own DEVS simulator called `pythonDEVS` [10], grafted onto the object-oriented scripting language Python.

3.2   Controlled Graph Rewriting with DEVS

At the heart of our approach is the embedding of graphs in DEVS events and of individual transformation rules into *atomic*DEVS blocks. Figure 5 shows how our approach comprises a number of transformations. First, we model a collection of transformation rules in domain-specific notation (shown on the top left of the figure). Each of these transformations is translated to a class with the same name as the rule (`pacDie` is shown here on the top right). The core of the generated code is the method `execute` which takes a (host) graph as argument and encodes the transformation rule (matching and re-writing). Second, we build a hierarchical model of the Modelled and Modular Timed Graph Transformation language, in the MoTif (Modular Timed model transformation) visual modelling language (shown at the bottom left of the figure). All building

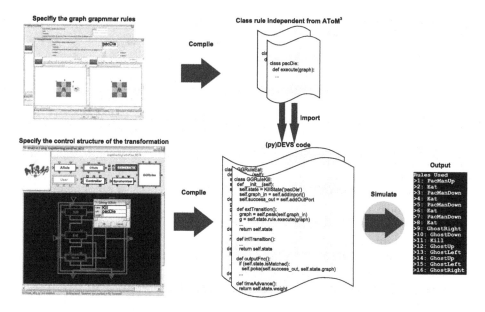

Fig. 5. DEVS-based Programmed Graph Rewriting Architecture

blocks have ports for incoming graphs (top left port), outgoing graphs in case of successful rule application (bottom left port), outgoing (unmodified) graphs in case of failed rule application (bottom right port), incoming transformation interrupt (top right port), incoming pivot (hint about where to start matching) information (left side port) and outgoing pivot information (right side port). These ports appear on both atomic (*ARule*: single rectangle frame) and coupled (*CRule*: double rectangle frame) transformation models which implies that they can be used interchangeably to build complex hierarchical transformation models. *ARules* contain a reference to the compiled rule class. Other special atomic models such as a **Synchronizer** block as well as default atomic and coupled models can be used to control the flow of the transformation. Third, the MoTif model gets compiled into a DEVS model. *CRules* get translated into *coupled*DEVS models. *ARules* models get translated into *atomic*DEVS models. In the latter, the `execute` method encoding the transformation is called in the `external transition` function of the *atomic*DEVS model. This transition function is triggered by the arrival of an external event (in which a to-be-transformed graph is embedded). Finally, all generated code is linked and presented to a DEVS simulator which performs the transformation and produces a trace.

3.3 The PacMan Case Study

The overall model of the PacMan game is shown in Figure 6.

The *coupled*DEVS block **User** is responsible for user (player) interventions. It can send the initial graph to be transformed, the number of rewriting steps to be performed (possibly infinite) and some control information. In the context of our previous work [6], the control information was in the form of key code presses to model the user interrupts of a game. All these events are received by the **Controller**, another *atomic*DEVS block. This block encapsulates the coordination logic between the external input and the transformation model. It sends the host graph through

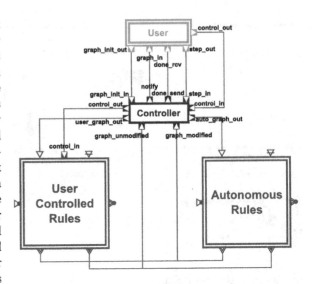

Fig. 6. Overall Transformation Model

its outport to a rule set (the **Autonomous Rules** *CRule*) until the desired number of steps is reached. If a control event is received however, the **Controller** sends the graph to another rule set (the **User Controlled Rules** *CRule*). The **Autonomous Rules** *CRule* expects a graph to perform the rewriting, whereas the **User Controlled Rules** *ARule* waits for a control, too. The details are omitted here to focus on the overall structure.

The model described in [6] does not model a realistic, playable game. When the user sends a key, the corresponding transformation rule is executed and the graph is sent to the **Autonomous Rules** until another key is received or the PacMan entity has been deleted. What prohibits this from being suitable for a playable game is:

- A rule consumes a fixed amount of time. From the graph rewriting perspective, this allows one to compute how long a transformation takes. From the input model perspective, it gives a way of quantifying the complexity of a model. This does however not take into consideration any notion of game levels or any real-time behaviour which such a game should have.
- The user sends information to the rewriting system to (1) configure the transformation engine and (2) to control the transformation execution abstracted to the specific domain of interest (PacMan movements). This model does not take into account any playability issues, such as the Ghost moving too fast versus a user reacting too slowly.

In the sequel we will present an extended model with focus on timing information. This will allow us, through simulation, to construct an optimally "playable" game.

4   Modelling Game *and* Player

The previous section showed how we can model both game syntax (using meta-modelling) and game dynamics (using programmed graph transformation) in an intuitive fashion suitable for non-software-experts. In our approach, the programmed graph transformation model gets compiled into a DEVS model which can subsequently be simulated.

In current graph transformation tools, the *interaction* between the user – the player, in the current context– and the transformation engine is hard-coded rather than explicitly modelled. Examples of typical interaction events are requests to step through a transformation, run to completion, interrupt an ongoing transformation, or change parameters of the transformation. In the context of the PacMan game, typical examples are game-events such as PacMan move commands. Also, if animation of a transformation is supported, the time-delay between the display of subsequent steps is coded in the rewriting engine.

In contrast, in our DEVS-based approach, the interaction between the user and the game is explicitly modelled and encapsulated in the *atomic*DEVS block **User** (see Figure 6). Note that in this interaction model, time is explicitly present.

4.1   Modelling the Player

With the current setup, it is impossible to evaluate the *quality* (playability) of a particular game dynamics model without actually *interactively* playing the game. This is time-consuming and reproducibility of experiments is hard to achieve. To support automatic evaluation of playability, possibly for *different types* of players/users, it is desirable to explicitly model player behaviour. With such a model, a complete game between a modelled player and a modelled PacMan game –an experiment– can be run *autonomously*. Varying either player parameters (modelling different types of users) or PacMan game parameters (modelling for example different intelligence levels in the behaviour of Ghosts) becomes straightforward and alternatives can easily be compared with respect to playability.

For the purpose of the PacMan game, player behaviour parameters could mean different user reaction speed or different levels of decision analysis (such as pathfinding). We have explored these two dimensions of behaviour. Section 5 will discuss reaction speeds more in-depth. Obviously, evaluating quality (playability) will require a precise definition of a *performance metric*. Also, necessary data to calculate performance metrics needs to be automatically collected during experiments.

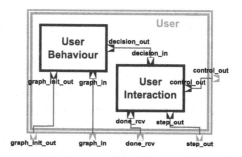

Fig. 7. Enhanced User Model

Explicitly modelling player behaviour can be done without modifying the overall model described in section 3.2 thanks to the modularity of DEVS. We simply need to replace the **User** block by a *coupled*DEVS block with the same ports as shown in Figure 7.

We would like to cleanly separate the way a player interrupts autonomous game dynamics (*i.e.,* Ghost moving) on the one hand and the player's decision making on the other hand. To make this separation clear, we refine the **User** block into two sub-models: the **User Interaction** and the **User Behaviour** *atomic*DEVS blocks. On the one hand, the **User Interaction** model is responsible for sending control information such as the number of transformation steps to perform next, or a direction key to move the PacMan. On the other hand, the **User Behaviour** block models the actual behaviour of the player (often referred to as "AI" in the game community). It is this block which, after every transformation step, receives the new game state graph, analyzes it, and outputs a decision determining what the next game action (such as PacMan move up) will be. Also, since it is the **User Interaction** block which keeps receiving the game state graph, we chose to give this block the responsibility of sending the initial host graph to the transformation subsystem.

The notion of Event-driven Graph Rewriting [11] can be found in the literature. It was proposed in the context of a meta-modelling editor: a graph rewriting rule would be triggered in response to a user action. This concept is incorporated in the **User Controlled Rules** *coupled*DEVS block where a rule gets triggered depending on the user action. In our approach the user and user interaction itself has been modelled in the **User** *coupled*DEVS block.

Different players may use different *strategies*. Each strategy leads to a different model in the **User Behaviour** block. We have modelled three types of players for our experiments: Random, Dummy, and Smart.

The Random player does not take the current game state graph into consideration but rather chooses the direction in which the PacMan will move in randomly. Note that this player may send direction keys requesting illegal Pac-Man moves such as crossing a boundary (wall). This is taken care of by our PacMan behaviour rules: the particular rule that gets triggered by that key will not find a match in the graph, hence PacMan will not move. However, time is progressing and if PacMan does not move, the ghost will get closer to it which will eventually lead to PacMan death.

The Dummy user does not make such mistakes. After querying the game state graph for the PacMan position, it moves to the adjacent grid node that has Food but not a Ghost on it. If no such adjacent grid node can be found, it randomly chooses a legal direction.

The Smart user is an improved version of the Dummy user. Whereas the Dummy user is restricted to making decisions based only on adjacent grid nodes, the Smart user has a "global" view of the board. The strategy is to compute the closest grid node with Food on it and move the PacMan towards it depending on the position of the Ghost. One way to implement this strategy is by using a path finding algorithm. Many solutions exist for such problems, including some efficient ones such as A* [12]. Modelling A* with graph transformation rules requires backtracking and is outside the scope of this paper. Our prototype implementation sidesteps the pathfinding problem by slightly modifying the meta-model of the PacMan formalism. Relative coordinates were added to the *gridNode* class with the condition that if a *gridNode* instance *g1* is associated with another instance *g2* via the *gridLeft* association, then $g1.x < g2.x$ and $g1.y = g2.y$. Similar conditions are defined for *gridRight*, *gridTop* and *gridBottom* associations. Therefore, the pathfinding only needs to compute the shortest Manhattan distance from PacMan to Food as well as a simple check for the grid node coordinates of the Ghost.

We compare the performance of different user behaviour types in Section 5.

Note that to match different user types, we need to model similar strategies for the Ghost to make the game fair. Indeed, a Smart user (controlling the PacMan) playing against a randomly moving Ghost will not be interesting nor will a Dummy user playing against a Smart Ghost. As players may become better at a game over time, game *levels* are introduced whereby the game adapts to the player's aptitude. This obviously increases game playability.

4.2 Modelling the Game

As long as the (modelled) player does not send a decision key to move the Pac-Man, thus changing the game state graph, the graph continues to loop between the **Controller** block and the **Autonomous Rules** block. If no instantaneous rule (**Kill** or **Eat**) matches, then it is the lower priority **Ghost Move** block that modifies the graph. In our earlier work [6], the graph received by this *CRule* was concurrently sent to the **Up**, **Down**, **Left** and **Right** *ARules* to make the ghost move. Non-deterministically, one of the matching rules got applied. This modelled a random movement of the Ghost. In order to generalize this behaviour to allow different strategies, a modification of the way the graph is sent to these *ARules* is necessary.

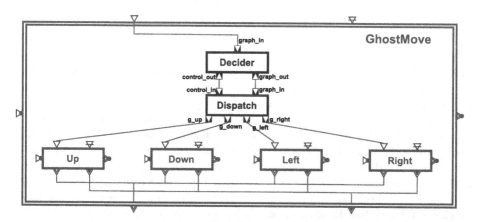

Fig. 8. Enhanced Ghost Behaviour Model

Figure 8 illustrates the modified topology of the Ghost movement model. The game state graph is received by a **Decider** *atomic*DEVS block. Similar to the **User Behaviour** block, it emits a direction that drives the movement of the Ghost. The Random, Dummy and Smart strategies are analogous to the player. The Random Ghost will randomly choose a direction, the Dummy Ghost will look for a PacMan among the grid nodes adjacent to the one the Ghost is on and the Smart Ghost has "global" vision and always decides to move towards the PacMan. The same argument previously made about optimal pathfinding and backtracking applies. Then, the **Decider** sends the graph and the decision (in the form of a key) to a **Dispatch** block and the rest of the behaviour is identical to that in the **User Controlled Rules** *CRule*.

4.3   Explicit Use of Time

We have now modelled both game and player, and the behaviour of both can use Random, Dummy, or Smart strategies. However, one crucial aspect has been omitted up to now: the notion of time. Time is critical for this case study since game playability depends heavily on the relative speed of player (controlling the PacMan) and game (Ghost). The speed is determined by both decision (thinking) and reaction (observation and keypress) times.

Timed Graph Transformation, as proposed by Gyapay, Heckel and Varró [13] integrates time in the double push-out approach. They extend the definition of a production by introducing, in the model and rules, a chronos element that stores the notion of time. Rules can monotonically increase the time. DEVS is inherently a timed formalism, as explained previously. In contrast with Timed Graph Transformation, it is the execution of a rule that can increase time and not the rule itself. Hence, the control flow (of the graph transformation) has full access to time. As pointed out in [13], time can be used as a metric to express how many time units are consumed to execute a rule. Having time at the level of the block containing a rule rather that in the rule itself does not lose this expressiveness.

We will now show how the notion of time from the DEVS formalism integrated in a graph transformation system can be used for realistic modelling of both player and game. We consider a game to be unplayable if the user consistently either wins or loses. The main parameter we have control over during the design of a PacMan game is the speed of the Ghost.

Each *atomic*DEVS block has a state-dependent *time advance* that determines how long the block stays in a particular state. **Kill** and **Eat** rules should happen instantaneously, thus their *time advance* is 0 whenever they receive a graph. In fact, all rules of the PacMan grammar have *time advance* 0. What consumes time is the decision making of both the player (deciding where to move the PacMan) and the game (deciding where to move the Ghost). For this reason, only the **Decider** and the **User Behaviour** blocks have strictly positive *time advance*.

To provide a consistent playing experience, the time for the Ghost to make a decision should remain almost identical across multiple game plays. The player's decision time may vary from one game to another and even within the same game. We have chosen a *time advance* for the **Decider** that is sampled from a uniform distribution with a small variance (interval radius of $5ms$). What remains is to determine a reasonable average of the distribution. To make the game playable, this average should not differ significantly from the player's reaction time. If they are too far apart, a player will consistently lose or win making the game uninteresting.

5   Simulation Experiments

In the previous section, we determined that the playability of the PacMan game depends on the right choice of the average *time advance* of the **Decider** block, *i.e.*, the response time of the Ghost. We will now perform multiple simulation experiments, each with a different average *time advance* of the **Decider** block. For each of the experiments, a playability performance metric (based on the duration of a game) will be calculated. The value of the **Decider** block's average *time advance* which maximizes this playability performance metric will be the one retained for game deployment. Obviously, the optimal results will depend on the type of player.

5.1   Modelling User Reaction Time

First of all, a model for player reaction time is needed. Different psychophysiology controlled experiments [14] give human reaction times (subjects between the ages of 17 and 20):

- the time of simple visuomotor reaction induced by the presentation of various geometrical figures on a monitor screen with a dark background
- the time of reaction induced by the onset of movement of a white point along one of eight directions on a monitor screen with a dark background.

The reaction time distribution can be described by an asymmetric normal-like distribution. The cumulative distribution function of frequencies for sensorimotor human reaction time is:

$$F(x) = e^{-e^{\frac{b-x}{a}}}$$

where a characterizes data scatter relative to the attention stability of the subject: the larger a is, the more attentive the subject is; b characterizes the reaction speed of the subject. For simulation purposes, sampling from such a distribution is done by using the Inverse Cumulative Method.

For our simulation, four types of users were tested: Slow with $a = 33.3$ and $b = 284$, Normal with $a = 19.9$ and $b = 257$, Fast with $a = 28.4$ and $b = 237$, VeryFast with $a = 17.7$ and $b = 222$. The parameters used are those of four example subjects in [14].

5.2   Simulation Results

For the simulations, we only consider the Smart user strategy. For each type of user (Slow, Normal, Fast and VeryFast), the *length of the simulated game* is measured: the time until PacMan is killed (loss) or no Food is left on the board (victory). To appreciate these results, the score is also measured for each run. Simulations were run for a game configuration with 24 gridNodes, 22 Food Pellets, 1 Ghost and 1 PacMan. The game speed (ghost decision time) was varied from 100*ms* to 400*ms*. Each value is the result of an average over 100 samples simulated with different seeds.

The following presents the simulation results obtained by means of the DEVS simulations of our game and player model. All figures show results for the four types of users (Slow, Normal, Fast and VeryFast). Figure 9 shows the *time until the game ends* as a function of the time spent on the Ghost's decision. The increasing shape of the curves imply that the slower the ghost, the longer the game lasts. This is because the user has more time to move the PacMan away from the Ghost. One should note that after a certain limit (about 310*ms* for the VeryFast user and 350*ms* for the Normal user), the curves tend to plateau. An explanation for this behaviour is simply that after a certain point, the Ghost decision time is too low and the user always wins. Therefore, the optimal average *time advance* value we are looking for is found in the middle of the steep slope of the plots.

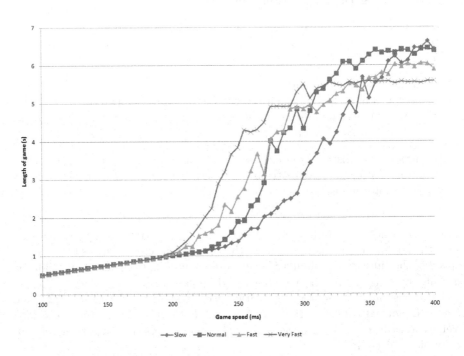

Fig. 9. Time till end

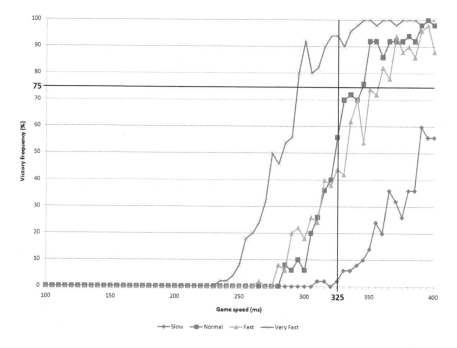

Fig. 10. Victory frequency

Figure 10 depicts the *frequency* with which a player will *win* a game (when playing a large number of games) as a function of the time spent on the Ghost's decision. We decided that we want to deploy a game where the user should be able to win with a probability of 75%. Thus, the optimal average Ghost *time advance* (decision time) was found to be 325ms.

To give further insight in the variability of the game experience, Figure 11 shows the *game length distribution* at the optimal *time advance* value. It is a unimodal distribution with a peak at 7.5s. This average is quite low, but not surprising given the small game board. Experience with the finally deployed real-time game application is consistent with this value.

5.3 Game Deployment

Having found a prediction for the optimal time the **Decider** block should spend on the choosing the next movement of the ghost entity, we can now test the simulated game with real users, in real-time. We simply *discard the player model* and deploy the real-time game model (by executing the translated programmed graph rewriting system in a real-time DEVS simulator). In an attempt to generate the application completely from models, we (mostly) synthesized (yet another model transformation) an Ajax/SVG-based application from the PacMan meta-model built in AToM[3].

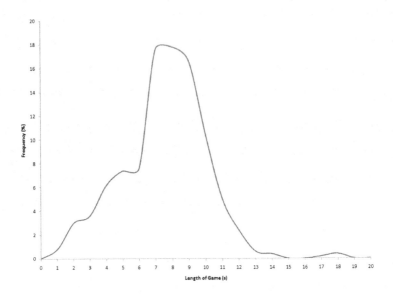

Fig. 11. Game length distribution; Normal user, game time advance $325ms$

6   Conclusions

In this article, we described the use of the Discrete-EVent system Specification (DEVS) formalism for the specification of complex control structures for programmed graph rewriting, with time. DEVS allows for highly modular, hierarchical modelling of timed, reactive systems. In our approach, graphs are embedded in events and individual rewrite rules are embedded in *atomic*DEVS models. A side-effect of this approach is the introduction of an explicit notion of time. This allows one to model a time-advance for every rule as well as to interrupt (pre-empt) rule execution.

We have shown how the explicit notion of time allows for the simulation-based design of reactive systems such as modern computer games. We used the well-known game of PacMan as an example and modelled its dynamics with programmed graph transformation based on DEVS. This allowed the modelling of player behaviour, incorporating data about human players' behaviour and reaction times. We used the models of both player and game to evaluate, through simulation, the playability of a game design. In particular, we proposed a playability performance metric and varied parameters of the PacMan game. This led to an "optimal" (from a playability point of view) game configuration. The user model was subsequently replaced by a web-based visual interface to a real player and the game model was executed using a real-time DEVS simulator.

The use of graph transformation at the heart of this approach allows non-software-experts to specify all aspects of the design in an intuitive fashion. The resulting simulations give quantitative insight into optimal parameter choices. This is an example of Modelling and Simulation Based Design, where the graph transformation rules and the timed transformation system are modelled, as well as the user (player) and the context. Having modelled all these aspects in the same model transformation framework, *MoTif*, allows for simulation-based design.

The decision about which next move the computer player (Ghost) should make was simplified by avoiding pathfinding concerns as mentioned in Section 4.1. We plan to investigate the specification of pathfinding strategies by means of graph transformation rules. This will require support for backtracking.

At the model structure level, it is noted how topologically similar the **User Controlled Rules** and **Ghost Move** *CRules* are. Re-use and parametrization of transformation models deserves further investigation.

Acknowledgments

The Canadian NSERC and MITACS agencies are gratefully acknowledged for partial support of this work.

References

1. Nickel, U., Niere, J., Zündorf, A.: Tool demonstration: The FUJABA environment. In: ICSE 2000, pp. 742–745 (2000)
2. Agrawal, A., Karsai, G., Kalmar, Z., Neema, S., Shi, F., Vizhanyo, A.: The design of a language for model transformations. Software and Systems Modeling (SoSyM) 5, 261–288 (2005)
3. Lengyel, L., Levendovszky, T., Mezei, G., Charaf, H.: Model transformation with a visual control flow language. International Journal of Computer Science (IJCS) 1, 45–53 (2006)
4. Schürr, A., Winter, A.J., Zündorf, A.: Graph grammar engineering with PROGRES. In: Proceedings of the 5th European Software Engineering Conference, pp. 219–234. Springer, Heidelberg (1995)
5. Schürr, A., Rötschke, T., Amelunxen, C., Königs, A.: MOFLON: A Standard-Compliant Metamodeling Framework with Graph Transformations. In: Rensink, A., Warmer, J. (eds.) ECMDA-FA 2006. LNCS, vol. 4066, pp. 361–375. Springer, Heidelberg (2006)
6. Syriani, E., Vangheluwe, H.: Programmed graph rewriting with DEVS. In: Applications of Graph Transformations with Industrial Relevance (AGTIVE), pp. 134–149 (2007)
7. Heckel, R.: Graph transformation in a nutshell. In: Proceedings of the School on Foundations of Visual Modelling Techniques (FoVMT 2004) of the SegraVis Research Training Network. ENTCS, vol. 148, pp. 187–198. Elsevier, Amsterdam (2006)
8. de Lara, J., Vangheluwe, H.: AToM³: A tool for multi-formalism and meta-modelling. In: Kutsche, R.-D., Weber, H. (eds.) ETAPS 2002 and FASE 2002. LNCS, vol. 2306, pp. 174–188. Springer, Heidelberg (2002)
9. Zeigler, B.P.: Multifacetted Modelling and Discrete Event Simulation. Academic Press, London (1984)

10. Bolduc, J.S., Vangheluwe, H.: The modelling and simulation package PythonDEVS for classical hierarchical DEVS. MSDL technical report MSDL-TR-2001-01, McGill University (2001)
11. Guerra, E., de Lara, J.: Event-Driven Grammars: Towards the Integration of Meta-modelling and Graph Transformation. In: Ehrig, H., Engels, G., Parisi-Presicce, F., Rozenberg, G. (eds.) ICGT 2004. LNCS, vol. 3256, pp. 54–69. Springer, Heidelberg (2004)
12. Hart, P., Nilsson, N., Raphael, B.: A formal basis for the heuristic determination of minimum cost paths. IEEE Transactions on Systems Science and Cybernetics 4, 100–107 (1968)
13. Gyapay, S., Heckel, R., Varró, D.: Graph transformation with time: Causality and logical clocks. In: Corradini, A., Ehrig, H., Kreowski, H.-J., Rozenberg, G. (eds.) ICGT 2002. LNCS, vol. 2505, pp. 120–134. Springer, Heidelberg (2002)
14. Zaitsev, A.V., Skorik, Y.A.: Mathematical description of sensorimotor reaction time distribution. Human Physiology 28(4), 494–497 (2002)

Live Model Transformations Driven by Incremental Pattern Matching

István Ráth, Gábor Bergmann, András Ökrös, and Dániel Varró

Budapest University of Technology and Economics,
Department of Measurement and Information Systems,
H-1117 Magyar tudósok krt. 2, Budapest, Hungary
bergmann.gabor@gmail.com, okrosa@gmail.com
rath@mit.bme.hu, varro@mit.bme.hu

Abstract. In the current paper, we introduce a live model transformation framework, which continuously maintains a transformation context such that model changes to source inputs can be readily identified, and their effects can be incrementally propagated. Our framework builds upon an incremental pattern matcher engine, which keeps track of matches of complex contextual constraints captured in the form of graph patterns. As a result, complex model changes can be treated as elementary change events. Reactions to the changes of match sets are specified by graph transformation rules with a novel transactional execution semantics incorporating both pseudo-parallel and serializable behaviour.

1 Introduction

Model transformations play a crucial role in modern model-driven system engineering. Tool integration based on model transformations is one of the most challenging tasks with high practical relevance. In tool integration, a complex relationship needs to be established and maintained between models conforming to different domains and tools. This *model synchronization* problem can be formulated as to keep a model of a *source language* and a model of a *target language* consistently synchronized while developers constantly change the underlying source and target models. Model synchronization is frequently captured by *transformation rules*. When the transformation is executed, *trace* signatures are also generated to establish logical correspondence between source and target models.

Traditionally, model transformation tools support the *batch execution* of transformation rules, which means that input is processed "as a whole", and output is either regenerated completely, or, in more advanced approaches, updated using trace information from previous runs. However, in software engineering using multiple domain-specific languages, models are *evolving* and changing continuously. In case of large and complex models used in agile development, batch transformations may not be feasible.

Incremental model transformations are aimed at updating existing target models based on changes in the source models (called *target incrementality* in [1]), and to minimize the parts of the source model that needs to be reexamined by a transformation when the source model is changed (*source incrementality*). To achieve target incrementality, an incremental transformation approach creates "change sets" which are merged

A. Vallecillo, J. Gray, A. Pierantonio (Eds.): ICMT 2008, LNCS 5063, pp. 107–121, 2008.

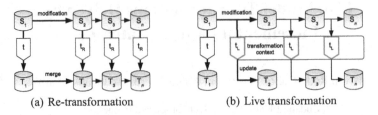

(a) Re-transformation   (b) Live transformation

Fig. 1. Incremental transformation approaches

with the existing target model instance. In order to efficiently calculate which source element may trigger changes (source incrementality), the *transformation context* has to be maintained, which describes the execution state of the model transformation system (e.g. variable values, partial matches). Depending on whether this is possible or not, there are two main approaches to incremental transformations, as discussed in Fig. 1 (adapted from [2]):

- Systems employing *re-transformations* lack the capability to maintain the transformation context over multiple execution runs, thus the entire transformation has to be re-run on the modified source models. This approach generates either new output models which must be merged with existing ones, or change sets which can be merged *in-situ*. As noted in [2], since the transformation context is lost, a merging strategy has to be employed. This involves the computation of which model elements are involved in the change, and which elements should be left untouched by the transformation. Thus, the feasibility of this approach depends heavily on the trace information. For instance, in case of graph transformation [3], negative application conditions (NACs) may be used to forbid the execution of a transformation rule twice on the same source element. An intelligent re-transformation based model synchronization approach has been proposed recently for ATL in [4], which targets bidirectionality rather than incrementality.

- In contrast, *live transformations* maintain the transformation context continuously so that the changes to source models can be instantly mapped to changes in target models. Live transformations are persistent and go through phases of execution whenever a model change occurs. Similarly to re-transformations, the information contained in trace signatures is used in calculating the source elements that require re-transformation. However, as the execution state is available in the transformation context, this re-computation can be far more efficient.

Related work in incremental transformations. In case of live transformations, *changes* of the source model are categorized as (i) an *atomic* model update consisting of an operation (e.g. create, delete, update) and operands (model elements); or, more generally, (ii) a complex *sequence* (set, transaction) of such atomic operations. To execute an incremental update, an atomic or complex model change has to be captured and processed. For this purpose, the following approaches have been proposed in case of *declarative transformation languages*:

- The Progres [5] graph transformation tool supports incremental attribute updates to invalidate partial matchings in case of node deletion immediately. On the other hand, new partial matchings are only lazily computed.
- The incremental model synchronization approach presented in [6] relies on various heuristics of the correspondence structure interconnecting the source and target models using triple graph grammars[7]. Dependencies between correspondence nodes are stored explicitly, which drives the incremental engine to undo an applied transformation rule in case of inconsistencies. Other triple graph grammar based approaches for model synchronization (e.g. [8]) do not address incrementality.
- In relational databases, materialized views, which explicitly store their content on the disk, can be updated by incremental techniques like Counting and DRed algorithms [9]. As reported in [10], these incremental techniques are also applicable for views that have been defined for graph pattern matching by the database queries of [11]. The use of non-materialized views have been discussed in [12].
- In [13], user-guided manipulation events are directly represented as model elements in the model store, while triple graph grammars [7] are extended to *event driven grammars* to determine the kind of event and the model elements affected. Change detection is directly linked to user interface events as this approach primarily targets (domain-specific) modeling environments. Note that this approach, *does not* rely on live transformations since the transformation context is not preserved; instead, the underlying ATOM3 [14] engine is started whenever an event from the UI is received. The idea, however, could be used in a live transformation environment.
- Triple graph grammar techniques are also used in [15] for tool integration based on UML models. The aim of the approach is to provide support for change synchronization between various languages in several development phases. Based on an integration algorithm, the system merges changed models on user request. Although it is not a live transformation approach, it could benefit from being implemented as such.
- [2] proposes a more general solution where *fact addition* and *fact removal* constitute an elementary change. Since the underlying TefKat [16] tool uses a transformation engine based on SLD resolution, a fact change may represent atomic updates (involving a single operation) as well as more complex changes, since a fact may encode information about multiple model elements (such as a complex pattern describing a UML class with attributes). This approach is only applicable to fully declarative transformation languages, since incremental updates involve the processing and modification of the SLD resolution tree (which, in broad terms, can be thought of as a special structure storing the whole transformation context).
- [17] describes a special application of incremental updates for the consistency checking of UML models. The approach provides a rule-based formalism to specify well-formedness constraints which are evaluated instantly after model modifications. Our demonstrating example illustrates how specialised transformations can be applied to a similar problem, but on a higher abstraction level.

Contributions of the paper. In the current paper, we present a novel approach to incremental model transformations based on incremental graph pattern matching and complex transaction handling. The main features of our contribution can be identified as follows: we support (i) atomic changes as well as model changes for complex constraints;

(ii) various styles of model transformation languages including fully declarative, partially declarative and procedural languages; and (iii) live transformations by preserving the transformation context. We discuss also how our incremental engine has been implemented and integrated as part of the VIATRA2 model transformation framework.

2   Preliminaries

In this section, we give a motivating example for live transformations. We also provide a brief introduction to the transformation language of the VIATRA2 framework.

2.1   Demonstrating Example

In this section, we demonstrate the technicalities of our approach using Petri nets, which are widely used to formally capture the dynamic semantics of concurrent systems due to their easy-to-understand visual notation and the wide range of available analysis tools. From a system modelling point of view, a Petri net model is frequently used for correctness, dependability and performance analysis in early stages of design.

Fig. 2(a) shows a simplified metamodel for Petri nets (captured in the VPM formalism [18] of VIATRA2). Petri nets are bipartite graphs, with two disjoint sets of nodes: Places and Transitions. Places may contain an arbitrary number of Tokens. Tokens are also modeled as objects to support visual representation. The Petri net concept can be extended by the notions of *place capacity* constraints which impose a limit on the number of Tokens a Place can hold.

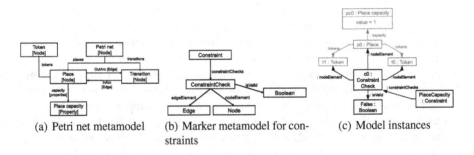

(a) Petri net metamodel   (b) Marker metamodel for constraints   (c) Model instances

Fig. 2. VIATRA metamodels and model instances

In the paper, we demonstrate our approach by the incremental validation of a complex dynamic modeling constraint for user editing events. In this use case, the user is editing models using a domain-specific editor which is capable of enforcing static type constraints so that only syntactically correct Petri net graphs can be produced. However, an advanced framework may go beyond this and provide immediate feedback if more dynamic constraints, such as a *capacity constraint* is violated (e.g. the user tries to assign too many tokens to a place).

In order to provide support for the editor, the modeling environment makes use of a *marker metamodel* which is a special type of trace model depicted in Fig. 2(b). A

Constraint denotes a particular run-time constraint being enforced within the editor, e.g. "PlaceCapacity". For each constraint, we explicitly mark all the (Petri net) elements, which are required to evaluate the constraint within a given context by a *ConstraintCheck* element. Each evaluation context of a *Constraint* is explicitly marked by a *ConstraintCheck* instance (i.e. separately for each Petri net place and its respective tokens in our case). The *isValid* relation indicates whether the constraint is valid *currently* for the context defined by the ConstraintCheck instance; the runtime environment makes use of this relationship to indicate graphical feedback to the user. In Fig. 2(c), place *p0* contains two tokens but has a capacity of 1, thus, the associated ConstraintCheck instance indicates that the PlaceCapacity constraint is violated in this context. In our demonstrating example used throughout the paper, we aim at providing an incremental evaluation of the capacity constraint in all contexts in response to elementary changes or complex transactions initiated by the user or another transformation.

2.2   Model Transformations in VIATRA

The transformation language of VIATRA2 consists of several constructs that together form an expressive language for developing both model to model transformations and code generators. Graph patterns (GP) define constraints and conditions on models, graph transformation (GT) [3] rules support the definition of elementary model manipulations, while abstract state machine (ASM) [19] rules can be used for the description of control structures.

Graph patterns are the atomic units of model transformations. They represent conditions (or constraints) that have to be fulfilled by a part of the model space in order to execute some manipulation steps on the model. The basic pattern body contains model element and relationship definitions. In VIATRA2, *patterns may call other patterns* using the *find* keyword. This feature enables the reuse of existing patterns as a part of a new (more complex) one. The semantics of this reference is similar to that of Prolog clauses: the caller pattern can be fulfilled only if their local constructs can be matched, and if the called (or referenced) pattern is also fulfilled. A *negative application condition* (NAC, defined by a negative subpattern following the *neg* keyword) prescribes contextual conditions for the original pattern which are forbidden in order to find a successful match. Negative conditions can be embedded into each other in an arbitrary depth (e.g. negations of negations).

Graph transformation (GT) [3] provides a high-level rule and pattern-based manipulation language for graph models. In VIATRA2, graph transformation rules may be specified by using a *precondition* (or left-hand side – LHS) pattern determining the applicability of the rule, and a *postcondition* pattern (or right-hand side – RHS) which declaratively specifies the result model after rule application. Elements that are present only in (the image of) the LHS are deleted, elements that are present only in the RHS are created, and other model elements remain unchanged. Further actions can be initiated by calling any ASM instructions within the *action* part of a GT rule, e.g. to report debug information or to generate code. In addition to graph transformation rules, VIATRA2 provides procedural constructs (such as simple model operations – new, delete, update) as well as pattern and scalar variables. Using these constructs, *complex model transformations* can be written.

3 Incremental Pattern Matching in VIATRA

Pattern matching plays a key role in the execution of VIATRA2 transformations. The goal is to find the occurrences of a graph pattern, which contains structural as well as type constraints on model elements. In the case of incremental pattern matching, the occurrences of a pattern are readily available at any time, and they are incrementally updated whenever changes are made. As pattern occurrences are stored, they can be retrieved in constant time – excluding the linear cost induced by the size of the result set itself –, making pattern matching a very efficient process. Generally speaking, besides memory consumption, the drawback is that these stored result sets have to be continuously maintained, imposing an overhead on update operations.

Our approach is based on the RETE algorithm [20], which is a well-known technique in the field of rule-based systems. This section is dedicated to giving a brief overview on how we adapted the concepts of RETE networks to implement the rich language features of the VIATRA2 graph transformation framework.

Tuples and Nodes. The main ideas behind the incremental pattern matcher are conceptually similar to relational algebra. Information is represented by a tuple consisting of model elements. Each node in the RETE net is associated with a (partial) pattern and stores the set of tuples that conform to the pattern. This set of tuples is in analogy with the relation concept of relational algebra.

The *input nodes* are a special class of nodes that serve as the underlying knowledge base representing a model. There is a separate input node for each entity type (class), containing unary tuples representing the instances that conform to the type. Similarly, there is an input node for each relation type, containing ternary tuples with source and target in addition to the identifier of the edge instance. Miscellaneous input nodes represent containment, generic type information, and other relationship between model elements.

Intermediate nodes store partial matches of patterns, or in other terms, matches of partial patterns. Finally, *production nodes* represent the complete pattern itself. Production nodes also perform supplementary tasks such as filtering those elements of the tuples that do not correspond to symbolic parameters of the pattern (in analogy with the projection operation of relational algebra) in order to provide a more efficient storage of models.

Joining. The key intermediate component of a RETE is the join node, created as the child of two parent nodes, that each have an outgoing RETE edge leading to the join node.

The role of the join node can be best explained with the relational algebra analogy: it performs a natural join on the relations represented by its parent nodes.

Figure 3(a) shows a simple pattern matcher built for the *sourcePlace* pattern, which describes a Place-Transition pair connected by an out-arc, illustrating the use of join nodes. By joining three input nodes, this sample RETE net enforces two entity type constraints and an edge (connectivity) constraint, to find pairs of Place and Transitions instances which fulfill the constraints described in the pattern.

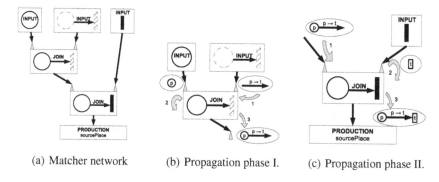

(a) Matcher network   (b) Propagation phase I.   (c) Propagation phase II.

Fig. 3. RETE matcher for the sourcePlace pattern

Updates after model changes. The primary goal of the RETE net is to provide incremental pattern matching. To achieve this, input nodes receive notifications about changes on the model, regardless whether the model was changed programmatically (i.e. by executing a transformation) or by user interface events.

Whenever a new entity or relation is created or deleted, the input node of the appropriate type will release an update token on each of its outgoing edges. To reflect type hierarchy, input nodes also notify the input nodes corresponding to the supertype(s). Positive update tokens reflect newly added tuples, and negative updates refer to tuples being removed from the set.

Each RETE node is prepared to receive updates on incoming edges, assess the new situation, determine whether and how the set of stored tuples will change, and release update tokens of its own to signal these changes to its child nodes. This way, the effects of an update will propagate through the network, eventually influencing the result sets stored in production nodes.

Figure 3(b) shows how the network in Fig. 3(a) reacts on a newly inserted out-arc. The input node for the relation type representing the arc releases an update token. The join node receives this token, and uses an effective index structure to check whether matching tuples (in this case: places) from the other parent node exist. If they do then a new token is propagated on the outgoing edge for each of them, representing a new instance of the partial pattern "place with outgoing arc". Fig. 3(c) shows the update reaching the second update node, which matches the new tuple against those contained by the other parent (in this case: transitions). If matches are found, they are propagated further to the production node.

More details of this incremental pattern matching approach can be found in [21], where initial investigations concerning the run-time performance of our implementation also have been presented. Our results indicate a significant efficiency increase over the conventional (local search-based) pattern matcher; in certain applications, the difference is two orders of magnitude. Additionally, it is worth pointing out that our RETE implementation significantly extends [22], the only existing RETE based approach in the field of graph (and model) transformation. In the future, we plan to incorporate another incremental approach [23] based on notification arrays to store a tree for partial matchings of a pattern.

4   Live Transformations Driven by Incremental Pattern Matching

Based on our incremental pattern matching technology introduced in Sec. 3, we now propose a novel approach to live model transformations.

4.1   Overview of the Approach

Model changes. In our approach, a model change is detected by a change in the *match set* of a graph pattern. The match set is defined by the subset of model elements satisfying structural and type constraints described by the pattern. Formally: a subgraph S of the model G is an element of the match set M(P) of pattern P, if S is isomorphic to P.

Changes in the matching set can be tracked using the RETE network. A model change occurs if the match set is expanded by a new match or a previously existing match is lost. Since a graph pattern may contain multiple elements, a change affecting any one of them may result in a change in the match set. The RETE-based incremental pattern matcher keeps track of every constraint prescribed by a pattern, thus it is possible to determine the set of constraints causing a change in the match set.

Our approach can be regarded as an extension of the *fact change* approach [2]. It provides support for the detection of changes of arbitrary complexity; not only atomic and compound model change facts (with simple and complex patterns respectively), but also operations, or sequences of operations can be tracked using this technique (either by representing operations directly in the model graph, or by using reference models).

Transformation context and efficient recomputation. Live transformation execution requires the continuous maintenance of the *execution context* to avoid the necessity of model merging in target models. In our approach, this context contains:

- *global variables*, which are persisted to enable the transformation engine to store (global) cached values.
- *pattern variables*, which are maintained by the incremental pattern matching engine after each atomic model manipulation operation. This means that the matches stored in a given pattern variable are always updated and the match set of any pattern can be retrieved in constant time.

As a result, the *computation* required to initialize and execute the incremental transformation sequence after a change is fast, since pattern matching, the most cost-intensive phase of the transformation, is executed in linear time with respect to the size of the matching set.

Explicit specification. In addition to targeting the incremental execution of model synchronization transformations, our approach is intended to support a broader range of live transformations. For this purpose, incremental transformation rules, called *triggers* are explicitly specified by the transformation designer. A trigger is defined in the form of a graph transformation rule: the precondition of its activation is defined in the form of a graph pattern, while the reaction is formulated by arbitrary (declarative or imperative) transformation steps.

In fact, not only tool integration, but many application scenarios can be formulated as incremental transformations, especially, in the context of domain-specific modeling such as (i) model execution (simulation), where triggers may be used to execute the dynamics semantics of a domain-specific language; (ii) constraint management, where incremental transformations are used to check and enforce the validity of a complex constraint; (iii) event-driven code generation, where the textual representation of abstract models may be incrementally maintained as the source model changes.

4.2 Triggers

In our approach, the basic unit of incremental transformations is the *trigger*. The formal representation of a trigger is based on a simplified version of the graph transformation rule: it consists of a *precondition pattern* and an *action* part consisting of a sequence of VIATRA2 transformation steps (including simple model manipulations as well as the invocation of complex transformations).

```
@Trigger(priority='10', mode='always', sensitivity='rise')
gtrule initPlace() = {
  precondition pattern pre(P) = {
    Place(P);
    Place.Place_Capacity(PC);
    Place.capacity(Cap,P,PC);
    neg pattern placeSet(P) = {
      Constraint.ConstraintCheck(CC);
      Constraint.ConstraintCheck.nodeElement(NE,CC,P);
    }
  }
  action {
    new(Constraint.ConstraintCheck(CC));
    new(Constraint.ConstraintCheck.nodeElement(NE, CC, P));
}}
```

Fig. 4. Place instance initialisation

In Fig. 4, a simple trigger is shown. It is automatically fired after the user creates a new Place and the modeling environment creates (as a complex model change involving multiple elements) an additional Capacity and a ConstraintCheck marker element for the new Place-Place_Capacity pair. As a common technique in graph transformation based approaches, we use a negative application condition to indicate that the action sequence should only be fired for new pairs without a marker element.

This simple example highlights a number of extensions that constitute our additions to the VIATRA2 transformation language: the new Trigger annotation is used to indicate that the graph transformation rule should be executed as an event-driven transformation. The annotation uses the following options (specified in a Java-like syntax):

- **Priority** (integer): Defines a precedence relation on multiple active triggers (triggers with higher priority value will run first).
- **Mode** (always | once): Defines whether a trigger is continuously scheduled for execution, or it is executed only once and then it becomes disabled.
- **Sensitivity** (rise | fall | both): *Rise* triggers are activated whenever a new match is encountered; *fall* triggers are executed when a previously existing match is lost; *both* triggers execute on rises and falls as well.

4.3 Execution Context

The system tracks changes changes in the match sets of patterns and executes the action sequences in a persistently maintained *execution context*. This context consists of *pattern variables* (continuously maintained by the RETE network) and *persistent variables* (called *ASM functions* in VIATRA2; essentially global associative arrays).

```
// An array to cache token numbers
asmfunction numberOfTokens / 1;

@Trigger(priority='10', mode='always', sensitivity='rise')
gtrule placeAdded() = {
 precondition pattern pre(CC) = {
  Constraint.ConstraintCheck(CC);
  Place(P);
  Constraint.ConstraintCheck.nodeElement(NE_P,CC,P);
 }
 action {
   // Initialize the 'numberOfTokens' array
   update numberOfTokens(P) = 0;
   // calculate the initial number of tokens
   forall T with find placeToken(P,T) do
    update numberOfTokens(P) = numberOfTokens(P)+1;
   // check the constraint's validity
   call constraintCheck(P,CC);
}}
```

Listing 1.1. Invoking constraint checking in the transformation context

In Listing 1.1, the *numberOfTokens* array is used in the persistent context to cache the amount of tokens assigned to a given place (the array is indexed by the Place reference). This trigger is fired after the ConstraintCheck marker element has been created by the trigger described in Fig. 4, and performs the necessary steps to set up the cache with the appropriate value (Listing 1.2; note that some pattern definitions have been omitted for space considerations).

```
rule constraintCheck(in P, in CC) = seq {
  // match the PlaceCapacity element storing the value
  // of P's capacity.
  choose PC with find placeCapacity(P,PC) do seq {
    if (numberOfTokens(P) <= value(PC)) seq {
      // delete a possible previous 'False' marking
      choose R find constraintFalse(CC,R) do delete(R);
      // create a new 'True' marking
      new ConstraintCheck.isValid(R,CC, Boolean.True);
    }
    else seq {
      choose R with find constraintTrue(CC,R) do delete(R);
      new ConstraintCheck.isValid(R,CC, Boolean.False);
}}}
```

Listing 1.2. Command sequence to check the validity of the capacity constraint

It is important to note that *pattern variables* (CC, P in the precondition, and T in patterns used in the action part) are also part of the maintained context, which makes the execution much more efficient. The underlying RETE-based pattern matcher maintains the matches for all involved patterns (*precondition, placeToken*, as well as *placeCapacity* and *constraintFalse / constraintTrue* in the constraintCheck rule) incrementally, thus the pattern matching operations (*forall* and *choose*, which pick all matches and one match, respectively) execute instantly, without any additional graph traversal.

4.4 Complex Change Detection

To detect complex model changes, the transformation developer can make use of the *rise* and *fall* triggers and some advanced VIATRA2 pattern language constructs.

Creation. In practical applications, a chain of triggers may be used to execute multiple incremental updates. For instance, after a Token instance has been added by the user, the system may execute a trigger similar to Fig. 4 to connect the new Token to the CapacityConstraint marker element. In reaction to that, after initPlace has reached the commit point, the tokenAdded() trigger (Listing 1.3) is activated.

```
@Trigger(sensitivity='rise')
 gtrule tokenAdded() = {
 precondition find connectedToken(P,CC,T) = {
  find placeToken(P,T);
  Constraint.ConstraintCheck(CC);
  Token(T);
  Constraint.ConstraintCheck.nodeElement(NE_Tok,CC,T);
 }
 action {
  update numberOfTokens(P) = numberOfTokens(P) + 1;
  call checkConstraint(P,CC);
}}
```

Listing 1.3. Trigger to handle the addition of Tokens

The *tokenAdded()* trigger updates the *numberOfTokens* array stored in the execution context, and initiates a constraint update which provides feedback to the user.

Deletions. To detect deletions, a trigger for the same precondition pattern as used in Listing 1.3 can be used in *fall* mode. In this case, the undef constant is assigned to the corresponding pattern variables to indicate that the model element identified by the pattern variable is no longer existent (Listing 1.4). However, other pattern variables (pointing to existing model elements) can be used in the action part in the usual way.

```
@Trigger(sensitivity='fall')
 gtrule tokenRemoved() = {
 precondition find tokenAdded.connectedToken(P,CC,T)
 action {
  // only act if token T has been lost (deleted)
  if (T == undef) seq {
   update numberOfTokens(P) = numberOfTokens(P) - 1;
   call checkConstraint(P,CC);
}}}
```

Listing 1.4. Handling token deletion

Attribute updates. The system also provides support for the incremental detection of attribute changes. VIATRA2 provides a *value* field for all node types; in this example, this value field of the *PlaceCapacity* property node is used to store the actual value of the capacity of the connected *Place*.

```
// associative array to cache place capacity values
asmfunction capacities / 1;

@Trigger(sensitivity='fall')
 gtrule capacityChanged() = {
  precondition pattern pre(P,PC) = {
    find placeCapacity(P,PC);
    // check condition to define a value constraint
    check(value(PC) == capacities(PC))
  }
  action {
    // check whether the attribute update caused the activation
    if (PC!=undef && P!=undef && value(PC) != capacities(PC)) seq {
     // update constraint validity
     choose CC with find placeConstraint(P,CC) do call checkConstraint(P,CC);
     // store new value
     update capacities(PC) = value(PC);
}}}
```

Listing 1.5. Handling attribute updates

In Listing 1.5, a *fall* trigger is defined for changes in the capacity value (the user may change that any time during modeling). The trigger is activated for changes in the match set of a complex pattern involving a *check condition*, which is a special feature of the VIATRA2 transformation language to define additional attribute constraints which cannot be expressed using structural graph patterns. The global array *capacities* is used to cache known capacity values; the trigger checks whether the cause of activation was a change in the attribute value and proceeds to update the constraint validity.

4.5   Transaction Management

In order to be able to perceive changes in the match set of a pattern over a complex model manipulation operation, such as the execution of a graph transformation rule or a complex editing operation, the model management system has to support transactions. A *transaction* is defined as a sequence of atomic model manipulation operations (e.g. create node, edge, instance-type-supertype relation, update attribute, etc.), followed by a commit command. The VIATRA2 framework ensures that all model manipulation occurs within a transaction.

The operational workflow of the live transformation system is shown in Fig. 5 from the viewpoint of transactions. After a transaction has reached its commit point, the system evaluates the changes in the match sets of precondition patterns of triggers registered in the trigger queue. The evaluation is linear, i.e. more registered triggers increase the execution time linearly (as future work, we will improve this). Since the RETE networks are updated after each atomic model manipulation operation, a match set may experience transient changes while a long transaction is running. In our approach, only the *effective* changes are considered; thus, even if a new match is generated while a

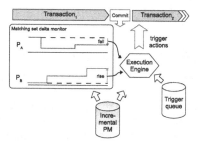

Fig. 5. Overview of incremental execution

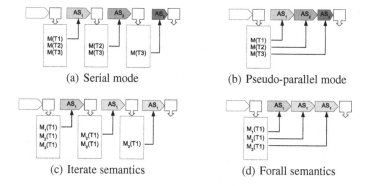

(a) Serial mode   (b) Pseudo-parallel mode

(c) Iterate semantics   (d) Forall semantics

Fig. 6. Execution semantics for multiple match set changes and execution modes for multiple trigger activation

transaction is running, if that match is subsequently lost, the system will not process it for triggers. This mechanism is provided by the matching set *delta monitor*, which computes the net changes that occurred during a transaction. After the changes have been evaluated, the execution engine processes triggers registered in the *trigger queue* and selects those with a precondition activated by the processed matching set changes, and prepares them for execution based on the current *execution mode*.

Execution modes. Action sequences of activated triggers can be executed in two modes (Fig. 6). In the depicted scenario, we assume that there are three active triggers (T1–3) with their action sequences (AS1–3 respectively). After a transaction, the system encounters a new match (M(T1)–M(T3)) for each of the three triggers.

In *serial mode* (Fig. 6(a)), the action sequences are executed in separated transactions according to the priority order. After each commit point, the system re-evaluates all trigger conditions. In this mode, *conflicts* between competing triggers are eliminated (since the checks may reveal, for instance, that M2 was invalidated while AS1 was executed). However, a circular activation of triggers may result in infinite loops in case of serial execution mode.

In contrast, *pseudo-parallel mode* (Fig. 6(b)), action sequences are executed in a single transaction with a common commit point. In this case, conflicts may occur, and they need to be accounted for by the transformation designer. On the other hand, the execution is faster than in serial mode, since no intermediate checks are performed. A similar race condition may arise for *multiple matches* for a single trigger. In Figures 6(d) and 6(c), trigger T1 has been activated for matchings M_1 - M_3. In *iterate mode*, we non-deterministically select one match, and execute its action sequence as a separate transaction. Then, if the rest of the matches are not invalidated, their respective actions are also executed one by one in separate transactions. In *forall mode*, all execution occurs in a single transaction with the possibility of conflicts which may cause a run-time error.

5   Conclusion

In the current paper, we presented a novel approach to live model transformations based on incremental graph pattern matching and complex transaction handling. Compared to existing incremental transformation approaches, the main added value of the current paper is (i) to preserve full transformation context in the form of pattern matches; (ii) to incorporate incremental reaction to complex model changes (both deletion and addition), and (iii) to provide incremental support for both declarative and imperative transformations with the help of complex transaction handling mechanism. Our approach is fully implemented and integrated to the VIATRA2 model transformation framework.

References

1. Czarnecki, K., Helsen, S.: Feature-based survey of model transformation approaches. IBM Systems Journal 45(3), 621–645 (2006)
2. Hearnden, D., Lawley, M., Raymond, K.: Incremental Model Transformation for the Evolution of Model-Driven Systems. In: Nierstrasz, O., Whittle, J., Harel, D., Reggio, G. (eds.) MoDELS 2006. LNCS, vol. 4199, pp. 321–335. Springer, Heidelberg (2006)
3. Ehrig, H., Engels, G., Kreowski, H.J., Rozenberg, G. (eds.): Handbook on Graph Grammars and Computing by Graph Transformation: Applications, Languages and Tools, vol. 2. World Scientific, Singapore (1999)
4. Xiong, Y., et al.: Towards automatic model synchronization from model transformations. In: Proceedings of the 22nd IEEE/ACM International Conference on Automated Software Engineering, pp. 164–173. ACM, New York (2007)
5. Schürr, A.: Introduction to PROGRES, an attributed graph grammar based specification language. In: Nagl, M. (ed.) WG 1989. LNCS, vol. 411, pp. 151–165. Springer, Berlin (1990)
6. Giese, H., Wagner, R.: Incremental Model Synchronization with Triple Graph Grammars. In: Nierstrasz, O., Whittle, J., Harel, D., Reggio, G. (eds.) MoDELS 2006. LNCS, vol. 4199, pp. 543–557. Springer, Heidelberg (2006)
7. Schürr, A.: Specification of graph translators with triple graph grammars. Technical report, RWTH Aachen, Fachgruppe Informatik, Germany (1994)
8. Klar, F., et al.: Model transformation in the large. In: Proc. of the 6th Joint Meeting of the European Software Engineering Conference and the ACM SIGSOFT Symposium On The Foundations of Software engineering, pp. 285–294. ACM, New York (2007)

9. Gupta, A., Mumick, I.S., Subrahmanian, V.S.: Maintaining views incrementally. In: ACM SIGMOD Proceedings, Washington, D.C., USA, pp. 157–166 (1993)

10. Varró, G., Varró, D.: Graph transformation with incremental updates. In: Proc. of the 4th Workshop on Graph Transformation and Visual Modeling Techniques, Barcelona, Spain. ENTCS, vol. 109, pp. 71–83. Elsevier, Amsterdam (2004)

11. Varró, G., Friedl, K., Varró, D.: Graph transformation in relational databases. Journal of Software and Systems Modelling 5(3), 313–341 (2006)

12. Jakob, J., Schürr, A.K., Non-materialized, A.: model view specification with triple graph grammars. In: Corradini, A., Ehrig, H., Montanari, U., Ribeiro, L., Rozenberg, G. (eds.) ICGT 2006. LNCS, vol. 4178, pp. 321–335. Springer, Heidelberg (2006)

13. Guerra, E., de Lara, J.: Event-driven grammars: Relating abstract and concrete levels of visual languages. Software and Systems Modeling 6(3), 317–347 (2007)

14. de Lara, J., Vangheluwe, H.: AToM3: A tool for multi-formalism and meta-modelling. In: Kutsche, R.-D., Weber, H. (eds.) ETAPS 2002 and FASE 2002. LNCS, vol. 2306, pp. 174–188. Springer, Heidelberg (2002)

15. Becker, S.M., Thomas Haase, B.W.: Model-based a-posteriori integration of engineering tools for incremental development processes. Software and Systems Modeling 4(2), 123–140 (2005)

16. The University of Queensland: TefKat homepage, http://tefkat.sourceforge.net/

17. Egyed, A.: Instant consistency checking for the UML. In: Proc. of the 28th International Conference on Software Engineering, pp. 381–390. ACM, New York (2006)

18. Varró, D., Pataricza, A.: VPM: A visual, precise and multilevel metamodeling framework for describing mathematical domains and UML. Journal of Software and Systems Modeling 2(3), 187–210 (2003)

19. Börger, E., Stärk, R.: Abstract State Machines. A method for High-Level System Design and Analysis. Springer, Heidelberg (2003)

20. Forgy, C.L.: Rete: A fast algorithm for the many pattern/many object pattern match problem. Artificial Intelligence 19(1), 17–37 (1982)

21. Bergmann, G., Ökrös, A., Ráth, I., Varró, D., Varró, G.: Incremental pattern matching in the VIATRA transformation system. In: 3rd International Workshop on Graph and Model Transformation. 30th International Conference on Software Engineering (accepted, 2008)

22. Bunke, H., Glauser, T., Tran, T.H.: An efficient implementation of graph grammars based on the RETE matching algorithm. In: Ehrig, H., Kreowski, H.-J., Rozenberg, G. (eds.) Graph Grammars 1990. LNCS, vol. 532, pp. 174–189. Springer, Heidelberg (1991)

23. Varró, G., Varró, D., Schürr, A.: Incremental graph pattern matching: Data structures and initial experiments. In: Graph and Model Transformation (GraMoT 2006). Electronic Communications of the EASST, vol. 4 (2006)

Semantics-Based Weaving of UML Sequence Diagrams

Roy Grønmo[1,2], Fredrik Sørensen[1], Birger Møller-Pedersen[1],
and Stein Krogdahl[1]

[1] Univ. of Oslo, Dept. of Informatics, Norway
[2] SINTEF ICT, Norway
{roygr,fredrso,birger,steinkr}@ifi.uio.no

Abstract. In this paper we briefly introduce an aspect language that can define cross-cutting effects on a set of UML 2.0 sequence diagrams. Our main contribution is to weave aspects and sequence diagrams at the model level. By basing the weaving upon a formal trace model for sequence diagrams, we ensure that the weaving is semantics-based. To avoid the intractability of working on complete trace sets, we define a lifeline-based weaving upon trace-based equivalence classes. A major challenge is to handle unbounded loops which produce infinite trace sets. We establish a systematic way to rewrite the original loop definition so that the weaving can be performed on a finite structure. A weaving tool has been implemented to validate the approach.

1 Introduction

Aspect-orientation for programming has emerged as a promising way to separately define cross-cutting parts of programs, in order to achieve separation of concerns. We believe that the same potential is there also for modeling. This paper explores aspect-oriented modeling for UML 2 sequence diagrams [13].

In aspect-oriented programming the *base program* is the main program upon which one or more aspects may define some cross-cutting code as additions or changes. An aspect is defined by a pair (*pointcut* and *advice*), where the *pointcut* defines where to affect the base program and the corresponding *advice* defines what to do in the places identified by the pointcut. Analogously we term our set of sequence diagrams as the *base model*, and we define an aspect diagram to consist of a pointcut diagram and an advice diagram, both based upon the concrete syntax of sequence diagrams.

In this paper we assume that the sequence diagrams are used as input for tools that automatically produce executable test code, e.g. to test if a sequence diagram is a correct refinement of another sequence diagram [12], or to test if a system specified by UML statecharts, class diagrams and object diagrams is consistent with sequence diagram specifications [14]. The test tools expect complete sequence diagrams. Therefore we need to weave the aspect and the base model, into a woven model, before generation of test code.

The woven model is not intended to be viewed (except for debugging) or further updated by the modeler. This means that the structure of the result is not a primary focus. It suffices that the woven model is semantically correct with respect to our formal model.

Many aspect-oriented approaches suffer because they rely on a pure syntactic pointcut matching and weaving. This paper gives part of an answer to the following question:

A. Vallecillo, J. Gray, A. Pierantonio (Eds.): ICMT 2008, LNCS 5063, pp. 122–136, 2008.

How can we use the trace-based formal model of STAIRS [15] to achieve a semantics-based matching and weaving algorithm for sequence diagrams?

The paper is organized as follows; Section 2 introduces the STAIRS formal model for sequence diagrams; Section 3 presents the matching and weaving approach; Section 4 shows how we may statically weave unbounded loops; Section 5 describes our tool implementation; Section 6 presents related work; and finally Section 7 provides the conclusions.

2 STAIRS

STAIRS gives the semantics of a sequence diagram by a set of traces that represents the set of possible execution runs. The trace set may be infinite while each individual trace is finite.

The syntax of a UML sequence diagram, called *interaction*, follows the EBNF of Figure 1 [15]. We focus on the operators seq, alt and loop. The first two operators are chosen because they are the basic operators from which we also may define several other operators. The loop is included since it provides some challenges in the context of semantics-based weaving (section 4).

Each message is represented by two events, a *transmission* event (!) and a *reception* event (?) (the transmitter and receiver lifelines are omitted for readability in the paper examples when this information is unambiguously defined by associated diagrams). An event takes place on a lifeline L1 if it is a transmission event on L1, e.g. !(signal,L1,L2), or a reception event on L1, e.g. ?(signal,L2,L1). We assume that the messages are complete (i.e. contain both events ! and ?) within each alt operand, loop operand, pointcut, advice and each sequence diagram in the base model.

The weak sequence operator, seq, of sequence diagrams imposes a partial order of events given by: 1) the transmission event must come before the reception event of the same message, and 2) all events are ordered for each lifeline in isolation. An intuitive idea behind this partial order is that messages are sent asynchronously and that they may happen in any order on different lifelines, but sequentially on the same lifeline. Figure 2 shows an interaction example and the corresponding arrows of its four partial order requirements.

Sequence diagrams allow *crossing messages*, i.e. two messages a and b are crossing only when they have events on the same two lifelines, and a has an event before b on one lifeline, while b has an event before a on the other lifeline, e.g. seq $[!(a, L1, L2), !(b, L1, L2), ?(b, L1, L2), ?(a, L1, L2)]$.

The alt operator defines alternative interactions for each operand, and the loop operator represents alternative interactions for each allowed repetition of the loop body.

Interaction → Event | WeakSeq | Alternatives | Loop	WeakSeq → "seq [" Interactions "]"
Event → Kind "(" Signal "," Transmitter "," Receiver ")"	Alternatives → "alt [" Interactions "]"
Interactions → Interaction | Interactions "," Interaction	Loop → "loop" Set? "[" Interaction "]"
Kind → "!" | "?"	*Signal* is the message content, *Transmitter* and *Receiver* are lifeline names.

Fig. 1. Syntax of interactions

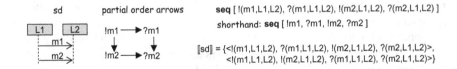

Fig. 2. Example: Sequence diagram, partial order, syntax and semantics

Notice that the `loop` operator has an optional parameter, `Set`, to define the possible iterations of the loop. This can be expressed in many different ways such as {1, 3, 5} or 2..* (0..* is the default).

We briefly explain the semantics operator, $[\![\ ]\!]$, while a precise definition is given in [15]. The semantics of an interaction i is $[\![i]\!] = (p, n)$, where p is the set of *positive traces* and n is the set of *negative traces*. *Positive traces* define valid behavior and *negative traces* define invalid behavior, while all other traces are defined as inconclusive. In this paper we concentrate on aspects that only affect positive traces, and we therefore use a simplified model without negative traces: that is $[\![i]\!] = p$. A *trace* is a sequence of events which we display as $\langle e_1, \ldots, e_n \rangle$, where e_i are events for all $i \in 1..n$.

The $[\![\ ]\!]$ operator produces one trace for each valid permutation of events that satisfy the two partial order requirements as explained for the `seq` operator above. The $[\![\ ]\!]$ operator produces the union of the traces for each operand of the `alt` operator and the union of traces for each possible number of iterations of a `loop`. n iterations of the loop are replaced by a weak sequence of n occurrences of the loop body before the semantics operator is applied to it. If the loop has no upper bound, called *unbounded loop*, then we will have infinitely many traces. Each message in the trace is dynamically given a unique identifier, which is shared between the transmission and reception events of the message. We say that two interactions i_1 and i_2 are *semantically equivalent* if they represent the same trace set (except for the dynamic identifiers), i.e. if $[\![i_1]\!] = [\![i_2]\!]$.

We define one trace to be *partial order equivalent (POE)* to another trace if they are both permutations of the same set of events with the same order on each lifeline. The $[\![\ ]\!]$ operator is used to define POE since it is defined to produce all such permutations:

Definition 1. *We say that two traces* $t^A = \langle t_1^A, \ldots, t_n^A \rangle$ *and* $t^B = \langle t_1^B, \ldots, t_n^B \rangle$ *are **partial order equivalent (POE)** if and only if:*

$$[\![seq[t_1^A, \ldots, t_n^A]]\!] = [\![seq[t_1^B, \ldots, t_n^B]]\!]$$

We let the function, `POE: Trace → TraceSet`, calculate all the POE traces of a given trace, $\text{POE}(\langle t_1^A, \ldots, t_n^A \rangle) = [\![seq[t_1^A, \ldots, t_n^A]]\!]$. The diagram in Figure 2 has two traces which are POE: $\langle !m1, ?m1, !m2, ?m2 \rangle$ and $\langle !m1, !m2, ?m1, ?m2 \rangle$. The function POE() of either of these two traces returns the set of both traces.

3   The Approach

This section explains how we perform the semantics-based weaving for finite traces where there are no unbounded loops, while section 4 covers unbounded loops. Finite loops can be seen as a set of alternatives, so we only have to cover the `seq` and `alt` operators.

The aspect diagrams are inspired by graph transformation [4] where the left part, the pointcut diagram, defines a pattern for which we are looking for matches or morphisms in the base model. The right part, the advice diagram, defines a replacement of the matches within the base model. This implies that messages present only in the pointcut and not in the advice, will be deleted, while messages present only in the advice and not in the pointcut, will be added. Both the pointcut and advice diagrams are based upon the graphical elements of sequence diagrams so that the modeler can work with an already familiar notation.

3.1 Syntactic-Based Matching Does Not Work

If the pointcut identifies only a single message to be matched, then there is no difference between syntactic-based and semantics-based matching. However, even for only two consecutive messages, as in the example in Figure 3, syntactic-based and semantics-based matching is different.

The pointcut of Figure 3 expresses that the message m1 from the lifeline L1 to the lifeline L2 is followed by the message m2 from L1 to L2. A weaving must replace all pointcut matches by an advice which adds the message new and an `alt` operator. The base model has two consecutive `alt` operators. An `alt` operator defines a choice of different alternatives, where the alternatives are given as operands separated by a dashed line. If we try to find matches of the pointcut within the base model with pure syntactic matching, then we do not find any matches. However, one possible execution trace chooses the second operands of the two `alt` operators, which then should result in a match of the specified pointcut.

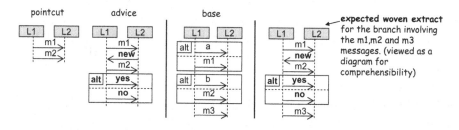

Fig. 3. *Example*: Aspect model, base model, and expected woven model(extract)

3.2 Lifeline-Based Matching

In order to make the matching semantics-based, we define matches directly on the base model traces. We need an injective mapping function, ϕ: Event → Event, which maps from pointcut events to base events. For each event, ϕ only maps the identifier, while it preserves all the other event properties (kind, signal, transmitter, receiver).

Definition 2. *We have a **match** if and only if a base trace contains a pointcut trace (where each event in the pointcut trace is mapped by ϕ)*

In theory we may calculate all the pointcut and base traces to find matches. In practice this is an intractable problem since the number of traces may have an exponential growth relative to the number of events in the diagram. In our first test implementation we were not able to handle a relatively small base model, consisting of eleven consecutive messages in the same direction between the same two lifelines, since there are as much as 58, 786 traces.

In an optimized weave algorithm we avoid calculating all the traces by instead working on the POE equivalence classes (abbreviated as *POE classes*) instead. This has a large impact on the performance since a POE class may represent thousands of actual traces, e.g. all the 58, 786 traces in the base model mentioned above belong to the same POE class. The set of POE classes, representing an interaction, is derived from an interaction by a tree-like traversal of the `alt` operands. Each valid combination of the `alt` operands represents a POE class. For each POE class, we only represent the event orders per lifeline, so that each event occurs only once. Hence, the optimized algorithm scales well and performs linearly wrt. to the number of alt operands and the number of events. The next lemma states that a lifeline-based matching wrt. to each POE class is sufficient to identify all the possible matches:

Lemma 1. *(**Lifeline-based matching**) For a base trace,* `bTrace`, *there exists a **match in one of its POE traces** (`POE(bTrace)`) if and only if*

1. $\forall l \in$ `Lifelines`: *the event order on l of* `POE(bTrace)` *contains the event order on l of the pointcut (where each event in the pointcut is mapped by ϕ) AND*
2. *there are no messages in* `POE(bTrace)` *having the reception event before the contained pointcut on one lifeline and the transmission event after the contained pointcut on another lifeline (match blocking messages).*

Proof: *If-direction*: Assume all the pointcut event orders per lifeline is contained within base event orders per lifeline, and that there are no match blocking messages in the base trace. No match blocking messages ensure that we may construct a matching base trace within `POE(bTrace)` as follows: select all the events on each lifeline prior to each lifeline match in one of the valid orders, then select all the events from the `pTrace` and persist their order (this will be the contained match), then proceed with any valid selection of the remaining events. *Only-if-direction*: Assume there is a pointcut trace contained in a base trace. No match blocking messages follow directly since such messages otherwise would split the match events. To get a contradiction, assume there is a lifeline on which the pointcut event order is not contained within the base event order of the same lifeline. Then there must be an intermediate event, not part of the match, between two of the matching base trace events on the lifeline. But then it would also be part of the match trace due the relationship between lifeline event orders and traces. □

Lemma 1 needs to exclude match blocking messages. Otherwise the if-direction of the lemma does not hold as we can see from Figure 4. The pointcut has a single trace: $\langle !a, ?a, !b, ?b \rangle$. None of the six shown base traces have a contained pointcut trace, and thus there are no matches (Def. 2). This is because the match blocking c message will always get its two events between the first and last events of the matched pointcut trace.

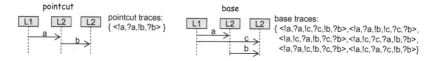

Fig. 4. c is a match blocking message

3.3 Lifeline-Based Weaving

The previous section showed that a lifeline-based matching of the POE classes is equivalent to a semantics-based matching on the traces. This section continues by defining a lifeline-based weaving. We calculate the POE classes of the base model, the single POE class of the pointcut and the POE classes of the advice. Since the pointcut is restricted to use only seq and events, it has always only one POE class.

The weave algorithm repeats the following three steps as long as there are unhandled matches in the base POE classes: 1) Identify a match in a base POE class (lifeline-based matching), 2) Perform lifeline-based weaving, according to Def. 3 below, for each of the advice POE classes. Add the results, a new POE class for each advice POE class, to the set of base POE classes, and 3) Remove the matched base POE class and repeat the three steps if there are more matches.

Definition 3. *Lifeline-based weaving for a matched base POE class (baseP) with match m and an advice POE class (advP). The resulting POE class, res, gets the initial value: res = baseP. Then the lifelines of res are updated according to three rules:*

(1) $\forall l \in baseP.LLs : m(l) \neq \langle \rangle \Rightarrow res.replaceEvts(l, m(l), advP.evts(l))$

(2) $\forall l \in advP.LLs \setminus baseP.LLs : res.addLL(l, advP.evts(l))$

(3) $\forall l \in baseP.LLs : (m(l) = \langle \rangle \wedge advP.evts(l) \neq \langle \rangle) \Rightarrow res.ins(l, advP.evts(l))$

Prerequisites of Def. 3: A POE class contains the following methods; LLs() retrieves the set of (non-empty) lifelines; replaceEvts(l,m(l),advP.evts(l)) replaces the match events by the advice events on lifeline l; advP.evts(l) retrieves the list of events of the advice on lifeline l; addLL(l,advP.evts(l)) adds l as a new lifeline with the advice events on l as the content; ins(l,advP.evts(l)) inserts the advice event list on lifeline l into an appropriate position on lifeline l (the details are given below). m(l) retrieves the event list of the match on the l lifeline, and ⟨⟩ denotes an empty event list.

Explanation of Def. 3: Each lifeline can be woven separately as defined by the three mutually exclusive rules. When a lifeline has matched events, **rule (1)**, then the matched events on this lifeline are simply replaced by the corresponding advice events (in some cases an empty list). When a lifeline has events in the advice and not in the base, **rule (2)**, then all of this advice lifeline is inserted as a new base lifeline. Figure 5 shows how the lifeline-based weaving works for rules 1 and 2.

The most difficult rule, **rule (3)**, is when a lifeline has no matched events, but have events in both the base and advice, e.g. the ?adv event in the advice of Figure 6 occurs on lifeline L3 with no events in the pointcut (the match part), and there is a !b event on

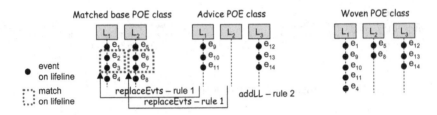

Fig. 5. The three rules for the lifeline-based weaving

the L3 lifeline in the base model. *Should the new event, ?adv, be placed before or after the !b event?*. Choosing to place ?adv before !b will produce the undesired woven diagram (Figure 6) which has no possible traces because there is a deadlock.

In many cases, a proper placement can be found by exploring the partial order relationships. Let po(e_1,e_2) denote a partial order where the event e_1 must happen before the event e_2. We will produce the union of the partial orders of the advice POE class and the matched base POE class:

$$\{po(!a, ?a), po(!adv, ?adv), po(!b, ?b), po(?a, !adv), po(?b, ?a)\}$$

Since partial order is a transitive relation, we may calculate the transitive closure, which will produce the pair po(!b,?adv). This defines a unique and proper position for ?adv on the base L3 lifeline in Figure 6. There are however cases, where there may be several position choices fulfilling the partial order requirements, e.g. add another event !(c,L3,L4) after !b on L3. In such cases we choose an arbitrary position among the choices except that we will avoid or minimize the number of crossing messages, and provide a warning message to the modeler.

We know that the transitive closure of the partial orders will not produce conflicting position instructions. Otherwise we get a contradiction: Assume there exists two events, e_1 and e_2, on the lifeline where the new advice event, new, shall be inserted, such that po(e_1,e_2). The only way to get a conflict is if both po(new,e_1) and po(e_2,new) are part of the transitive closure. But then also the pairs po(e_1,new) and po(new,e_2) must belong to the transitive closure. This is a contradiction, and we may conclude that we will not encounter conflicting partial order requirements for new advice events.

When there are no more unhandled matches, the woven result is a set of POE classes. Finally, we need to go from POE classes to a woven interaction. Each POE class is represented by a single seq operator with the lifeline events as operands in one of the legal orders (the choice is insignificant). Then all these seq operators are used as operands inside an outermost alt operator to represent the woven interaction.

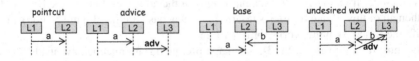

Fig. 6. Placement of a new event on a lifeline with no events in the pointcut

pointcut POE class	base POE classes	woven POE classes	woven interaction
L1: <!m1,!m2> L2: <?m1,?m1>	L1: <!a,!b,!m3> L2: <?a,?b,?m3>	*The three non-matching POE classes are kept*	alt [...,seq[!m1,?m1, !new,?new, !m2,?m2,
	L1: <!a,!m2,!m3> L2: <?a,?m2,?m3>		!yes,?yes,
advice POE classes		L1: <!m1,?new,!m2,!yes,!m3> L2: <?m1,!new,?m2,?yes,?m3>	!m3,?m3], seq[!m1,?m1,
L1: <!m1,?new,!m2,!yes> L2: <?m1,!new,?m2,?yes>	L1: <!m1,!b,!m3> L2: <?m1,?b,?m3>		!new,?new, !m2,?m2,
L1: <!m1,?new,!m2,!no> L2: <?m1,!new,?m2,?no>	L1: <!m1, !m2, !m3> L2: <?m1,?m2, ?m3>	L1: <!m1,?new,!m2,!no,!m3> L2: <?m1,!new,?m2,?no,?m3>	!no,?no, !m3,?m3]]

Fig. 7. Lifeline-based weaving on POE classes

Figure 7 shows our proposed weaving on the example in Figure 3. Each POE class is represented by its event order on each of the two lifelines L1 and L2. The only base POE class with a match is woven for each of the two advice POE classes, resulting in five woven POE classes. The final woven interaction (Figure 7) is semantically equivalent to the expected woven result (Figure 3).

3.4 Discussion

We have described the matching strategy as a *random matching*. Find any match, perform weaving and repeat the process. If our weaving terminates, then we are guaranteed that there will not exist any matches in the woven model. Consider an example of an aspect a,a → b (shorthand notation for an aspect: pointcut → advice), and a base model a,a,a,a, where the a's and b's are messages in the same direction between the same two lifelines. A random matching strategy gives one of the following three alternative derivations with two different end results: 1) a,a,a,a ⇒ a,b,a, 2) a,a,a,a ⇒ a,a,b ⇒ b,b, and 3) a,a,a,a ⇒ b,a,a ⇒ b,b. Klein et al. [10] suggest a *left-most matching* strategy leading to the unique derivation alternative 3. Our weaving supports the left-most matching by choosing the top-most matches of each lifeline.

We define a *plain additive aspect* to be an aspect that does not delete events. For such aspects we will mark all the events in a treated match and exclude them from possible future matches. This ensures a terminating weaving process for a lot of aspects that would otherwise never terminate, e.g. a,a → a,a,b.

Our weaving algorithm uses the lifeline-based matching for performance reasons. The remainder of this paper will, however, refer to matches according to the equivalent trace-based match definition (Def. 2) to ease the presentation.

4   Weaving Unbounded Loops

This section describes how, and under which conditions, we can do the weaving also for unbounded loops. Loops without an upper bound are troublesome because they produce an infinite trace set.

We classify unbounded loops as two types relative to a pointcut. The two loop types need different kinds of treatment. Figure 8 shows a pointcut to the left and two unbounded loops to the right:

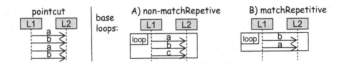

Fig. 8. Loop types with respect to pointcut

- *non-matchRepetitive*. A loop which cannot produce any matches on its own. Such a loop may however be part of a match in combination with trace events outside of the loop. The loop in Figure 8A is non-matchRepetitive since the c message prevents the loop to produce matches only from loop events no matter how many iterations we use.
- *matchRepetitive*. A loop which produces matches on its own after some number of iterations. Such a loop has infinitely many matches since the number of iterations is infinite. The loop in Figure 8B is matchRepetitive since we get the first match by three iterations. Thus, there will be n matches after $n * 3$ iterations for all $n > 0$.

We will treat the loops by rewriting them into an expanded, but semantically equivalent (except possibly some weaving) interaction structure. After the rewrite we have isolated or woven a remaining unbounded loop such that we are guaranteed it will not take part in further matches. The treatment of loops happens before the rest of the weaving process, and each loop is treated individually and in isolation from the rest of the model. This means that we cannot ensure a left-most matching for unbounded loops, but restrict ourselves to cases where it is acceptable with a random matching strategy. When all the unbounded loops are treated, they will be ignored while we perform ordinary weaving for the surrounding finite parts of the interaction.

We now introduce three conditions under which we are able to present (terminating) algorithms to statically weave unbounded loops: 1) The unbounded loop bodies contain no `alt` or `loop` operators, 2) the aspect is *plain additive*, and 3) the pointcut is *connected*.

A diagram is *connected* if and only if every involved lifeline has a *path* to any other involved lifeline in the diagram. There is a path between two lifelines if there is a message from one of them to the other. Furthermore this path relation is both reflexive, symmetric and transitive. In Figure 9A both the pointcut and base models are connected, while both the pointcut and base models are disconnected in Figure 9B since neither of L1 and L2 has no path to neither of L3 and L4.

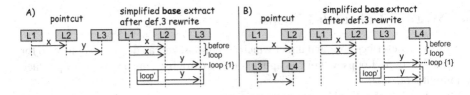

Fig. 9. Correctness of loop rewrite depends on connected pointcuts

We need a way to differentiate the two loop types. The following lemma proves it is sufficient to consider the loop with an upper bound equal to the number of messages in the pointcut. If that bounded loop has a match, then it is matchRepetitive, otherwise it is non-matchRepetitive (numP returns the number of messages within the pointcut diagram):

Lemma 2. *An unbounded loop lp = loop[body] is **matchRepetitive** for a pointcut pd if and only if there exist at least one match in the bounded loop* $lp^b =$ loop *{numP}[body].*

Proof: *If-direction*: Since *lp* has a match after *b* iterations, it is by definition matchRepetitive. *Only-if-direction*: Let *n* be the fewest number of iterations for *lp* which gives a match. Such a matching trace must involve at least one event from all iterations, otherwise we could exclude iterations not contributing to the match and get a match within fewer iterations than *n*. The pointcut trace which equals the match involves a number of messages which all have two events. Since the match need to involve both the transmission and reception events of a message, we know that each iteration contributes with at least two events in the matching trace. The length of the pointcut trace is twice the number of messages, which means that *n* cannot be larger than the number of messages within the pointcut. □

If we apply this lemma to the example pointcut that contains four messages in Figure 8, then it is sufficient to consider the bounded loop of four iterations for any loop to determine if it is matchRepetitive or not. Now that we have a systematic way to determine the loop type relative to a pointcut, the next two sections show how to perform a static weaving for non-matchRepetitive and matchRepetitive loops.

4.1 Non-matchrepetitive Loops

From the definition of a non-matchRepetitive loop, we know that possible matches include preceding or succeeding (of the loop) trace events or both. Matches starting in the preceding trace events may be ended by loop trace events, and matches starting in the loop trace events may be ended by succeeding trace events. By looking at the proof of lemma 2 we deduce that the maximum number of loop iterations involved in the match, is numP-1.

We translate the syntactic representation of the loop into a semantically equivalent form (Def. 4):

Definition 4. *An unbounded, non-matchRepetitive loop,* loop *[body], has the following rewrite expression:*

$$alt[\text{ loop}\{0..((numP-1)*2-1)\}[body],$$
$$seq[\text{loop}\{numP-1\}[body], loop'[body], loop\{numP-1\}[body]]]$$

The remaining unbounded loop, *loop'*, can no longer be part of a match, if all the surrounding finite parts are woven. *loop'* is always preceded by numP-1 loop iterations, which prevents any matches to end in the unbounded loop. Similarly the unbounded loop is always followed by numP-1 loop iterations, which prevents that matches start in the unbounded loop. This claim that the remaining unbounded loop cannot contain matches rely on the two conditions of connected pointcut (connected blocking match) and that the aspect is plain additive (the blocking match is maintained by the weaving).

Figure 9A illustrates why the rewrite expression works. We have a pointcut with two consecutive messages x,y, an original base model (not shown) $x, x,$ loop $[y]$, and a simplified extract of the base model showing the second alt operand result of the rewrite. After the rewrite, the remaining unbounded loop is prefixed by loop $\{1\} [y] = y$. It is easy to see that preceding x messages are matched in the preceding bounded loop, and that this match effectively blocks possible matches ending in the remaining unbounded loop.

With a slight modification to the example in Figure 9A, we get the disconnected pointcut (and disconnected base model) in Figure 9B. Now we may (depending on the advice) get a match starting with one of the x messages and ending with the y message in the unbounded loop which illustrates that the rewrite expression does not always ensure a proper result for disconnected pointcuts.

4.2 MatchRepetitive Loops

The base model example and associated aspect in Figure 10 is adopted from Klein et al. [9]. The base model starts with a login attempt from Customer to Server. At the end the Server finally answers with an ok message to indicate successful login. In between these two events there may be zero or more iterations of a loop. The loops first message, tryAgain, informs of login failure, while the second message, newAttempt, is a new customer login attempt.

The aspect in Figure 10 expresses that whenever the message newAttempt is followed by tryAgain, then add another message saveAttempt, in between the two messages matched by the pointcut, to log the failed attempt. Since we only want to log bad attempts, we need to ensure that the the message newAttempt is followed by tryAgain. A syntactic-based pointcut matching fails to find matches within our base model, since the two messages come in a different order syntactically. However we easily observe that they will occur in an execution involving two or more iterations.

We now use lemma 2 to check if our base model loop example is matchRepetitive (tA=tryAgain and nA=NewAttempt):

$$numP = 2 \qquad [\![pointcut]\!] = \{\langle !nA, ?nA, !tA, ?tA\rangle\}$$
$$[\![\texttt{loop}\ \{2\}\ [seq\ [!tA, ?tA, !nA, ?nA]]]\!] = \{\langle !tA, ?tA, \underbrace{!nA, ?nA, !tA, ?tA}_{match}, !nA, ?nA\rangle\}$$

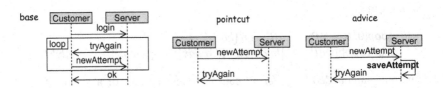

Fig. 10. Base model: login w/ loop, Aspect: logging

This bounded loop has a single trace with a match, meaning that our base model loop is matchRepetitive. This means that there are matches for every even iteration. In a first weaving attempt we make a new loop with a woven body for all even iterations. Such a loop is produced by expanding the loop body to two iterations and weaving the loop body (sA = saveAttempt):

$$\text{loop}\,[\text{seq}\,[!tA, ?tA, !nA', ?nA', \textbf{!sA}, \textbf{?sA}, !tA', ?tA', !nA, ?nA]]$$

This weaving attempt is not good enough, since this loop still is matchRepetitive and has match(es) for all iterations greater than or equal to 2. This happens because the end part of the loop body together with the beginning part of the loop body makes a match, which we miss when only weaving the loop body without taking into account that it may have repetitions. Since the pointcut is connected and there is a marked match within the loop, we know that additional matches are restricted to be only within the part after the match combined with the part before the match.

To fix the problem of missed matches, we permute the loop so that a match part makes up the beginning of the loop body. Then we also need to insert a prefix and a postfix so that the semantics of the loop is not changed, resulting in the following rewrite expression (before/after is the sequence of events relative to the match in the loop body):

$$\text{seq}\,[before, \text{loop}\,[\text{seq}\,[match, after, before]]\,, match, after]$$

For the example in Figure 10 we get the following woven rewritten structure, where the permutation resulted in one additional match/weaving in the loop body:

$$\text{seq}[\ !tA, ?tA,$$
$$\text{loop}\,[\text{seq}\,[!nA', ?nA', \textbf{!sA}, \textbf{?sA}, !tA', ?tA', !nA', ?nA', \textbf{!sA}, \textbf{?sA}, !tA', ?tA']]\,,$$
$$\text{seq}\,[!nA', ?nA', \textbf{!sA}, \textbf{?sA}, !tA', ?tA']\,, !nA, ?nA]$$

This structure is now fine for all the original even iterations. However, we have lost all the original iterations of odd numbers. By appending the loop $\{0..1\}\,[body]$ to the end, we also get the odd iterations, and this is a bounded loop for which we can generate all traces. In general, the appended loop should be loop $\{0..(numP - 1)\}\,[body]$.

We have only considered unbounded loops with cardinality $0..*$, where $*$ is unbounded. Other unbounded loops may easily be translated into finite loops combined with $0..*$ loops by rewrites from loop $\{n..*\}\,[body]$ to seq $[\text{loop}\,\{n\}\,[body]\,, \text{loop}\,[body]\,]$, and using the alt operator to split loops of the form loop $\{2, 10, 20..*\}$.

5 Implementation

We have a tool implementation of the full approach described in this paper. The tool uses the Eclipse-based SeDi sequence diagram editor v.1 [11] to define base, pointcut and advice diagrams. The weaving has been verified to behave correctly on the paper examples, by manually investigating the woven textual interactions. We are currently implementing a translation from textual interactions to graphical diagrams for easier manual validation purposes.

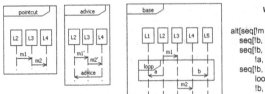

Fig. 11. Weave tool: From aspect and base model to woven interaction

In [5] we have described how to define a single aspect to weave cross-cutting behavior into 40 sequence diagrams of an SMS-based buddy positioning service. The aspect definition uses some additional constructs, outside the scope of this paper, such as decomposition, negative application conditions, wildcards and an insertRest operator.

Automata-based weaving attempts (Grosu and Smolka [6], Klein et al. [10,9]) achieve semantics-based weaving of UML 2 sequence diagrams. In contrast to our approach they cannot handle loops leading to irregular trace expressions. *Example* (from [10]): Figure 11 shows an aspect that matches an m1 message followed by an m2 message. The base represents an unbounded sequence diagram since it has a loop that leads to an irregular expression. n loop iterations means that there are also n a messages and n b messages, and these messages may have an arbitrary order. There is an m1 message before the base loop and an m2 message after the base loop, and independent of the number of loop iterations there will always be a match in the base.

The woven interaction of Figure 11 shows that our weaving tool produces the expected result. The outermost alt operator contains four alternatives representing the POE classes of 0, 1, 2, and 2+ loop iterations, and all of these POE classes have the advice message added exactly once in an appropriate position. We need to emphasize that the ?advice message is defined to be inserted directly after the !m1 message on the L2 lifeline, which means that ?advice must come before all the !a messages. Although it looks odd that the ?advice event is placed before the corresponding !advice in the latter POE class, this is allowed for textual interactions, and will be sorted out by the ⟦ ⟧ operator when making traces. Notice also that we indicate the messages that have been matched and the loops that are treated, by the prime (').

6   Related Work

In this paper we have restricted the base model to use only the seq, alt and loop operators. However, the results are directly applicable to other operators that can be defined with seq and alt, e.g. opt (optional) and par (parallel). The strict operator is not supported. It represents a strict sequence of events also across lifelines, which is in strong contrast to our approach.

The pointcut model in AspectJ [8] cannot express matching based on a sequence of events, which is necessary to encounter the problem of syntactic-based matching described in this paper.

Klein et al. [9], Stein et al. [17] allow the match to contain additional events in between the explicit pointcut events, called *general part* matching in [9]. Our matching definition in this paper corresponds to the *enclosed part* matching, while our full aspect language includes the *arbitrary events symbol* [5] to support *general part* matching.

Clarke and Walker [2] model aspects using sequence diagrams. Their intention is to map the aspects onto an aspect-oriented programming language, such as AspectJ, and not to produce woven sequence diagrams as in our approach.

Deubler et al. [3], Solberg et al. [16] and Jayaraman et al. [7] all define syntactic-based approaches for sequence diagrams. Deubler et al. can only match single events. The approach taken by Jayaraman et al. is similar to ours in that they define aspects similar to graph transformation rules directly upon sequence diagram syntax.

Avgustinov et al. [1] have a trace-based run-time matching of events to execute some extra code when a match occurs. Since this happens during run-time and not statically as in our approach, the aspects are restricted to additive parts that are inserted entirely after the already executed match part (excluding aspects like in Figure 10). While performance is a major issue in run-time weaving, our weaving is static and termination within reasonable time is sufficient.

7   Conclusions

We have demonstrated that it is possible to do semantics-based aspect weaving for UML 2.0 sequence diagrams based upon a formal trace model for these. In our semantics-based weaving the matching is defined at the trace level ('what' the sequence diagrams really describe), and not at the syntactic level ('how' the sequence diagrams are described), but still with the convenience for the developer that the advice specifications can be done by means of syntactic elements of sequence diagrams.

We have proven that the semantics-based matching is equivalent to a lifeline-based matching upon trace-based equivalence classes, and our lifeline-based weaving algorithm will thus produce the same result as a pure trace-based implementation. While a pure trace-based implementation performs in exponential time wrt. to the number of events, the lifeline-based implementation performs in linear time wrt. the number of events and the number of `alt` operands.

Klein et al. [10] have an automata-based (and semantics-based) weaving that fails to handle cases of infinite loops leading to non-regular trace expressions. Such loops impose no problem in our solution.

Acknowledgment. The work reported in this paper has been funded by The Research Council of Norway, grant no. 167172/V30 (the SWAT project). We thank Mass Soldal Lund for valuable discussions and implementation help.

References

1. Avgustinov, P., Tibble, J., de Moor, O.: Making trace monitors feasible. In: The 22nd Annual ACM SIGPLAN Conference on Object-Oriented Programming, Systems, Languages and Applications, OOPSLA (2007)
2. Clarke, S., Walker, R.J.: Composition Patterns: An Approach to Designing Reusable Aspects. In: The 23rd International Conference on Software Engineering (ICSE) (2001)

3. Deubler, M., Meisinger, M., Rittmann, S., Krüger, I.: Modeling Crosscutting Services with UML Sequence Diagrams. In: Briand, L.C., Williams, C. (eds.) MoDELS 2005. LNCS, vol. 3713. Springer, Heidelberg (2005)
4. Ehrig, H., Ehrig, K., Prange, U., Taentzer, G.: Fundamentals of Algebraic Graph Transformation. Springer, Heidelberg (2006)
5. Grønmo, R., Sørensen, F., Møller-Pedersen, B., Krogdahl, S.: A Semantics-based Aspect Language for Interactions with the Arbitrary Events Symbol. In: European Conference on Model Driven Architecture — Foundations and Applications (ECMDA 2008) (2008) (in press)
6. Grosu, R., Smolka, S.A.: Safety-Liveness Semantics for UML 2.0 Sequence Diagrams. In: Fifth International Conference on Application of Concurrency to System Design (ACSD) (2005)
7. Jayaraman, P., Whittle, J., Elkhodary, A.M., Gomaa, H.: Model Composition in Product Lines and Feature Interaction Detection Using Critical Pair Analysis. In: Engels, G., Opdyke, B., Schmidt, D.C., Weil, F. (eds.) MODELS 2007. LNCS, vol. 4735. Springer, Heidelberg (2007)
8. Kiczales, G., Hilsdale, E., Hugunin, J., Kersten, M., Palm, J., Griswold, W.G.: An Overview of AspectJ. In: Knudsen, J.L. (ed.) ECOOP 2001. LNCS, vol. 2072. Springer, Heidelberg (2001)
9. Klein, J., Fleurey, F., Jézéquel, J.-M.: Weaving multiple aspects in sequence diagrams. In: Trans. on Aspect Oriented Software Development III (2007)
10. Klein, J., Hélouët, L., Jézéquel, J.-M.: Semantic-based weaving of scenarios. In: The 5th International Conference on Aspect-Oriented Software Development (2006)
11. Limyr, A.: Graphical editor for UML 2.0 sequence diagrams. Master's thesis, Department of Informatics, University of Oslo (2005)
12. Lund, M.S.: Operational analysis of sequence diagram specifications. PhD thesis, Department of Informatics, University of Oslo, Norway (2008)
13. O.M.G. (OMG). UML 2.0 Superstructure Specification, OMG Adopted Specification ptc/03-08-02 (August 2003)
14. Pickin, S., Jard, C., Jéron, T., Jézéquel, J.-M., Traon, Y.L.: Test Synthesis from UML Models of Distributed Software. IEEE Trans. Software Eng. 33(4) (2007)
15. Runde, R.K., Haugen, Ø., Stølen, K.: Refining UML interactions with underspecification and nondeterminism. Nordic Journal of Computing 2(12) (2005)
16. Solberg, A., Simmonds, D., Reddy, R., Ghosh, S., France, R.B.: Using Aspect Oriented Techniques to Support Separation of Concerns in Model Driven Development. In: 29th Annual International Computer Software and Applications Conference (COMPSAC) (2005)
17. Stein, D., Hanenberg, S., Unland, R.: Join Point Designation Diagrams: a Graphical Representation of Join Point Selections. International Journal of Software Engineering and Knowledge Engineering 16(3), 317–346 (2006)

Translation of QVT Relations into QVT Operational Mappings

Raphael Romeikat, Stephan Roser, Pascal Müllender, and Bernhard Bauer

Programming Distributed Systems Lab,
University of Augsburg, Germany
{romeikat,roser,bauer}@ds-lab.org,
p_muellender@users.sourceforge.net

Abstract. Model transformations play a key role in Model-Driven Engineering solutions. To efficiently develop, specify, and manage model transformations, it is often necessary to use a combination of languages that stand for different transformation approaches. To provide a basis for such hybrid model transformation specification solutions, we developed and implemented a translation of the declarative QVT Relations into the imperative QVT Operational Mappings language.

1 Introduction

Model Driven Engineering (MDE) treats models as primary development artifacts as they are used for model and code generation. MDE uses models to raise the level of abstraction at which developers create and evolve software [8] and reduces complexity of the software artifacts by separating concerns and aspects of a system under development [9]. Largely automated model transformations refine abstract models to more concrete models or simply describe mappings between models of the same level of abstraction.

Model transformations are considered as a kind of metaprogramming since they are specified on the basis of metamodels. People developing model transformations have to respect the rich semantics of the metadata upon which the model transformations operate [4]. Not surprisingly, various authors suggest to use different model transformation approaches for the diverse transformation problems. Declarative transformation approaches are best applied to specify simple transformations and relations between source and target model elements, while imperative approaches lend themselves for implementing complex transformations that involve detailed model analysis [7]. As it is done with other programming languages, it seems beneficial to use several model transformation language to solve complex problems [11]. In the OMG standard for model transformations QVT [12], the imperative *QVT Operational Mappings (OM)* language is defined as an extension of the declarative *QVT Relations (Relations)* language.

Having a closer look at model transformation approaches, one can observe that the various approaches and their implementations support model transformation features like automatic updates, directionality, traceability, etc. to a

A. Vallecillo, J. Gray, A. Pierantonio (Eds.): ICMT 2008, LNCS 5063, pp. 137–151, 2008.

different extent [7,11]. In the case of the QVT standard, update is automatically supported by the Relations language, while the user of OM has to implement this transformation feature by hand. The Relations language also allows to specify bidirectional transformations, which reduces effort in model synchronization scenarios. In OM it is in general necessary to specify multiple unidirectional transformations. However, it may not be possible and sensible for people using model transformation languages to construct complex transformations using a fully declarative approach [7].

Though the QVT standard allows to extend Relations with OM (hybrid transformation approach), no engine exists that can execute such a hybrid approach. Some MDE platforms will only provide one optimized execution engine onto which the transformation programs of different model transformation languages are mapped. When implementing such an approach, it is a good heuristic to map declarative and hybrid languages onto imperative languages and provide an execution engine for the imperative language. It is expected that e.g. translating Relations into OM does not expose obstacles [11]. However, the advanced features such as multidirectionality, automatic traceability, special transformation scenarios, etc., that are only supported natively by the Relations language and not by the OM language, have to be translated into imperative OM code and separate transformations.

In this paper we develop a translation of Relations into OM and implement it as a higher-order model transformation. Higher-order transformations take transformations as input and produce other transformations as output [2]. Our translation allows model transformation developers to specify the 'easy' things in a declarative way and profit from the additional features of Relations like support for model synchronization and model updates. By using our translation, one can implement 'hard' model transformation code in OM, execute the Relations code on a possibly optimized OM engine, and use tool support that is available for OM like debuggers, profilers, etc.. We implement our translation approach to show its feasibility and evaluate it with a UML to RDBMS transformation.

This paper is structured as follows: Section 2 gives an introduction to QVT and the Relations and the OM language. Section 3 describes the approach we follow for the translation and Section 4 presents the details of the translation. Section 5 describes the implementation, evaluates our Relations to OM translation and compares it with related work. The paper concludes with a summary in Section 6.

2   Basics

The OMG adopted the Meta Object Facility (MOF) 2.0 Query/View/Transformation specification (QVT) [12] as standard for model transformations. The QVT specification defines a hybrid transformation language. The three transformation languages *Relations*, *Core*, and *Operational Mappings (OM)* provide declarative and imperative transformation constructs. The languages *Relations* and *Core* can be used to specify declarative transformations. QVT provides two options to extend declarative specifications with imperative transformation constructs, the *OM* language and *Black Box* operations.

2.1   UML to RDBMS Transformation Example

This paper presents a translation of Relations into OM, which we illustrate via the UML to RDBMS transformation described in the QVT specification [12].

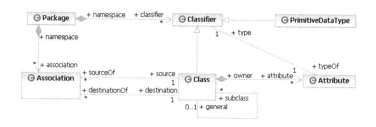

Fig. 1. Simple UML metamodel

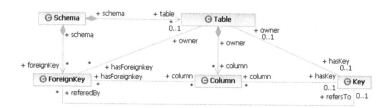

Fig. 2. Simple RDBMS metamodel

The UML to RDBMS transformation maps persistent classes of a UML model to tables of a model of a relational database management system (RDBMS). Figures 1 and 2 show the respective metamodels. The transformation basically works as follows: A persistent class maps to a table. Attributes of the persistent class map to columns of the table. An association between two persistent classes maps to a foreign key relationship between the corresponding tables.

2.2   QVT Relations

Listing 1.1 depicts an excerpt of the UML to RDBMS model transformation implemented in Relations. We will explain the concepts of Relations on the basis of this code.

In the Relations code the transformation *UmlToRdbms* is specified between the candidate models *uml* and *rdbms* as a set of relations that must hold for the transformation to be successful. A candidate model is any model that conforms to a model type. For example, the element types of the *uml* model are restricted to those within the *SimpleUML* metamodel. Relations in a transformation like

PackageToSchema or *ClassToTable* declare constraints that must be satisfied by the elements of the *uml* and *rdbms* models. The relation *ClassToTable* is presented in more detail now.

First, a source and a target domain are declared that match elements in the *uml* and *rdbms* models respectively. *ClassToTable* is further constrained by two sets of predicates, a *when* clause and a *where* clause. The *when* clause specifies the conditions under which the relationship must hold, i.e. the relation *ClassToTable* must hold only when the *PackageToSchema* relation holds between the *Package* containing the *Class* and the *Schema* containing the *Table*. The *where* clause specifies the condition that must be satisfied by all model elements participating in the relation. Whenever the *ClassToTable* relation holds, the relation *AttributeToColumn* must also hold.

Listing 1.1. UML to RDBMS transformation in QVT Relations

```
1  transformation UmlToRdbms(uml: SimpleUML; rdbms: SimpleRDBMS) {
2      key Table {schema, name};
       ...
4      top relation PackageToSchema {...}
       top relation ClassToTable {
6          cn, prefix: String;
           checkonly domain uml c:Class {
8              namespace = p:Package {},
               kind = 'Persistent',
10             name = cn
           };
12         enforce domain rdbms t:Table {
               schema = s:Schema {},
14             name = cn,
               column = cl:Column {
16                 name = cn+'_tid',
                   type = 'NUMBER'
18             },
               hasKey=k:Key {
20                 name = cn+'_pk',
                   column = cl
22             }
           };
24         when {
               PackageToSchema(p, s);
26         }
           where {
28             prefix = '';
               AttributeToColumn(c, t, prefix);
30         }
       }
32     top relation AssocToFKey {...}
       ...
34 }
```

Each of the domains is also associated with several object template expressions used to match patterns in the candidate models. A template expression match for the *uml* domain results in a binding of the matching classes to the root variable c of the *uml* domain. Such template expression matches are only performed with regard to to the free variables of the domain. For the *uml* domain this applies to the variables c, p, and cn. The variable p is not free as it already has a binding resulting from the evaluation of the *when* clause expression. Pattern matching proceeds by filtering any class with its *kind* property not set to *'Persistent'*. As *cn* is free, it gets a binding to the value of the name property for all remaining classes. Matching proceeds to the property pattern *namespace = p:Package*. As *p* is already bound in the *when* clause, the pattern only matches those classes whose *namespace* property has a reference to the same package that is bound to *p*. The three variables *c*, *p*, and *cn* make a three tuple and each valid match results in a unique tuple representing the binding.

The *uml* domain is marked *checkonly* and the *rdbms* domain is marked *enforce*. Thus, when executing the transformation in the direction of the *uml* domain, no elements are created in the *uml* model. If for example a table in *rdbms* exists with no corresponding class in *uml*, this is simply reported as an inconsistency. If the transformation is executed in the direction of the enforced domain *rdbms*, elements are created or modified in the target model *rdbms* so the relations between the candidate models hold. For example, for each valid class there must exist at least one valid table that satisfies the *where* clause. Otherwise, tables are created and properties are set as specified in the template expression associated with the *rdbms* domain. Also, for each valid table there must exist at least one valid class that satisfies the *where* clause. Otherwise, tables are deleted from the *rdbms* model so there it is no longer a valid match.

To create objects in the target model, object template expressions of the target domain are used. The template associated with *Table* specifies that a table object is created with the properties *schema*, *name*, *column*, and *hasKey* set to values as specified in the template expression. When creating objects, Relations ensures that duplicate objects are not created if the required objects already exist. The existing objects are updated. For this purpose, the concept of *key* is used defining a set of properties that uniquely identify an object instance. A *Table* is uniquely identified by its name and the *schema* it *belongs* to.

2.3   QVT Operational Mappings

OM is the target language of our translation. In the following, we shortly introduce the basic language concepts of OM. The concepts and the presented language constructs are used to specify the Relations into OM translation in Sections 3 and 4. Listing 1.2 illustrates a short example of OM code.

Listing 1.2. QVT Operational Mappings example

```
1  modeltype UML "strict" SimpleUml;
2  modeltype RDBMS "strict" uses SimpleRDBMS;
   transformation UmlToRdbms(in uml:UML,out rdbms:RDBMS) {
4    main() {
       uml.objectsOfType(Package)->map packageToSchema();
6    }
     mapping Package::packageToSchema() : Schema {
8      init { ... }
       population { ... }
10     end { ... }
     }
12 }
```

An operational transformation represents the definition of a unidirectional transformation that is expressed imperatively. It defines a signature indicating the models involved in the transformation. The signature of the *UmlToRdbms* transformation declares that an *rdbms* model of type *RDBMS* is produced from an *uml* model of type *UML*. The *UML* and *RDBMS* symbols represent model types. The model types are defined by the metamodels *SimpleUML* and *SimpleRDBMS*.

A operational transformation defines an entry operation for its execution named *main*. The main operation first retrieves the list of objects of type *Package* and then applies a mapping operation called *packageToSchema* on each *Package* of the list. A mapping operation like *packageToSchema* is an operation that implements a mapping between one or more source model elements into one or more target model elements. The *init* section contains some code to be executed before the instantiation of the declared outputs. The *population* section contains code to populate the result parameters and the *end* section contains additional code to be executed before exiting the operation. Between the *init* and the *population* sections, there is an implicit instantiation section which creates all output parameters that have a null value at the end of the *init* section.

3   Translation Approach

In this section we describe requirements, restrictions, and challenges for the translation of Relations into OM and introduce the overall translation algorithm.

3.1   Transformation Execution Direction

A crucial difference between the two languages is the execution direction of the transformation. OM transformations are unidirectional. Their execution direction is explicitly defined by their imperative statements, specifying which models are read and which ones are written. Relations transformations can be executed in any direction by selecting one of the candidate models as target. One may change the execution direction of a Relations transformation by selecting another target model, which is not possible in OM. The QVT specification does not clarify whether multiple target models are supported in the enforce mode. Examples are only provided for transformations with one target model. Hence, the described translation algorithm is restricted to one target model, which is is assumed to be the last parameter of the transformation and to appear as enforce domain in at least one relation. The translation algorithm generates the operational transformation in one direction towards the target model.

3.2   Model Transformation Execution Semantics

In the translation of programming languages into other programming languages, it is not sufficient to only map statements of the source language onto statements of the target language. The crucial and normally more challenging part is to develop an accurate mapping of the execution semantics. This is also the main challenge when translating Relations into OM.

Relations performs a model transformation in a declarative way based on a powerful pattern matching mechanism and OCL constraints on the candidate models. This facilitates developing a consistent transformation for the user, but at the same time involves complex execution semantics with nested loops of object tuples for the execution engine [12]. In contrast, a transformation in OM is defined as sequence of statements executed by the engine step by step in the defined order. When performing a translation from Relations into OM, the transformation semantics must remain the same in spite of the different programming paradigms. The following aspects of the execution semantics have to be considered when translating Relations into OM:

Rule Scheduling. Relations uses implicit rule scheduling which is based on the dependencies among the relations. OM uses explicit internal scheduling where the sequence of applying the transformation rules is specified within the transformation rules. Our Relations into OM translation has to make the implicit rule scheduling of the Relations execution semantics explicit in the OM transformations. This has to be done in a way that has no (bad) side effects on the pattern matching and binding of the variables in the transformation occurs.

Pattern Matching. Relations uses pattern matching to find bindings of source and target model elements to the variables declared by the transformation. Pattern matching is based on the internal rule scheduling of Relations. When translating this mechanism to OM, the expressions in the relation domains must be organized into a sequential order and one has to take care that in the final OM code only variables are accessed that have been bound or at least defined before (cp. [12, p.17f]). Hence, we deal with pattern matching at various points in our translation; the most important issues are described in the Sections 3.3 and 4.4.

Check-Before-Enforce Semantics. The Relations semantics first performs a step where it checks whether a valid match exists in the target model that satisfies the relationship with the source model. Based on the checking results, the enforcement semantics modifies the target model so it satisfies the relationship with the source model. Through this check-before-enforce semantics Relations provides support for both generating new and updating existing target models. OM does not support updates of existing models automatically by its execution semantics. In OM this has to be implemented in the model transformation. The *generation* scenario can be realized by translating the checking semantics into rules that generate new model transformation elements. For *update* scenarios this has to be enhanced with functionality to modify and delete model elements.

3.3   Overall Translation Algorithm

Algorithm 1 gives an overview about the different steps performed during the translation. The algorithm first translates the transformation declaration. Before the relations are translated one after another, they are sorted topologically to account for dependencies between them.

The main building blocks of a relation are domains, when clause, and where clause. In order to address the challenges and to keep the relational execution semantics in the imperative environment, it is essential to translate the building blocks in the designated sequence. The main issue is to ensure that assigned expressions only contain variables that have been bound before. For this purpose, the algorithm stores all variable values for each relation at all times in order to determine which variables have already been bound and which ones are still free.

Algorithm 1. Translation algorithm overview

 1: **procedure** RELATIONSTOOPERATIONALMAPPING($RelTrans$) : $OperationMapping$
 2:      $OmTrans \leftarrow \emptyset$
 3:      $OmTrans \leftarrow$ TRANSLATETRANSFORMATIONDECLARATION($RelTrans$)
 4:      $Relations \leftarrow$ SORTRELATIONSTOPOLOGICALLY($RelTrans$)
 5:      **for all** $relation \in Relations$ **do**
 6:          $OmTrans \leftarrow OmTrans \cup$ TRANSLATERELATIONDECLARATION($relation$)
 7:          $OmTrans \leftarrow OmTrans \cup$ TRANSLATEDOMAINDECLARATION($relation$)
 8:
 9:          $OmTrans \leftarrow OmTrans \cup$ TRANSLATEWHENCLAUSE($relation$)
10:          $OmTrans \leftarrow OmTrans \cup$ TRANSLATESOURCEDOMAINS($relation$)
11:
12:          $OmTrans \leftarrow OmTrans \cup$ TRANSLATEWHERECLAUSE($relation$)
13:          $OmTrans \leftarrow OmTrans \cup$ TRANSLATETARGETDOMAIN($relation$)
14:      **end for**
15:      **return** $OmTrans$
16: **end procedure**

---

4   Realizing the Translation

In this section, the rules of the translation algorithm that implement the Relations into OM translation are presented. The structure of this section is aligned with the steps of the overall translation algorithm (cp. Algorithm 1).

The translation rules we describe in this paper cover all Relations language concepts that are relevant for the UML to RDBMS transformation. These are transformation and modeltypes, relations and domains, when and where clauses, pattern matching and restriction expressions, as well as keys and object creation.

4.1   Transformation Declaration

First, the transformation declaration is translated from Relations into OM. Lines 1 to 3 of Listing 1.3 depict the OM transformation declaration that is generated in the UML to RDBMS Relations example (cp. Listing 1.1). As a relational transformation is bidirectional, the direction of the parameters must be determined for OM. Source models are translated into *in* parameters. If the target model is only used as *enforce* domain, it is translated into an *out* parameter; if it is used as *checkonly* domain in one or more relations, it is translated into an *inout* parameter. Each parameter of the relational declaration is also translated into a *modeltype* reference to import the respective metamodel packages. According to the Relations specification, type checking for the modeltypes is *strict*. This implies that all objects passed as parameter of the translation must be instances of the respective *modeltype*; subclasses of that type are not allowed.

4.2   Calculate Relations Topology Tree

In Relations it is not necessary to specify an explicit sequence of execution as rule scheduling automatically considers dependencies between relations. This is e.g. the case if a relation occurs as precondition in the when clause of another relation. In OM rule scheduling is explicit. OM requires a *main* operation as an entrance point as shown in lines 4 to 8 of Listing 1.3. For each toplevel relation in Relations, invocations are generated in that *main* operation that specify in which sequence the OM mappings are executed. If there are no dependencies between the toplevel relations, the respective OM mappings can be executed in arbitrary sequence. Otherwise, the correct sequence of execution is determined by a topological sorting algorithm in an iterative process.

That sorting algorithm regards the dependencies between the toplevel relations as a directed acyclic graph (DAG) whereas a node represents a relation and an edge represents a dependency between two relations. The initial structure of the DAG is built as follows. For each relation, a node is added. If a relation R1 is referenced in the when clause of another relation R2, an edge from R1 to R2 is added. If the where clause of R2 contains a reference to R3, an edge from R2 to R3 is added. For each toplevel relation, the algorithm now determines the number of incoming edges. In the first iteration, all toplevel relations are determined that have no incoming edges, which means they are not dependent from any other relation. The respective nodes and outgoing edges are removed from the DAG. This may result in some more toplevel relations that have no incoming edges, which are then processed in the same way in the next iteration. The algorithm terminates as soon as there are no toplevel relations with zero incoming edges left. Finally, calls to the respective OM mappings are generated in the main operation according to the determined sequence.

4.3   Relation and Domain Declarations

Relation declarations are translated into OM mapping declarations (cp. lines 9, 10, and 31 of Listing 1.3). For each domain in a relation, the algorithm generates a parameter with same type and name in the respective OM mapping. In doing so, the translation differentiates between the three kinds of domains.

- **Primitive domains** represent simple datatypes and are translated into *inout* parameters in OM.
- The **enforce domain** is translated into the *result* variable in OM. If the relation is not top level, the *result* variable has already been bound before

the OM mapping is executed. For this reason, the generated mapping requires a parameter to which the previously bound result is passed and which initializes the *result* variable in the init block.

- All other domains are **checkonly domains**. The first one is translated into the context variable, which is then accessible using the *self* keyword in OM. Any further checkonly domains are translated into *in* parameters.

Listing 1.3. UML to RDBMS transformation in QVT Operational Mappings

```
1  modeltype SimpleUML "strict" uses UmlMM;
2  modeltype SimpleRDBMS "strict" uses RdbmsMM;
   transformation UmlToRdbms(in uml: SimpleUML, out rdbms: SimpleRDBMS) {
4    main() {
       uml.objects[Package]->map PackageToSchema();
6      uml.objects[Class]->map ClassToTable();
       uml.objects[Association]->map AssocToFKey();
8    }
   mapping Package :: PackageToSchema () : Schema {...}
10 mapping Class :: ClassToTable () : Table {
     when {
12     self.kind = 'Persistent';
       self.namespace <> null;
14     self.namespace.resolveoneIn(PackageToSchema) <> null;
     }
16   population {
       self.map AttributeToColumn(result);
18     result.schema := self.namespace.resolveoneIn(PackageToSchema);
       result.name := self.name;
20     var cl := object Column {
         name := self.name + '_tid';
22       type := 'NUMBER';
       };
24     result.column += cl;
       result.hasKey := object Key {
26       name := self.name + '_pk';
         column := cl;
28     }
     }
30 }
   mapping Association :: AssocToFKey () : ForeignKey {...}
32 }
```

4.4   When Clause and Source Domains

In Relations, statements and OCL constraints in the source domains and in the when clause are used for filtering candidate models from the source domains. This is done by assigning objects and values to bound variables of a source domain. The purpose of unbound variables is to temporarily store values for the reuse in other domains of the relation, which e.g. allows for adopting a value from a source to the target domain. OCL constraints over the relation domains that are compliant with the QVT specification are supported by our algorithm.

Translating the When Clause. The when clause of a relation references other relations to represent preconditions of that relation. For each reference, the algorithm generates a call to the respective OM mapping. The sorting algorithm ensures that the called mapping has been executed before the calling mapping.

The execution semantics of Relations performs a pattern matching of the passed variables to the model elements for which the referenced relation holds. In OM, *resolve* expressions are used to perform such pattern matching. An appropriate *resolveIn* expression is generated in the *population* body of OM if a set of objects is passed; otherwise, a *resolveOneIn* expression is generated. This can be seen with the variable *s* in the relation call *PackageToSchema(p,s)* in the when clause (cp. lines 8 and 25 of Listing 1.1). As *s* is assigned to the bound variable *namespace* in the source domain, the *resolveIn* expression is performed on the respective variable *self.namespace* in OM (cp. line 18 of Listing 1.3).

Translating the Source Domain. An assignment to a bound variable according to pattern matching semantics filters model elements from the candidate models. Therefore, a respective condition is generated in the *when* block of OM. If a single value or object is assigned, the statement is adopted straightforward. In the example, the variable *kind* is used to filter all classes having that variable set to the value *'Persistent'*. This is translated into the operational statement *self.kind='Persistent'* (cp. line 12 of Listing 1.3). If a set is assigned to such a variable, an *xselect* condition is generated in OM instead. That *xselect* iterates over the candidate models and uses a condition that corresponds to the assigned set. The algorithm also considers cases that are not covered by the example such as multiple assignments to the same bound variable, which are translated into one combined expression using the logical *and* operator.

Assignments to unbound variables according to pattern matching semantics are not translated directly. Whenever such a variable is used at another place in the relation, the assigned value is used by the translation algorithm instead of the variable itself. This eliminates those variables in OM. The variable *cn* in lines 10 and 14 of Listing 1.1 gives an example. It is used to store the value of the attribute *name* of a *Class* and assign it to the variable *name* of the respective *Table*. The translation of such an assignment affects the target domain.

Furthermore, each variable bound to an object template must not be null. Therefore, respective conditions are generated in the *when* block of OM.

4.5   Where Clause and Target Domain

For candidate models that do match in the Relations source domain, the respective target models are generated according to the statements and OCL constraints in the where clause and the target domain. The respective model elements are created, changed, or deleted. If a target model does not exist, it is created from scratch.

Translating the Where Clause. In contrast to the when clause, a relation reference in the where clause represents a postcondition of the relation. Such a reference is directly translated into an invocation of the respective OM mapping at the beginning of the *population* block; cp. *AttributeToColumn(c,t)* in line 29 of Listing 1.1. Here, the passed variable *c* in the where clause represents the source domain and is therefore translated to the *self* attribute in OM. For the passed variable *t*, the algorithm generates the *result* attribute.

Translating the Target Domain. Variable assignments that modify the target model still remain to be translated. An example is given by the variable *cn* in lines 10 and 14 of Listing 1.1. In the source domain *uml*, the root variable *c* is represented by the variable *self* in OM. The attribute *name* is assigned to the variable *cn*. In the target domain *rdbms*, the root variable *t* is represented by the variable *result* in OM and the value of *cn* is assigned to the target variable *name*. The algorithm generates the respective assignment *result.name:=self.name* in the *population* body of OM (cp. line 19 of Listing 1.3).

If the assigned value occurs within an object template in the source and in the target domain, the translation is more complicated as the assignment happens within a set of objects. In this case, an appropriate *xcollect* expression is generated in OM and the *+=* operator instead of *:=* is used. That *xcollect* adds for each object in the source domain a respective object in the target domain.

In either case, an object expression is generated whenever an object template is used and its bound variable is bound for the first time. Thus, a new object must be instantiated in the imperative environment, which is e.g. the case with the variable *c1* in line 20 of Listing 1.3.

4.6   Updates of Existing Target Models

Updates of existing target models are automatically supported by the Relations semantics. In OM updates must be specified in the transformation explicitly. Model elements in Relations are uniquely identified by a set attributes specified by *key* expressions (cp. line 2 of Listing 1.1). For this purpose, the algorithm generates queries in OM that search for those model elements in the target model which have the same values for the identifying attributes as the respective model elements in the source model. These queries are performed before model element instantiation. The result object of an OM mapping is initialized with the result of the respective query as illustrated in Listing 1.4. If no respective model element is found, a new instance is created in the implicit instantiation section.

Listing 1.4. Updating an existing target model in QVT Operational Mappings

```
1  query findTable(name: String, schema: Schema): Table {
2    rdbms.objects()[Table]->xselectOne(t | t.name = name and t.schema = schema);
3  }
4  mapping Class::ClassToTable(): Table {
5    init {
6      result := findTable(self.name, self.namespace.resolveone(Schema));
7    }
8  }
```

Relations also supports the deletion of model elements which are no longer valid. In OM the deletion of model elements must also be specified explicitly, which is not a trivial task. One approach is to delete all objects from the target model that cannot be found in the trace data of the transformation execution after all mappings have been executed (cp. Listing 1.5). However, there are issues with regard to object expressions as they do not generate trace data according to the QVT specification [12]. Object expressions could be realized as mappings that do generate trace data. This again involves issues since the transformations would increase in length, for example.

Listing 1.5. Deleting objects in QVT Operational Mappings

```
1  main() {
2    uml.objects()[Package]->map PackageToSchema();
     uml.objects()[Class]->map ClassToTable();
4    uml.objects()[Association]->map AssocToFKey();
     rdbms.objects()->xselect(obj | obj.invresolve(true) = null)->forEach(obj) {
6      dest.removeElement(obj);
     };
8  }
```

A second approach is tagging all model elements that should not be deleted, which applies to model elements that are bound by the queries and that are newly created. A effective implementation of that approach depends on the concrete transformations and is not further regarded in this paper.

5   Implementation and Evaluation

In this section we present the implementation of the compiler and evaluate it with respect to the experience gained in the UML to RDBMS example.

5.1   Implementation

In order to demonstrate our translation approach, we developed an implementation of our algorithm as Eclipse plugin under the GNU General Public License [14]. The compiler is called QVT-Rel2Op and performs a translation from Relations to OM as described in Sections 3 and 4.

For this purpose, the compiler frontend takes two inputs: the Relations transformation as a textfile and the respective metamodels as emof models. A parser [13] generates a representation of the Relations transformation as emof model, which is passed to the compiler backend. In the backend an oAW workflow controls the further steps of the translation. The translation logic is implemented in Java and subsequently generates the respective OM transformation as emof model. A code generator and a beautifier generate a textual representation of that emof model and return an OM textfile as the result of the compilation.

The compiler implements important features of the Relations language. These are transformations, modeltypes, relations, domains, when clauses, where clauses, pattern matching, restriction expressions, keys, and object creation. However, some restrictions are made to the relational transformation. The compiler only allows two non-primitive domains, one source and one target domain. The check-only mode of Relations is not supported. For each binding of the root variable of the source domain, only one binding in the target domain is allowed.

5.2   Evaluation

Besides some other small examples, the UML to RDBMS transformation was taken to evaluate our translation approach and implementation. For this purpose, we executed a series of Relations transformations with ModelMorf [15], which is an execution engine for Relations. We then used our compiler to generate the respective OM transformation and executed the resulting transformation with SmartQVT [6], which is an execution engine for OM.

As SmartQVT does not support *resolveIn* expressions, a minor modification of the translation was required. For this purpose, the compiler offers a compatibility mode that generates appropriate *resolve* expressions instead, which are supported by SmartQVT. This works fine if all OM mappings return different object types. Finally, we compared the results of both transformations to each other and observed that the generated OM transformation returns the same results as the Relations transformation. This indicates that our algorithm correctly translates the relational execution semantics into the imperative environment.

We also compared our translation approach and implementation to others. As described in [10], there exist model transformation compilers for imperative model transformations. Thereby, languages like ATL or OM are mapped onto the ATL VM language [5,10], which serves as a basis for the execution of imperative model transformations. Other implementations compile model transformations into Java code. SmartQVT [6] generates Java code to execute OM transformations. [1] compiles model transformations defined by a combination of graph transformation and abstract state machine rules into transformer plugins for the EJB 3.0 platform. [17] provides an overview and comparison of further graph-based approaches compiling transformation rules into native executable code (Java, C, C++). Higher-order model transformations are also an elegant way to specify the semantics of model transformation languages [3]; the QVT specification [12] e.g. describes a translation of the Relations to the Core language. Other objectives of higher-order model transformation are to refactor and improve model transformations, increase the performance of model transformations, and maintain or upgrade model transformations [3,16].

6   Conclusions

In this paper we presented a higher-order model transformation that takes Relations model transformations as input and produces OM model transformations as output. Our implementation is a first realization of translating QVT declarative specifications into QVT operational specifications. Hence, it provides the basis for realizing the development of hybrid model transformations with QVT. Translating Relations into OM and not the other way round seems to be the natural way of realizing a hybrid approach for two reasons: first, all features of the declarative language can be translated into the imperative language without restrictions, which is not the case for the other direction [11]; second, hybrid approaches normally use declarative relations first, which are manually refined into operational rules later on [16].

Our translation allows developers to specify the 'easy' things in Relations and extend and execute their transformations as OM. It saves them implementing update functionality in OM code and gives them means to specify bidirectional transformations instead of several unidirectional OM transformations. This is especially beneficial in synchronization and conformance checking scenarios. The generated code can be executed on an optimized OM engine and developers can use tool support that is available for OM (editors, debuggers, profilers, etc.).

As future work, we will apply our approach and implementation to further transformations and case studies in order to gather more experience and address further scenarios. Moreover, we will realize further concepts of the Relations language such as in-place updates or support for multiple source domains.

References

1. Balogh, A., Varró, G., Varró, D., Pataricza, A.: Compiling model transformations to EJB3-specific transformer plugins. In: 21st ACM SAC, pp. 1288–1295 (2006)
2. Bézivin, J.: On the unification power of models. Software and System Modeling 4(2), 171–188 (2005)
3. Bézivin, J., et al.: Model Transformations? Transformation Models! In 9th MoDELS Conference. In: Nierstrasz, O., Whittle, J., Harel, D., Reggio, G. (eds.) MoDELS 2006. LNCS, vol. 4199, pp. 440–453. Springer, Heidelberg (2006)
4. Czarnecki, K., Helsen, S.: Feature-based survey of model transformation approaches. IBM Systems Journal 45(3), 621–645 (2006)
5. Eclipse Project, A.T.L.: Use Case - QVT to ATL Virtual Machine Compiler, http://www.eclipse.org/m2m/atl/usecases/QVT2ATLVM/
6. France Telecom R&D. SmartQVT, http://smartqvt.elibel.tm.fr/
7. Gardner, T., Griffin, C., Koehler, J., Hauser, R.: A review of OMG MOF 2.0 Query / Views / Transformations Submissions and Recommendations towards the final Standard. In: 1st MetaModelling for MDA Workshop, pp. 178–197 (2003)
8. Greenfield, J., Short, K., Cook, S., Kent, S.: Software Factories: Assembling Applications with Patterns, Models, Frameworks, and Tools. Wiley, Chichester (2004)
9. Hailpern, B., Tarr, P.: Model-driven development: The good, the bad, and the ugly. IBM Systems Journal 45(3), 451–461 (2006)
10. Jouault, F., Kurtev, I.: On the architectural alignment of ATL and QVT. In: 21st ACM Symposium on Applied Computing, pp. 1188–1195. ACM Press, New York (2006)
11. Jouault, F., Kurtev, I.: On the interoperability of model-to-model transformation languages. Science of Computer Programming 68(3), 114–137 (2007)
12. OMG. Meta Object Facility (MOF) 2.0 Query/View/Transformation Specification - Final Adopted Specification. ptc/07-07-07 (July 2007)
13. Sourceforge. QVT Relations Parser, http://sourceforge.net/projects/qvtparser/.
14. Sourceforge. QVT Relations to Operational Mappings (2007), http://sourceforge.net/projects/qvtrel2op/
15. TRDDC. ModelMorf, http://www.tcs-trddc.com/ModelMorf/
16. Varró, D., Pataricza, A.: Generic and Meta-transformations for Model Transformation Engineering. In: 7th UML Conference. LNCS, pp. 290–304 (2004)
17. Varró, G., Schurr, A., Varró, D.: Benchmarking for Graph Transformation. In: IEEE Symposium on VL/HCC, pp. 79–88. IEEE, Los Alamitos (2005)

Composition Techniques for Rule-Based Model Transformation Languages

Dennis Wagelaar*

Vrije Universiteit Brussel, Pleinlaan 2, 1050 Brussels, Belgium
`dennis.wagelaar@vub.ac.be`

Abstract. Model transformation languages have matured to a point where people have started experimenting with model transformation definitions themselves in addition to the language they are written in. In addition to the transformation language properties, the properties of model transformation definitions themselves become important, such as scalability, maintainability and reusability. Composition of model transformations allows for the creation of smaller, maintainable and reusable model transformation definitions that can scale up to a larger model transformation. There are two kinds of composition for model transformations. External composition deals with chaining separate model transformations together by passing models from one transformation to another. Internal composition composes two model transformation definitions into one new model transformation, which typically requires knowledge of the transformation language. This paper focuses on internal composition for two rule-based model transformation languages. One is the ATLAS Transformation Language, which serves as our implementation vehicle. The other is the QVT Relations language, which is a standard transformation language for MOF. We propose a composition technique called module superimposition. We discuss how module superimposition interacts with other composition techniques in ATL, such as helpers, called rules and rule inheritance. Together, these techniques allow for powerful composition of entire transformation modules as well as individual transformation rules. By applying superimposition to QVT Relations, we demonstrate that our composition technique is relevant outside the ATL language as well.

1 Introduction

Model transformations have become increasingly commonplace in model-driven engineering, with a number of stable model transformation languages and tools available. The OMG has even released the MOF Query/View/Transformation standard transformation language [1]. This means that people have started experimenting with model transformations themselves in addition to transformation languages. Whereas the focus initially lay on the expressiveness of transformation languages, other properties are starting to become important, such

---

* The author's work is part of the VariBru project, which is funded by the Institute for the encouragement of Scientific Research and Innovation of Brussels (ISRIB).

A. Vallecillo, J. Gray, A. Pierantonio (Eds.): ICMT 2008, LNCS 5063, pp. 152–167, 2008.

as scalability, maintainability and reusability of model transformation definitions. As model-driven engineering becomes more mature, the model transformation definitions used typically become more elaborate. During the evolution of a model transformation definition, exceptions to the standard transformation scenario are discovered. All these exceptions are then integrated back into the original model transformation definition. In order to keep such model transformation definitions maintainable, they eventually have to be split up into separate model transformation definitions of a manageable size. Those separate model transformation definitions have be composed in order to achieve the intended transformation result.

Perhaps the most straightforward method of composition is to chain several model transformations together by providing the output of one transformation as input for another transformation. Another method is to compose the rules from a number of transformation definitions into one transformation. The latter method typically requires the model transformations that will be composed to be expressed in the same language. There has been at least one workshop on the topic of model transformation composition [2], where these two methods were labelled as *internal* and *external* transformation composition, respectively. We believe that both composition methods are necessary and complement each other, as we will also demonstrate in this paper.

The focus of this paper lies on internal transformation composition, which means that the composition method is specific to the domain of a particular transformation language. We propose a composition technique called *module superimposition*. Module superimposition allows one to overlay several transformation definitions on top of each other and then execute them as one transformation. We will discuss our composition technique based on two rule-based transformation languages. The first language is the ATLAS transformation language (ATL) [3], which has been used as an implementation vehicle for our experiment. The second language is the QVT Relations [1] standard language, which currently exists as a specification. By translating our composition technique to QVT Relations, we demonstrate that our composition technique is relevant outside the ATL language as well.

The rest of this paper is organised as follows: first, we briefly explain the ATLAS transformation language. After that, we introduce module superimposition for ATL. We discuss module superimposition semantics by means of a higher-order transformation that performs module superimposition. Next, we discuss how module superimposition interacts with other composition techniques in ATL. We will also discuss how module superimposition applies to QVT Relations. We will then discuss related work, followed by the conclusion and future work.

2   ATLAS Transformation Language

The ATLAS Transformation Language (ATL) [3] historically served as a submission to the QVT Request For Proposals [4]. As a consequence, ATL shows similarities to QVT Relations, save some limitations: ATL transformations are unidirectional.

Output models are write-only and always start off as empty models. All navigation in ATL is done on read-only input models. QVT checking transformations are typically implemented as ATL *queries*, while enforcing transformations are represented in ATL as *modules*. Furthermore, ATL is a *hybrid* language, providing declarative as well as imperative language constructs. For the purpose of explaining our composition technique, we will only discuss ATL transformation modules.

2.1   Modules

An ATL transformation module has a number of input models and typically one output model. It contains a number of *rules* that define the mapping from source elements to target elements. ATL has two kinds of rules: *matched* rules and *called* rules. These compare to QVT *top-level* relations and *non-top-level* relations in that matched rules are automatically triggered, while called rules must be invoked from a matched rule. Listing 1.1 shows an example ATL module that copies a UML Model element to another UML Model element.

```
module UML2Copy;
create OUT: UML2 from IN: UML2;
rule Model {
    from s: UML2!"uml::Model"
    to t: UML2!"uml::Model" (
        name <- s.name,
        visibility <- s.visibility,
        viewpoint <- s.viewpoint)
}
```

Listing 1.1. UML2Copy transformation module

The UML2Copy module has one output model named "OUT" of model type "UML2" and one input model "IN", which is also of model type "UML2". In ATL, models and model types are bound to concrete models and meta-models at run-time. ATL does not perform any type-checking at compile-time and allows the developer to use any meta-class or property name. Only at run-time, ATL resolves meta-classes and properties by their name in the bound meta-model. In our example, the model type "UML2" is (intended to be) bound to the Eclipse UML2 meta-model.

The transformation module has one *matched* rule named "Model". Since ATL transformations are unidirectional, ATL rules don't have a **domain** construct like QVT relations. Instead, ATL rules have a **from** part and a **to** part. The **from** part specifies which model elements from the input model(s) trigger the matched rule. The **to** part creates one or more model elements in the output model. In the example, any instance of the meta-class "uml::Model" from the "UML2" meta-model triggers the rule, where the "uml::" prefix specifies that the "Model" meta-class is inside the "uml" package. ATL uses '<-' to specify assignment: the Model copy has the same name, visibility and viewpoint values as the original Model instance. Listing 1.2 shows how multiple matched rules interact.

```
module UML2ExtendedCopy;
create OUT: UML2 from IN: UML2;
rule Model {
    from s: UML2!"uml::Model"
    to t: UML2!"uml::Model" (
        name <- s.name,
        visibility <- s.visibility,
        viewpoint <- s.viewpoint,
        packagedElement <- s.packagedElement)
}
rule Package {
    from s: UML2!"uml::Package" (
        s.oclIsTypeOf(UML2!"uml::Package"))
    to t: UML2!"uml::Package" (
        name <- s.name,
        visibility <- s.visibility,
        packagedElement <- s.packagedElement),
}
```

Listing 1.2. UML2ExtendedCopy transformation module

The "Model" rule now includes an assignment of the "packagedElement" property. The "packagedElement" property refers to a collection of packaged model elements in the source model. Each of those model elements may separately match against a rule in the transformation module. Normally, the target element "t" of the "Model" rule is supposed to contain the target "packagedElement" elements, just like the source element "s" contains the source "packagedElement" elements. ATL automatically translates assignments of source elements to their target element counterparts whenever those source elements trigger a matched rule in the transformation module.

This kind of source-to-target element tracing [5] is defined by the **from** element and the first **to** element[1]. This tracing information is used to translate an assignment of source elements to target elements: the target "packagedElement" collection in the "Model" rule will not contain the elements of "s.packagedElement", but rather the target elements that trace back to the elements of "s.packagedElement".

The "Package" rule copies all instances of "uml::Package" that satisfy the additional condition "s.oclIsTypeOf(UML2!uml::Package)". This additional condition is necessary to prevent the rule from triggering against subclasses of "uml::Package", such as "uml::Model".

---

[1] Tracing information for the other **to** elements is also recorded, but must be retrieved explicitly in ATL via an API call.

3   Module Superimposition

While ATL transformation modules are normally run by themselves, that is one transformation module at a time, it is also possible to *superimpose* several transformation modules on top of each other. The end result is a transformation module that contains the union of all transformation rules. It is also possible for a transformation module to *override* rules from the transformation modules it is superimposed upon. Rule overriding is done by *name*: superimposed rules with the same name as an existing rule override the existing rule. This allows for rule-level adaptation of one transformation module by another and improves reusability of transformation modules.

Fig. 1 shows an example of a typical use case for superimposition: the transformation rules of the UML2Copy transformation module are reused and overridden where necessary by the UML2Profiles transformation module. While the UML2Copy transformation module given earlier in this paper contains only one rule, the real UML2Copy includes a transformation rule for every metaclass of which it must copy the instances [2]. This amounts to approximately 200 rules for the entire UML2 meta-model. Any refinement transformation basically needs to copy all meta-class instances, except for the few meta-class instances that are refined. The UML2Profiles transformation module applies a profile to the "uml::Model" instance, provided it was not yet applied. All other elements should just be copied. To achieve this, the UML2Profiles module is superimposed on the UML2Copy module. It overrides the "Model" rule, which copies each "uml::Model" instance, by a version that checks that the profile we want to apply has already been applied. It also introduces a new rule "ModelProfile", which checks that the profile we want to apply has **not** been applied and then applies the profile. The resulting transformation module contains all rules from Fig. 1 that are not ~~struck out~~.

ATL has a number of other constructs besides matched rules, such as lazy rules, called rules, helper attributes and helper methods. Similar to matched rules, all of these constructs have a *name* that is registered in a global ATL namespace during execution. Module superimposition therefore also applies to all these constructs. Note that attribute and method helpers also have a *context* in addition to their name: multiple helpers with the same name can exist as long as they have a different context. This is taken into account by module superimposition, which overrides helpers by name *and* context. Also note that each named ATL construct has its own distinct namespace in ATL, such that name clashes between rules and helpers, for example, are avoided. As such, it is impossible to override a rule by a helper with module superimposition.

Note that superimposition is a load-time construct: there is no real transformation module that represents the result of superimposing several modules on top of each other. Instead, several modules are simply *loaded* on top of each other, overriding existing rules and adding new rules. As normally each ATL

---

[2] http://ssel.vub.ac.be/viewvc/UML2CaseStudies/uml2cs-transformations/
UML2Copy.atl?revision=7380&view=markup

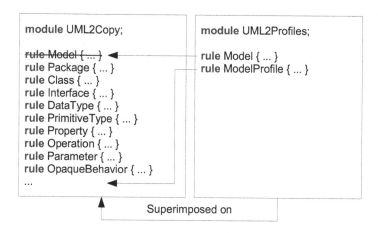

Fig. 1. ATL superimposition example

transformation is compiled to ASM format before it is executed, this load-time superimposition approach significantly improves scalability. Only the ATL modules that have changed need to be recompiled, regardless of the other ATL modules it will be combined with. The performance overhead of the superimposition itself is minimal. The ATL engine already keeps an internal look-up table of available rules and helpers when loading a transformation module. Module superimposition simply updates that table as new modules are loaded on top of the previously loaded modules. In addition, it updates the "main" procedure of the first loaded transformation to include any new rules/helpers for every superimposed transformation module.

3.1   Usage Scenarios

Module superimposition is a good way to achieve a specific "base behaviour" of the transformation engine, such as copying the input model to the output model. Superimposition can deal with non-standard situations, such as having multiple input (and/or output) models. Our example UML2Copy transformation is meant to only copy elements from the model "IN" to the model "OUT". Listing 1.3 shows the UML2Profiles transformation module that is superimposed on UML2Copy.

UML2Profiles adds an extra input model, "ACCESSORS". The "ACCESSORS" model refers to the UML profile that is applied to "OUT". The elements of the "ACCESSORS" model should not be copied, but should instead be referenced from the "OUT" model. This is achieved by checking that only elements contained in the "inElements" helper attribute match the **from** part from each rule. The "inElements" helper is provided by the UML2Copy module and contains all elements from "IN".

By separating the general copying functionality (UML2Copy) from the specific refinement functionality (UML2Profiles), we have achieved better scalability in

```
module UML2Profiles ;
create OUT: UML2 from IN: UML2 , ACCESSORS : UML2;
helper def: accessorsProfile : UML2!"uml::Profile" =
    UML2!"uml::Profile". allInstances ()
    ->select (p|p.name='Accessors ')->first ();
rule Model {
    from s: UML2!"uml::Model" (
        if thisModule.inElements->includes(s) then
            s.profileApplication ->select (a|
                a.appliedProfile=thisModule.accessorsProfile)
            ->notEmpty ()
        else false endif)
    to t: UML2!"uml::Model" (
        name <- s.name ,
        visibility <- s.visibility ,
        viewpoint <- s.viewpoint ,
        profileApplication <- s.profileApplication )
}
rule ModelProfile {
    from s: UML2!"uml::Model" (
        if thisModule.inElements->includes(s) then
            s.profileApplication ->select (a|
                a.appliedProfile=thisModule.accessorsProfile)
            ->isEmpty ()
        else false endif)
    to t: UML2!"uml::Model" (
        name <- s.name ,
        visibility <- s.visibility ,
        viewpoint <- s.viewpoint ,
        profileApplication <- s.profileApplication ),
        pa : UML2!"uml::ProfileApplication " (
        applyingPackage <- s,
        appliedProfile <- thisModule.accessorsProfile )
}
```

Listing 1.3. UML2Profiles transformation module

our development process where we don't have to recompile ±200 copying rules each time we change a refinement rule. We have also achieved better maintainability, since it's much easier to find a specific transformation rule within a small, specific transformation module. Maintainability is also improved by reduced code duplication in all available refinement transformation modules; all copying code is now centralised. Finally, reusability is improved by the ability to extend and adapt general transformation modules, such as UML2Copy.

Another usage scenario is the generation of platform ontologies from Java API models expressed in UML [6]. In this scenario, a general transformation module UMLtoAPIOntology.atl is superimposed by either UMLToPackageAPI-Ontology.atl or UMLToClassAPIOntology.atl to create either a package-level or a class-level ontology of the input Java API model[3].

Yet another scenario is provided by the configuration language of our instant messenger case study[4]. The configuration language meta-model is split up in a general "Transformations" package and a specific "InstantMessenger" package. The ConfigToBuildFile.atl transformation module has also been split up in two parts: one for each meta-model, where ConfigToBuildFile.atl for "Instant-Messenger" can be superimposed on ConfigToBuildFile.atl for "Transformations". This allows for reuse of the general "Transformations" infrastructure in other configuration languages and generators.

3.2   Semantics

An important aspect of the module superimposition semantics is that any combination of superimposed modules can be rewritten as a single transformation module. We have expressed the rewriting of two combined modules as a single module in a higher-order ATL transformation module. The start of this module is shown in Listing 1.4.

```
module Superimpose;
create OUT: ATL from IN: ATL, SUPER: ATL;
helper def: inElements: Set(ATL!ATL::LocatedElement) =
    ATL!"ATL::LocatedElement".allInstancesFrom('IN')
    ->reject(o|o.isOverridden())->asSet()->union(
        ATL!"ATL::LocatedElement".allInstancesFrom('SUPER')
        ->reject(s|if s.oclIsKindOf(ATL!"ATL::Rule")
            or s.oclIsKindOf(ATL!"ATL::Helper") then
              s.isOverriding()
            else false endif));
```

Listing 1.4. Superimpose transformation module

This higher-order transformation module superimposes the "SUPER" transformation module on the "IN" transformation module and writes the result into the "OUT" transformation module[5]. It copies all the elements in `inElements` directly to "OUT". "`inElements`" is a helper attribute that contains all elements from "IN" that are not overridden, and all elements from "SUPER" excluding overriding rules and helpers. There are special transformation rules for overridden rules and helpers. The transformation rule in Listing 1.5 deals with overridden matched rules.

The "`OverriddenMatchedRule`" transformation rule transforms the overridden matched rule from "IN" to "OUT" using all the property values from the

---

[3] http://ssel.vub.ac.be/ssel/research:mdd:platformkit:ontologies
[4] http://ssel.vub.ac.be/ssel/research:mdd:casestudies
[5] The ATL meta-model can be found at http://tinyurl.com/2t5mcp

```
helper def: realInElements: Set(ATL!"ATL::LocatedElement") =
    ATL!"ATL::LocatedElement".allInstancesFrom('IN');
rule OverriddenMatchedRule {
    from s: ATL!"ATL::MatchedRule" (
        if thisModule.realInElements->includes(s) then
            s.oclIsTypeOf(ATL!"ATL::MatchedRule") and
            s.isOverridden()
        else false endif)
    using { o: ATL!"ATL::MatchedRule" = s.overriddenBy(); }
    to t: ATL!"ATL::MatchedRule" (
        name <- o.name,
        ...)
}
```

Listing 1.5. OverriddenMatchedRule transformation rule

overriding matched rule "o". As a consequence, the output matched rule "t" will have all the properties of "o", but it will still occur in the same place in "OUT" as "s" did in "IN". This is achieved by ATL's implicit tracing mechanism, which maps all "s" references to "t" references. This becomes clearer when looking at Listing 1.6, which shows the transformation rule that deals with the transformation module element.

The "Module" transformation rule copies only the transformation module element from "IN". The contained elements are retrieved from the "SUPER" transformation module in the **using** part. They are then appended to the (ordered) list of existing elements. In the case of overridden matched rules, the overridden rule is already contained in "s.elements". After the assignment, "elements" contains the same ordered list, except that its elements are all mapped to their "OUT" counterparts by the ATL tracing mechanism.

The full higher-order transformation is split up in two parts: ATLCopy.atl and Superimpose.atl, where ATLCopy.atl is a simple copying transformation and Superimpose.atl provides the special transformation rules for superimposition[6]. As a proof of concept, Superimpose.atl is superimposed on ATLCopy.atl and then applied to ATLCopy.atl and itself. The result is a single transformation module, ATLSuperimpose.atl, that represents the composition of ATLCopy.atl and Superimpose.atl.

3.3   Interaction with Other Composition Techniques

Module superimposition interacts with other composition techniques in ATL, such as helpers and called rules. In addition to the normal matched rules in ATL, module superimposition also allows for reusing and overriding called rules and helpers.

Called rules allow for functional composition in ATL. Called rules can be invoked (with side-effects) and return a value. With module superimposition,

---

[6] http://ssel.vub.ac.be/viewvc/atl-superimposition-semantics/

```
rule Module {
    from s: ATL!"ATL::Module" (
        thisModule.realInElements->includes(s))
    using {
        superElements: Sequence(ATL!"ATL::ModuleElement") =
            ATL!"ATL::Module".allInstancesFrom('SUPER')
            ->collect(m|m.elements
                ->select(e|not e.isOverriding()))
            ->flatten();
        superInModels: Sequence(ATL!"OCL::OclModel") =
            ATL!"ATL::Module".allInstancesFrom('SUPER')
            ->collect(m|m.inModels)->flatten();
        superOutModels: Sequence(ATL!"OCL::OclModel") =
            ATL!"ATL::Module".allInstancesFrom('SUPER')
            ->collect(m|m.outModels)->flatten();
        superLibraryRefs: Sequence(ATL!"ATL::LibraryRef") =
            ATL!"ATL::Module".allInstancesFrom('SUPER')
            ->collect(m|m.libraries)->flatten(); }
    to t: ATL!"ATL::Module" (
        name <- s.name,
        ...,
        libraries <- s.libraries->union(superLibraryRefs),
        inModels <- s.inModels->union(superInModels),
        outModels <- s.outModels->union(superOutModels),
        elements <- s.elements->union(superElements))
}
```

Listing 1.6. Module transformation rule

it is possible to replace parts of the function invocation chain by overriding called rules. It is also possible to invoke called rules from other modules in the superimposition stack. This introduces dependencies on the other modules, however, and should be used with care. It is advisable to limit invocation of called rules in other modules to the modules "below" (i.e. modules that are superimposed upon, not the superimposing modules).

Module superimposition has a similar effect on helpers as on called rules. Helpers are different from called rules in that they can have a context, however. The ATL engine keeps track of helper attributes and methods per context. That way, it is possible to define multiple helpers with the same name and a different context. Depending on the context, the corresponding version of the helper is used. As a consequence, superimposition can override helpers per context in ATL, leaving helpers with another context in place.

ATL supports another decomposition construct called *rule inheritance* [7]. Rule inheritance allows one to define general transformation rules that can be extended by specific rules. A sub-rule is required to specify a **from** part that matches the same or less elements than its super-rule. It can then inherit the **to** part from its super-rule and add its own entries to the **to** part. It is currently not possible to separately superimpose sub- and super-rules. Only the sub-rules can be manipulated by module superimposition. This is because the ATL compiler inlines the super-rules into the sub-rules. No super-rules exist in the ATL bytecode. In addition, it is not possible to inherit from super-rules in another module. This is because module superimposition is performed *after* the compiler does its work. The compiler only operates on a single module at a time.

3.4   Superimposition of QVT Relations Transformations

Module superimposition can be used for other languages than ATL, as long as the transformation language has the concepts of rules and modules that contain those rules. QVT Relations is such a transformation language. In the Relations language, a transformation between models is specified as a set of relations that must hold for the transformation to be successful. Each model in the transformation conforms to a model type, which is a specification of the kind of model elements that can occur in a conforming model. A model type is typically represented by a meta-model. The models in a transformation are named and are bound to a specific model type. Listing 1.7 shows our UML2Copy example as a Relations specification.

```
transformation UML2Copy (IN: UML2, OUT: UML2) {
  top relation Model {
    domain IN s: uml::Model {
      name = n,
      visibility = v,
      viewpoint = vp,
      profileApplication = pa}
    domain OUT t: uml::Model {
      name = n,
      visibility = v,
      viewpoint = vp,
      profileApplication = pa}} ... }
```

Listing 1.7. UML2Copy QVTR transformation

Note that a special "inElements" helper is not necessary. A QVT relation is already defined on the basis of models, not meta-models, so we can explicitly target elements from the model 'IN'. In our example, we only gave a relation for the "uml::Model" meta-class and omitted the other relations. We still need one relation for each meta-class in the UML2 meta-model, just like in our ATL version of the transformation. Each of these relations follow the same pattern as the given "Model" relation. Now let's consider the same scenario, in which we superimpose the Relations version of UML2Profiles on UML2Copy. Listing 1.8 shows UML2Profiles as defined in QVT Relations.

The illustration of superimposition in Fig. 1 is also valid for QVT Relations. A QVT *transformation* is the equivalent of an ATL *module* and a QVT *relation* is the equivalent of an ATL *rule* for the purpose of superimposition. When the two relations "Model" and "ModelProfile" are superimposed on UML2Copy, the "Model" relation is overridden and the "ModelProfile" relation is added to the base transformation.

4   Related Work

In the domain of model transformation languages, (internal) composition techniques are relatively new. In graph transformations [8], *negative application conditions* (NACs) are used to inhibit a transformation rule from triggering. A NAC essentially is another (partial) transformation rule that is composed with the base transformation rule. It overrides the behaviour of the base transformation rule. As graph transformations are in-place transformations without implicit tracing mechanism [5], there is no difference between applying one rule after the other or applying them "together" like rules in an ATL module[7]. In ATL (and QVT Relations), two or more models are involved and transformation rules interact through implicit tracing. The Epsilon transformation language[8] uses transformation *strategies* to specify the default behaviour for elements that don't match against any transformation rule. Strategies are defined in Java as engine plug-ins. With module superimposition, such default behaviour can be defined directly in ATL as a normal transformation module.

In the domain of program transformation, the Conditional Transformations approach (CTs) has a special composition mechanism for combining multiple transformations into one transformation [10]. The CT approach is similar to graph transformations in that each transformation consists of one rule. Instead of negative application conditions, CTs use logic *conditions*. The CT composition mechanism allows for the composition of multiple CT rules. The result is a transformation with multiple rules, not unlike ATL or QVT Relations. The composed CT is a *sequence* of rules, where the rule sequence may be an AND-sequence or an OR-sequence. The AND and OR refer to the trigger condition of the rules: in an AND-sequence, all rule conditions must hold for the transformation to be executed. In an OR-sequence, individual rules may trigger while others do not. CT composition achieves the same goal as module superimposition, since it can combine pre-existing transformation rules in any way. Because the nature of CT rules is very different from ATL rules, the composition mechanisms are different as well. CT rules are independently defined and may be applied in sequence, while ATL rules are defined in combination and interact via the implicit ATL tracing mechanism.

In the domain of aspect-oriented programming languages, Hyper/J [11] follows an approach similar to superimposition. Hyper/J can merge Java implementations of multiple software dimensions into one Java program. Hyper/J claims

---

[7] The order in which rules are applied can be important, however [9]

[8] http://www.eclipse.org/gmt/epsilon/

to be a symmetric composition approach, in which all dimensions are at the same "level". This is in contrast to superimposition, where one module is superimposed on top of another. Superimposition therefore also allows for overriding. The Composition Filters (CF) [12] approach to aspect-oriented programming includes a "superimposition" language construct. In CF, superimposition refers to *filter modules*, which can be distributed and put on top of object classes. Multiple filter modules can be superimposed on top of each other as well. A filter module can manipulate messages going into or out of objects.

```
transformation UML2Profiles(IN:UML2,ACCESSORS:UML2,OUT:UML2){
  top relation Model {
    domain IN s: uml::Model {
      name = n,
      visibility = v,
      viewpoint = vp,
      profileApplication = p}
    domain OUT t: uml::Model {
      name = n,
      visibility = v,
      viewpoint = vp,
      profileApplication = p}
    domain ACCESSORS accessorsProfile: uml::Profile {
      name = 'Accessors'}
    when {p->select(a|
      a.appliedProfile=accessorsProfile)->notEmpty()}}
  top relation ModelProfile {
    domain IN s: uml::Model {
      name = n,
      visibility = v,
      viewpoint = vp,
      profileApplication = p}
    domain OUT t: uml::Model {
      name = n,
      visibility = v,
      viewpoint = vp,
      profileApplication = p->union(Set{
        pa: uml::ProfileApplication {
          applyingPackage = t,
          appliedProfile = accessorsProfile}})}
    domain ACCESSORS accessorsProfile: uml::Profile {
      name = 'Accessors'}
    when {p->select(a|
          a.appliedProfile=accessorsProfile)->isEmpty()}} }
```

Listing 1.8. UML2Profiles QVTR transformation

5 Conclusion and Future Work

This paper has presented an approach for *internal* composition of model transformations written in a rule-based model transformation language. Our composition approach, called *module superimposition*, allows for the composition of two or more transformations into one single transformation. It therefore allows one to split up a model transformation into multiple, reusable and maintainable transformations that can later be composed into one single transformation. Module superimposition is implemented for the ATLAS transformation language, but is also applicable to the QVT Relations language. Module superimposition has been applied in our MDE case study[9] on UML 2.x refinement transformations, Java API model to platform ontology transformations [6] as well as the build script generators for our case study's configuration language.

As module superimposition is a load-time composition technique, operating on the compiled ATL bytecode, it improves ATL's scalability. When changing one ATL transformation module, one only has to re-compile that particular module. This means that compiler performance no longer has to degrade with increasing transformation code size, as long as transformation code is separated into multiple transformation modules. The performance overhead of the superimposition itself is minimal. Module superimposition simply updates the internal ATL rule/helper look-up table as new modules are loaded on top of the previously loaded modules.

One main use case of module superimposition is to achieve a *base behaviour* from the transformation engine. By default, ATL does not transform anything in the input models and will simply give back an empty output model. For refinement or refactoring transformations, most elements should simply be copied and only a few elements are modified. In ATL, this means that every refinement/refactoring transformation consists mostly of copying rules. ATL refining mode has been introduced to tackle this issue, but it cannot deal with customised copying requirements. Module superimposition allows one to modularise all copying rules into a separate copying transformation. That copying transformation may include any special conditions that can be expressed in ATL. By separating the base behaviour from the specific behaviour, we achieve better maintainability through reduced code duplication in the transformation modules. Finally, reusability is improved by the ability to extend and adapt general transformation modules. We intend to investigate more use cases of module superimposition in the future. A candidate use case we are currently looking into is the leverage of ATL's implicit tracing mechanism to automatically "update" models that refer to the model being transformed.

Module superimposition works at the granularity of transformation rules in ATL and relations in QVT Relations. It allows one to add new rules/relations and to override existing ones. As ATL already supports decomposition of transformation rules into helpers and called rules, our module superimposition approach can leverage this decomposition. In addition to overriding and adding

---

[9] http://ssel.vub.ac.be/ssel/research:mdd:casestudies

standard matched rules, it is possible to override and add helpers and called rules as well. Deletion of rules and helpers is not directly supported, but it is possible to replace the trigger condition with a condition that never triggers.

It is currently not possible to separately superimpose sub- and super-rules in ATL rule inheritance. Only the sub-rules can be manipulated by module superimposition, because the ATL compiler in-lines the super-rules into the sub-rules. In the future, the implementation of ATL rule inheritance can be changed to dynamic look-up of super-rules after a transformation module has been compiled. This allows superimposition of super-rules as well as rule inheritance across superimposed modules.

There is currently a QVT Relations compiler in development that targets the ATL virtual machine[10]. Module superimposition operates on the bytecode that goes into the ATL virtual machine, which makes it easier to port the implementation of module superimposition to QVT Relations. As soon as the QVT Relations compiler is released, an implementation of module superimposition for QVT Relations may become available shortly after.

Acknowledgement

The author would like to thank Frédéric Jouault for reviewing a draft of this paper and his discussions on the topic. Thanks also go to the review committee for providing many helpful comments. Thanks go to the ATL community for trying out module superimposition and helping to iron out any issues.

References

1. Object Management Group, Inc.: Meta Object Facility (MOF) 2.0 Query/View/-Transformation Specification, Final Adopted Specification, ptc/05-11-01 (2005)
2. Kleppe, A.G.: First European Workshop on Composition of Model Transformations - CMT 2006. Technical Report TR-CTIT-06-34, Enschede (2006)
3. Jouault, F., Kurtev, I.: On the Architectural Alignment of ATL and QVT. In: Proceedings of the 21st Annual ACM Symposium on Applied Computing (SAC 2006), Dijon, France (2006)
4. Object Management Group, Inc.: Request for Proposal: MOF 2.0 Query / Views / Transformations RFP, ad/2002-04-10 (2004)
5. Czarnecki, K., Helsen, S.: Feature-based survey of model transformation approaches. IBM Systems Journal 45(3), 621–645 (2006)
6. Wagelaar, D., van Der Straeten, R.: Platform Ontologies for the Model-Driven Architecture. European Journal of Information Systems 16, 362–373 (2007)
7. Kurtev, I., van den Berg, K., Jouault, F.: Evaluation of rule-based modularization in model transformation languages illustrated with ATL. In: SAC 2006: Proceedings of the 2006 ACM symposium on Applied computing, pp. 1202–1209. ACM Press, New York (2006)
8. Mens, T., Gorp, P.V.: A Taxonomy of Model Transformation. Electr. Notes Theor. Comput. Sci. 152, 125–142 (2006)

---

[10] http://wiki.eclipse.org/M2M/Relational_QVT_Language_%28QVTR%29

9. Mens, T., Taentzer, G., Runge, O.: Detecting Structural Refactoring Conflicts Using Critical Pair Analysis. Electr. Notes Theor. Comput. Sci. 127(3), 113–128 (2005)
10. Kniesel, G., Koch, H.: Static Composition of Refactorings. Science of Computer Programming 52, 9–51 (2004)
11. Ossher, H., Tarr, P.: The Shape of Things To Come: Using Multi-Dimensional Separation of Concerns with Hyper/J to (Re)Shape Evolving Software. Comm. ACM 44, 43–50 (2001)
12. Bergmans, L., Akşit, M.: Composing Crosscutting Concerns Using Composition Filters. Comm. ACM 44, 51–57 (2001)

Approaches for Model Transformation Reuse: Factorization and Composition

Jesús Sánchez Cuadrado and Jesús García Molina

University of Murcia, Spain
{jesusc, jmolina}@um.es
http://gts.inf.um.es/

Abstract. Reusability is one of the principal software quality factors. In the context of model driven development (MDD), reuse of model transformations is also considered a key activity to achieve productivity and quality. It is necessary to devote important research efforts to find out appropriate reusability mechanisms for transformation tools and languages. In this paper we present two approaches for reusing model transformation definitions. Firstly, we tackle the creation of related model transformations, showing how the factorization of common parts can be achieved. Secondly, we describe a proposal on the composition of existing, separated transformation definitions so that they can be used to solve a concrete transformation problem. We illustrate both proposals with examples taken from the development of a software product line for adventure games, which has been implemented using the modularization mechanisms of the RubyTL transformation language.

1 Introduction

Reusability is one of the principal software quality factors because the reuse of software assets reduces development effort and cost, and improves quality aspects such as maintainability, reliability and correctness. In the same way, in model driven development (MDD), the reuse of model transformation definitions is also considered a key activity to achieve productivity and quality [1]. However, it is still necessary to gain more experience on transformation reuse in real projects, and to devote important research efforts to discover appropriate reusability mechanisms for transformation tools and languages.

Two points of view can be considered in the practice of software reuse: developing artifacts *for reuse* and developing new systems *with reuse* of existing artifacts. Languages and tools must support mechanisms for creating and specifying reusable artifacts, as well as mechanisms for specializing and integrating them for building a new system. Transformation reuse follows the same principles as software reuse. So, good abstractions are essential for creating reusable transformations. Current approaches are focused on reusing single rules or patterns [2][3][4]. However, practical development of large systems requires reuse to be tackled at a coarser-grained level. Transformation definitions should be reusable

A. Vallecillo, J. Gray, A. Pierantonio (Eds.): ICMT 2008, LNCS 5063, pp. 168–182, 2008.

as a whole, and mechanisms for their specialization, integration and adaptation must be provided.

In this paper we address two model transformation reuse techniques: factorization and composition. The first deals with developing reusable transformation definitions and the second with the adaptation and integration activities. When related transformation definitions are created, they can have duplicated code. We will show how factorization of common parts in a new transformation definition, intended *for reuse*, removes the duplicated code. With regard to developing *with reuse*, we will tackle the problem of composing several, independent transformation definitions for solving a specific transformation problem. Throughout the paper we will analyze some issues related to constraints for reuse imposed by the specification of source and target metamodels in the transformation definition.We will propose solutions in the context of the RubyTL transformation language [5].

The paper is organized as follows. The next section motivates the interest in factorization and composition of model transformation definitions. Then, Section 3 introduces the example that will be used through the paper. Section 4 gives a brief explanation of the modularity mechanism provided by RubyTL. Sections 5 and 6 explain our approaches for factorization and composition in model-to-model transformations respectively. Finally, in Section 7 the related work is presented, and Section 8 presents some conclusions.

2   Motivation

Tackling large projects using MDD implies managing complex metamodels and transformations of considerable size. To deal with this complexity, decomposition in smaller parts, finding commonalities and reusing common parts are needed. Implementation of software product lines (SPL) using MDD [6] is a clear example of this situation. Model transformation languages should provide reuse mechanisms, allowing us to create transformation definitions that can be used to create different products, and that can be extended to fulfill the requirements of a concrete product.

In our experiments, which integrate software product lines and model driven development, we have had to face three problems related to transformation definition reuse.

1. *Factorizing common parts* of transformation definitions.
2. *Adapting and composing* several transformation definitions.
3. *Variability* in transformation definitions, that is, the need to attach an aspect to a transformation definition to implement a certain product variant [6]. In this paper we will not address this issue because of lack of space. In any case, we have been able to address it successfully using the phasing mechanism explained in Section 4.

In this paper, we will focus on the last two problems. Next, we set out our proposal for factorization and composition. We also introduce two key concepts in our proposal: *metamodel compatibility* and *metamodel extension*.

2.1   Transformation Factorization

Transformation factorization is the process of finding common functionality shared between two or more transformation definitions, and of extracting the common parts to a base transformation definition. The non-common functionality is implemented by other transformation definitions which reuse the base transformation definition, and add their specific functionality.

Nevertheless, for a transformation definition to be reused, it is not enough that it provides the required functionality, but some kind of compatibility between metamodels of both transformation definitions must be satisfied. A transformation definition T_1 can only be directly reused within another transformation definition T_2 if each source and target metamodel of T_2 is "compatible" with the corresponding metamodel of T_1.

In Section 5, where factorization of transformation definitions is addressed using an example, we will propose an approach to deal with metamodel compatibility which relies on the notion of model type [7].

2.2   Transformation Composition

As is noted in [8], transformation definitions can be composed in several ways, such as chaining definitions written in different languages (external composition), or composing rules from two or more transformation definitions written in the same language (internal composition). Internal composition requires proper modularity mechanisms and composition operators. The composition unit can be a rule [2][4][3], or some coarser-grained construct.

Our proposal relies on a phasing mechanism [9], which is a mechanism for internal transformation composition. It is coarse-grained because it uses the concept of *phase* as composition unit, which encapsulates a set of rules aimed to perform a well-defined transformation task. The mechanism provides operators to allow transformation definitions to be composed by means of the trace information. In this paper, we will tackle the problem of composing transformation definitions whose source metamodels are the same (or at least compatible) and whose target metamodels are completely independent. Each one of the target metamodels represents a concern in the system being generated, but at some point these concerns must be connected.

This issue arises frequently, for instance in the MDA approach when several platform specific models (PSM) are derived from the same PIM. To be able to generate a complete and meaningful architecture, the bridges between the architectural elements must be established. Our approach to solving this problem will rely on creating an *extension* of the PSM metamodels, which will be in charge of adding the metaclasses needed to establish the bridge.

We define a metamodel MM_{ext} as an *extension* of another metamodel MM_{base} when: MM_{ext} imports MM_{base} and at least one of its metaclasses is related to another metaclass of MM_{base} (either having a reference or inheriting from it).

In Section 6 we will explain the approach in detail, highlighting the problems involved at model transformation language level, and proposing a solution using the RubyTL transformation language.

3   Running Example

To show the problems involved in the reuse of transformation definitions, and to illustrate our solution, we have developed a small, but non-trivial, case study. In this case study, we are interested in developing a software product line for interactive fiction games (also known as text adventures). In this kind of games, the player is presented with a text describing a situation or a room. The player interacts with the game by writing simple commands such as "get key" or "go north". A feature model has been used to describe the game requisites and to express commonalities and variabilities in the domain. Figure 1(a) shows an excerpt of it, while Figure 1(b) shows an screenshot of the user interface.

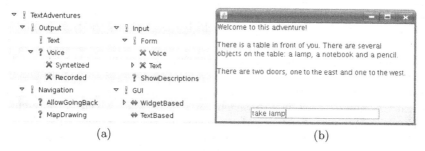

(a)   (b)

Fig. 1. (a) Simple feature model for text adventure games. (b) Screenshot of the user interface of a game generated with this SPL.

As can be seen in the feature model, a game must have input and output components (for the user to interact with the game), there is a navigation mechanism so that the user can go from one room to another (e.g. a variation must allow the user to go back to an already visited room) and a graphical user interface.

A DSL has been developed to describe a specific game, using a metamodel to represent its abstract syntax. In this DSL, the concepts involved in the description of an adventure are present, such as rooms, objects, exits, actions, etc. The example below shows a concrete syntax for the description of a room that is present in the game.

```
room 'table_and_notebook' do
    text %{ There is a table in front of you. There are
            several objects on the table: a lamp, a notebook and a pencil.
            There are two doors, one to the east and one to the west. }
    object 'lamp' do
      allowed_actions :take
      description "a normal lamp"
    end
    exit :west, :goto => 'dark_room'
end
```

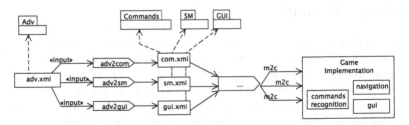

Fig. 2. Transformation flow for our software product line for adventure games. Dashed lines represents conformance relationships, while solid lines connect an input or output model with a transformation.

The game implementation is generated automatically from this DSL using a model-to-model transformation approach. Figure 2 shows the transformation flow, where three model-to-model transformations are involved to transform the initial DSL (Adv) into the game implementation. The game architecture, independent from an implementation technology, is represented by three metamodels, each one representing a game concern. One concern is the command interface (i.e. which commands are valid in each game situation), which is represented by the Commands metamodel. Another concern is the game navigation (i.e. the mechanism in charge of moving the user from one room to another), which is represented by a state machine-like metamodel (SM). Finally, the user interface is also represented, by the GUI metamodel. These metamodels are instantiated by the adv2com, adv2sm and adv2gui model-to-model transformations respectively.

We will use this example product line to drive the discussion of the rest of the paper. From the example, we will identify general problems regarding transformation reuse, and we will derive general solutions for them.

4   Phasing Mechanism

In [9] we presented a modularity mechanism for rule-based model transformation languages, which allows decomposition and composition of model transformation definitions. This mechanism is based on the idea of *phase*. In this section we give a brief introduction, using RubyTL as the implementation language.

With a phasing mechanism, a transformation definition is organized as a set of phases, which are composed of rules. Executing a transformation definition consists of executing its phases in a certain order. The execution of a phase means executing its rules as if they belonged to an isolated transformation definition, without conflicts with rules defined in other phases. A transformation definition is therefore seen as a phase, so allowing the same composition operators as for phases. Also, the mechanism provides a DSL to set the phase execution order explicitly.

One composition operator we have defined is a new kind of rule, called *refinement rule*, which matches against the trace information, instead of the source model. There is a match if a source instance of the metaclass specified in the rule's source pattern (i.e. rule's *from* part), has a trace relationship with one target instance of the metaclass specified in the rule's target pattern (i.e. rule's *to* part). Thus, for each match, the refinement rule is executed, but instead of creating a new target element as usual, the element matched by the target pattern is used. This means that no new target elements are created, but the rule works on existing elements, refining them.

Since a transformation definition is a form of phase, importing a separate transformation definitions within another transformation integrates seamlessly with the whole mechanism. RubyTL provides an `import` statement, which is in charge of resolving the dependency with an external definition by treating it as a phase.

The next example shows an example of phase usage. The `adv2com` transformation definition is extended to implement the `ShowDescriptions` feature, which implies creating a *describe* command for each available object in a room.

```
import 'm2m://adv2com'

phase 'show_descriptions' do
  refinement_rule 'refine_room' do
    from Adv::Room
    to   Command::CommandSet
    mapping do |room, command_set|
      command_set.validCommands = room.availableObjects
    end
  end

  rule 'obj2command' do
    from Adv::Object
    to   Command::Command
    mapping do |room, input|
      command.words << Input::Word.new(:value => 'describe')
      command.words << Input::Word.new(:value => object.name)
    end
  end
end

scheduling do
  execute 'adv2input'
  execute 'show_descriptions'
end
```

First of all, the `adv2com` definition is imported, so that it can be scheduled as a normal phase. Secondly, the `show_descriptions` phase contains a refinement rule that refines the `Room` to `CommandSet` mapping, so that the set of valid commands is extended. Note that no new `CommandSet` elements are created, but the match is against those `Room` objects that are related by the trace to already created `CommandSet` objects. Finally, the `scheduling` block is in charge of setting the order in which phases are executed.

5   Transformation Factorization

In this section, we will show how to factorize common parts of two transformation definitions into a base transformation, which is then reused so that code duplication is avoided.

In the game, each room has an associated set of valid commands the user can issue, which are derived by the adv2com transformation. It creates the com.xmi model, conforming to the Commands metamodel, which represents an implementation independent view of a command-based interface. From this model, a concrete implementation must be generated.

The implementation of the Input feature (see Figure 1(a)) requires dealing with different technologies to handle whether speech or written text is used to enter commands to the game. A model-to-model transformation approach has been used to tackle this issue. Commonalities in speech and text recognition technologies have been studied in order to reuse as many transformation definitions and metamodels as possible.

In particular, we have detected commonalities in the way the text or speech structure is recognized. Some speech recognition technologies use a special kind of grammar (JSGF, Java Speech Grammar Format), which is very similar to an EBNF grammar, but adding special constructs, such as the possibility of attaching a weight to a grammar element. Moreover, EBNF grammars are classic artifacts for representing text recognizers.

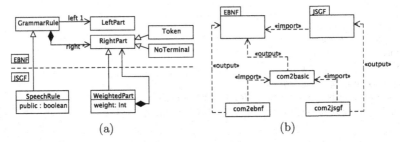

Fig. 3. (a) Excerpts of the EBNF and JSGF metamodels. (b) Relationships between reused transformations and their metamodels.

A metamodel to represent an EBNF grammar has therefore been created. In order to depict JSGF grammars, an extension of the former metamodel has also been created. As explained in Section 2.2 this means that the JSGF contains metaclasses which inherit from metaclasses defined in the EBNF metamodel (Figure 3(a) shows an excerpt of both metamodels and their inheritance relationships). The text feature is implemented as a model-to-model transformation from the Commands metamodel to EBNF (com2ebnf), while the speech feature is implemented as another model-to-model transformation from the Commands metamodel to JSGF (com2jsgf). Since JSGF has been modelled as an extension of EBNF, both transformation definitions share most of the functionality.

Our approach for *factorizing* the common parts of the transformations relies on creating a base transformation, which is imported by the concrete transformations that implement the non-common functionality. This schema is illustrated in Figure 3(b).

The `com2jsgf` transformation outputs models conforming to both JSGF and EBNF metamodels (i.e. JSGF is an extension of EBNF, so JSGF models can be used where EBNF models are expected), and it reuses `com2basic`, whose output model must conform to the EBNF metamodel. The constraint for reuse regarding metamodel conformance is that the metamodels used by one transformation provide the classifiers expected by the reused transformation, that is, metamodels must be compatible in some way.

To formalize this constraint we rely on the model type concept. In [7] a formalization of model types is presented, where the type of a model is seen as the set of the types of all objects belonging to the model. This definition allows models to conform to several metamodels.

At this point, we will address the compatibility problem posed in Section 2.1. From a transformation language point of view, the type of a model is the set of classifiers that are used within the transformation. In the same way as the previous definition, a transformation input or output model can conform to several metamodels. However, the problem arises when two metamodels contain a classifier with the same name, because the name clash prevents the transformation language from knowing which of them is being referred to by the name.

Usually, transformation languages define one namespace for each input or output model, which is bound at launch time to the concrete metamodel, so that classifiers are referenced through the corresponding namespace. If a metamodel imports another metamodel, when it is bound to the namespace the transitive closure on classifiers can be made to give access to the imported metamodel's classifiers. However, this approach has two problems: (1) it does not prevent name clashes, and (2) models conforming to several non-related metamodels cannot be handled.

We propose allowing several namespaces to be defined for each model, reflecting the fact that the model conforms to several metamodels, so that each metamodel is handled by its corresponding namespace. Thus, when a transformation is going to be launched these bindings must be established in some way. In our tooling [10] we use a DSL to set the models to be used in a transformation execution, and to bind the namespaces with the metamodels. The piece of DSL below shows how the concrete metamodels (`jsgf.ecore` and `ebnf.ecore`) are bound to the namespaces EBNF and JSGF expected by the transformation definition. Moreover, since the `com.xmi` model conforms to only one metamodel, a classic approach can be used (i.e. only one namespace per model).

```
model_to_model :com2jsgf do
  sources :namespace => 'Commands',
          :metamodel => 'commands.ecore',
          :model     => 'com.xmi'
```

```
targets :model => 'jsgf.xmi',
        :namespaces => {
            'JSGF' => 'jsgf.ecore'
            'EBNF' => 'ebnf.ecore' }

transformation 'm2m://com2jsgf.rb'
end
```

In this way, the transformation definition that creates a JSGF model to implement speech recognizers (com2jsgf in Figure 2) expects a metamodel to be bound to the Commands namespace, while it expects the EBNF and JSGF target namespaces to be bound too.

Below, an excerpt of the com2jsgf transformation definition is shown. It reuses the com2basic transformation definition using an import statement as explained in Section 4. Since the com2basic transformation definition may expect different namespace names to be bound (e.g. it may name the target namespace as EGrammar instead of EBNF), the import statement must provide a renaming facility. In our implementation, the binding between the current namespaces and the ones expected by the reused transformation is made using the map statement.

```
transformation 'com2jsgf'
source 'Adv'
target 'EBNF', 'JSGF'

import 'm2m://com2basic' do
  map 'Commands' => Commands
  map 'EGrammar' => EBNF
end

phase 'voice2grammar' do
 ... Transformation rules creating JSGF and EBNF elements...
end

scheduling do
  execute 'basic-grammar'
  execute 'voice-grammar'
end
```

It is also worth noting that the transformation definition does not know whether it receives one model conforming to two metamodels, or two models conforming to one metamodel each. Also, it does not specify a specific version of the metamodel, but different versions of the metamodel are allowed (for instance, several versions of UML can be handled). All these versions must have at least the classifiers used in the transformation rules, and the classifiers' properties used within the rules. A formalization on these constraints is made in [7].

6 Transformation Composition

This section presents an approach for composing independent transformation definitions, so that their relationships can be established. We illustrate it with an example intended to bridge the game concerns introduced in Section 3.

As explained in Section 3, we have defined three separate model transformations to instantiate each of the three concerns of our game architecture. These concerns, depicted as the Commands, SM and GUI metamodels, are completely independent of each other (i.e. they do not have references between them). Thus, they can be reused in contexts different from this transformation flow (e.g. a command-based input interface can also be used in command-line applications).

However, since each part of the game must interact with other parts, the three transformation definitions need to be composed to generate the bridges between the different parts. As a result of this composition, model elements of different metamodels must be connected. Typically, a connection between a model element a_1 and another model element a_2 implies that either the a_1's metaclass or the a_2's metaclass contains a reference to the other metaclass. This problem will always arise when we need to relate elements that belong to independent metamodels, as occurs in this case.

The challenge is to reuse the metamodels and their associated transformations, while being able to establish connections between them. We propose to extend the metamodels which must contain the connections, creating a new metamodel where, for each metaclass that needs to be related with another metaclass, a new metaclass inheriting from it is created. This new metamodel represents the connections between concerns in the architecture, and is usually small, because it only defines the minimum number of metaclasses to establish the connections. Another approach would be to use model weaving techniques [11] to represent these relationships, but the problems involved at model transformation level would be the same.

Figure 4 shows our approach to create a new metamodel (ExtSM) which extends the original SM metamodel to bridge states with the set of available commands for this particular game state. A subclass of SM::State is created, also called State, which has a reference to the CommandSet metaclass in the Command metamodel.

Once metamodels are integrated, transformations need to be integrated as well, so that bridges can be instantiated. Our strategy relies on importing and executing the transformation definitions that are going to be bridged in the context of another definition, which is actually in charge of locating the join

Fig. 4. Schema for creating a new metamodel bridging the SM and Command metamodel

points and instantiating the connections. It is important to notice that each transformation is imported as a black-box, which creates a piece of target model as a result, that must be integrated with the other transformation execution results. Since the interface of a transformation definition are the mappings it defines (i.e. its rules are "private"), rule-level composition mechanisms such as rule inheritance [2][4] or pattern factorization [3] cannot be applied.

According to the scheme shown in 2, the adv2sm transformation instantiates State objects conforming to the SM metamodel. However, we need to have State objects from the ExtSM metamodel instantiated by adv2sm, but its transformation rules have fixed metaclasses in their *to part*. This problem is similar to that of object oriented languages, where object creation statements using concrete classes limit reusablity and extensibility.

We propose to tackle this issue using an approach inspired by the factory patterns [12]. RubyTL allows a hook to be specified in an instantiation statement (typically the to part of a rule). The hook definition takes a base metaclass, which is used as the default metaclass in the case of the hook never being filled. When the transformation is imported into another transformation module, such a hook can be filled with the concrete metaclass to be instantiated, which must be a child metaclass of the base metaclass specified in the hook definition. The following piece of transformation shows the definition of a hook on the room2state rule: the hook is called vstate and its base class is SM::State.

```
top_rule 'sm' do
  from Adv::Adventure
  to   SM::StateMachine
  mapping do |adv, machine|
    machine.name   = adv.name
    machine.states = adv.rooms
  end
end

rule 'room2state' do
  from Adv::Room
  to   hook(SM::State => :vstate)
  mapping do |situation, state|
    state.name = situation.name
  end
end
```

Once the problem related to model elements instantiation has been solved, the next step is to actually integrate the transformation definitions. As explained above, we propose to define an "integration" transformation definition , which is in charge of composing and adapting the adv2sm, adv2com and adv2ui transformation definitions. It imports these three transformation definitions, and the integration is performed in three steps:

1. The target metamodel for state machines is an extension of the original one (as shown in Figure 4).
2. The adv2sm is parametrized by means of the **vstate** hook, so that the type of states can vary.
3. The "integration" transformation locates the join points using a **refinement rule** to match against the trace information (e.g. any *state* created from the same *room* as a another *command set* must be bridged). Then, new elements are created (either by other rules or imperatively) to adapt the existing model elements.

The following piece of code corresponds to our implementation in RubyTL of the "integration" transformation definition.

```
transformation 'integration'
source 'Adv'
target 'SM', 'ExtSM', 'Commands', 'GUI'

import 'm2m://adv2com'
import 'm2m://adv2ui'
import 'm2m://adv2sm' do
  map      'SM'     => SM
  factory :vstate => ExtSM::State
end

phase 'merge' do
  refinement_rule 'merge_rule' do
    from Adv::Room
    to   ExtSM::State, Comands::CommandSet, UI::CompositePanel
    mapping do |situation, command_set, state, ui|
      cconnector             = ExtSM::CommandConnector.new
      cconnector.commandSet = command_set
      state.input            = cconnector

      gconnector             = ExtSM::GUIConnector.new
      gconnector.gui         = ui
      state.ui               = bconnector
    end
  end
end

scheduling do
  execute 'adv2input'
  execute 'adv2sm'
  execute 'adv2ui'
  execute 'merge'
end
```

The third import statement binds SM namespace in the adv2sm transformation with the current SM namespace. Moreover, it parametrizes adv2sm so that instead of creating `SM::State` objects it creates `ExtSM::State` objects. Notice that although `adv2sm` has been bound to use the SM metamodel, it can create model elements conforming to `ExtSM::State` because such a metaclass is a subclass of `SM::State`.

Finally, the refinement rule is in charge of bridging related elements, creating the proper connector objects imperatively, and linking them to the state. It is worth noting that this rule matches to existing target elements, which are related to the same source element by the trace information. In this way, the join point to weave the elements is defined based on the trace information.

7   Related Work

We have illustrated this paper with an example product line which has been implemented using the approach proposed by Voelter in [13]. In this proposal, variability in transformation is a key issue. Although we have not explained in detail how to implement variability in transformations, the mechanism explained Section 4 can be used for this purpose.

In [14] an infrastructure for defining model transformation chains is presented. It studies the problems involved in reusing transformations written in different languages within a transformation chain. However, it does not propose any concrete mechanism to compose transformation definitions, although it mentions as future work relying on trace information to achieve composition.

Transformation reuse at rule-level has been addressed in several works. In [2], an study of rule-based mechanisms to modularize transformation definitions is presented. Transformation languages such as Tefkat [4], ATL [15], Viatra [3] or QVT[16] provide mechanisms for fine-grained reuse, that is, reuse of rule definitions. On the other hand, reuse at a coarse-grained level has not been extensively treated. In [17] an approach based on the transformation pattern is presented. Instead of establishing constraints on the source and target metamodels, transformations are created to adapt models to the expected metamodel. Higher-order transformations is also a means to tackle transformation reuse [15][18]. Regarding model transformation languages and their mechanisms for coarse-grained reuse, we have compared RubyTL with oAw's Xtend [13] and ATL [15].

Xtend is an imperative model transformation language, based on transformation functions, which includes explicit support for transformation aspects. This mechanism is suitable for factorizing common transformation code but not for composition of transformations using the strategies explained in 6.

The ATL language provides a facility called *superimposition* which allows several transformations to be superimposed on top of each other, yielding a final transformation containing the union of all transformation rules and helpers. It is a white-box mechanism, like a form of copy-paste, which is well-suited to reusing rules within related transformations, especially when combined with rule inheritance. On the other hand, it is not a good mechanism for composing independent transformations, since they would need to expose their implementation.

In ATL, naming conflicts are solved by adding the metamodel package name as part of the classifier's name. The problem of this approach is that it does not permit metamodel variation [14], since it relies on the package name, making it impossible to use different versions of the same metamodel.

Finally, regarding QVT, it provides reuse mechanisms at rule level, such as rule inheritance [16], but it does not provide any coarser-grained composition mechanism. Also, with respect to the notion of model type explained in Section 2, our approach coincides with that adopted by the QVT specification (in particular with effective type conformance). However, we propose to allow a model to conform to several metamodels, while in QVT a model can conform only to one metamodel.

8   Conclusions and Future Work

Model transformation reuse is an important issue for model driven development to succeed when applied to large projects. Techniques and constructs at model transformation level are needed for abstracting, selecting, specializing and integrating reusable transformation definitions.

In this paper, we have presented two approaches intended to factorize and compose transformation definitions. Through a running example we have shown the problems involved and how to solve them in RubyTL. Anyway, the approaches are applicable to other languages. Beyond addressing factorization and composition of model transformations, other important contributions of this work are:

- We have shown the constraints regarding metamodels and transformation reuse, and we have tackled these contraints using the idea of model type.
- We have given a proposal to make model element creation independent of the concrete types set in transformation rules, so that a black box approach for transformation composition can be achieved.
- We have illustrated our approach with a small, but not trivial implementation of a software product line using MDD. It is available for download at *http://gts.inf.um.es/age*.

Regarding future work, an interesting issue to be studied is whether it is possible to achieve external transformation composition using these approaches. We are studying how to "connect" different languages by means of trace information.

Acknowledgments

This work has been partially supported by Fundación Seneca (Murcia, Spain), grant 05645/PI/07. Also, we would like to thank pure-systems for supporting us by letting us use its variability managment tool: pure::variants.

References

1. Krueger, C.W.: Software reuse. ACM Comput. Surv. 24(2), 131–183 (1992)
2. Kurtev, I., van den Berg, K., Jouault, F.: Rule-based modularization in model transformation languages illustrated with ATL. Sci. Comput. Program 68(3), 111–127 (2007)
3. Balogh, A., Varró, D.: Pattern composition in graph transformation rules. In: European Workshop on Composition of Model Transformations, Bilbao, Spain (July 2006)
4. Lawley, M., Raymond, K.: Implementing a practical declarative logic-based model transformation engine. In: SAC 2007: Proceedings of the 2007 ACM symposium on Applied computing, pp. 971–977. ACM, New York (2007)
5. Sánchez, J., García, J., Menarguez, M.: RubyTL: A Practical, Extensible Transformation Language. In: Rensink, A., Warmer, J. (eds.) ECMDA-FA 2006. LNCS, vol. 4066, pp. 158–172. Springer, Heidelberg (2006)
6. Voelter, M., Groher, I.: Product line implementation using aspect-oriented and model-driven software development. In: SPLC 2007: Proceedings of the 11th International Software Product Line Conference (SPLC 2007), Washington, DC, USA, pp. 233–242. IEEE Computer Society, Los Alamitos (2007)
7. Steel, J., Jzquel, J.-M.: On model typing. Journal of Software and Systems Modeling (SoSyM) 6(4), 452–468 (2007)
8. Kleppe, A.: MCC: A model transformation environment. In: Rensink, A., Warmer, J. (eds.) ECMDA-FA 2006. LNCS, vol. 4066, pp. 173–187. Springer, Heidelberg (2006)
9. Cuadrado, J.S., Molina, J.G.: A phasing mechanism for model transformation languages. In: SAC 2007: Proceedings of the 2007 ACM symposium on Applied computing, pp. 1020–1024. ACM Press, New York (2007)
10. Cuadrado, J.S., Molina, J.G.: Building domain-specific languages for model-driven development. IEEE Softw. 24(5), 48–55 (2007)
11. Fabro, M.D.D., Bézivin, J., Valduriez, P.: Weaving models with the eclipse amw plugin. In: Eclipse Modeling Symposium, Eclipse Summit Europe 2006, Esslingen, Germany (2006)
12. Gamma, E., Helm, R., Johnson, R., Vlissides, J.: Design Patterns: Elements of Reusable Object-Oriented Software. Addison Wesley, Reading (1995)
13. Voelter, M., Groher, I.: Handling variability in model transformations and generators. In: Proceedings of the 7th OOPSLA Workshop on Domain-Specific Modeling (DSM07) (2007)
14. Vanhooff, B., Ayed, D., Van Baelen, S., Joosen, W., Berbers, Y.: UniTI: A Unified Transformation Infrastructure. In: Engels, G., Opdyke, B., Schmidt, D.C., Weil, F. (eds.) MODELS 2007. LNCS, vol. 4735, pp. 31–45. Springer, Heidelberg (2007)
15. Jouault, F., Kurtev, I.: Transforming Models with ATL. In: Bruel, J.-M. (ed.) MoDELS 2005. LNCS, vol. 3844. Springer, Heidelberg (2006)
16. OMG. Final adopted specification for MOF 2.0 Query/View/Transformation (2005), www.omg.org/docs/ptc/05-11-01.pdf
17. Willink, E.D., Harris, P.J.: The side transformation pattern: Making transforms modular and reusable. Electr. Notes Theor. Comput. Sci. 127(3), 17–29 (2005)
18. Oldevik, J., Haugen, O.: Higher-order transformations for product lines. In: SPLC 2007: Proceedings of the 11th International Software Product Line Conference, Washington, DC, USA, pp. 243–254. IEEE Computer Society, Los Alamitos (2007)

Code Generation by Model Transformation
A Case Study in Transformation Modularity

Zef Hemel, Lennart C.L. Kats, and Eelco Visser

Software Engineering Research Group, Delft University of Technology,
The Netherlands
Z.Hemel@tudelft.nl, L.C.L.Kats@tudelft.nl,
visser@acm.org

Abstract. The realization of model-driven software development requires effective techniques for implementing code generators. In this paper, we present a case study of *code generation by model transformation* with Stratego, a high-level transformation language based on the paradigm of rewrite rules with programmable strategies that integrates model-to-model, model-to-code, and code-to-code transformations. The use of *concrete object syntax* guarantees syntactic correctness of code patterns, and enables the subsequent transformation of generated code. The composability of strategies supports *two dimensions of transformation modularity*. *Vertical* modularity is achieved by designing a generator as a pipeline of model-to-model transformations that gradually transforms a high-level input model to an implementation. *Horizontal* modularity is achieved by supporting the definition of plugins which implement all aspects of a language feature. We discuss the application of these techniques in the implementation of WebDSL, a domain-specific language for dynamic web applications with a rich data model.

1   Introduction

Model-driven software development aims at improving productivity and maintainability of software by raising the level of abstraction from source code in a general purpose language to high-level, domain-specific models such that developers can concentrate on application logic rather than the accidental complexity of low-level implementation details. The essence of the approach is to shift the knowledge about these implementation details from the minds of programmers to the templates of *code generators* that automatically translate models into implementations. Since the code generators themselves need to be developed and maintained as well, effective languages and tools for implementing generators are crucial for realizing model-driven software development. Many paradigms and technologies for transformation and generation are under development. In order to compare the various proposals, large scale case studies are needed. To this end we are developing WebDSL, a domain-specific language (DSL) for modeling dynamic web applications with a rich data model. In earlier work we described the development of WebDSL as a case study in domain-specific language engineering, i.e. a method to find the design of a new DSL [24].

A. Vallecillo, J. Gray, A. Pierantonio (Eds.): ICMT 2008, LNCS 5063, pp. 183–198, 2008.

In this paper, we discuss a case study in *code generation by model transformation*, an approach to the organization of DSL implementations that we use in the implementation of WebDSL. We have implemented the approach with the Stratego/XT program transformation system [23,5]. Stratego is a high-level transformation language that integrates model-to-model, model-to-code, and code-to-code transformations. The language provides *rewrite rules* for the definition of basic transformations, and *programmable strategies* for building complex transformations that control the application of rules. The use of *concrete object syntax* [22] in the definition of transformation rules improves the readability of rules, guarantees syntactic correctness of code patterns, *and* supports the subsequent transformation of generated code, which is not the case for text-based template engines such as Velocity [19] or xPand [25].

The composability of strategies supports *two dimensions of transformation modularity* used to realize separation of concerns in DSL implementations. First, *vertical modularization* is used to reduce the semantic gap between input and output model. Rather than directly generating code from the input model, the generator is constructed as a pipeline of model-to-model transformations that gradually transform a high-level input model to a low-level implementation model. Since even the generated code has a structured model representation to which transformations can be applied, any restrictions in modularity of the target language can be alleviated by extending it with new constructs to support better modularity. For example, we have created an extension of Java with partial classes, interface extraction, and name generation in order to simplify code generation rules.

Secondly, the approach supports *horizontal modularization*, that is, the separate definition of all transformations for a single language construct. This is the basis for *meta-model extensibility* through *generator extensibility*. The basic transformation pipeline provides an implementation for a base language. Extensions to the base language are implemented as plug-ins that extend the basic pipeline. Combining horizontal and vertical extensibility makes it possible to implement new domain-specific abstractions as plug-ins to the base language.

In the next section we give a brief introduction to WebDSL and the architecture of its implementation. In the rest of the paper we discuss the core ideas of the code generation by model transformation approach, i.e., code generation by rewriting (Section 3), model-to-model transformations to reduce input models to implementation models (Section 4), the role of semantic analyses and annotations (Section 5), and modularity and extensibility of the transformations (Section 6). We compare the approach to related work in Section 7.

2   WebDSL

WebDSL is a domain-specific language for the implementation of dynamic web applications with a rich data model. The language provides sub-languages for the specification of data models and for the definition of custom *pages* for viewing

```
entity Blog {                          define view page blog(b : Blog) {
  title   :: String (name)               main()
  entries <> List<BlogEntry>             title{ text(b.title) }
}                                        define body() {
                                           section{
entity BlogEntry {                           header{ output(b) }
  blog     -> Blog                           for(entry : BlogEntry in b.entries
              (inverse=Blog.entries)                   order by entry.created desc) {
  title   :: String (name)                     section {
  author  -> User                                header { output(entry) }
  created :: Date                                par{ "by " output(entry.author)
  content :: WikiText                                 " at " output(entry.created) }
}                                                par{ output(entry.content) } } } } } }
```

Fig. 1. Example WebDSL data model and page definition

and editing objects in the data model. Fig. 1 illustrates this by means of a data model and view page for a blogging application.

The data model introduces *entity* definitions (e.g., `Blog`, `BlogEntry`), consisting of *properties* with a name and a type. Types of properties are either value types (indicated by `::`) or associations to other entities defined in the data model. Value types are basic data types such as `String` and `Date`, but also domain-specific types such as `WikiText` that carry additional functionality. Associations are composite (the referrer owns the object, indicated by `<>`) or referential (the object may be shared, indicated by `->`). The `inverse` annotation on a property declares a relation with automatic synchronization of two properties.

Page definitions consist of the name of the page, the names and types of the objects used as parameters, and a presentation of the data contained in the parameter objects. For example, the `blog(b : Blog)` definition in Fig. 1 creates a page showing all blog entries for blog `b`. WebDSL provides basic markup operators such as `section`, `header`, and `list` for defining the structure of a page. Data from the object parameters (and the objects they refer to) are injected in the page by data access operations such as `output`. Collections of data can be presented using the iterator construct `for`, which can filter and sort the elements of a collection. It is also possible to present content conditionally on some property of an object, for example, whether the user has the right access control permissions. User-defined *templates* allow the developer to define reusable chunks of WebDSL code. For example, the `main()` template used in Fig. 1 defines a general set-up for the page (navigation sidebars and menus) that is shared among many pages of the application. Finally, WebDSL supports separation of concerns by means of a module mechanism, and a separate sub-language for access control, which is beyond the scope of this paper.

The architecture of the WebDSL generator follows the four-level model organization of Bézivin [3] as illustrated in Fig. 2. At the M_3 level we find the SDF metametamodel, which is the grammar of the Syntax Definition Formalism SDF, which is defined in (and thus conforms to) itself [21]. At the M_2 level we find the WebDSL meta-model, i.e., the grammar of WebDSL defined in SDF. At the M_1 level we find WebDSL models of web applications, consisting of entity and page definitions. At the M_0 level we find the actual web applications consisting of Java classes and XHTML pages, which represent the models at the M_1 level.

In the implementation of WebDSL that we have realized [24], the M_0 systems are based upon the Java/Seam architecture, consisting of high-level application frameworks, such as the Java Persistence API (JPA), JavaServer Faces (JSF), and the Seam web framework. For each entity definition, a corresponding entity class is generated with fields, getters, and setters for the properties of the entity, annotated for object-relational mapping according to the JPA. For each page definition, a JSF XHTML page, a Seam Java bean class, and an accompanying interface are generated. In the following sections we discuss the organization of the generator as a pipeline of model-to-model transformations, and the techniques used to realize these transformations. The transformations are expressed in the Stratego transformation language [23,5], which is based on the paradigm of rewrite rules with programmable rewriting strategies.

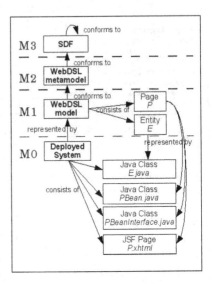

Fig. 2. Organization of models and artifacts of the WebDSL generator

3   Code Generation by Rewriting

WebDSL is a textual, domain-specific language and its M_2 meta-model is a grammar describing the valid sentences of that language. From the grammar, we automatically generate a parser, which transforms the textual representation of a model to an abstract syntax tree (AST). The AST conforms to a regular tree grammar, another M_2 meta-model that defines a set of valid trees, and which is obtained automatically from the grammar. All subsequent transformations are applied to the AST corresponding to the textual representation of the model. The WebDSL generator transforms high-level models into Java code and XML files. These target languages are also described by a grammar and a derived abstract syntax definition. All transformations are expressed in Stratego, which can apply transformations to any models with an abstract syntax definition.

The WebDSL generator can be decomposed into three main steps, which can be expressed and combined in Stratego as a *strategy*. A strategy is essentially a function that controls the order of application

```
webdsl-to-seam =
  import-modules
  ; generate-code
  ; output-generated-files
```

of more basic transformations. The basic strategy `webdsl-to-seam` is defined as a sequence of three steps, which are applied to the input model. First, starting with the main module of an application, all imported modules are parsed. Next, the combined model is transformed to a model of the generated Java and XML files. Finally, these code models are written to files and packaged for deployment to a web server. In later sections we will discuss refinements of this basic strategy.

3.1   Code Generation Rules

The elementary transformations that are combined by strategies are rewrite rules of the form L : p1->p2 where s. The name L of a rule can be used to invoke it in a strategy. When applied, the left-hand side pattern p1 is matched against the subject term, binding any variables in the pattern to corresponding sub-terms of the subject term. When the match succeeds, and the condition s succeeds as well, the subject term is replaced with the instantia-

```
parameter-to-bean-property :
  |[ x : srt ]| ->
  <emit-java-code> |[
    @Partial class x_PageBean {
      @RequestParameter("~x") private Long x#Id;
      private t _#x;
      public void set#x(t x) { _#x = x; }
      public t   get#x()     { return x; }
      @Partial void initializeParameter() { bstm* }
    }
  ]|
  where bstm*      := <parameter-to-initialization>
    ; t            := <defined-java-type> srt
    ; x_PageBean := <CurrentPageBean>
```

Fig. 3. Rewrite rule transforming WebDSL source to Java target code using concrete syntax

tion of the right-hand side pattern p2. Rewrite rules are used for code generation by translating a fragment of the source language on the left-hand side to a fragment of the target language on the right-hand side. This is illustrated in Fig. 3 with a rewrite rule that rewrites a WebDSL page parameter, such as b : Blog in the page definition of Fig. 1, into a fragment of Java code that includes fields, accessors, and initialization code implementing the processing of a page parameter in a Seam page bean.

Rewrite rules in Stratego can make use of the *concrete syntax* of the transformed language [22] using the |[and]| quotation construct. For example, a Java return statement can be expressed as |[return true;]|, rather than the abstract syntax form Return(Some(Lit(True()))). A language's concrete syntax is usually more concise and more familiar than its abstract syntax. The Stratego compiler parses concrete syntax quotations at compile-time, checking their syntax and replacing them with equivalent abstract syntax fragments.

Using *meta-variables* in concrete syntax fragments (written in *italics*), the rule in Fig. 3 matches any parameter x of type (or "sort") srt. In the where clause of the rule, a number of meta-variables are set for use in the produced Java fragment. For instance, t is set to the Java equivalent of WebDSL type srt, and $x\_PageBean$ is set to the current page bean.

In Stratego, the application of rewrite rules is under the control of *programmable strategies*, such that transformations can be explicitly staged. For example, the WebDSL generate-code transformation strategy uses a top-down traversal to visit all model elements for which code needs to be generated. This is expressed using the generic topdown traversal strategy as follows:

```
generate-code = topdown(try(argument-to-bean-property <+ ...))
```

Different rewrite rules are combined using the `<+` operator, which tries to apply each rule in the given order. Using the `try` strategy, the `generate-code` strategy will *try* to apply these rules, but will not fail if no rules are applicable, so that the `topdown` traversal will proceed even if none of the rules match.

3.2   Transforming Generated Code

In Stratego, generated code has a structured representation just like the input model of the generator — as opposed to the flat textual representation produced by traditional template engines. Therefore, additional transformations can be applied to generated code. This enables the use of an enriched version of the target language in generation, reducing the semantic gap between model and code, and thus simplifying the generator by capturing common generation patterns, and ensuring separation of concerns in their implementation.

For instance, in Fig. 3, the generated Java code takes the form of a *partial class*. That is, the rule defines only part of the generated class, as indicated by the `@Partial` annotation. In a later stage of the code generation process, all partial class fragments for the same class are merged. This approach eliminates the need for maintaining an aggregated model at this stage of the generator. In particular, the generated fragment is not used locally to replace the model fragment. Rather, in this case using `emit-java-code`, all code fragments are collected centrally for later assembly. Similarly, the generated `initializeParameter` method is a `@Partial` method, so that it can be extended for other page parameters. The order in which the statements of partial methods are merged is unspecified, thus no dependencies between statements in different definitions of a partial method should exist, an invariant that should be maintained by the developer of the generator.

Another extension of Java that is designed to simplify code generation, is the `#` identifier concatenation operator. It is used to generate the names of accessors, field, and classes that are commonly built up from different parts. For example, for accessors, `get#x` is used to generate a 'get' accessor for meta-variable x. In a later stage of the generator, such concatenations are evaluated and capitalized according to the Java conventions (e.g., using *camelCase* for method names).

Generated page bean classes require a matching interface definition. This interface is automatically generated in a separate generation stage: after merging all partial classes, such an interface is extracted from each generated class annotated with a `@RequiresInterface` annotation.

4   Semantic Analysis and Annotation

Not all models that conform to the WebDSL syntax are valid. For instance, identifiers may refer to a nonexisting entity, property, or function. Such models violate the static semantic constraints of WebDSL. A

```
webdsl-to-seam =
  import-modules
  ; typecheck
  ; generate-code
  ; output-generated-files
```

separate typechecking stage of the generator checks these constraints, and reports any violations found. The semantic information gathered at this stage is also used to provide context information for other transformations, as we will discuss in the next section.

Typechecking involves a *context-sensitive* global-to-local transformation in which type information is propagated from the declaration site of an identifier to its use sites. Stratego provides support for such transformations through its mechanism of *dynamic rewrite rules* [6], which allows the definition of new rewrite rules at run-time. For example, the `typecheck-variable` rule in Fig. 4 defines the checking

```
typecheck-variable :
  Var(x) -> Var(x){Type(t)}
  where if not(t := <TypeOf> x) then
          typecheck-error(|
            ["Undeclared variable ",x," referenced"])
        end
declare-page-argument :
  |[ x : srt ]| -> |[ x : srt ]|
  where if not(<TypeExists> srt) then
          typecheck-error(|
            ["Illegal type ",srt," for parameter ",x]]
        else
          rules( TypeOf : x -> srt )
        end
```

Fig. 4. Typechecking with dynamic rules

of the *use* of a variable with abstract syntax `Var(x)`. The dynamic rule `TypeOf` is used to rewrite the identifier `x` to its type `t`. If this fails an error is reported. Otherwise, the variable is *annotated* with its type. The `TypeOf` rule is *defined* when a variable declaration, which may be a page parameter or a local variable, is encountered. For example, the `declare-page-argument` rule checks that the type used in the declaration of a page parameter is a valid type (using the `TypeExists` dynamic rule). If the type does exist, the `rules` construct is used to define a new instance of the `TypeOf` rule specific to the values of `x` and `srt` encountered in the declaration. Dynamic rule *scopes* are used to limit the scope of rules to the traversal of a fragment of the model. For example, the `TypeOf` rule for a page parameter is valid only during the traversal of that page. Similarly, functions and `for` loops also define a local scope.

5   Model-to-Model Transformations

Extending the target language helps in simplifying the translation from models to code. However, directly translating input models to code may still require complex transformations, in particular, when adding higher-level abstractions. Instead of a complex model-to-code translation, the WebDSL generator pipeline consists of several stages of model-to-model transformations that reduce models in the full WebDSL language to *core* WebDSL, which is domain-specific, yet relatively close to the

```
webdsl-to-seam =
  import-modules
  ; typecheck
  ; normalize-syntax
  ; expand-page-templates
  ; derive
  ; merge-emitted-decs
  ; generate-code
  ; merge-partial-classes
  ; output-generated-files
```

target platform. As a result, only normalized core language constructs have to be transformed to the target platform during code generation, which improves retargetability. All the abstractions built on top of the core language can be ignored by the back-end. Staging the transformations in a pipeline is a case of *vertical modularity*; each stage is a separately defined transformation that is only concerned with one aspect of the code generator. In this section we illustrate this with a discussion of typical transformations applied in such a pipeline: syntactic normalization, and the implementation of user-defined and generative abstractions. We also discuss the problem of preserving or reproducing the annotations produced by semantic analyses.

5.1   Syntactic Normalization

Syntactic abstractions, also known as syntactic sugar, provide new language constructs that support expression of functionality that is already provided by the base language in a more compact manner. The implementation of such abstractions can often be realized by means of simple local-to-local transformation rules (Fig. 5), but sometimes, more complex local-to-global rules (Fig. 7) are needed.

```
NormalizeSyntax :
  |[ text(e1,e2,e*){} elem* ]| ->
  |[ text(e1) text(e2,e*){} elem* ]|
NormalizeSyntax :
  |[ for(x : srt in e1
            order by e2){elem*} ]| ->
  |[ for(x : srt in e1
            where true
            order by e2){elem*} ]|
normalize-syntax =
  topdown(repeat(NormalizeSyntax))
```

Fig. 5. Local-to-local syntactic normalization rules

A local-to-local rewrite replaces a model fragment with another without using or producing other parts of the model, as illustrated by the examples in Fig. 5. The first rule normalizes applications of the `text` construct with multiple arguments to a list of applications of `text` with a single argument. More precisely, it splits off the first argument of a multi-argument application. Repeated application of the rule ensures that only singleton applications remain. For example, the application `text(blog.title, ": ", blog.author)` is reduced to `text(blog.title) text(": ") text(blog.author)`. Similarly, the second rule rewrites an occurrence of the `for` statement without a `where` clause to one with the universally valid `where true` clause. These normalizations ensure that later stages of the code generator only need to deal with one syntactic variant, i.e., singleton applications of `text`, and `for` statements with a `where` clause. The application of normalization rules is controlled by the `normalize-syntax` strategy, which performs a top-down traversal, which repeatedly applies rules to each element.

A local-to-global transformation rewrites a local element, but also produces elements that should be placed elsewhere in the model. An example of such a transformation is the lifting of list comprehensions. These provide declarative manipulations and queries on lists and sets, i.e., a combined map, filter and sort operation. As an example, consider the expression in Fig. 6, which retrieves the list of blog entries created after `date`, sorted in reverse chronological order. Such expressions can be computed by means of the `for` *statement* of WebDSL, as shown in the second part of Fig. 6. Statements, however, may not be used as expressions.

```
[e.title
 for(e : BlogEntry in b.entries
     where e.created > date
     order by e.created desc)]
```

```
globals { function lcf_33
(b : Blog, date : Date) {
  var y : List<String> := [];
  for(e : BlogEntry in b.entries
      where e.created > date
      order by e.created desc)
  { y.add(e.title); } } }
```

Fig. 6. List comprehension and implementation

The transformation in Fig. 7 *lifts* a list comprehension to a new global function definition and replaces the expression with a call to the generated function The free variables of the list comprehension expression are extracted and passed as parameters to the generated function. The `emit-webdsl-dec` rule takes the newly defined function

```
Lift :
  |[ [e for(x : srt in e2 where e3 order by e4)] ]| ->
  |[ x_fun(arg*) ]|
  where x_fun     := <newname> "lcf"
      ; free-vars := <collect-free-vars> (e,e2,e3,e4)
      ; param*    := <map(build-param)> free-vars
      ; arg*      := <map(build-arg)> free-vars
      ; <emit-webdsl-dec> |[
          globals {
            function x_fun(param*) : List<srt> {
              var y : List<srt> := [];
              for(x : srt in e2 where e3 order by e4)
                { y.add(e); }
              return y; } } ]|
```

Fig. 7. Local-to-global syntactic normalization

and stores it in a dynamic rule. Declarations emitted in this manner are merged into the model during the `merge-emitted-decs` generator stage. (A pattern also applied in the form of partial classes during code generation).

In a global-to-local transformation, constructs are locally transformed using (global) context information. The typechecking rules in the previous section are an example. Another example is the expansion (inlining) of user-defined templates by the `expand-page-templates` strategy. It collects top-level and local template definitions and replaces calls to these template definitions by their bodies, substituting actual parameters for formal parameters. This mechanism allows WebDSL developers to capture reoccurring patterns in page definitions for reuse.

5.2 Generative Abstractions

Generative abstractions are abstractions that explicitly invoke the generator to derive some functionality. Here we discuss an example of type-based derivation. Consider the edit page in Fig. 9, which provides an interface for editing the values of the properties of a `BlogEntry`. Depending on the type of the property, a different interface element is used; a simple string input box for `title`, a select box for `author`, and

```
DeriveInput :
  |[ input(e){} ]| ->
  |[ select(s : srt, "Select", e) ]|
  where SimpleSort(srt) := <get-type> e
      ; <defined-entity> SimpleSort(srt)
DeriveOutput :
  |[ output(e){} ]| ->
  |[ navigate(x_view(e)){text(e.name)} ]|
  where SimpleSort(s) := <get-type> e
      ; <defined-entity> SimpleSort(s)
      ; x_view := <view-page-for-entity> s
```

Fig. 8. Type-based derivation

a text area for `content`. The definition of the edit page in Fig. 9 simply invokes input(e.*prop*) to declare an edit interface for property *prop*. The specific implementation for each input type is derived from the type of the expression. For example, the `DeriveInput` rule in Fig. 8 derives for an `input` of a property with a 'defined entity' type a select box for that type. Similarly, the `DeriveOutput` rule derives a rendering mechanism for an expression based on its type. For example, the use of output(e.author)

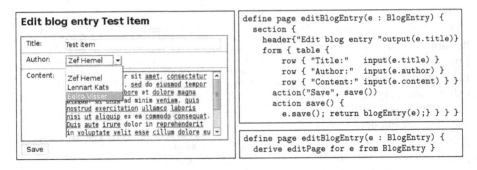

Fig. 9. Screenshot of an edit page with low-level and high-level page definition

in a page definition results in a link (`navigate`) to the view page for the object that is referred to by `e.author`. The `e.author.name` property of that object is used as anchor for the link.

The next step in generative abstraction is the generation of complete page definitions. The structure of an edit page can often be fairly straightforward, say a table with a row for each property with an appropriate input interface. Such a structure can be derived automatically from the declaration of the entity. The implementation of `editBlogEntry` in the lower right of Fig. 9 uses the `derive` construct to automatically generate the implementation of the body of the edit page from the `BlogEntry` entity. The `derive-page` rule in Fig. 10 implements this derivation. The rows of the table are generated by a map of the `derive-edit-row` transformation over the properties of the entity *srt*, which are obtained by applying the

```
derive-page :
  |[ derive editPage for x from srt ]| ->
  |[ section{ header{"Edit " srt " " text(x.name)}
       form { table { row* }
         action("Save", save()) } }
     action save() {
       x.save(); return x_view(x); } ]|
  where x_view := <decapitalize-string> x
      ; prop* := <entity-properties> srt
      ; row*  := <map(derive-edit-row(|x))> prop*
derive-edit-row(|x) :
  |[y k srt (anno*)]| -> |[row{x_text input(x.y)}]|
  where x_text := <concat-strings> [x, ": "]
```

Fig. 10. Rules to derive edit page elements

dynamic rule `entity-properties`.

5.3 Restoring Annotations

As a model undergoes transformation, type annotations may be lost. Rewrite rules may introduce new variables or entire fragments of code that do not include type annotations. For example, the `derive-edit-row` rule in Fig. 10 does not attach a type annotation to the expression of the `input` element it generates. Defining the rules to create correct type annotations would

```
webdsl-to-seam =
  import-modules        ; typecheck
  ; normalize-syntax    ; typecheck
  ; expand-page-templates ; typecheck
  ; derive              ; typecheck
  ; merge-emitted-decs
  ; generate-code
  ; merge-partial-classes
  ; output-generated-files
```

be quite tedious and would require duplication of the knowledge encapsulated in the typechecking rules. Following the principle of separation of concerns, the typechecking rules are used to introduce type annotations in freshly generated code. A question then is what the granularity of applying typechecking rules should be. Since the type checker is currently defined as a complete traversal over the model, reapplying the type checker after each application of a transformation rule would be prohibitive. Instead, we take a rather course grained approach, re-applying the type checker after each transformation stage, as illustrated in the strategy above. This strategy requires these stages to be designed such that no transformation opportunities are missed by missing type annotations. Combination of analysis and transformation in an efficient way is a topic for research; it would be desirable to automatically infer an optimal incremental analysis strategy.

6   Transformation Modularity and Extensibility

Since its conception, the WebDSL generator has grown more and more complex. Initially, the generator was constructed in a centralized fashion, with a single *"God rule"* associated with each generated artifact. Much like a "God class", an anti-pattern in object-oriented programming, such a God rule dispatches a large number of smaller transformation rules to generate a monolithic target artifact (e.g., a Java class). As new language extensions were added, these rules grew to a size that they would no longer fit on a single screen. As such, this pattern was quickly identified as a code smell that hindered the extensibility and maintainability of the generator.

```
Derive :
  |[ input(e){} ]| -> |[ inputDate(e){} ]|
  where SimpleSort("Date") := <type-of> e

Derive :
  |[ output(e){} ]| -> |[ outputDate(e){} ]|
  where SimpleSort("Date") := <type-of> e

GenerateXML :
  .. generate xhtml controls for
  inputDate and outputDate ...

GenerateJavaExpr :
  |[ Date(d) ]| ->
  |[ org.webdsl.tools.Utils.parseDate(e1) ]|
  where e1 := <expression-to-java> d

GenerateJavaExpr :
  |[ now() ]| -> |[ new java.util.Date() ]|
```

Fig. 11. Modular definition of the primitive type `Date`

The employment of God rules was the unfortunate result of the structure of the target metamodel: Java provides only limited means of modularization of classes. Other platforms, such as C#, offer partial classes (but not partial methods), that can help further subdivide classes into smaller units. The lack of such a construct makes it difficult to decompose rewrite rules that generate large classes. This platform limitation can be resolved by extension of the target language, in the form of partial classes and methods. In a separate generator stage (`expand-partial-classes`), all partial classes and methods are merged for processing with a regular Java compiler.

To support both modularity and extensibility of transformation definitions, Stratego provides the notion of *strategy and rule definition extension*. Strategies and rules can be extended by declaring a new instance with the same name. All such definitions are merged together, and evaluated in an unspecified order when invoked, until one of the definitions succeeds or all fail. The different stages of the generator make use of this facility, by defining rules that are extended in separate transformation modules. For example, Fig. 11 shows an implementation of an extension of WebDSL with a `Date` value type that makes use of this facility. It extends the definition of the `Derive` rule used in the derivation stage, and a number of rules in the code generation stage. (Not shown here are the mappings to the Java `Date` type and the corresponding JPA annotations.) Another, more elaborate extension that has been implemented is the addition of access control constraints to the model, which is outside the context of this paper.

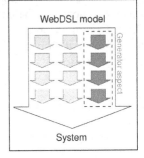

Fig. 12. Dimensions of modularity

As seen in the preceding section, transformations for an aspect of the generator can be divided into different stages. This *vertical modularity* helps in separation of concerns and retargetability. Further modularity can be achieved in a second dimension, by subdividing rules that operate on a single level. This is a form of *horizontal modularity* and is supported by rule definition extension and generation of partial artifacts. Horizontal modularity is essential for the extensibility of the generator. Fig. 12 illustrates the two dimensions of the transformation architecture. Highlighted is a horizontal extension of the generator (such as the `Date` extension), which consists of a number of vertical transformation stages.

The definition extension feature of Stratego elegantly combines rewrite rules that operate on different elements of a source model. However, it will only evaluate a single rule if multiple rules are applicable to the same element (e.g., a page parameter that has different rules to generate Java and JSF code for the same page parameter). While Stratego does not offer a direct facility for this, we build upon the notion of strategy extension to accomplish this, as shown below.

By use of a `fail` statement at the end of each definition of `GenerateCode`, all alternatives will "fail", ensuring each will be tried.

```
GenerateCode =
    page-to-java; fail
GenerateCode =
    parameter-to-bean-property; fail
```

The result of the applications can then be collected as a side effect using dynamic rules (e.g., using `emit-java-code` in Fig. 3). This pattern efficiently achieves the desired composition of definitions. Direct language support and accompanying compile-time checks for this within Stratego could prove useful, and could prevent subtle bugs that may occur if an extension programmer now forgets to include `fail` at the end of a definition, or mistypes its name.

7   Discussion

Since the advent of model-driven engineering, several modeling methodologies and model transformation approaches have been introduced. A classification of a number of such systems is given in [7]. Various MDE toolkits provide model transformation and code generation facilities, many of which are based on OMG's MDA (openArchitectureWare [8], AMMA [12], AndroMDA [2]). These generally consist of a metamodeling language (MOF [16], Ecore, KM3 [9]), model transformation language (ATL [11], xTend [8]), code generation language (TCS [10], xPand [25], Velocity [19]), and a language to define the sequence of transformations (oAW's workflow language, Groovy scripting language).

Model management can be based on any algebraic datastructure such as trees, graphs, hypergraphs, or categories [4]. Most current MDE toolkits are based on graphs, while Stratego/XT uses trees. By combining trees with dynamic rules, graphs *can* be represented in Stratego, which makes it possible to model context-sensitive information that cannot easily be expressed using just trees.

Consistency management is an important issue in MDE [14]. It is possible to keep models consistent as part of transformations, but in practice this also tends to make transformations much more complex. In our approach we chose to separate the concern of typechecking from the model transformation at hand. The drawback of this approach is that models need to be reanalyzed after applying transformations. Incremental analysis and transformation techniques are an important research topic. By analyzing models before any transformations are performed, we detect inconsistencies early and can report them to the developer. However, problems that occur while the system is running turn out to be difficult to trace back to errors in the model. In the future, we intend to investigate the feasibility of origin tracking [20] to achieve code-to-model traceability.

Transformation languages such as ATL and xTend allow transformations to be separated in modules, similarly to Stratego. However, extensibility of transformations is more difficult to realize, especially if transformation extensions have to operate on the same modeling elements, which is forbidden in ATL, for instance. In existing MDE toolkits, vertical modularity in transformations is often realized using a separate workflow language, such as the oAW workflow language and Groovy in AndroMDA. Stratego not only integrates model-to-model and model-to-code transformations, but also the overall generator workflow. Thus, a single transformation composition language is used for micro and macro compositions.

Some approaches [26] generate partial artifacts through the use of partial classes, which are then combined by the regular compiler for the target language. However, these approaches only work if the target language supports these features. In our approach, code is treated as a model, while most MDE approaches generate code through the use of textual template engines, which produce plain text, not amenable to further transformation. By treating generated code as a model, it is possible to extend the target language and add convenient language features such as partial classes and methods, and interface extraction.

Many (visual) languages for modeling web applications have been developed, including WebML [13], MIDAS [17], OOWS [15], Netsilon [18], and UWE [1]. UWE generates JSP code via a model representation conforming to a JSP metamodel. Netsilon uses an intermediate language for code generation in order to increase retargetability of the generator. The other approaches use textual, usually template-based code generation.

8   Conclusions

In this paper we presented a case study of the *code generation by model transformation* approach applied in the development of WebDSL. WebDSL is a substantial DSL code generator, consisting of a total of 1300 rules and strategies (see Fig. 13). It has been employed for a number of web applications, most significantly the webdsl.org project website (which is currently used in production). The site features a generic project management interface, including a wiki-based documentation system, an issue tracker, blogs, and discussion forums. Fig. 13 gives an indication of the scale of the project: it is defined using 146 page and entity definitions, written in a total of 2366 lines of text. The code generated from these definitions spans nearly 80.000 lines of code. Even if this is not the volume of code one would produce manually for such an application, it seems justified to conclude that an order of magnitude reduction in code can be achieved. As such, we believe that employment of the WebDSL generator enables a significant gain in productivity, resulting from the high level of abstraction it provides.

We have shown how a pipeline of model-to-model transformations helps achieve high-level abstractions in models. By applying two-dimensional modularity—vertically in stages and horizontally in a core language and extensions—we ensure maintainability and extensibility of the generator. We have also demonstrated the benefits of generating models, rather than text, and how this technique aids horizontal modularity. The modular design of WebDSL provides a solid foundation for further research into higher-level domain-specific abstractions for web-based software systems. The approach should also be usable in the implementation of other DSLs. The approach can be further improved by research into incrementality of analysis and transformations, and the application of origin tracking.

134	**Modeling elements**
103	core model elements
1298	**Rules and Strategies**
459	in code generation stage
318	in model-to-model stage
277	in typechecking
126	rules for access control
	webdsl.org application
2366	lines in webdsl.org model
38395	lines of generated Java code
39216	lines of generated JSF code

Fig. 13. WebDSL statistics

Acknowledgments. This research was supported by NWO/JACQUARD project 638.001.610, *MoDSE: Model-Driven Software Evolution.*

References

1. Kraus, A.K.A., Koch, N.: Model-driven generation of web applications in UWE. In: Model-Driven Web Engineering (MDWE 2007), Como, Italy (July 2007)
2. AndroMDA.org. AndroMDA documentation (2007), http://galaxy.andromda.org

3. Bézivin, J.: On the unification power of models. Software and System Modeling 4(2), 171–188 (2005)
4. Bézivin, J.: Model Driven Engineering: An Emerging Technical Space. In: Lämmel, R., Saraiva, J., Visser, J. (eds.) GTTSE 2005. LNCS, vol. 4143, pp. 36–64. Springer, Heidelberg (2006)
5. Bravenboer, M., Kalleberg, K.T., Vermaas, R., Visser, E.: Stratego/XT 0.16. Components for transformation systems. In: Partial Evaluation and Program Manipulation (PEPM 2006), Charleston, South Carolina. ACM, New York (2006)
6. Bravenboer, M., van Dam, A., Olmos, K., Visser, E.: Program transformation with scoped dynamic rewrite rules. Fund. Informaticae 69(1–2), 123–178 (2006)
7. Czarnecki, K., Helsen, S.: Feature-based survey of model transformation approaches. IBM Systems Journal 45(3), 621–645 (2006)
8. Efftinge, S., Friese, P.: openArchitectureWare (2007), http://www.eclipse.org/gmt/oaw
9. Jouault, F., Bézivin, J.: KM3: a DSL for metamodel specification. In: Gorrieri, R., Wehrheim, H. (eds.) FMOODS 2006. LNCS, vol. 4037, pp. 171–185. Springer, Heidelberg (2006)
10. Jouault, F., Bézivin, J., Kurtev, I.: TCS: a DSL for the specification of textual concrete syntaxes in model engineering. In: Generative programming and component engineering (GPCE 2006), pp. 249–254. ACM Press, New York (2006)
11. Jouault, F., Kurtev, I.: Transforming Models with ATL. In: Bruel, J.-M. (ed.) MoDELS 2005. LNCS, vol. 3844, pp. 128–138. Springer, Heidelberg (2006)
12. Kurtev, I., Bézivin, J., Jouault, F., Valduriez, P.: Model-based DSL frameworks. In: Companion to OOPSLA 2006, pp. 602–616. ACM Press, New York (2006)
13. Brambilla, P.F.M., Comai, S., Matera, M.: Designing web applications with WebML and WebRatio. In: Rossi, G., et al. (eds.) Web Engineering: Modelling and Implementing Web Applications. Human-Computer Interaction Series. Springer, Heidelberg (2007)
14. Mens, T., van Gorp, P.: A taxonomy of model transformation. In: Graph and Model Transformation (GraMoT 2005), vol. 152, pp. 125–142 (March 2006)
15. Pastor, V.P.O., Fons, J.: OOWS: A method to develop web applications from web-oriented conceptual models. In: Web Oriented Software Technology (IWWOST 2003), pp. 65–70 (2003)
16. Object Management Group (OMG). Meta object facility (MOF) core specification. OMG available specification. Version 2.0 (January 2006), http://www.omg.org
17. Cáceres, B.V.P., Marcos, E.: A MDA-Based approach for web information system development. In: Proceedings of Workshop in Software Model Engineering (2003)
18. Pierre-Alain Muller, F.F., Studer, P., Bézivin, J.: Platform independent web application modeling and development with Netsilon. Software and Systems Modeling 4(4), 424–442 (2005)
19. The Apache Foundation. Velocity User Guide (2007), http://velocity.apache.org/engine/devel/user-guide.html
20. van Deursen, A., Klint, P., Tip, F.: Origin tracking. Journal of Symbolic Computation 15(5/6), 523–545 (1993)
21. Visser, E.: Syntax Definition for Language Prototyping. PhD thesis, University of Amsterdam (September 1997)
22. Visser, E.: Meta-programming with Concrete Object Syntax. In: Batory, D., Consel, C., Taha, W. (eds.) GPCE 2002. LNCS, vol. 2487, Springer, Heidelberg (2002)
23. Visser, E.: Program Transformation with Stratego/XT. In: Lengauer, C., Batory, D., Consel, C., Odersky, M. (eds.) Domain-Specific Program Generation. LNCS, vol. 3016, pp. 216–238. Springer, Heidelberg (2004)

24. Visser, E.: WebDSL: A case study in domain-specific language engineering. In: Generative and Transformational Techniques in Software Engineering (GTTSE 2007). LNCS. Springer, Heidelberg (2008)
25. Voelter, M., Groher, I.: Handling variability in model transformations and generators. In: Domain-Specific Modeling (DSM 2007) (2007)
26. Warmer, J.B., Kleppe, A.G.: Building a flexible software factory using partial domain specific models. In: Domain-Specific Modeling (DSM 2006), Portland, Oregon, USA, pp. 15–22 (October 2006)

Application of Reflection in Model Transformation Languages

Ivan Kurtev

Software Engineering Group, University of Twente,
P.O. Box 217, 7500 AE, Enschede, the Netherlands
kurtev@ewi.utwente.nl

Abstract. Computational reflection is a well known technique applied in many existing programming languages ranging from functional to object-oriented languages. In this paper we study the possibilities and benefits of introducing and using reflection in rule-based model transformation languages. The paper identifies some language abstractions to achieve structural and behavioral reflection. Every reflective feature is motivated by examples of problems derived from the experience with currently used transformation languages. Example solutions are given by using an experimental language with reflective capabilities.

The paper also outlines possible implementation strategies for adding reflection to a language and discusses their advantages and disadvantages.

Keywords: reflection, model transformation languages, MDE, MISTRAL.

1 Introduction

Computational reflection is a technique applied in many programming languages to solve non-trivial problems. Usually, adding reflective capabilities to a language is motivated by the need to improve certain quality attributes in the programs such as run-time adaptability, long-term maintainability, modularity and composability, and others.

Reflection may be applied to languages based on different paradigms. It was first proposed by Brian Smith in the context of Lisp [21] and later was successfully introduced in object-oriented languages [16] Smalltalk, CLOS, Java [3], etc.

The problems that may be tackled by using reflection also span a wide spectrum. It was shown that debugging and tracing may benefit from reflective techniques [15]. Composition Filters approach to object composition [1] is based on a restricted reflection on message passing between objects. The application of reflection in aspect-oriented programming is well studied in number of works [20, 22]. A limited form of reflection (*introspection*) was introduced in the Java language. The reflective API available in ECore [2] allows building generic model editors.

The ability of reflection to be applied across diverse types of languages to solve a significant number of problems is appealing. The quality characteristics that a reflective program may expose are often required in model transformation specifications. Therefore, it is worth studying how reflection may be applied in current

A. Vallecillo, J. Gray, A. Pierantonio (Eds.): ICMT 2008, LNCS 5063, pp. 199–213, 2008.

model transformation languages in the context of Model Driven Engineering (MDE). More importantly, we look for problems that are difficult to solve with the available techniques in the majority of these languages.

In this paper we study the possibilities for adding reflection to an experimental model transformation language called MISTRAL [11]. We are driven by a set of problems encountered in our experience with current transformation languages. The introduced reflective features aim at solving these problems in a concise manner that improves the quality of the solution. The most important problems we address are: achieving flexible trace generation in model transformations, improving change impact analysis and change propagation when source or target models change, and achieving better composability and adaptability of existing transformation specifications. We also aim at a conceptual solution that is applicable to both imperative and declarative transformation languages.

We present a set of features in the structure and in the behavior of transformation programs that may be exposed to metaprograms written on the base of metainterfaces on these features. A set of examples is presented that illustrate the motivation and the applicability of the proposed reflective features.

The paper is organized as follows. Section 2 gives background knowledge about reflection and how reflection can be applied on model transformation languages. The identified features are included and implemented in an experimental model transformation language named MISTRAL. The language is presented in Section 3. Section 4 presents several examples of application of reflection. Section 5 discusses various implementation options to introduce reflection. Section 6 concludes the paper and outlines future work.

2   Identifying Reflection Features in Transformation Languages

This section gives a short theoretical overview on reflection and the relevant concepts. We apply the theoretical framework described in section 2.1 to the domain of model transformation languages. We make assumptions about the structures and operations available in a model transformation execution environment that make our approach general enough and applicable to a number of languages (section 2.2). Section 2.3 gives a two-dimensional space that serves as a guiding framework for designing reflective infrastructures.

2.1   Background

Reflection is a capability to perform computation about another computation. Usually a computation is a result of executing a program written in a programming language. A running program may expose some aspects of its execution environment via some interface. It is said that the running program resides at the *base level* of computation and is called *base program*. Another program may be written that accesses and eventually changes the exposed elements of the execution environment for the base program. Such a program is called *metaprogram* and the level of computation is called *metalevel*[1].

The relation between base and metalevel is causal [16]. This means that changes in the base level are accessible in the metalevel and changes made in the metalevel affect the base level.

There are two orthogonal classification schemes for reflection. They are based on the ability of the metaprogram to access various aspects of the base program and the ability to read and alter the base level. If the metaprogram is capable of accessing the structure of the base program then it performs *structural reflection*. If the metaprogram accesses a representation of the runtime behavior of the base program then it performs *behavioral reflection*.

The ability of the metaprogram to read data about the execution environment and the program is known as *introspection*. The ability to alter the execution environment is called *intercession*. Intercession may affect both the structural part and the behavioral part of the base level. Concerning the structural part the metaprogram may change the structure of the running program. Concerning the behavioral part the metaprogram may change the runtime structures of the running program and change its behavior at run time. We study all types of reflection: structural, behavioral, introspection, and intercession.

2.2 Towards a Common Model of Execution of Model Transformation Programs

The success of applying reflection in object-oriented languages is due to the possibility to find a common computational model valid for a large set of OO languages. The computation model consists of objects that exchange messages. The typical representation of an object-based execution environment includes interfaces to objects and representation of messages.

An important research question in this paper is if it is possible to find such a concise and yet expressive enough computational model for executing model transformations. We claim that it is possible under certain assumptions.

We make the following assumptions:

- The transformation language operates on models that conform to metamodels. The transformation language by itself is defined by a metamodel;
- The language is rule-based. Transformation specification consists of transformation rules executed on tuples of source elements. Every rule may create new elements, update existing elements, and delete elements. Creation and update involve setting property values;

The majority of transformation languages satisfy the assumptions. Usually they operate in an ECore or MOF based metamodeling environment. The abstract syntax of the language is expressed in a metamodel. Furthermore, transformation rule is the most commonly found modular unit that has effects on the model elements. A transformation execution consists of events: executions of transformation rules. Execution

---

[1] The term *metalevel* used in this paper is different from the same term used to denote a layer in a metamodeling architecture.

of a rule involves: identifying matches of the rule source and executing the effects of the rule per match. Effects are creation, deletion, and update of model elements. The events may occur in various orders. For example, in ATL [6], a declarative transformation is executed in the following order: matching of all the rules, for every match the creation of new elements is executed, property values are assigned. In case of an imperative language such as QVT Operational Mappings [19] the order of matching, creation, and property value assignment may differ. Regardless the order of events, however, the set of event types is stable across the languages. This is our starting point for identifying the aspects that should be exposed during a model transformation execution.

2.3   Reflection in the Common Execution Model

McAffer [17] proposes two approaches for designing the metalevel. The first one considers the language elements that should be exposed. This corresponds to identifying the elements used in structural reflection. The second approach considers the events observed during the program execution. This corresponds to identifying elements used in behavioral reflection.

Clearly, both approaches may be combined. They also span the dimension of introspection/intercession options. The two dimensions usually give us a large solution space ranging from a limited *structural introspection* to a difficult to design and control *behavioral intercession*.

Table 1. Example operations on transformation and rule

	Structural	Behavioral

Introspection	*Transformation*
	  • Navigate transformation definition
	Rule
	  • Navigate the rule structure
	  • Navigate data related to a rule match (source element, created target elements)
		Transformation
		  • Check the status of the transformation(started, in execution, executed)
		  • Check the currently executed rule
		Rule
		  • Check the rules status
		  • Check the current match being executed

Intercession	*Transformation*
	  • Change the transformation at run time
	Rule
	  • Change the rule structure at run time
		Transformation
		  • Start/stop transformation execution
		Rule
		  • Execute rule
		  • Mark rule as executed

We will give an example of possible structures and operations by considering two constructs found in transformation languages and the relevant events: transformation specification and transformation rule. We place them in a two-dimensional space where the first dimension denotes the structural/behavioral dichotomy and the second dimension denotes introspection/intercession dichotomy. The space consists of four points shown as cells in Table 1. In each cell we consider transformation and rule constructs. Constructs are shown in italic. Below them a bulleted list indicates possible operations on them.

Table 1 shows that even for two constructs with only part of the possible operations we have 12 operations (see the bulleted elements). The implementation of the metalevel usually involves intercepting the relevant events in the execution (behavioral introspection) and *reification* of the relevant data as *metaobjects*. The term *metaobject* should be interpreted in the broad sense as a data structure (not necessary implemented in an OO language). Metaobjects may be queried by the metaprogram, may be changed (example of structural intercession), and operations may be applied on them that eventually affect the program behavior (behavioral intercession).

3 MISTRAL: An Experimental Language with Reflective Features

MISTRAL is initially described in [11] without having a complete execution engine. Recently we implemented an experimental interpreter for the language. Here we briefly describe the language constructs and their meaning.

Consider the following code fragment that is used in a transformation for flattening class hierarchies in UML class models. Only the identification of attributes of a class (including the inherited attributes) is shown.

```
1.    transformation Flattening
2.    input s : UML
3.    output t : UML
4.
5.    allAttributesOfRoot ModelElementRule {
6.       source [class : UML!Class condition{class.extends->isEmpty()}]
7.       target [attr : Sequence(UML!Attribute) = class.attribute]
8.    }
9.
10.   allAttributesOfNonRoot ModelElementRule {
11.      source [class : UML!Class condition{class.extends->size() > 0}]
12.      target [attr : Sequence(UML!Attribute) = class.attribute->union(
13.                      transformation.trace(class.extends->first(), 'attr')
14.                                  )]
15.   }
```

A transformation declares a number of input and output models that are assigned to a variable typed by the corresponding metamodel (lines 1-3). Output models do not exist in advance and are created after the execution of the transformation. The elements of the input models may be changed.

Every transformation contains named model element rules (*allAttributesOfRoot*, *allAttributesOfNonRoot*). Model element rules have a source that is identified by a single variable of a given type and an optional condition over the values of the variable. The purpose of a model element rule is to execute actions enumerated in its target. Actions are executed for every match of the rule source. Two types of actions are supported: *instantiation* and *update* (not shown in this sample). Instantiation action causes creation of new elements. The types of the elements are types from a metamodel and the built-in OCL types.

The example code determines the total set of attributes per class including the locally defined and the inherited attributes. Rule *allAttributesOfRoot* determines the attributes of root classes. The total set of attributes is represented in the target of the rule as variable *attr* of type *Sequence*. It has an initialization expression. Rule *allAttributesOfNonRoot* determines the attributes of classes that extend other classes. The set of the attributes is the union of the locally defined and the inherited attributes. The inherited attributes are obtained by navigating to the parent class and invoking the resolution function that returns target elements for a given source. The resolution function is called 'trace'. It accepts two arguments: the source element and the identifier of the target element. An example invocation is given in line 13.

The current implementation of the language supports rules that match single source element. A source element may be matched by multiple rules. Target model elements are navigable during the transformation execution. If a slot value of a target element is requested but not yet assigned the value will be calculated on demand and assigned.

MISTRAL is a declarative language. The rule execution order and the action execution order within a rule are decided by the interpreter at runtime. As explained in [11] if a transformation does not change the source model by using update actions the transformation execution is deterministic.

During the design of the metalevel of MISTRAL it was difficult to decide on language constructs and execution events that should be exposed to the metacomputations. One extreme approach is to include a very rich set covering most aspects of the language definition and execution. Another approach is to select a set of concrete problems that need to be solved with reflection and to choose only the necessary features. We chose the second approach since it is problem driven and gives a clear motivation in the metalevel design. We performed 4 case studies all implemented with various forms of reflection. Three of them are detailed in Section 4. In this section we give the language constructs and execution events accessible in the metalevel.

Language constructs:

- transformation definition;
- rule definition;

Execution events:

- rule execution on a particular element;
- action execution (only instantiation execution is supported);
- slot assignment;
- model element slot access;
- invocation of resolution algorithm by calling *trace* function;

We placed every construct and event in the two-dimensional space according to Table 1. Partial results are shown in Table 2.

Table 2 shows that we do not support any structural intercession, i.e. the transformation specification cannot be changed at runtime. On the other hand transformation definition as a whole and every rule can be navigated and read (structural introspection).

Table 2. Reflective features in MISTRAL

	Structural	Behavioral

Introspection	*Transformation definition*
	   • Navigate transformation definition
	Rule definition
	   • Navigate the rule structure
	Rule execution
	Action execution
	Invocation of resolution algorithm
		Transformation
		Rule definition
		Rule execution
		   • Access the set of rules that match the source element
		   • Access data related to a rule match (source element, created target elements)
		Action execution
		   • Access to the matched element and rule
		Invocation of resolution algorithm
		   • Access function arguments

Intercession	*Transformation*
	Rule definition
	Rule execution
	Action execution
	Invocation of resolution algorithm
		Transformation
		Rule definition
		Rule execution
		   • Specify partial rule execution order per match
		Action execution
		Invocation of resolution algorithm
		   • Change function argument
		   • Calculate and return function value

The most interesting part is the possibility to alter the execution behavior at runtime (behavioral intercession). By default, the rule execution order is chosen by the engine. We provide a possibility to obtain all the rules that match a given source element and to specify complete or partial order of executing these rules. Furthermore, when the trace function is invoked the invocation event is reified and passed as a metaobject. The metaobject may be altered and the metaprogram may provide its own resolution algorithm that replaces the default one.

3.2 Expressing Metaprograms

The reflective features are implemented by introducing new rule types generally called *metarules*, and new variables with reserved names that refer to objects accessible during the transformation execution.

Variables. Two variables are introduced: *transformation* and *this*.

The variable *transformation* may be used everywhere in the transformation specification. During the execution it refers to the transformation definition. It is accessible as an ordinary model. OCL can be used for navigating over the definition. The transformation definition cannot be changed.

The variable *this* may be used in the context of a rule. During the execution it refers to a representation of the rule. Via the variable a transformation definition may access the name of the rule, the source definition, etc. Function *value* can be invoked on *this* variable. It takes as argument an identifier that refers to the rule source or to the target elements and returns the element currently assigned to the identifiers in the context of the rule match.

For example, in the context of rule *allAttributesOfRoot this.name* is evaluated to "allAttributesOfRoot". The property *name* is defined in the metamodel of MISTRAL [18]. The expression *this.value('class')* is evaluated to the value of the variable *class* for the concrete match of the rule. Variables *transformation* and *this* allow structural introspection. Function *value* allows introspection of run-time data.

Metarules. Several types of metarules are introduced to allow behavioral reflection. We follow the syntactical conventions used in the base programs.

Execution Rule

This rule may be invoked in the context of a source element. It allows specifying execution order on the rules that match the source element. The syntax is as follows:

```
ruleName ExecutionRule {
    source
    target[listOfRuleNames]
}
```

source has the same syntax as the source of model element rules (see for example lines 6 and 11). The target specifies an ordered list of rule names. If a source element is matched by the source of an execution metarule then during the execution of the transformation the set of rules that will be executed on this element is obtained. Rules are executed in the order specified in *listOfRuleNames*. In general, this order is partial, that is, not all the applicable rules are listed there. Not listed rules may be executed in an order decided by the transformation engine.

Instantiation Rule

This rule is called every time before executing an instantiation action. The syntax is the following:

```
ruleName InstantiationRule (inputParameters) {
    source
    target
}
```

The syntax of source and target does not differ from the syntax used in model element rules. The rule source matches elements in the source model. It will be executed only for those source elements. In that way the developer may narrow the scope of the rule. The rule accepts two input parameters: the first one is bound to the rule being executed and the second one is bound to the instantiation action being executed. These parameters give access to the context of the instantiation.

Slot Assignment Rule

This rule is called every time before assigning a value to a slot in the context of a target action. The syntax is the following:

```
ruleName SlotAssignmentRule (inputParameters) {
    source
    target
}
```

The execution semantics of this rule is similar to the semantics of instantiation rule. The difference is that three parameters are passed: the rule being executed, the identifier of the object that possesses the slot, and the assignment expression.

4 Example Applications

During the design of MISTRAL we performed four case studies that use reflection. We present three of them. The fourth one is about manipulation of invocations to the resolution algorithm. It is skipped due to lack of space.

4.1 Generation of Trace Links Based on Introspection

Most transformation languages and their engines support trace links between source and target elements. However, there may be cases in which the transformation developer prefers to create their own trace structure. This problem is already analyzed in [7, 12]. It is desirable to create a generic trace capturing functionality that is independent from the concrete transformation definition and may be reused in multiple transformations.

```
1.   transformation UML2Java
2.   input s : UML
3.   output t : Java
4.
5.   copyPackage ModelElementRule {
6.       source [sp : UML!Package]
7.       target [tp : Java!Package {name = sp.name}]
8.   }
9.
10.  copyClass ModelElementRule {
11.      source [sc : UML!Class]
12.      target [tc : Java!Class {name = sc.name, isPublic = true, isStatic = false,
13.             field = sc.attribute->collect(a | transformation.trace(a, 'f')) ,
14.             method = sc.attribute->collect(a |
15.                     Sequence{transformation.trace(a, 'getter'),
16.                             transformation.trace(a, 'setter')})->flatten()}]
17.  }
18.
19.  transformAttribute ModelElementRule {
20.      source [sa : UML!Attribute]
21.      target [f : Java!Field{name   = sa.name, isPublic = false,
22.             type = transformation.trace(sa.type, 'tc'),
23.             owner = transformation.trace(sa.owner, 'tc')},
24.          getter : Java!Method{name   = 'get_'+sa.name, isPublic = true,
25.             returnType = f.type, owner = f.owner},
26.          setter : Java!Method{name   = 'set_'+sa.name, isPublic = true,
27.             owner = f.owner}]
28.  }
```

In this section we illustrate how such functionality may be specified by using introspection. Consider a transformation that transforms UML class models to Java programs. We require that every UML attribute is transformed to a private field and two methods for getting and setting the value of the field. For brevity we do not give the metamodels of UML and Java. The code above shows a part of the transformation specification.

We aim at producing a second output model that contains traces between source and target elements. The metamodel for traces expressed in KM3 [8] is:

```
package Traces{

  class Trace {
    attribute ruleName : String;
    attribute sourceName : String;
    attribute targetName [1-*]: String;
  }
}

package PrimitiveTypes {
  datatype String;
}
```

The idea is that for every execution of a rule over a source node we create an instance of class *Trace* that contains the name of the rule, the name of the source element, and a list of the names of the target elements. This may be done by introducing a new instantiation in every rule that uses the identifiers of the source and target elements per a concrete rule. However, such functionality depends on a particular rule and needs changes for every new rule. A generic solution may be obtained by using the variable *this*. The following instantiation named *trace* (line 8) needs to be added in every rule (we show only the new signature of the transformation and the first rule):

```
1.   transformation UML2Java
2.   input s : UML
3.   output t : Java, traces : Traces
4.
5.   copyPackage ModelElementRule {
6.       source [sp : UML!Package]
7.       target [tp : Java!Package {name = sp.name},
8.              trace : Traces!Trace in traces {ruleName = this.name,
9.                 sourceName = this.value(this.source.variableName).name,
10.                targetName = this.target->select(t |
11.                       t.identifierName <> 'trace')->collect(t |
12.                       this.value(t.identifierName).name)}]
13. }
```

A new output model is declared in line 3 that will contain traces. The new instantiation specified in lines 8-12 creates a new trace and puts it in the extent denoted with the variable *traces* (please note the keyword **in** on line 8). It should be noted that the new code does not use any details from the hosting rules. The concrete details about the elements are obtained by the function *value*. The navigation expressions `this`.source.variableName and `this`.target rely on knowledge from the Mistral metamodel.

4.2 Generation of Execution Trace

A declarative language like MISTRAL usually does not rely on explicit specification of the control flow. The execution engine detects dependencies among rules at runtime and orders the execution of instantiations and slot assignments. Typically the execution order and the dependencies are not kept after the execution. Their externalization, however, may help in solving several problems. In this example we show how the execution trace can be captured by intercepting execution events. Instantiation rules and slot assignment rules are used for this purpose.

Consider the previous example of transforming UML to Java. We introduce two metarules: one for intercepting instantiations and one for intercepting slot assignments.

```
catchInstantiation InstantiationRule (rule : Mistral!Rule,
                                       instantiation : Mistral!Instantiation) {
    source[s : SimpleUML!UMLModelElement]
    target [e : ExecutionEvents!InstantiationEvent in events{ruleName = rule.name,
                   sourceName = s.name,
                   id = instantiation.identifierName,
                   targetClassName = instantiation.type.elementName}]
}

catchAssignment SlotAssignmentRule (rule : Mistral!Rule,
                                    id : Mistral!String,
                                    assignment : Mistral!SlotAssignment) {
    source[s : SimpleUML!UMLModelElement]
    target [e : ExecutionEvents!PropertyAssignment in events {sourceName = s.name,
                   ruleName = rule.name,
                   id = id,
                   slotName = assignment.name}]
}
```

catchInstantiation rule is invoked before executing an instantiation from a given rule on a given source node. The source node is bound to the source variable *s*. The context rule and the instantiation are passed as parameters. The source of the rule may have a condition thus limiting the scope of the rule only on some source nodes. When the rule is executed a new instance of the class *InstantiationEvent* will be created. It will store info about the name of the rule, the name of the source, the identifier of the target element, and the target class name. Clearly, this is just one possibility to store information about instantiation events.

Similarly, *catchAssignment* rule is invoked every time before an assignment is performed. Again the source node is passed to the rule and the context of the execution is passed as three parameters.

We envisage two applications of these metarule types. The may be used for performing debugging of transformations. They may also be used to capture the execution order and the dependency among the execution events. This information, combined with information about the access to the source and target model elements and a trace record (like in the previous example) allows performing change impact analysis and change propagation when the source model is changed. We intend to report about this application of reflection in another paper.

4.3   Controlling Aspect Weaving at Shared Join Points

The last example we give is inspired by a common problem in Aspect-Oriented Programming (AOP) [9]. Aspects are modular constructs that encapsulate behavior usually scattered across multiple locations in a program. They are integrated in designated points (called *join points*) by a process called *aspect weaving*. In general, aspects do not know about each other and more than one aspect may be woven in a single join point. Possibly, aspect interference may occur. This problem is known as weaving of aspects at shared join points [5]. Usually it requires some policy of ordering of the weaving.

In this example we implement aspects as transformation rules that change a Java program. The process of weaving is actually the process of executing the transformation rules. Consider the following two rules that implement logging aspect and synchronization aspect.

```
1.   addLogConcern ModelElementRule {
2.     source[sourceMethod : Java!Method condition{(sourceMethod.name = 'methodA')
3.                                   or (sourceMethod.name = 'methodC')}]
4.     target[logInvocation : Java!MethodCall{variableName='Log',
5.                                   methodName = 'log'},
6.        update sourceMethod{statements =
7.           Sequence{logInvocation}->union(sourceMethod.statements)}
8.        ]
9.   }
10.
11. addSynchConcern ModelElementRule {
12.     source[sourceMethod : Java!Method]
13.     target[obtainLockInvocation : Java!MethodCall{variableName = 'Lock',
14.                                   methodName = 'getLock'},
15.        releaseLockInvocation : Java!MethodCall{variableName = 'Lock',
16.                                   methodName = 'releaseLock'},
17.        update sourceMethod{statements =
18.        Sequence{obtainLockInvocation}->union(sourceMethod.statements)->union(
19.                                   Sequence{releaseLockInvocation})}
20.        ]
21. }
```

Rule *addLogConcern* creates a Java method call that implements the logging functionality (lines 4-5). Then the method call is inserted before the statements of the selected Java method. This is done by using *update* action that modifies the slot value of the source node (line 6).

Rule *addSynchConcern* inserts two method calls in an existing method. The first one is inserted in the beginning and is responsible to obtain a synchronization lock. The second one is inserted in the end and releases the lock.

The logging aspect is applied to methods with name *methodA* or *methodC*. The synchronization aspect is applied to all the methods in the base program. Apparently these two aspects have shared join points. The question is in which order the aspects are applied at their shared join points. This problem is studied in [10] and several solutions are proposed. Assume that for some methods we want to apply first the logging aspect and then the synchronization aspect while for other methods we reverse the order. MISTRAL is a declarative language and the order of rule execution cannot be controlled. However, even with the possibility to order rules the problem cannot be completely solved. Rule ordering ensures a global order valid for all source nodes, whereas we require finer control at the level of a single node.

The execution metarule can be applied in this situation. It allows to select a node and to specify a partial order of execution of the rules that match the node. We apply the following execution rule:

```
orderConcerns ExecutionRule {
    source [sourceMethod : Java!Method condition{sourceMethod.name = 'methodA'}]
    target [addSynchConcern, addLogConcern]
}
```

The rule specifies that for all methods with name *methodA* first the synchronization aspect is applied and then the logging aspect. If there are other rules matching that method then their order is up to the execution engine. Execution metarule implements behavioral intercession in MISTRAL.

5 Discussion

In our experience with reflection we encountered two main issues: how to design the metalevel and which implementation approach to choose.

5.1 Design of the Metalevel

Before implementing a reflective framework the first step is the identification of the elements to be exposed to the metalevel. The classification used in Table 1 and 2 partially helps in this. In our approach we started with a set of cases with problems and used them as a criterion for selecting among the possible reflective features. This approach, however, may be not sufficient if a general-purpose reflective mechanism is required.

Unfortunately, there is no much experience in using reflection in current model transformation languages. The most commonly found form of reflection is structural introspection over model elements based on the reflective API of ECore. Some languages [13, 23] allow expressions to be specified at places where a class or a feature is expected. This increases the genericity of programs.

We are not aware of any work that generally treats the problem of introducing reflection in transformation languages. It should be noted that we have not experimented with transformation languages that are embedded DSLs in a language with reflective features. Such a language is RubyTL [4] implemented in the context of Ruby. The authors of RubyTL report on the possibility to introspect the language constructs, a capability provided by Ruby. This corresponds to the capability provided by the variables *transformation* and *this* in our work.

5.2 Implementing Reflection

In general, there are three ways to introduce reflection in a language: using preprocessing, modifying the language interpreter, and modifying the language compiler.

- *Using preprocessing.* This approach is employed in [14]. The language is syntactically extended and the new constructs are translated to the existing constructs by including a preprocessing phase. This approach does not require changing the interpreter/compiler of the language. In the context of MDE, this approach may be applied by using a higher-order transformation (HOT) that translates the reflective program to a non-reflective one. Jouault [7] applies HOT to achieve flexible traceability. He does not extend the transformation language with new features though. The shortcoming of the preprocessing approach lies in the fact that it deals with static aspects of reflection and is limited to source code manipulation. In case of reflection upon the runtime behavior of the transformation engine changes in the engine may be required.
- *Changing the interpreter.* The current prototype of the MISTRAL engine is implemented as an interpreter and we had to change it to introduce the forms of

behavioral reflection we presented. The major disadvantage in this approach is that it slows down the execution of the transformation even in cases when no reflection is performed. This is due to the fact that the interpreter is checking every time if a reflection feature is requested when the interpreter evaluates expressions that are exposed to metacomputations.

- *Changing the compiler.* This approach overcomes the problems of the interpreter-based execution. During compilation the compiler may analyze the reflective code and introduce the invocations to the metalevel only when necessary. An application of this idea is reported in [22] and applied for the Java reflective framework Reflex.

6 Conclusions

In this paper we studied the possibilities to employ reflection in the current rule-based model transformation languages. The design of the metalevel was motivated by a number of cases studies. The reflective features were considered from a more general perspective in a two dimensional space that gives us a reasoning framework about the possible solutions. The reflective capabilities were implemented in an experimental model transformation language by modifying the language interpreter. It was possible to solve the problems formulated in the case studies.

The solution proposed here cannot be considered as a general-purpose reflective framework. It was driven by concrete needs. We believe, however, that the introduced reflective extensions allow solving other problems as well. This hypothesis will be addressed in the future research.

The major benefit of using refection is achieving transformation solutions with better quality. We were able to specify generic and reusable trace generation functionality. This should help us in improving traceability and change management in model transformations. Reflection may provide fine control during execution and as we suggested in the paper other technologies (e.g. AOP) may benefit from this.

References

1. Aksit, M., Wakita, K., Bosch, J., Bergmans, L., Yonezawa, A.: Abstracting Object Interactions Using Composition Filters. In: ECOOP Workshop 1993, pp. 152–184 (1993)
2. Budinsky, F., Steinberg, D., Raymond Ellersick, R., Ed Merks, E., Brodsky, S.A., Grose, T.J.: Eclipse Modeling Framework. Addison Wesley (2003)
3. Chiba, S.: Load-Time Structural Reflection in Java. In: Bertino, E. (ed.) ECOOP 2000. LNCS, vol. 1850, Springer, Heidelberg (2000)
4. Cuadrado, J.S., Molina, J.G., Tortosa, M.M.: RubyTL: A Practical, Extensible Transformation Language. In: Rensink, A., Warmer, J. (eds.) ECMDA-FA 2006. LNCS, vol. 4066, pp. 158–172. Springer, Heidelberg (2006)
5. Havinga, W., Nagy, I., Bergmans, L., Aksit, M.: Detecting and resolving ambiguities caused by inter-dependent introductions. In: AOSD 2006, pp. 214–225 (2006)
6. Jouault, F., Kurtev, I.: Transforming Models with ATL. In: Bruel, J.-M. (ed.) MoDELS 2005. LNCS, vol. 3844, pp. 128–138. Springer, Heidelberg (2006)

7. Jouault, F.: Loosely Coupled Traceability for ATL, accepted for the ECMDA Workshop on Traceability, Nuremberg, Germany (2005)
8. Bézivin, J., Jouault, F.: KM3: A DSL for Metamodel Specification. In: Gorrieri, R., Wehrheim, H. (eds.) FMOODS 2006. LNCS, vol. 4037. Springer, Heidelberg (2006)
9. Kiczales, G., Hilsdale, E., Hugunin, J., Kersten, M., Palm, J., Griswold, W.G.: An Overview of AspectJ. In: Knudsen, J.L. (ed.) ECOOP 2001. LNCS, vol. 2072, p. 327. Springer, Heidelberg (2001)
10. Kojarski, S., Lorenz, D.H.: Awesome: an aspect co-weaving system for composing multiple aspect-oriented extensions. In: OOPSLA 2007, pp. 515–534 (2007)
11. Kurtev, I.: Adaptability of Model Transformations, PhD thesis, University of Twente, the Netherlands (2005)
12. Kurtev, I., van den Berg, K., Jouault, F.: Rule-based modularization in model transformation languages illustrated with ATL. Sci. Comput. Program. 68(3), 138–154 (2007)
13. Lawley, M., Steel, J.: Practical Declarative Model Transformation with Tefkat. In: Bruel, J.-M. (ed.) MoDELS 2005. LNCS, vol. 3844, pp. 139–150. Springer, Heidelberg (2006)
14. Leitner, A., Eugster, P., Oriol, M., Ciupa, I.: Reflecting on an Existing Programming Language. In: TOOLS Europe 2007. JOT, vol. 6(9) (2007)
15. Lewis, B., Ducassé, M.: Using events to debug Java programs backwards in time. In: OOPSLA Companion 2003, pp. 96–97 (2003)
16. Maes, P.: Computional reflection. PhD thesis, Artificial intelligence laboratory, Vrije Universiteit, Brussels, Belgium (1987)
17. McAffer, J.: Engineering the meta-level. In: Kiczales (ed.) Reflection 1996, San Francisco, CA, USA, pp. 39–61 (1996)
18. Mistral web site, http://www.vf.utwente.nl/~kurtev/mistral/
19. OMG. MOF 2.0 Query/Views/Transformations RFP. OMG document ad/2002-04-10 (2002)
20. Pawlak, R., Seinturier, L., Duchien, L., Floring, G.J.: A flexible solution for aspect-oriented programming in Java. In: 3rd International Conference on Metalevel Architectures and Advanced Separation of Concerns, Japan (2001)
21. Smith, B., Reflection, C.: semantics in Lisp. In: Proceedings of the 14th Annual ACM Symposium on Principles of Programming Languages, pp. 23–35 (January 1984)
22. Tanter, E., Noyé, J., Caromel, D., Cointe, P.: Partial behavioral reflection: spatial and temporal selection of reification. In: OOPSLA 2003, pp. 27–46 (2003)
23. Pataricza, A., Varró, D.: Generic and Meta-transformations for Model Transformation Engineering. In: Baar, T., Strohmeier, A., Moreira, A., Mellor, S.J. (eds.) UML 2004. LNCS, vol. 3273. Springer, Heidelberg (2004)

Proofs-as-Model-Transformations

Iman Poernomo

Department of Computer Science,
King's College London
Strand, London, WC2R2LS
iman.poernomo@kcl.ac.uk

Abstract. This paper provides an overview of how to develop model transformations that are "provably correct" with respect to a given functional specification. The approach is based in a mathematical formalism called Constructive Type Theory (CTT) and a related synthesis formal method known as proofs-as-programs. We outline how CTT can be used to provide a uniform formal foundation for representing models, metamodels and model transformations as understood within the Object Management Group's Meta-Object Facility (MOF 2.0) and Model Driven Architecture (MDA) suite of standards [6, 8]. CTT was originally developed to provide a unifying foundation for logic, data and programs. It is higher-order, in the sense that it permits representation and reasoning about programs, types of programs and types of types. We argue that this higher-order aspect affords a natural formal definition of metamodel/model/model instantiation relationships within the MOF. We develop formal notions of models, metamodels and model transformation specifications by utilizing the logic that is built into CTT. In proofs-as-programs, a functional program specification is represented as a special kind of type. A program is provably correct with respect to a given specification if it can be typed by that specification. We develop an analogous approach, defining model transformation specifications as types and provably correct transformations as inhabitants of specification types.

1   Introduction

This paper outlines how a formal software verification and synthesis approach can be applied to the problem of developing model transformations in the Model Driven Architecture (MDA) strategy [6]. Our intent is to develop model transformations that are correct with respect to a given pre- and post-condition specification. A plethora of formal methods are available that might serve our purpose. We employ a theory previously developed as a unifying foundation of mathematics and programming, Constructive Type Theory (CTT), and a related synthesis formal method known as proofs-as-programs [2, 10].

In its simplest form, the MDA process involves a transformation between two models, of the form

$$PIL \xrightarrow{T} PSL$$
$$T(PIM) = PSM$$
(1)

A. Vallecillo, J. Gray, A. Pierantonio (Eds.): ICMT 2008, LNCS 5063, pp. 214–228, 2008.
© Springer-Verlag Berlin Heidelberg 2008

A transformation T takes as input a model PIM, written in a source modelling language PIL, and outputs a new model PSM, written in a (possibly different) target modelling language PSL. The transformation might serve any number of purposes. It might describe how the PIM should be implemented for a particular middleware and platform, so that the resulting PSM contains specific implementation decisions that are to be realized by the system programmers. The transformation T should be applicable to any PIM written using the PIL. It is therefore defined as a general mapping from elements of the language PIL to elements of the language PSL.

The intention of MDA is to enable designers to focus most of their work on providing a robust, architecturally sound PIM. Then, given a particular platform and PSL choice, a designer applies a (possibly off-the-shelf) transformation to automatically obtain an appropriate PSM.

The methodology is powerful and useful. It can also be dangerous. There is already significant uptake of the strategy from within the enterprise software engineering sector. If a large community of developers agree to use the standard, then refinement-based development becomes a practical reality. Ideally, this will result in better software quality. However, because MDA is essentially an informal approach, it does not guarantee correct model transformations. Currently, given a specification, a transformation is developed by hand with little certification that the specification is met. Testing is still limited: an important research subarea concerns the development of an adequate range of tests [5], often involving a metamodel instance generation problem.

Using MDA without formal grounding can be dangerous. In fact, if model transformations are incorrect, the MDA process can result in software of a lower quality than that produced by traditional software development. This paper provides an overview of how higher-order constructive type theory (CTT) can be used to develop correct-by-construction MDA model transformations. CTT was originally developed to provide a unifying foundation for logic, data and programs. It is higher-order, in the sense that it permits representation and reasoning about ordinary programs, types of programs, types of types and programs that manipulate other programs and types.

We will consider transformations of the form (1) as higher-order typed functional programs. The input type will represent the PIL and the output type will represent the PSL. In MDA, the OMG defines these two languages as metamodels within the Meta-Object Facility (MOF 2.0). Consequently, we need to understand how the MOF 2.0 metamodelling hierarchy can be given a shallow embedding within CTT.

We believe that CTT is a "natural" formalism for representing the MDA and MOF. This is because the MDA and MOF are intrinsically higher-order. Metamodels are classifiers of classifers and so define types of types. Model transformations are programs that manipulate classifiers, and so, from a mathematical perspective, are functions that manipulate types. The nature of CTT also provides a convenient "built-in" logic, permitting types to include statements and constraints about instantiating terms, in a way that parallels the MOF and MDA use of logical model constraints in the definition of metamodels and model transformations. Our approach will exploit the proofs-as-programs paradigm property of CTT [10]. At its simplest, the type theory of the lambda-calculus can be regarded as both a proof system and an executable pure functional programming language. A provably correct functional program can be obtained from the inhabiting term of its behavioural specification, treated as a type.

The paper proceeds as follows. Section 2 describes the MOF and explains how it is used to write metamodels within the MDA approach. Section 3 sketches the constructive type theory we use and the proofs-as-programs idea. Section 4 outlines our type theoretic encoding of the MOF and MDA. Conclusions and a discussion of future work is provided in Section 5.

This paper assumes the reader is familiar with the UML representation of classes, class relationships and class objects and has a partial familiarity with the MOF specification document [8]. A detailed study of constructive type theory can be found in [2] or [10] (we follow the formulation of the latter here). More details of our type theoretic treatment of the third and fourth level of the MOF 1.4 are given in [9], which might also serve as a detailed account of our type theory.

2   The MOF

The MOF 2.0 specification consists of two metamodelling languages, the EMOF and CMOF [8]. The former is a subset of, and may be defined reflexively within, the latter. For the purposes of illustrating our formalism, we will consider the subset of the CMOF that permits a UML class-style representation of metamodel grammars. We do not treat a number of other useful features present in the MOF 2.0, such as reflection.

Metamodelling in the MOF is commonly done according to a four level hierarchy, as depicted in [7, pp. 30–31] (the MOF 2.0 permits an any number of levels greater than two). The M_0 level consists of model instances. These might be data values, instantiated class objects, instantiated database tables, algorithms, XML code or function definitions. The M_1 level consists of models, which may also be considered as metamodel instances. This level includes elements such as UML diagrams, class, module and type declarations, database table declarations or XML schema. The M_2 level consists of metamodels, which may also be considered as MOF model instances. This level consists of metamodel descriptions, defining the syntax and semantics of M_1 elements. This level includes languages such as the UML, the XML, Java, the B specification language or *Casl* algebraic specification language. The M_3 level is the MOF language itself, used to define M_2 level elements.

UML-style classes, class associations or class object can be defined at any level in the MOF hierarchy, to serve different purposes. For instance, classes at the M_3 are used to type modelling languages, while classes at the M_2 level are used within modelling languages to type models. The levels are then related by an object-oriented-style class/object instantiation relationship. Class elements of level M_{i+1} provide type descriptions of level M_i objects. M_i objects instantiate M_{i+1} classes.

An important aspect of the MOF hierarchy is that M_1 and M_2 level information can be encoded in two separate ways: as model elements *or* object instances. This enables the MOF hierarchy to treat types as classifications and as forms of data. The principle works as follows. The MOF language is defined by a set of related model elements at the M_3 level. A metamodel is defined at the M_2 level by a set of MOF objects that instantiate the MOF model elements. This MOF object representation of a metamodel can also be rewritten as a M_2 metamodel that provides type descriptions via a set of model elements. A model at the M_1 level is understood as a set of elements that instantiate the classifiers of an M_2 level metamodel. Finally, these M_1 level elements can also be rewritten to form M_1 level model classifiers that specify the required form of an M_0 level model instantiation.

2.1   Object-Based Metamodels

The M_3 level MOF model consists in a set of associated M_3 level classes, "meta-metaclasses", hereafter referred to as MOF classes. The MOF classes classify the kinds of elements that make up a M_2 level metamodel. Metamodels are collections of associated M_2 instances of these MOF classes, in the same sense that, for example, a collections of M_0 UML objects represent an instance of a M_1 UML class diagram.

The MOF specification defines both the structure of MOF metamodels, consisting of roles and relationships, together with a structural semantics, consisting of constraints that must apply to any instances of the type structure. The MOF defines a set of associated M_3 level classes, the most important of which are as follows: Classifier (a general supertype of all metamodel classifiers), Class (typing all metamodel classifiers that are not basic data types), Datatype (a type of datatypes), Property (a type of attributes that may be associated with a metamodel classifier) and Association and AssociationEnd (typing associations that might hold between metamodel classifiers). The classes are related to each other in the obvious way and have a range of associated attributes treating, for instance, private and public accessibility and inheritance hierarchies. An important attribute of Property is the boolean isComposite. If the property is set to true, then the owning classifier contains the property and no cyclic dependencies via properties are permitted. If the property is false, then the property is a reference, and cyclic dependencies are permitted [8, pp. 36–37].

The MOF permits constraints to be associated with any of the elements of a metamodel. These can be written in an informal language, such as English, or a formal language, such as the Object Constraint Language (OCL). The MOF model employs constraints in two distinct ways. The MOF model itself has a set of constraints that are defined for each of its classes. These constraints define a static structural semantics of the model that specifies how M_2 metamodels should be formed. Also, the model contains a class called Constraint that is associated with all other classes of the model. Instances of this class are used to write a semantics for M_2 metamodels that, in turn, is used to specify how M_1 instantiating models must behave.

For the purposes of this paper, we may consider the simplified notion of a MOF metamodel as a collection of associated MOF class object instances. These instances are M_2 level objects.

Definition 1 (Metamodel). *A metamodel M is a set of* Classifer, Class, Datatype, Attribute, Association, AssociationEnd *and* Constraint M_2 *level objects. Objects within M may only refer to each other.*

2.2   Class-Based Description of Metamodels

A metamodel specification consists in a set of M_2 level objects. This is a data-centric view of a metamodel. When considering a metamodel as a model of models, we need to use this data to classify models. The MOF achieves this by means of an equivalent representation of a metamodel, as M_2 level *classes*, whose M_1 level object instances are *models*.

Given a metamodel MO represented as a set of M_2 level objects, we can build an equivalent M_2 level *class-based* representation MC as follows. Each Class M_2 object o in MO corresponds to a M_2 class toClass(o), whose class attributes each correspond to the M_2 level Attribute objects associated with o. Similarly, for each Association object a in MO that defines a relation between two Class objects o_1 and o_2, we add a class association in the metamodel MC between the classes that correspond to o_1 and o_2. Each Constraint object associated with an object o is mapped to a UML-style *note* that is associated with toClass(o). The contents of the note are the same as the contents of the constraint.

A class-based representation is important as it prescribes how the metamodel should be used as a typing structure for M_1 level models. It is important to note that, according to the MOF, not every collection of M_2 level classes defines a metamodel. To be valid, a metamodel must also have an object-based representation that instantiates the MOF model.

3   Constructive Type Theory

This section presents a brief summary of the constructive type theory (CTT) that shall be used to formalize. We define a version of Martin-Löf's predicative type theory with dependent sum and product types [4], and explain how the CTT provides an uniform framework for treating functions, types, proofs and programs.

We work with a lambda calculus whose core set of terms, P, are given over a set of variables, V:

$$P ::= V | \lambda V.\, P | (P\ P) | \langle P, P \rangle | \mathsf{fst}(P) | \mathsf{snd}(P) | \mathsf{inl}(P) | \mathsf{inr}(P) |$$
$$\mathsf{match}\ P\ \mathsf{with}\ \mathsf{inl}(V) \Rightarrow P \mid \mathsf{inr}(V) \Rightarrow P |$$
$$\mathsf{abort}(P) | \mathsf{show}(V, P) | \mathsf{select}\ (P)\ \mathsf{in}\ V.V.P$$

The evaluation semantics of lambda abstraction and application are standard and widely used in functional programming languages such as *SML*: $\lambda x.\, P$ defines a function that takes x as input and will output $P[a/x]$ when applied to

a via an application $(\lambda\ x.\ P)a$. The calculus also includes pairs $\langle a, b\rangle$, where $\mathsf{fst}(\langle a, b\rangle)$ will evaluate to the first projection a (similarly for the second projection). Case matching provides form of conditional, so that $\mathsf{match}\ z\ \mathsf{with}\ \mathsf{inl}(x) \Rightarrow P \mid \mathsf{inr}(y) \Rightarrow Q$ will evaluate to $P[x/a]$ if z is $\mathsf{inl}(a)$ and to $Q[y/a]$ if z is $\mathsf{inr}(a)$. $\mathsf{show}(a, P)$ is a form of pairing data a with a term P. Terms leading to inconsistent state are represented $\mathsf{abort}(p)$. Evaluation is assumed to be *lazy* – that is, the operational semantics is applied to the outermost terms, working inwards until a neutral term is reached. We write $a \triangleright b$ if a evaluates to b according to this semantics.

The lambda calculus is a programming language. We can compile terms and run them as programs. Like most modern programming languages, our calculus is typed, allowing us to specify, for example, the input and output types of lambda terms. The terms of our lambda calculus are associated with the following kinds of types: basic types from a set BT, functional types $(A \to B)$, product types $(A * B)$, disjoint unions $(A|B)$, dependent product types $(\prod x : t.a)$ where x is taken from V, and dependent sum types $(\Sigma x : t.b)$ where x is taken from V. The intuition behind the first four types should be clear. For example, if a term t has type $(A \to B)$, then t is a function that can accept as input any value of type A to produce a value of type B. A dependent product type expresses the dependence of a function's output types on its input term arguments. For example, if a function f has dependent product type $\prod x : T.F(x)$, then f can input any value of type T, producing an output value of type $F(arg)$. Thus, the final output type is parameterized by the input *value*. Typing rules provide a formal system for determining what the types of lambda terms should be. The core typing rules are displayed in Fig. 1. Further rules may be included in a straightforward way to accommodate recursion.

It is not permissible to define a totality of the collection of all types, as this results in an inconsistent theory. Instead, we employ a common solution, defining a predicative hierarchy of type universes of the form:

$$\text{TYPE}_0, \text{TYPE}_1, \text{TYPE}_2, \ldots$$

The typing rules for the universes, omitted for reasons of space, may be found in [9]. In these rules, the first universe TYPE_0 is the type of all types generated by the basic types and the typing constructors.

To encode objects and classes, we will require record types. These types have the usual definition – see, for example, [2] or [9]. A record type is of the form $\{a_1 : T_1; \ldots; a_n : T_n\}$, where $a_1, \ldots, a_n$ are labelling names. A record is a term $\{a_1 = d_1; \ldots; a_n = d_n\}$ of a record type $\{a_1 : T_1; \ldots; a_n : T_n\}$, where each term d_i is of type T_i. The term $\{a_1 = d_1; \ldots; a_n = d_n\}.a_i$ evaluates to the value d_i associated with the label a_i in the left hand side record.

To treat cyclic dependencies within metamodels, we require *co-inductive types*. Co-induction over record types essentially allows us to expand as many references to other records as we require, simulating navigation through a metamodel's cyclic reference structure. For the purposes of this paper, these types are abbreviated by means of mutually recursive definitions, of the form

$$\frac{}{x : A \vdash x : A} \ (\text{Ass-I})$$

$$\frac{\Delta, x : s \vdash p : A}{\Delta \vdash \lambda x : s.\, p : \prod x : s \bullet A} \ (\textstyle\prod\text{-I})$$

$$\frac{\Delta_1 \vdash p : \prod x : s \bullet A \quad \Delta_2 \vdash c : s}{\Delta_1, \Delta_2 \vdash (p\, c) : A[c/x]} \ (\textstyle\prod\text{-E})$$

$$\frac{\Delta, x : s \vdash p : A \quad x : s \text{ is not free in } A}{\Delta \vdash \lambda x : s.\, p : s \to A} \ (\to\text{-I})$$

$$\frac{\Delta_1 \vdash p : s \to A \quad \Delta_2 \vdash c : s}{\Delta_1, \Delta_2 \vdash (p\, c) : A} \ (\to\text{-E})$$

$$\frac{\Delta \vdash p : P[a/y]}{\Delta \vdash \mathsf{show}(a, p) : \Sigma y : s \bullet P} \ (\Sigma\text{-I})$$

$$\frac{\Delta_1 \vdash p : \Sigma y : s \bullet P \quad \Delta_2, x : P[z/y] \vdash q : C}{\Delta_1, \Delta_2 \vdash \mathsf{select}\ (p)\ \text{in}\ z.x.q : C} \ (\Sigma\text{-E})$$

$$\frac{\Delta \vdash a : A \quad \Delta' \vdash b : B}{\Delta, \Delta' \vdash \langle a, b \rangle : (A * B)} \ (\text{prod-I})$$

$$\frac{\Delta \vdash p : (A_1 * A_2)}{\Delta \vdash \mathsf{fst}(p) : A_1} \ (\text{prod-E}_1) \qquad \frac{\Delta \vdash p : (A_1 * A_2)}{\Delta \vdash \mathsf{snd}(p) : A_2} \ (\text{prod-E}_2)$$

$$\frac{\Delta \vdash p : A_1}{\Delta \vdash \mathsf{inl}(p) : (A_1 | A_2)} \ (\text{union-I}_1) \qquad \frac{\Delta \vdash p : A_2}{\Delta \vdash \mathsf{inr}(p) : (A_1 | A_2)} \ (\text{union-I}_2)$$

$$\frac{\Delta \vdash p : A | B \quad \Delta_1, x : A \vdash a : C \quad \Delta_2, y : B \vdash b : C}{\Delta_1, \Delta_2, \Delta \vdash \mathsf{match}\ p\ \text{with}\ \mathsf{inl}(x) \Rightarrow a \mid \mathsf{inr}(y) \Rightarrow b : C} \ (\text{union-E})$$

$$\frac{\Delta \vdash a : \bot}{\Delta \vdash \mathsf{abort}(a) : A} \ (\bot\text{-E})$$

Fig. 1. Typing rules for our lambda calculus

$$\mathrm{T} \equiv F(\mathrm{U}) : \textsc{Type}_i$$

$$\mathrm{U} \equiv G(\mathrm{T}) : \textsc{Type}_i$$

This is a notational convenience: the formal treatment of co-induction, and associated co-inductive recursion schemes, is given in [9]. This paper does not treat inheritance in metamodelling: we have equipped our type theory with a notion of subtyping to treat inheritance [9].

3.1 Proofs-as-Programs

The Curry-Howard isomorphism shows that constructive logic is naturally embedded within our type theory, where proofs correspond to terms, formulae to types, logical rules to typing rules, and proof normalization to term simplification. Consider a constructive logic whose formulae, WFF are built from exactly the same predicates that occur in our type theory. We can define an injection

A	$\mathsf{asType}(A)$
$Q(x)$, where Q is a predicate	$Q(x)$
$\forall x : T.P$	$\prod x : T.\mathsf{asType}(P)$
$\exists x : T.P$	$\Sigma x : T.\mathsf{asType}(P)$
$P \wedge Q$	$\mathsf{asType}(P) * \mathsf{asType}(Q)$
$P \vee Q$	$\mathsf{asType}(P)|\mathsf{asType}(Q)$
$P \Rightarrow Q$	$\mathsf{asType}(P) \rightarrow \mathsf{asType}(Q)$
$\perp$	$\perp$

Fig. 2. Definition of asType, an injection from WFF to types of the lambda calculus

asType, from well-formed formulae WFF to types of the lambda calculus as in Fig. 2.

The isomorphism tells us that logical statements and proofs correspond to types and terms:

Theorem 1 (Curry-Howard isomorphism). *Let* $\Gamma = \{G_1, \ldots, G_n\}$ *be a set of premises. Let* $\Gamma' = \{x_1 : G_1, \ldots, x_n : G_n\}$ *be a corresponding set of typed variables. Let* A *be a well-formed formula. Then the following is true. Given a proof of* $\Gamma \vdash_{\mathsf{Int}} A$ *we can use the typing rules to construct a well-typed proof-term* $p : \mathsf{asType}(A)$ *whose free proof-term variables are* Γ'. *Symmetrically, given a well-typed proof-term* $p : asType(A)$ *whose free term variables are* Γ', *we can construct a proof in constructive logic* $\Gamma \vdash A$.

Theorem 2 (Program extraction). *Let* $\Gamma = \{G_1, \ldots, G_n\}$ *be a set of premises. Let* $\Gamma' = \{x_1 : G_1, \ldots, x_n : G_n\}$ *be a corresponding set of typed variables. Let* $\forall x : T.\exists y : U.P(x, y)$ *be a well-formed* $\forall\exists$ *formula.*

There is a mapping extract *from terms to terms such that, if* $\vdash p : asType(\forall x : T.\exists y : U.P(x, y))$ *is a well typed term, then* $\vdash \forall x : T.P(x, \mathsf{extract}(p)x)$ *is provable.*

The proof of the theorem follows standard previous presentations, but requires an extension to deal with co-inductive types. The implication of this theorem is that, given a proof of a formula $\forall x : T.\exists y : U.P(x, y)$, we can automatically extract a function that f that, given input $x : T$ will produce an output fx that satisfies the constraint $P(x, fx)$.

Our notion of proofs-as-model-transformations essentially follows from this theorem. A model transformation of the form (1) can be specified as a constraint in the OCL over instances of an input PIM and an output PSM. Assuming we can develop types and to represent the PIM and PSM metamodels, and that the constraint can be written as a logical formula over a term for the metamodels, we can then specify the transformation as an $\forall\exists$ formula. Then, in order to synthesize a provably correct model transformation, we prove the formula's truth and apply the extraction mapping according to Theorem 2.

The main technical challenges posed by this approach are 1) the extract map is a non-trivial extension of the usual extraction map used in similar proofs-as-programs approaches, modified to suit our more complicated type theory and 2) the way in which MOF-based metamodels can be formalized as types is not clear. Space does not permit us to describe the extraction mapping, but essentially it is developed using the generic machinery of [10]. The latter challenge is now addressed.

3.2   Metaclass Structures as Record Types

We first describe how the *structure* of classes and objects can represented within our type theory. Our encoding is standard (see, e.g., [13]). We define classes as recursive record types, with objects taken as terms of these types. We restricted our attention to classes with attributes but without operations, we will not deal with representing operations within class types. Our representation can be easily extended to this (again, see [13]).

First, recall that we shall treat the associations of a class in the same way as attributes. That is, if class M_1 is associated with another class M_2 with n the name of the end of the association at M_2, then we treat this as an attribute $n : M_2$ within M_1 if the multiplicity of n is 1, and $n : [M_2]$ otherwise.

Essentially, the idea is to map a class C with attributes and associations $a_1 : T_1, \ldots, a_n : T_n$ to a record type definition

$$C \equiv \{a_1 : T_1; \ldots; a_n : T_n\}$$

where each a_i is an element of *String* corresponding to the attribute name a_i and each T_i a type corresponding to the classifier T_i. The class can reference another class or itself through the attribute types. The mapping therefore permits mutual recursion between class definitions. That is, each T_i could be C or could refer to other defined class types.

The encoding of classes is purely structural and does not involve a behavioural semantics. A semantics is instead associated with a structural class type through a logical specification in a way now described.

4   The MOF and MDA within CTT

If we can encode the MOF within our CTT, it is possible to apply proofs-as-programs to develop provably correct model transformations via extraction from proofs. Following previous work by the author [9], metamodel/model/model instantiation relationships of the MOF can treated using terms and types within the CTT's predicative type hierarchy. This framework enables us to define a higher order type for any metamodel MODELLANG, so that ⊢ *model* : MODELLANG is derivable if, and only if, the term *model* corresponds to a well formed model instance of the metamodel. Model transformations should then be representable as functions within the CTT that are typed by metamodel types.

The main concepts of the MOF have obvious formal counterparts within the CTT. Classes and objects are treated using recursive records. The four levels of the MOF are corresponding to the CTT's predicative hierarchy of type universes. The CTT's typing relation allows us to systematically treat MOF model/metamodel/model/model instantiation relationships as follows. The M_3 level MOF classes are defined through TYPE_2 class types, M_2 level metamodel classifiers are given a dual representation as objects of the MOF class types and as TYPE_1 class types. M_1 level model entities are given a dual representation as terms of the metamodel types and as as TYPE_0 types, M_0 level implementations of models are instantiating terms of TYPE_0 types. This section outlines how to formalize the MOF classes and metamodels at levels M_3 and M_2.

4.1   Encoding of the MOF

The structure of MOF metamodels was defined as a set of M_3 level classes. It is possible to define a set of mutually recursive TYPE_2 level record types that encode these classes. A metamodel, considered as a set of M_2 level objects that instantiate the MOF classes, is then formally understood as a set of mututally recursive TYPE_1 level terms of these types.

For the purpose of illustration, the type of the MOF classifier class is as follows.

Definition 2 (MOF classifier type). *A MOF classifier is encoded by the following record type,* $\text{CLASSIFER} \equiv \Sigma x : \text{CLASSSTRUCT}.\text{MClassCst}(x)$ *where* CLASSSTRUCT *stands for the record*

$$\{ name : String; isAbstract : Bool;$$

$$supertype : \text{CLASSIFER}; attributes : [\text{ATTRIBUTE}]\}$$

and $\text{MClassCst}(x)$ *is a statement about* $x : \text{CLASSSTRUCT}$ *that formalize the constraints given in the OMG standard.*

A similar encoding is made for the other MOF elements: a record type, used to define the element's structure, is paired with constraints over the structure using a dependent sum, used to formally specify the element's semantics.

The type of all MOF-based metamodels, METAMODEL, can be defined as a fixed point corresponding to mutually recursive set of MOF class instances. The definition follows from the MOF, where a metamodel is understood to consist of a set of associated metaclasses.

4.2   Metamodels as Types

Recall that metamodels have a dual representation, as M_2 level objects and as M_2 level classes. This dual representation is formalized by means of a transformation between instantiating METAMODEL terms and TYPE_1 level types. The transformation is twofold: (1) A *reflection map* ϕ is applied to obtain a set of mutally recursive record types from a metamodel term. The map essentially obtains a type structure for the metaclasses and associations of the metamodel. (2) The constraints specified by the MOF metamodel description as `Constraint` objects are formalized as a specification over the type structure obtained from the reflection map. The transformation then uses this information to build a dependent sum type that represents the metamodel. The mapping is omitted for reasons of space – see [9] for details.

Definition 3 (Metamodel types). *Given a* METAMODEL *instance* a : METAMODEL*, the type* $\phi(a)$ *is called the metamodel structure type for* a*, and represents the structure of the metamodel, when considered as a collection of* M_2 *level classifiers. The general form of a metamodel type is* $\Sigma x : \phi(a).P(x)$ *for a generated predicate* P *and* a : METAMODEL.

Given a metamodel type $\Sigma x : \phi(a).P(x)$, the predicate P should be a formal specification of the `Constraints` objects that form part of the MOF metamodel for a. In general, when using our approach for formalizing MOF-based metamodels, it is not possible to automatically generate P, because the OMG specification permits `Constraints` to take any form. However, if we assume the constraints are always written in a subset of first order logic, such as the OCL, then it is possible to generate P in a consistent manner.

4.3   Metamodelling and Modelling Process

Given a typical, informal, MOF-based specification of a metamodel, consisting of metaclasses, meta-associations and constraints, it is quite straightforward to develop an instance of METAMODEL. The process is straightforward because MOF-based metamodel specifications, such as the OMG's definition of the UML, usually make use of OCL constraints. These can be readily translated into logical constraints in the METAMODEL Then, by application of ϕ, a TYPE$_1$ level type can be produced that defines the structure of the metamodel.

For example, given a MOF-compliant definition of the simple database meta-model of Fig. 3, it is possible to develop a metamodel term rdb that will yield a TYPE$_2$ dependent sum of the form $\Sigma x : \phi(rdb).P(x)$ where $\phi(rdb)$ is a coinductive record[1]

$$\text{RDB} \equiv \{\textsf{nes} : [\text{NAMEDELEMENT}]; \textsf{tables} : [\text{TABLE}]; \textsf{keys} : [\text{KEY}]; \textsf{columns} : [\text{COLUMN}]\}$$

built from the following types

$$\text{NAMEDELEMENT} \equiv \{name : String\}$$

$$\text{TABLE} \equiv \{name : String; tablecolumns : [\text{COLUMN}]; keys : [\text{KEY}]]\}$$

$$\text{KEY} \equiv \{name : String; keyColumns : [\text{COLUMN}]\}$$

$$\text{COLUMN} \equiv \{name : String\}$$

and P is a formula that is derived from `Constraint` metaobjects that were associated with the metamodel.

---

[1] We write this record informally here as a record: formally, it would involve a μ constructor, following [9]. The idea is that a term instance of this metamodel type will consist of a record of metaclass term instances that can mutually refer to each other. This also allows us to represent shared data, as in the case where the same column is referenced by a key and by a table.

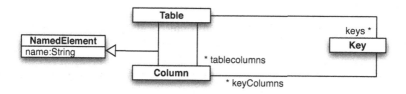

Fig. 3. Fragment of the DB metamodel

Similarly, given the OMG's definition of the UML, it is possible to develop a metamodel term *uml* that will yield a TYPE$_2$ dependent sum of the form $\Sigma x : \phi(uml).P(x)$ where $\phi(uml)$ is a fixed point, written in a recursive style as

$$\text{NAMEDELEMENT} \equiv \{name : String\}$$

$$\text{CLASS} \equiv \{name : String; isAbstract : Boolean; tag : String; super : Class;$$
$$attrs : [\text{ATTRIBUTE}]\}$$

$$\text{PRIMITIVETYPE} \equiv \{name : String\}$$

$$\text{TYPE} \equiv \{name : String\}$$

$$\text{TYPEELEMENT} \equiv \{name : String; type : \text{TYPE}\}$$

$$\text{ATTRIBUTE} \equiv \{name : String; type : \text{TYPE}; multiplicity : \text{MULTIPLICITYKIND}\}$$

$$\text{MULTIPLICITYKIND} \equiv \{lowerBound : int; upperBound : int; ordered : Boolean;$$
$$unique : Boolean\}$$

and P is a formula that is derived from `Constraint` metaobjects that were associated with the metamodel. As required, this corresponds to the standard equivalent M_2 level class-based metamodel diagram.

4.4   Proofs-as-Model-Transformations

Given a way of representing MOF metamodels and models within our type theory, we can then apply the proofs-as-programs approach entailed in Theorem 2 to extract correct model transformations. First, we specify transformations as $\forall\exists$ types of the form

$$\forall x : \text{PIL}.I(x) \rightarrow (\exists y : \text{PSL}.O(x,y))$$

where PIL and PSL are source and target metamodel types, $I(x)$ specifies a precondition on the input model x for the transformation to be applied, and $O(x,y)$ specifies required properties of the output model y. We use typing rules to obtain an inhabiting term for such a transformation type. Then, by virtue of Curry-Howard isomorphism and proofs-as-programs, this term can be transformed into a model transformation function f such that, given any PIM x satisfying the precondition $I(x)$, then the postcondition $O(x, fx)$ will be satisfied.

4.5   Example

Consider the following toy UML-to-relational-database model transformation specification: For each non abstract class of the UML model which is taged "CMP" persistent a table is created in the RDB model. This table has the same name as the class and holds one column per attributes of the class. Columns have the name of its corresponding attribute.

The transformation has UML models as its input and RDB models as output. The precondition of the transformation is class name uniqueness, sketched in OCL as

```
UMLModel->instanceof(Class)->forall(c1,c2 | c1.name = c2.name
    implies c1 = c2)
```

The postcondition of the transformation is

```
UMLModel->instanceoff(Class)->select(c |   c.isAbstract == false
  c.tag == 'CMP')->forall(c | RDBMModel->instanceof(Table)->one(t |
      t.name == c.name attributes->forall(a |
        t.columns->one( | col.name == a.name))))
```

The specification of the transformation is given as follows

$$\forall x : \text{UML}.\forall c : \text{CLASS}.c \in x.\text{classes} \wedge$$
$$c.\text{isAbstract} = false \wedge c.\text{tag} =' CMP' \rightarrow$$
$$\exists y : \text{RDB}.!\exists t : \text{TABLE}.t \in y.\text{tables} \wedge t.\text{name} = c.\text{name} \wedge$$
$$\forall a : \text{ATTRIBUTE}.a \in c.\text{attribs} \wedge$$
$$!\exists col : \text{COLUMN}.col \in t.\text{columns} \wedge col.\text{name} = a.\text{name} \quad (2)$$

where
$$!\exists y : T.P(y) \Leftrightarrow \exists y : T.P(y) \wedge \forall z : T.P(z) \rightarrow z = y$$

This specification can then be proved using just over 100 applications of the typing rules of Fig. 1. Semi-automatic use of tactics in a theorem proving environment such as PVS should reduce the burden of proof on a human developer. Then, by application of the extraction mapping, we can obtain a lambda term whose input type is UML and whose output is RDB, $\lambda x : \text{UML}.F(x.classes)$, where F is an extracted function of the form

```
F: [Class] -> [Tables]
F hd::tl ->
 if hd.tag = 'CMP'
  {name = hd.name; columns = v}::F(tl)
  where v = [{name = a.name}] a over all hd.attribs
  else F(tl)
 [a] -> if a.tag = 'CMP' then {name = a.name; columns = v}
  else []
```

This extracted function is the required model transformation.

5   Related Work and Conclusions

We have attempted to demonstrate that constructive type theory is a natural choice to formally encode the higher-order structure of the MOF. To the best of our knowledge, constructive type theory has not been used previously as a framework to treat metamodelling.

Favre [3] developed a methodology for writing correct transformations between UML-based metamodels. Transformations are understood formally in terms of the *Casl* algebraic specification language, so a notion of formal correctness is present and transformations are proved correct. The work has yet to be generalized to arbitrary MOF metamodels.

Akehurst et al. have used relational algebras to formalize metamodels and model transformations [1]. Thirioux et al. have a similar approach based on typed multigraphs [14]. Their framework forms an algebra with operations corresponding to the classification relationship between metamodels and models. From a type theoretic perspective, their formalisation is first order, and based in set theory. As a result, their model of the higher order nature of the MOF and model transformations is "flattened" into a single type universe (sets).

Structured algebraic specification languages that have been used for formalizing object-oriented specification should have the potential for formal metamodelling. We know of two approaches. Ruscio et al. have made some progress towards formalizing the KM3 metamodelling language using the Abstract State Machines [12]. Rivera and Vallecillo have exploited the class-based nature of the Maude specification language to formalize metamodels written in the KM3 metamodelling language [11]. Their treatment of the dual, object- and class-based, representation of metamodels is similar to ours, involving an equivalence mapping. The intention was to use Maude as a means of defining dynamic behaviour of models, something that our approach also lends itself to. Their work has the advantage of permitting simulation via rewriting rules.

Our experience with the small transformation described above is that, while the proof steps are often relatively trivial, there are a great many of them and the process of manual proof is laborious. We expect a tactic-based theorem prover will improve efficiency of the development process. A tactic is essentially a script that automates a sequence of proof steps. There are three robust tactic-based tools based on higher order lambda calculus: Nuprl, Coq and PVS. All three systems are equipped with advanced semi-automatic theorem provers and have been shown to be effective in the synthesis and verification of complex industrial software systems. A full implementation of our approach within Nuprl forms part of ongoing research by the author's group.

References

[1] Akehurst, D.H., Kent, S., Patrascoiu, O.: A relational approach to defining and implementing transformations between metamodels. Software and System Modeling 2(4), 215–239 (2003)

[2] Constable, R., Mendler, N., Howe, D.: Implementing Mathematics with the Nuprl Proof Development System. Prentice-Hall, Englewood Cliffs (1986) (Accessed May 2003), http://www.cs.cornell.edu/Info/Projects/NuPrl/book/doc.html

[3] Favre, L.: Foundations for mda-based forward engineering. Journal of Object Technology 4(1), 129–153 (2005)

[4] Martin-Löf, P.: Intuitionistic Type Theory. Bibliopolis (1984)

[5] Mottu, J.-M., Baudry, B., Le Traon, Y.: Mutation Analysis Testing for Model Transformations. In: Rensink, A., Warmer, J. (eds.) ECMDA-FA 2006. LNCS, vol. 4066, pp. 376–390. Springer, Heidelberg (2006)

[6] Mukerji, J., Miller, J.: MDA Guide Version 1.0.1. Object Management Group (2003)

[7] OMG. Meta Object Facility (MOF) Specification. Object Management Group (2000)

[8] OMG. Meta Object Facility (MOF) Core Specification, Version 2.0. Object Management Group (January 2006)

[9] Poernomo, I.: A Type Theoretic Framework for Formal Metamodelling. In: Reussner, R., Stafford, J.A., Szyperski, C.A. (eds.) Architecting Systems with Trustworthy Components. LNCS, vol. 3938, pp. 262–298. Springer, Heidelberg (2006)

[10] Poernomo, I., Crossley, J., Wirsing, M.: Adapting Proofs-as-Programs: The Curry-Howard Protocol. Monographs in computer science. Springer, Heidelberg (2005)

[11] Rivera, J., Vallecillo, A.: Adding behavioural semantics to models. In: The 11th IEEE International EDOC Conference (EDOC 2007), Annapolis, Maryland, USA, pp. 169–180. IEEE Computer Society, Los Alamitos (2007)

[12] Ruscio, D.D., Jouault, F., Kurtev, I., Bézivin, J., Pierantonio, A.: Extending AMMA for supporting dynamic semantics specifications of DSLs. Technical Report 06.02, Laboratoire d'Informatique de Nantes-Atlantique (LINA), Nantes, France (April 2006)

[13] Simons, A.J.H.: The theory of classification. part 3: Object encodings and recursion. Journal of Object Technology 1(4), 49–57 (2002)

[14] Thirioux, X., Combemale, B., Crégut, X., Garoche, P.-L.: A framework to formalise the mde foundations. In: Proceedings of TOWERS 2007, Zurich, June 25 2007, pp. 14–30 (2007)

Analysing Graph Transformation Rules through OCL

Jordi Cabot[1], Robert Clarisó[1], Esther Guerra[2], and Juan de Lara[3]

[1] Universitat Oberta de Catalunya (Spain)
{jcabot,rclariso}@uoc.edu
[2] Universidad Carlos III de Madrid (Spain)
eguerra@inf.uc3m.es
[3] Universidad Autónoma de Madrid (Spain)
jdelara@uam.es

Abstract. In this paper we present an approach to the analysis of graph transformation rules based on an intermediate OCL representation. We translate different semantics of rules into OCL, together with the properties of interest (like rule applicability, conflict or independence). The intermediate representation serves three purposes: (i) allows the seamless integration of graph transformation rules with the MOF and OCL standards, and enables taking into account meta-model and OCL constraints when verifying the correctness of the rules; (ii) permits the interoperability of graph transformation concepts with a number of standards-based model-driven development tools; and (iii) makes available a plethora of OCL tools to actually perform the rule analysis.

1 Introduction

Model-Driven Development (MDD) is a software engineering paradigm where models play a fundamental role. They are used to specify, simulate, test, verify and generate code for the application to be built. Most of these activities are model manipulations, thus, model transformation becomes a crucial activity. Many efforts have been spent in designing specialized languages for model transformation, ranging from textual to visual; declarative to imperative through hybrid; semi-formal to formal. The OMG vision of MDD is called Model-Driven Architecture (MDA) and is founded on standards like QVT [17] for the transformations and MOF and OCL for modelling and meta-modelling.

Graph Transformation [8,18] is a declarative, rule-based technique for expressing model transformations. It is gaining increasing popularity due to its visual form (making rules intuitive) and formal nature (making rules and grammars amenable to analysis). For example, it has been used to describe the operational semantics of Domain Specific Visual Languages (DSVLs) [14], taking the advantage that it is possible to use the concrete syntax of the DSVL in the rules, which then become more intuitive to the designer.

As models and meta-models can be expressed as graphs (with typed, attributed nodes and edges), graph transformation can be used for model manipulation. The main formalization of graph transformation is the so called algebraic

A. Vallecillo, J. Gray, A. Pierantonio (Eds.): ICMT 2008, LNCS 5063, pp. 229–244, 2008.

approach [8], which uses category theory in order to express the rewriting. Prominent examples of this approach are the double [8] and single [9] pushout (DPO and SPO), which have developed interesting analysis techniques, e.g. to check independence between pairs of derivations [8,18], or to calculate critical pairs (minimal context of pairs of conflicting rules) [12]. However, graph grammar analysis techniques work with simplified meta-models (so called type graphs), with neither inheritance, cardinalities nor textual OCL-like constraints.

In this paper, our goal is to advance in the integration of graph transformation and MDD. We propose using OCL as an intermediate representation of both the semantics of graph transformation rules and the analysis properties of interest. Representing rules with OCL, concepts like attribute computation and attribute conditions in rules can be seamlessly integrated with the meta-model and OCL constraints during the rule analysis. Specifying the rules and the properties in OCL makes available a plethora of tools, able to analyze this kind of specifications. A secondary effect is that graph transformation is made available to the increasing number of MDA tools that the community is building and vice-versa. For example, using such tools, it could be possible to generate code for the transformations, or apply metrics and redesigns to the rules.

More in detail, we use OCL to represent (DPO/SPO) rules with negative application conditions and attribute conditions. These rules may have objects with abstract typing, which can be matched to objects of more concrete types [13]. In addition, we have represented a number of analysis properties with OCL, taking into account both the rule structure and the rule and meta-model constraints such as rule applicability (whether there is a model satisfying the rule and the meta-model constraints), weak executability (whether the rule's post-condition and the meta-model constraints are satisfiable by some model) and correctness preserving (if a rule applied to a legal model always yields a legal model) among others. As a proof of concept, we have checked these properties using the UMLtoCSP tool [6]

Paper Organization. Section 2 introduces graph transformation using a production system example. Section 3 presents our translation of graph transformation rules into OCL. Section 4 shows the encoding of some analysis properties. Section 5 presents the use of the UMLtoCSP tool for checking some properties. Section 6 compares with related work and Section 7 ends with the conclusions.

2   Graph Transformation by Example

In this section we give an intuition on graph transformation by presenting some rules that belong to a simulator of a DSVL for production systems. Fig. 1 shows the DSVL meta-model. It defines different kinds of machines (concrete subclasses of *Machine*) that can be connected through conveyors. These can be interconnected and contain pieces (the number of pieces they actually hold is stored in attribute *nelems*), up to its maximum capacity (attribute *capacity*). The last two OCL constraints to the right of the figure guarantee that the number of elements of a conveyor is equal to the number of pieces connected to it and

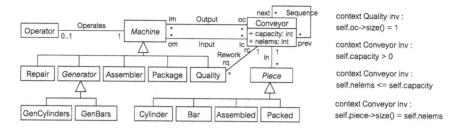

Fig. 1. Meta-model of a DSVL for production systems

never exceeds its capacity. Human operators are needed to operate the machines, which consume and produce different types of pieces from/to conveyors.

Fig. 2 shows a production model example using a visual concrete syntax. It contains six machines (one of each type), two operators, six conveyors and five pieces. Machines are represented as decorated boxes, except generators, which are depicted as semi-circles with an icon representing the kind of piece they generate. Operators are shown as circles, conveyors as lattice boxes, and each kind of piece has its own shape. In the model, the two operators are currently operating a generator of cylindrical pieces and a packaging machine respectively. Even though all associations in the meta-model are bidirectional, we have assigned arrows in the concrete syntax, but of course this does not affect navigability.

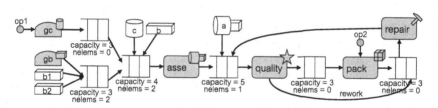

Fig. 2. Example production system model

We use graph transformation techniques for the specification of the DSVL operational semantics. A graph grammar is made of a set of rules and an initial graph to which the rules are applied. Each rule is made of a left and a right hand side (LHS and RHS) graphs. The LHS expresses pre-conditions for the rule to be applied, whereas the RHS contains the rule's post-conditions. In order to apply a rule to the *host graph*, a morphism (an occurrence or match) of the LHS has to be found in it (if several are found, one is selected randomly). Then, the rule is applied by substituting the match by the RHS. The grammar execution proceeds by applying the rules in non-deterministic order, until none is applicable.

Next, we show some of the rules describing the DSVL operational semantics. Rule "assemble" specifies the behaviour of an assembler machine, which converts one cylinder and a bar into an assembled piece. The rule is shown in concrete syntax to the left of Fig. 3, and in abstract syntax to the right. It can be applied if an occurrence of the LHS is found in the model (e.g. it could be applied to the model in Fig. 2). Then, the elements in the LHS that do not appear in the RHS are deleted, whereas the elements in the RHS that do not appear in the LHS are newly created. Our rules may include attribute conditions (which must be satisfied by the match) and attribute computations, both expressed in OCL. Attributes referenced to the right of an assignment in an attribute computation refer to the value of the attribute before the rule application.

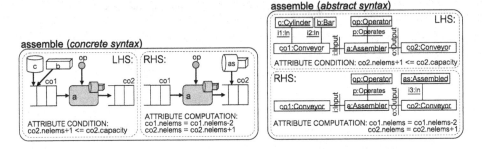

Fig. 3. Assemble rule in concrete syntax (left) and abstract syntax (right)

There are two main formalizations of algebraic graph transformation, DPO and SPO. From a practical point of view, their difference is that in DPO, deletion has no side effects. When a node in the host graph is deleted by a rule, it can only be connected with those edges explicitly deleted by the rule. When applying the rule in Fig. 3, if piece "b" in the match is connected to more than one conveyor (should it be allowed by the meta-model), then the rule cannot be applied as edges would become dangling in the host graph. This condition is called *dangling edge* condition. In SPO, dangling edges are removed by the rewriting step. Therefore in DPO, in addition to positive pre-conditions, a LHS also imposes implicit negative pre-conditions in case the rule deletes some node.

A match can be non-injective, which means for example that two nodes with compatible type in the rule may be matched to a single node in the host graph. If the rule specifies that one of them should be deleted and the other one preserved, DPO forbids applying the rule at such match, while SPO allows its application and deletes both nodes. This is called the *identification condition*.

Fig. 4 shows further rules for the DSVL. Rule "move" describes the movement of pieces through conveyors. The rule has a negative application condition (NAC) that forbids moving the piece if the source conveyor is the input to any kind of machine having an operator. Note that this rule uses abstract nodes: piece "p" and machine "m" have abstract types, and are visually represented with asterisks. Abstract nodes in the rule can get instantiated to nodes of any concrete subtype [13]. In this way, rules become much more compact. Rule "change" models an operator changing to a machine "m1" if the machine has some piece waiting to be processed and it is unattended. Rule "rest" models the break pause of an operator, which is deleted, while rule "work" creates a new operator in an unattended machine.

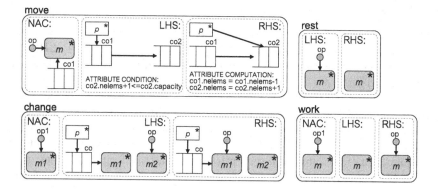

Fig. 4. Additional rules for the DSVL simulator

3   From Graph Transformation to OCL

This section presents a procedure to translate graph transformation rules into an OCL-based representation. The procedure takes as input a graph transformation system, made of a set of rules; together with the MOF-compliant meta-model used as a context for the rules. As output, the method generates a set of semantically-equivalent declarative operations (one for each rule) specified in OCL. Declarative operations are specified by means of a contract consisting of a set of pre and post-conditions. Roughly speaking, pre-conditions will define a set of conditions on the source model that will hold iff the rule can be applied, namely if the model has a match for the LHS pattern and no match for any NAC, while post-conditions will describe the new state of the model after the operation execution as stated by the difference between the rule's RHS and LHS.

More precisely, the input of the procedure is a tuple $(MM, ruleStyle, GTS = \{r_j\}_{j \in J})$, where MM is a meta-model (possibly restricted by OCL well-formedness rules), $ruleStyle$ is a flag indicating DPO or SPO semantics, and GTS is a set of graph transformation rules. We represent DPO and SPO rules as $r = (LHS, RHS, ATT_{COND}, ATT_{COMP}, \{NAC^i, ATT^i_{COND}\}_{i \in I})$, where LHS, RHS and NAC^i are models conformant to MM. Instances are identified across models by their object identifiers, e.g. the preserved elements by the rule have the same object identifiers in LHS and RHS. ATT_{COND}, ATT^i_{COND} and ATT_{COMP} are sets of OCL expressions. The first two contain attribute conditions for the LHS and the i-th NAC, the latter contains attribute computations to state the new values for the attributes in the RHS.

Next subsections use this formalization to translate the GTS in terms of a set of OCL operations. The name of the operations will be the name of the corresponding rule. All operations will be attached to an artificial class $System$, typically used in the analysis phase to contain the operations describing the behaviour of the system [15]. Alternatively, each operation could be assigned to one of the existing classes in the meta-model.

3.1   Translating the Left-Hand Side

A rule r can be applied on a host graph (i.e a model) if there is a match, that is, if it is possible to assign objects of the host graph to nodes in the LHS such that (a) the type in the host graph is compatible with the type in the LHS, (b) all edges in LHS may be mapped to links in the host graph and (c) the attribute conditions evaluate to true when symbols are replaced by the concrete attribute values in the model. It is possible that the same object is assigned to multiple nodes in LHS (non-injective match) as long as conditions (a-c) are satisfied.

When defining the translation for condition (a) we must explicitly encode the set of quantifiers implicit in the semantics of graph transformation rules: when checking if the host graph contains a match for LHS we have to try assigning each possible combination of objects from compatible types in the model to the set of nodes in the pattern. Thus, we need one quantifier for each node in LHS. In terms of OCL, these quantifiers will be expressed as a sequence of embedded *exists* operators over the population of each node type (retrieved using the predefined *allInstances* operation).

Once we have a possible assignment of objects to the nodes in LHS we must check if the objects satisfy the (b) and (c) conditions. To do so, we define an auxiliary query operation *matchLHSr*. This operation returns true if a given set of objects complies with the pattern structure defined in LHS and satisfy its ATT_{COND} conditions. In particular for each edge e linking two objects o_1 (of type t_1) and o_2 (of type t_2) in LHS, *matchLHSr* must define a $o_1.nav_{t2} -> includes(o_2)$ condition stating that o_2 must be included in the set of objects retrieved when navigating from o_1 to the related objects in t_2; the right association end to use in the navigation nav_{t2} is extracted from the MM according to the type of e and the type of the two object participants. ATT_{COND} conditions, already expressed using an OCL-like syntax in r, are directly mapped as a conjunction of conditions at the end of *matchLHSr*.

Let $L = \{L_1, \ldots, L_n\}$ denote the set of nodes in LHS and $E = \{(L_i, L_j)\}$ the set of edges. Then, according to the previous guidelines, the LHS pattern of r will be translated into the following equivalent pre-condition:

---

context System::r()
pre: $L_1.type$::allInstances()−>exists(L_1 |
   ...
     $L_n.type$::allInstances()−>exists(L_n | matchLHSr($L_1, \ldots, L_n$)))

---

context System::matchLHSr($L_1 : L_1.type, \ldots, L_n : L_n.type$)
body: $L_1.nav_{L2.type}$−>includes(L_2) and
   ...and
    $L_i.nav_{Lj.type}$−>includes(L_j) and ATT_{COND}

---

where $L_i.type$ returns the *type* of the node and the identifier of the node is used to name the variable in the quantifier. Note that $L_i.type$::allInstances() returns all direct and indirect instances of the $L_i.type$ (that is, it returns also the instances of its subtypes) and thus abstract objects can be used in the definition of r.

As an example, the pre-condition for the *rest* rule would be:

---

context System::rest()
pre: Operator::allInstances()−>exists(*op* |
      Machine::allInstances()−>exists(*m* | matchLHSrest(*op*, *m*))

---

context System::matchLHSrest(op: Operator, m: Machine)
body: op.machine−>includes(m)

---

where *matchLHSrest* is called for every possible combination of operators and machines in the model (because of the two nested *exists*). If one of such combinations satisfies *matchLHSrest* the pre-condition evaluates to true, meaning that "rest" can be applied on the model.

3.2 Translating the Negative Application Conditions

In presence of $NACs$ the pre-condition of r must also check that the set of objects of the host graph satisfying LHS do not match any of the NACs.

The translation of a NAC pattern is almost equal to the translation of a LHS pattern: an existential quantifier must be introduced for each new node in the NAC (i.e. each node not appearing also in the LHS pattern) and an auxiliary query operation ($matchNACr$) will be created to determine if a given set of objects satisfy the NAC pattern. $MatchNACr$ is specified following the same procedure used to define $matchLHSr$.

Within the pre-condition, the translation of the $NACs$ is added as a negated condition immediately after the translation of the LHS pattern.

Let $N = \{N_1, \ldots, N_m\}$ denote the set of nodes in a NAC that do not appear also in LHS. The extended pre-condition for r (LHS + NAC) is defined as:

---

context System::r()
pre: $L_1.type$::allInstances()−>exists(L_1 |
      ...
    $L_n.type$::allInstances()−>exists(L_n | matchLHSr($L_1, \ldots, L_n$)
    and not ($N_1.type$::allInstances()−>exists(N_1 |
      ...
    $N_m.type$::allInstances()−>exists(N_m |
    matchNACr($L_1, \ldots, L_n, N_1, \ldots, N_m$))...)

If r contains several $NACs$ we just need to repeat the process for each NAC, creating the corresponding $matchNAC_ir$ operation every time.

As an example, the translation for the LHS and NAC patterns of the "work" rule would be:

---

context System::work()
pre: Machine::allInstances()−>exists(m | matchLHSwork(m)
　　　　and not Operator::allInstances()−>exists(op1|matchNACwork(m,op1)))

---

context System::matchLHSwork(m:Machine):Boolean **body:** true

---

context System::matchNACwork(m:Machine, op1:Operator):Boolean
body: m.operator−>includes(op1)

Note that for this rule, *matchLHSwork* simply returns true since as long as a machine object exists in the host graph (ensured by the existential quantifier in the pre-condition), the LHS is satisfied. The additional condition is here imposed by the NAC, stating that no operator may be working on that machine.

3.3　Translating the Right-Hand Side

The effect of rule r on the host graph is the following: (1) the deletion of the objects and links appearing in LHS and not in RHS, (2) the creation of the objects and links appearing in RHS but not in LHS and (3) the update of attribute values of objects in the match according to the ATT_{COMP} computations.

Clearly, when defining the OCL post-condition for r we will need to consider not only the RHS pattern (the *new* state) but also the LHS (and NAC) patterns (the *old* state) in order to compute the differences between them and determine how the objects evolve from the old to the new state. In OCL, references to the old state (i.e. references to the values of objects and links in the state *before* executing the operation) must include the @*pre* keyword (for instance, a post-condition expression like $o.atr_1 = o.atr_1@pre + 1$ states that the value of atr_1 for object o is increased by one upon completion of the operation)

Therefore, the translation of the RHS pattern requires, as a first step, to select a set of objects of the host graph that are a match for the rule. Unsurprisingly, this initial condition is expressed with exactly the same OCL expression used to define the pre-condition (where the goal was the same: to determine a match for r). The only difference is that in the post-condition, all references to attributes, navigations and predefined properties will include the @*pre* keyword. Next, the selected set of objects are passed to an auxiliary operation *changeRHSr*, in charge of performing the changes defined in the rule.

Table 1. OCL expressions for changeRHSr

Element	$\exists$ in LHS?	$\exists$ in RHS?	Update	OCL Expression
Object o of type t	No	Yes	Insert o	$o.\text{oclIsNew}()$ and $o.\text{oclIsTypeOf}(t)$
Object o of type t	Yes	No	Delete o	$t::\text{allInstances}()->\text{excludes}(o)$
Link l between (o_1, o_2)	No	Yes	Insert l	$o_1.nav_{t2}->\text{includes}(o_2)$
Link l between (o_1, o_2)	Yes	No	Delete l	$o_1.nav_{t2}->\text{excludes}(o_2)$

---

context System::rest()
pre: Operator::allInstances−>exists(op|
         Machine::allInstances−>exists(m|matchLHSrest(op,m)))
post: Operator::allInstances@pre−>exists(op|
         Machine::allInstances@pre−>exists(m|
         matchLHSrest'(op,m) and changeRHSrest(op,m)))

---

context System::matchLHSrest(op: Operator, m: Machine):Boolean
body: op.machine−>includes(m)

---

context System::matchLHSrest'(op: Operator, m: Machine):Boolean
body: op.machine@pre−>includes(m)

---

context System::changeRHSrest(op: Operator, m: Machine):Boolean
body: Operator::allInstances()−>excludes(op)

---

context System::work()
pre: Machine::allInstances()−>exists(m|matchLHSwork(m) and not (
         Operator::allInstances()−>exists(op1|matchNACwork(m,op1)))
post: Machine::allInstances()@pre−>exists(m|matchLHSwork'(m) and not
         (Operator::allInstances@pre()−>exists(op1|matchNACwork'(m,op1)))
         and changeRHSwork(m)

---

context System::matchLHSwork(m:Machine):Boolean **body:** true

---

context System::matchLHSwork'(m:Machine):Boolean **body:** true

---

context System::matchNACwork(m:Machine, op1:Operator):Boolean
body: m.operator−> includes(op1)

---

context System::matchNACwork'(m:Machine, op1:Operator):Boolean
body: m.operator@pre−> includes(op1)

---

context System::changeRHSwork(m:Machine):Boolean
body: op.oclIsNew() and op.oclIsTypeOf(Operator) and
         m.operator−>includes(op)

ChangeRHSr will be defined as a conjunction of conditions, one for each difference between the RHS and LHS patterns. Table 1 shows the OCL expressions that must be added to *changeRHSr* depending on the modifications performed by r on the host graph. Moreover, all ATT_{COMP} are added as additional computations at the end. Again, in the computations all references to previous attribute values are extended with the @pre keyword. As usual, we assume in the definition of the post-condition for r that all elements not explicitly modified in the post-condition remain unchanged (*frame problem*).

As an example, we show the complete operations generated for the "rest" and "work" rules. The translation for the other rules in the running example can be found in the extended version of this paper [23].

3.4   Taking into Account DPO and SPO Semantics

The behaviour of the rules is slightly different depending on whether DPO or SPO semantics are assumed. The two main differences we must consider in our translation are the *dangling edge* condition and the *identification* condition.

In DPO, the *dangling edge* condition states that when a node is deleted, it can only be connected to other nodes by the edges that are explicitly deleted by the rule. With SPO semantics, all edges are implicitly removed when deleting the node. This is the common assumption in UML/OCL specifications [19] and thus with SPO we do not need to modify the translation patterns provided so far (for instance, in the "rest" operation it is assumed that all links connecting object op with other objects are implicitly removed when deleting it). Instead, under DPO semantics we must refine the generated pre-condition to ensure that the objects deleted by the rule have no other links except for those appearing in LHS and not in RHS. Therefore, for each deleted object o instance of a type t and for each type t_i related with t in MM we must include in $matchLHS$ the following conditions:

- $o.nav_{ti}->isEmpty()$ (when LHS does not include edges relating o with nodes of type t_i)
- $o.nav_{ti}->excludingAll(o_1, o_2, \ldots, o_n)->isEmpty()$ (when LHS includes edges relating o with a set of $\{o_1, o_2, \ldots, o_n\}$ nodes of type t_i)

The *identification* condition states that two nodes of the LHS cannot be matched into the same object in the host graph if one of the nodes does not appear in the RHS pattern (i.e. it is deleted). With SPO semantics, the object in the host graph is simply removed. Again, the SPO semantics coincide with the default UML/OCL behaviour. If two OCL variables point to the same object and one of the variables is used to define that the pointed object is removed, the other automatically becomes undefined. Instead, to enforce the DPO semantics we need an additional condition in the $matchLHS$ operation. Given that L_1 and L_2 are two nodes in the LHS pattern, $L_1.type = L_2.type$ and L_1 but not L_2 appear in RHS (or the other way around), the condition $L_1 <> L_2$ should be added in $matchLHS$. This condition forces the problematic existential quantifiers to map to two different objects when evaluating the pre-condition.

4   Formalization of Rule Properties with OCL

Translating a graph grammar into a set of operations with OCL pre/post-conditions allows the analysis of relevant properties of the rules. The properties under analysis will take into account the meta-model invariants that restrict the possible set of legal instantiations (i.e. models) of the meta-model.

The following notation will be used to express these concepts: I denotes an instantiation of the meta-model, while I' represents the modified instantiation after invoking an operation. An instantiation I is called *legal*, noted as $\mathsf{INV}[I]$, if it satisfies all the invariants of the meta-model, i.e. both the graphical restrictions such as multiplicity of roles in associations and the explicit OCL well-formedness rules. By $\mathsf{PRE}_r[I]$ we denote that an instantiation I satisfies the pre-condition of an operation r. Regarding post-conditions, we write $\mathsf{POST}_r[I, I']$ to express that instantiation I' satisfies the post-condition of an operation r assuming that I was the instantiation before executing the operation.

Two families of properties will be studied. First, it is desirable to verify that for each rule there exists at least one valid model where it can be applied, as otherwise the rule is useless. Second, it is interesting to check whether different rules may interfere among them, making the order of application matter. Within each family of properties, several notions will be presented, each with a trade-off between precision and the complexity of its analysis. The list, with its formalization, is the following:

- **Applicability (AP):** Rule r is *applicable* if there is at least one legal instantiation of the meta-model where it can be applied.

$$\exists I : \mathsf{INV}[I] \wedge \mathsf{PRE}_r[I]$$

- **Weak executability (WE):** r is *weakly executable* if the post-condition is satisfiable in some legal instantiation.

$$\exists I, I' : \mathsf{INV}[I] \wedge \mathsf{INV}[I'] \wedge \mathsf{POST}_r[I, I']$$

- **Strong executability (SE):** r is *strongly executable* if, for any legal instantiation that satisfies the pre-condition, there is another legal instantiation that satisfies the post-condition.

$$\forall I : \exists I' : (\mathsf{INV}[I] \wedge \mathsf{PRE}_r[I]) \rightarrow (\mathsf{INV}[I'] \wedge \mathsf{POST}_r[I, I'])$$

- **Correctness preserving (CP):** r is *correctness preserving* if, applied to a legal instantiation of the meta-model, cannot produce an illegal one.

$$\forall I, I' : (\mathsf{INV}[I] \wedge \mathsf{PRE}_r[I]) \rightarrow (\mathsf{POST}_r[I, I'] \rightarrow \mathsf{INV}[I'])$$

- **Overlapping rules (OR):** Two rules r and s overlap if there is at least one legal instantiation where both rules are applicable.

$$\exists I : \mathsf{INV}[I] \wedge \mathsf{PRE}_r[I] \wedge \mathsf{PRE}_s[I]$$

- **Conflict (CN):** Two rules r and s are in conflict if firing one rule can disable the other, i.e. iff there is one legal instantiation where both rules are enabled, and after applying one of the rules, the other becomes disabled.

$$\exists I, I' : \mathsf{INV}[I] \wedge \mathsf{INV}[I'] \wedge \mathsf{PRE}_r[I] \wedge \mathsf{PRE}_s[I] \wedge \mathsf{POST}_r[I, I'] \wedge \neg\mathsf{PRE}_s[I']$$

– **Independence (IN):** Two rules r and s are *independent* iff in any legal instantiation where both can be applied, any application order produces the same result. Four instantiations of the model will be considered to characterize this property: before applying the rules (I), after applying both rules (I''), after applying only rule r (I'_r) and after applying only rule s (I'_s).

$$
\begin{array}{ccc}
I & \xrightarrow{\ r\ } & I'_r \\
\Big\downarrow{\scriptstyle s} & & \Big\downarrow{\scriptstyle s} \\
I'_s & \xrightarrow{\ r\ } & I''
\end{array}
\qquad
\begin{aligned}
\forall I : \exists I'_r, I'_s, I'' : (\mathsf{INV}[I] \wedge{}& \mathsf{PRE}_r[I] \wedge \mathsf{PRE}_s[I]) \rightarrow \\
(\mathsf{INV}[I'_r] \wedge{}& \mathsf{POST}_r[I, I'_r] \wedge \mathsf{PRE}_s[I'_r] \wedge \\
\mathsf{INV}[I'_s] \wedge{}& \mathsf{POST}_s[I, I'_s] \wedge \mathsf{PRE}_r[I'_s] \wedge \\
\mathsf{INV}[I''] \wedge{}& \mathsf{POST}_r[I'_s, I''] \wedge \mathsf{POST}_s[I'_r, I''])
\end{aligned}
$$

A model I satisfying $\mathsf{PRE}_r[I]$ may admit non-determinism in the execution of r, if it contains more than one match of r. The difference between SE and CP is that the former requires one such application to be valid, while for CP all of them have to be valid. If a rule does not satisfy CP, it means that it is underspecified regarding the OCL meta-model invariants. Notice that the attribute condition in rule "assemble" in Fig. 3 is necessary to ensure that the rule satisfies CP.

The term *critical pair* is used in graph transformation to denote two direct derivations in conflict (applying one disables the other), where the starting model is minimal [8,12]. The set of critical pairs gives all *potential* conflicts, and if empty, it means that the transformation is confluent (i.e. a unique result is obtained from its application). For technical reasons, any attribute computation is usually modeled as a rewriting of edges [8]. This means that any two rules changing the same attribute of the same node will be reported as conflicting. This does not mean that one rule disables the other, but however ensures confluency. On the contrary, our CN condition is more precise about attribute computations and considers the OCL invariants, but by itself does not ensure confluency.

IN allows applying each pair of rules in any order, obtaining the same result. This is a strong version of the local Church-Rosser theorem in DPO [8], where we require rule independence for every valid model I, and ensures confluency.

5   Tool Support

Existing tools for the validation and verification of UML/OCL models (e.g. [11,7,4,1,6]) can be used to prove the correctness properties of graph transformation rules once translated into declarative OCL operations.

Each tool follows a different approach and internal formalism to cope with the verification process, with its own set of advantages and drawbacks: bounded verification, need of user guidance, termination and so forth. Moreover, the richness of constructs in OCL constitutes a challenge for all existing tools. As a result, the degree of support for some OCL constructs varies from one tool to another. An example is the support for the operator @pre in the post-condition, which must be used in the verification of properties that use POST_r. Therefore some tools may have to be adapted for the verification of those properties. All these issues should be taken into account by the designer when choosing a particular tool to verify the graph transformation rules.

As an example, we show in this section how our UMLtoCSP tool can be used to check properties of the rules of our running example. UMLtoCSP always proceeds by searching a possible instantiation of the (meta-)model consistent with all the invariants. Then, to analyze rules, pre-conditions of the corresponding operations for each rule must be added as additional invariants on the model. If after adding these additional invariants a valid instantiation still exists (i.e. the model is still strongly satisfiable [22]) we may conclude that the property is satisfied by the rule. To check properties involving post-conditions of operations, two valid instantiations (one representing the initial state and the other the final one) must be computed.

First, we use UMLtoCSP to check whether rules "change" and "move" overlap. To prove so, UMLtoCSP automatically computes the match on the left of Fig. 5. Notice that in this match of the "move" operation, the source and destination conveyors are mapped to the same conveyor object, as there is no constraint forbidding this choice. In fact, this instantiation helps us to detect a problem in our system definition: non-injective matches are inadequate for rule "move", which in this case may be solved by adding an additional invariant to the meta-model stating that a conveyor cannot be next to itself. On the other hand, the image in the right of Fig. 5 depicts a conflict between rules "work" and "change": both rules can be applied on the model but applying rule "work" would disable rule "change".

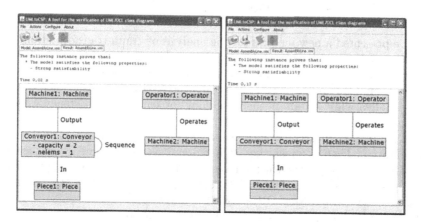

Fig. 5. Examples of an overlapping between rules "change" and "move" (left) and a conflict between rules "change" and "work" (right) as computed by UMLtoCSP

6   Related Work

There are two main sources of related work: those analysing rules using DPO and SPO theory, and those that translate rules to other domains for analysis.

In the former direction, graph transformation has developed a number of analysis techniques [8,12,18], but they usually work with simple type graphs. Our present work redefines some of these analysis properties, but taking into consideration a full-fledged meta-model, as well as OCL constraints in rules. Some preliminary efforts to integrate graph transformation with meta-modelling can be found in [13], where type graphs were extended with inheritance, and [20], were edge inheritance and edge cardinalities were incorporated into type graphs.

Regarding the transformation of graph rules into other domains, their translation into OCL pre- and post-conditions was first presented in [5]. Here we give a more complete OCL-based characterization of rules that considers both DPO and SPO, NACs, and that encodes the LHS's matching algorithm as additional pre-conditions (in [5] the match is passed as parameter to the OCL expressions, assuming an external mechanism). Besides, we exploit the resulting OCL expressions in order to enable the tool-assisted analysis of different rule properties.

Transformations to other domains can be found in [3], where rules are translated into Alloy in order to study the applicability of sequences of rules and the reachability of models; in [2], where rules are translated into Petri graphs to check safety properties; and in [21], where they are transformed into Promela for model-checking. However none of these approaches supports the analysis taking a meta-model into account or allowing OCL constraints in rules. Besides, our use of OCL as intermediate representation has the benefit that it is tool independent and we can easily integrate attribute conditions and meta-model constraints.

7   Conclusions and Future Work

We have presented a new method for the analysis of graph transformation rules that takes into account the (meta-)model structure and well-formedness OCL constraints during the verification process. This way, properties like applicability, which are fundamental to detect inconsistencies in graph transformation rules, can be studied while simultaneously checking for semantic consistency with the meta-model definition.

Our method translates the graph transformation rules into an OCL-based representation. Then, the resulting OCL expressions are combined with the OCL constraints specified for the (meta-)models and passed on to existing OCL tools for their joint verification. The translation supports rules with NACs, attribute conditions and distinguishes DPO and SPO semantics.

We believe this translation can useful for other purposes as well. Indeed, once the graph transformation rules are expressed in OCL, we can benefit from all tools designed for managing OCL expressions (spawning from code-generation to documentation, metrics analysis,...) when dealing with the rules.

As future work we would like to extend our set of correctness properties (e.g. including validation aspects, where an initial host graph is passed as an additional parameter to the verification tool) and to apply our approach to other graph transformation-based techniques, like triple graph grammars. Additionally, we plan to improve the efficiency of our approach by developing some heuristics to bound the search space explored during the verification process depending on the graph rule structure.

Acknowledgments. Work supported by the Spanish Ministry of Education and Science, projects MOSAIC (TSI2005-08225-C07-06), MODUWEB (TIN2006-09678) and TIN2005-06053, and an UOC-IN3 research grant.

References

1. Anastasakis, K., Bordbar, K., Georg, G., Ray, I.: UML2Alloy: A Challenging Model Transformation. In: Engels, G., Opdyke, B., Schmidt, D.C., Weil, F. (eds.) MOD-ELS 2007. LNCS, vol. 4735, pp. 436–450. Springer, Heidelberg (2007)
2. Baldan, P., Corradini, A., König, B.: A Static Analysis Technique for Graph Transformation Systems. In: Larsen, K.G., Nielsen, M. (eds.) CONCUR 2001. LNCS, vol. 2154, pp. 381–395. Springer, Heidelberg (2001)
3. Baresi, L., Spoletini, P.: On the Use of Alloy to Analyze Graph Transformation Systems. In: Corradini, A., Ehrig, H., Montanari, U., Ribeiro, L., Rozenberg, G. (eds.) ICGT 2006. LNCS, vol. 4178, pp. 306–320. Springer, Heidelberg (2006)
4. Brucker, A.D., Wolff, B.: The HOL-OCL book. Tech. Rep. 525, ETH Zurich (2006)
5. Büttner, F., Gogolla, M.: Realizing Graph Transformations by Pre- and Postconditions and Command Sequences. In: Corradini, A., Ehrig, H., Montanari, U., Ribeiro, L., Rozenberg, G. (eds.) ICGT 2006. LNCS, vol. 4178, pp. 398–413. Springer, Heidelberg (2006)
6. Cabot, J., Clarisó, R., Riera, D.: UMLtoCSP: A tool for the formal verification of UML/OCL models using constraint programming. In: Proc. ASE 2007, pp. 547–548 (2007)
7. Clavel, M., Egea, M.: A rewriting-based validation tool for UML+OCL static class diagrams. In: Johnson, M., Vene, V. (eds.) AMAST 2006. LNCS, vol. 4019, pp. 368–373. Springer, Heidelberg (2006)
8. Ehrig, H., Ehrig, K., Prange, U., Taentzer, G.: Fundamentals of Algebraic Graph Transformation. Springer, Heidelberg (2006)
9. Ehrig, H., Heckel, R., Korff, M., Löwe, M., Ribeiro, L., Wagner, A., Corradini, A.: Algebraic Approaches to Graph Transformation - Part II: Single Pushout Approach and Comparison with Double Pushout Approach. In: [18], pp. 247–312 (1999)
10. Ermel, C., Hölscher, K., Kuske, S., Ziemann, P.: Animated simulation of integrated UML behavioral models based on graph transformation. In: Proc. IEEE VL/HCC 2005, pp. 125–133 (2005)
11. Gogolla, M., Bohling, J., Richters, M.: Validating UML and OCL models in USE by automatic snapshot generation. SoSyM 4(4), 386–398 (2005)
12. Heckel, R., Küster, J.-M.-., Taentzer, G.: Confluence of typed attributed graph transformation systems. In: Corradini, A., Ehrig, H., Kreowski, H.-J., Rozenberg, G. (eds.) ICGT 2002. LNCS, vol. 2505, pp. 161–176. Springer, Heidelberg (2002)
13. de Lara, J., Bardohl, R., Ehrig, H., Ehrig, K., Prange, U., Taentzer, G.: Attributed graph transformation with node type inheritance. Theor. Comput. Sci. 376(3), 139–163 (2007)
14. de Lara, J., Vangheluwe, H.: Defining visual notations and their manipulation through meta-modelling and graph transformation. J. Vis. Lang. Comput. 15(3-4), 309–330 (2004)

15. Larman, C.: Applying UML and Patterns: An Introduction to Object-Oriented Analysis and Design, 3rd edn. Prentice-Hall, Englewood Cliffs (2004)
16. Mens, T., Taentzer, G., Runge, O.: Analysing refactoring dependencies using graph transformation. SoSyM 6(3), 269–285 (2007)
17. QVT standard specification, http://www.omg.org/docs/ptc/05-11-01.pdf
18. Rozenberg, G. (ed.): Handbook of Graph Grammars and Computing by Graph Transformations, Foundations, vol. 1. World Scientific, Singapore (1997)
19. Sendall, S., Strohmeier, A.: Using OCL and UML to Specify System Behavior. In: Clark, A., Warmer, J. (eds.) Object Modeling with the OCL. LNCS, vol. 2263, pp. 250–280. Springer, Heidelberg (2002)
20. Taentzer, G., Rensink, A.: Ensuring Structural Constraints in Graph-Based Models with Type Inheritance. In: Cerioli, M. (ed.) FASE 2005. LNCS, vol. 3442, pp. 64–79. Springer, Heidelberg (2005)
21. Varró, D.: Automated formal verification of visual modeling languages by model checking. SoSyM 3(2), 85–113 (2004)
22. Cabot, J., Clarisó, R., Riera, D.: Verification of UML/OCL Class Diagrams Using Constraint Programming. MoDeVVa 2008. ICST Workshop (to appear, 2008),http://gres.uoc.edu/pubs/MODEVVA08.pdf
23. Cabot, J., Clarisó, R., Riera, D.: Analysing Graph Transformation Rules Through OCL (extended version), http://gres.uoc.edu/UMLtoCSP/ICMT08.pdf

Extracting Object Interactions Out of Software Contracts Using Model Transformations*

Andrés Vignaga, Daniel Perovich, and María Cecilia Bastarrica

Department of Computer Science, Universidad de Chile
{avignaga,dperovic,cecilia}@dcc.uchile.cl

Abstract. One popular approach to object design proposes to identify responsibilities from software contracts, apply a number of principles to assign them to objects, and finally construct an object interaction that realizes the contract. This three-step activity is currently a manual process that is time-consuming and error-prone, and is among the most challenging activities in object-oriented development. In this paper, we present a model transformation that partially automates this activity. Such a transformation is modularized in three stages. The first stage automatically transforms a software contract to a trace of state modification actions. In the second stage the designer manually extends the trace with design decisions. Finally, the extended trace is automatically transformed to an object interaction in the third stage. A prototype of the whole transformation was developed and successfully applied to a case study from the literature. Our technique allows the extraction of valuable information from software contracts, provides a bridge between analysis and design artifacts, and significantly reduces the effort of interaction design.

1 Introduction

Responsibility-Driven Design (RDD) [26] is a popular approach to object design. Its core activity is the definition of object interactions from a system behavioral specification, by identifying and assigning *responsibilities* to objects. A responsibility is a '*knowing*' or '*doing*' obligation of an element. Different methods base their design stage on such an approach. One of those methods is [11], which is oriented to information-intensive software systems.

An object interaction specifies how messages are exchanged over time between object roles within a collaboration [16]. In turn, a possible approach to a system behavioral specification involves treating the system as a black box and identifying its public operations [5], usually called *system operations*. Conceptually, the state of a system is specified by a Domain Model, and a system operation can be understood as a command or partial function that operates on that state. Larman in [11] further proposes to identify system operations from use case scenarios, and to specify their semantics using software contracts [14]. In that

* The work of A. Vignaga and D. Perovich was partially funded by CONICYT Chile.

A. Vallecillo, J. Gray, A. Pierantonio (Eds.): ICMT 2008, LNCS 5063, pp. 245–259, 2008.

context, a software contract for a system operation expresses a binary relation between its input and output state.

In [11], the purpose of object design is the realization of every use case. A use case realization embodies an object interaction for each system operation identified for the use case, and a proper class model enabling these interactions. Building an object interaction essentially involves three steps: (*i*) identify responsibilities, (*ii*) assign them to objects, and (*iii*) express them as message flows. In step (*i*) responsibilities are identified by inspecting pre- and postconditions of the software contract associated to the system operation. In step (*ii*) participating objects are determined, as responsibilities are distributed among them. General Responsibility Software Assignment Patterns (GRASP) reduce the search space, and allow to avoid common pitfalls. In (*iii*) responsibilities are expressed as message flows among the participating objects and the interaction is effectively defined. This involves the creation of a UML interaction diagram expressing the result. During such a process, a designer can probe the decisions made during the previous step and apply corrective actions if required. As a consequence, steps (*ii*) and (*iii*) are usually carried out concurrently.

This approach exhibits a number of shortcomings. In step (*i*), no systematic technique is provided for responsibility identification, and thus it heavily relies on the designer's intuition about the problem. For step (*ii*) GRASP provides different design alternatives. In some cases GRASP can be applied straightforwardly, but in others, the designer needs to make trade-off decisions. In step (*iii*), no systematic technique is proposed for expressing responsibilities as flows of messages. A designer must repeatedly figure out the set of messages that are required for fulfilling each responsibility. Additionally, the representational gap between software contracts and object interactions is significative: software contracts are declarative analysis artifacts expressed as text, while object interactions are imperative design models expressed as diagrams. In most practical cases such a gap is even more significant since contracts are seldom specified due to a poor cost/benefit ratio; building a precise and useful contract is usually costly, and extracting information from it is performed ad hoc. Therefore, designing an object interaction is one of the most challenging activities in object-oriented development. Currently, this activity is a manual process that is time-consuming and error-prone, and whose success highly depends on the designer's skills.

In this paper, we present a technique which partially automates the generation of an object interaction from a software contract. We understand the steps already discussed as concerns that do not need to be sequentially addressed. Our technique interleaves these concerns and is organized in three stages, as shown in Fig. 1. In the first stage, we express contracts for system operations using a relational model transformation language. An engine capable of executing such specifications on a model of a source state will then be able to produce a model of the target state. Particularly, the engine modifies, or more concretely, performs a set of actions on the source state in order to produce the proper target state. Such a set of actions can be regarded as a trace of the execution leading from the source to the target state, and hence as a set of 'doing' responsibilities.

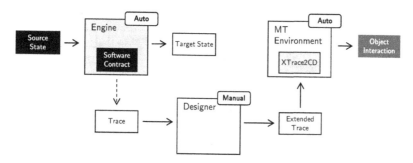

Fig. 1. The three stages of the technique. Black boxes are inputs, dark greyed boxes are outputs, and light grayed boxes are specific tools.

In the second stage the designer applies GRASP and augments the trace with responsibility assignments. Although a default assignment might be automatically chosen, manual intervention provides flexibility. In the third stage we apply another model transformation to the extended trace for producing the object interaction, in the form of a UML communication diagram. Such a transformation encodes the knowledge about generating message flows, but also identifies and assigns other responsibilities from the Domain Model if required.

Current work on MDE technologies tends to focus on producing implementation and deployment artifacts from detailed design models [7]. Our technique provides a bridge between analysis and design artifacts, allowing a significant reduction in the effort for interaction design. It also increases the value of contracts as it presents a systematic technique for extracting information from them. A prototype of the whole transformation which is detailed in [24] was successfully applied to the complete case study introduced in [11].

The rest of the paper is organized as follows. In Sect. 2 we motivate our technique by discussing manual interaction design on a concrete example. Section 3 describes our technique and noteworthy details are presented in Sect. 4. Related work is presented in Sect. 5, and Sect. 6 concludes and suggests further work.

2   Motivating Example

In this section we use an example for motivating the addressed problem and informally explaining the manual generation of object interactions. The example is based on the NextGen Point-of-Sale (POS) system introduced in [11]. A POS system is a computerized application used to record sales and handle payments in a retail store, which is deployed on each register. A Domain Model for a POS is illustrated in Fig. 2. The main use case in such a system is *Process Sale*, which deals with customers buying products at the store. Its main success scenario involves creating a new sale using system operation `makeNewSale()`, adding products to that sale using `enterItem()`, ending the sale using `endSale()`, and recording the payment using `makeCashPayment()`. Handling check payments belongs to an alternative scenario. In what follows we only focus on `enterItem()`.

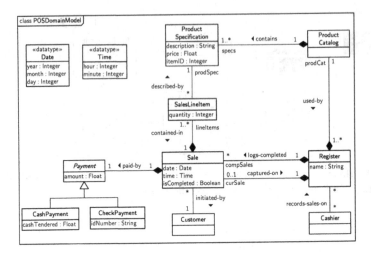

Fig. 2. Domain Model for the POS system

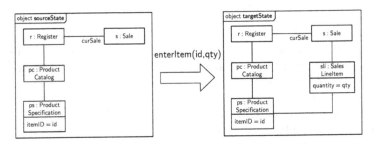

Fig. 3. Snapshots exemplifying the effect of `enterItem()` on the system state

The semantics of `enterItem(id,qty)` system operation can be specified using a software contract. Different versions of such a contract with varying degrees of formality are shown in [24]. Textually, its precondition requires a sale s to be underway, a product specification ps with itemID equal to parameter id in the product catalog, and a positive value for qty. In turn, the postcondition ensures that s has a new line item and its quantity attribute equals qty, and there is a link relating such line item and the product specification identified by id. By inspecting this contract, it can be *deduced* that such specification can be realized by the following sequence of actions on a system state, also called a *trace*: (*i*) create an instance sli of class SalesLineItem, (*ii*) set sli.quantity to qty, (*iii*) link sli to s, and (*iv*) link sli to ps. The effect on a sample state of such realization scheme is shown using a visual contract [13] in Fig. 3; sourceState represents a canonical state satisfying the preconditions discussed above, and the result of executing `enterItem()` on that particular state is represented by targetState.

The design of a system operation raises a number of design problems. Some of them are independent of the particular system operation, for example, which

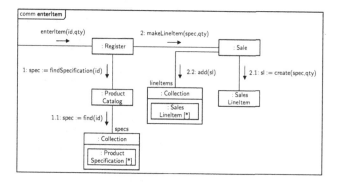

Fig. 4. Object interaction for `enterItem()`

class should handle the system operation call. Other problems are specific to the operation and are introduced by the trace, for example, which class should create instances of class SalesLineItems. GRASP address these problems by suggesting a reduced set of different solutions to each of them. Applying GRASP means choosing one of the solutions. The alternatives are discussed in a later section. The application of GRASP for `enterItem()` is as follows. Applying GRASP *Controller* class Register is chosen for handling the system operation. Action (*i*) in the trace introduces the problem of defining the responsible for creating line items. By GRASP *Creator* class Sale is chosen. Action (*ii*) introduces the problem of setting an attribute of a line item. By GRASP *Expert* class Sale is the responsible. In turn, the problem of linking sales to line items is introduced by action (*iii*). Again by *Expert*, class Sale is chosen. Finally, action (*iv*) introduces the problem of linking line items to product specifications, which in turn introduces a number of subproblems. By *Expert*, a sale is chosen as the responsible for handing the product specification to a line item. The product specification must be found and by *Expert* the catalog is chosen as the responsible for doing that. Similarly, by *Expert* again, the register is chosen as the responsible for retrieving a specification from the catalog and also passing it to the sale. Figure 4 illustrates an object interaction which fulfills the contract and reflects the responsibility assignment just discussed.

3   From Software Contracts to Object Interactions

In this section we present an overview of the technique while the next section discusses some noteworthy details. An operational description of the automated stages is presented in [24].

The purpose of the first stage is to find a sequence of atomic state changes needed to achieve the same effect as the system operation would have. A system operation is a partial function $O : State \hookrightarrow State$. A software contract defines a relation $R \subseteq State \times State$ such that $O(\sigma_1) = \sigma_2$ iff $(\sigma_1, \sigma_2) \in R$, provided that the contract is not underspecified. A contract may be expressed in a relational

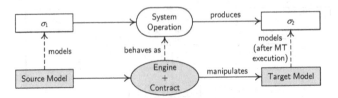

Fig. 5. A system operation transforms system state σ_1 to σ_2. A relational engine transforms models that model such states. **Target Model** is a copy of **Source Model** and thus models σ_1 before the engine executes; **Target Model** models σ_2 only after the execution.

model transformation language [4]. Specifications expressed in relational languages are in its pure form non-executable, however they can be given executable semantics [6]. Different languages [1,8,12] propose their own execution semantics, however they share the same underlying principle. Relation R has an associated transformation $\vec{R} : State \times State \hookrightarrow State$ where $\vec{R}$ looks at a pair of models (ϕ_1, ϕ_2) and figures out how to modify ϕ_2 so as to enforce the relation R, returning the modified version, so that $(\phi_1, \vec{R}(\phi_1, \phi_2)) \in R$ [19]. If a system operation contract is executed by an engine, with both source and target models modeling the same state, then the target model will be modified so as to make both of them satisfy every relation in the contract. This means that the engine exhibits the same behavior as the system operation specified by the contract, that is $\vec{R}(\sigma_1, \sigma_1) = O(\sigma_1)$; see Fig. 5. Even more important is that the engine knows how to manipulate the (copy of the) source state for transforming it into the target state. Such a manipulation can be expressed in terms of actions on the system state and is the main result of the first stage. Such actions represent 'doing' responsibilities and we call them the *trace* of the transformation, as discussed in Sect. 2. For expressing such actions we defined a Domain Specific Language (DSL) which is presented in the next section. The present stage is aligned with the notion of diagram reconciliation, where it is assumed as possible to discover what changed in a model during a transformation [2]. These actions can also be regarded as the difference between the two models of states.

The purpose of the second stage is to generate an *extended trace* consisting of a trace and design decisions; the trace from the first stage is augmented with responsibility assignments resulting from the application of GRASP. The responsibilities we address are: (*a*) to receive and coordinate the system operation, (*b*) to create a new instance of a class, and (*c*) to know a value which is calculated using attributes of different objects. For (*a*), GRASP *Controller* needs to be applied. Alternatives are an object representing the overall system, or an object representing the use case within which the system operation is called. In the POS example of Sect. 2 the former alternative was chosen. For (*b*), GRASP *Creator* proposes to assign such a responsibility to a particular class. It needs to be applied to every class involved in a *CreateAction* within the trace. In the POS example, a new SalesLineItem needs to be created and class Sale is its creator. For (*c*), GRASP *Expert* proposes to assign such a responsibility to the class that has the information necessary to fulfil it. In many cases, a class has all the information required and the assignment can be done straightforwardly, but in other cases the information is distributed among several objects. In the POS example, the responsibility of obtaining the product specification corresponding to the new line item is distributed among the register, the product catalog and the current sale. The process of augmenting the trace can be regarded as a model transformation which is currently performed manually but which is intended to be fully interactive. Such interactivity provides high flexibility to the designer. However, the structure of the Domain Model provides valuable information that helps in choosing among alternatives. For example, it tells who is the owner of certain attributes (for applying *Expert*), and who and how is associated to a class that needs to be instantiated (for applying *Creator*). Therefore, this transformation could be partially automated by defining default choices (not necessarily optimal, though) for each case.

The purpose of the third stage is to produce an object interaction that fulfills the software contract and thus realizes the behavior of the associated system operation. This is achieved by applying a model transformation that processes the extended trace. Based on the models of system states (i.e. snapshots) involved in the first stage, the transformation generates a graph as the basis of the expected communication diagram, and transforms actions to flows of messages among participating objects (i.e. nodes in the generated graph) using responsibility assignments explicitly found in the extended trace and implicitly found in the Domain Model.

4   Technical Details

4.1   Deriving the Trace

We assume a loose semantic interpretation for the contracts of the system operations, and express them using a relational model transformation language; for example, Fig. 6 shows the contract for `enterItem()` using QVT-like syntax. A software contract is defined as one or more binary relations between the source state and the target state. Each relation is a pair of predicates, one over the source state (i.e. precondition) and the other over both states (i.e. postcondition). Contracts built on multiple relations tend to be simpler, as disjunctions occurring in the precondition can be split across several relations, and their associated implication connectives for case analysis are no longer needed in the postcondition. For example, the single-relation contract on the left can be expressed as the two relations on the right:

$$\textbf{pre:} \;\; P_1 \vee P_2 \qquad\qquad\qquad \textbf{pre:} \;\; P_1 \qquad \textbf{pre:} \;\; P_2$$
$$\textbf{post:} \; P_1 \rightarrow Q_1 \wedge P_2 \rightarrow Q_2 \qquad \textbf{post:} \; Q_1 \qquad \textbf{post:} \; Q_2$$

These predicates use specification variables [10] for relating both states. Such variables are initialized when checking the precondition on the source state and their values are used when enforcing the postcondition. By this means, a postcondition can also express properties about the source state. This leads to more compact expressions, and avoids the use of constructs for accessing the source

```
 1  transformation enterItem(sourceState:POSDomainModel, targetState : POSDomainModel) {
 2      key Register(name);
 3      key ProductSpecification(itemID);
 4      key Sale(date, time);
 5      input parameter id : Integer;
 6      input parameter qty : Integer;
 7
 8      top relation SystemOperation {
 9          vname : String;
10          vdate : Date;
11          vtime : Time;
12
13          checkonly domain sourceState r : Register {
14              name = vname;
15              curSale = s : Sale {date = vdate, time = vtime},
16              prodCat = pc : ProductCatalog {
17                  prodSpec = ps : ProductSpecification {itemID = id}
18              }
19          };
20          enforce domain targetState r' : Register {
21              name = vname,
22              curSale = s' : Sale {
23                  date = vdate,
24                  time = vtime,
25                  lineItem = sli' : SalesLineItem {
26                      quantity = qty,
27                      prodSpec = ps' : ProductSpecification {itemID = id}
28                  }
29              }
30          };
31          when { qty > 0 }
32      }
33  }
```

Fig. 6. Transformation for `enterItem()` in QVT Relations

state such as OCL's @pre or JML's \old. For example, assuming sli as a known instance of SalesLineItem, the contract on the left can be expressed with specification variables as the contract on the right:

pre: $qty > 0$ **post:** $sli.quantity = sli.quantity@pre + qty$	**var:** $q:Integer$ **pre:** $qty > 0 \wedge sli.quantity = q$ **post:** $sli.quantity = q + qty$

Also, as a system operation may have arguments and a result, predicates can refer to input parameters and the postcondition must specify the returned values whenever required.

For processing a contract, a canonical state is chosen to feed the relational transformation engine. Such a state must satisfy the preconditions and conform to the Domain Model, and can be regarded as the left part of a visual contract [13]. Provided that both source and target models model the canonical state, while processing the contract, the engine enforces every relation in it in sequence by manipulating the target model, according to the structure specified by the Domain Model. Such a manipulation takes the form of a sequence of actions on the model of the system state. They correspond to a subset of UML actions [9] formalized in [22], and allow creating objects, linking and unlinking pairs of objects, and setting values of attributes. Explicit object deletion is not supported; an object is implicitly deleted when unreachable.

An engine must decide which actions are required and this cannot be achieved for arbitrary boolean expressions within postconditions. Their form is restricted to expressions that reduce to a conjunction of terms of the form: (i) result $=$ $\langle$exp$\rangle$, (ii) $\langle$obj$\rangle$.$\langle$prop$\rangle$ $=$ $\langle$exp$\rangle$, or (iii) $\langle$obj$\rangle$.$\langle$prop$\rangle$ $\neq$ $\langle$exp$\rangle$. Terms as (i) are used for specifying the returned value, and terms of the form (ii) and (iii) suffice for deriving any of the state manipulation actions. In (ii), when prop is an attribute, and hence exp reduces to a data value, a **setAction** is induced. In the example of Fig. 6, this is the case for lines 23, 24 and 26. Otherwise prop must be a role of an association end opposite to obj, and exp reduces to an object, namely obj'. A **linkAction** involving obj and obj' is induced (lines 25 and 27 in the example). When at most one object can be linked to either obj or obj', **unlinkAction**s are also required for disconnecting them from the already connected object. Additionally, when obj' does not exist in the target state, a **createAction** is induced (line 25 in the example). In (iii), exp must reduce to an object and prop can only be an opposite role, and hence an **unlinkAction** is induced. Clearly, incomplete traces are obtained from underspecified contracts. Finally, the sequential order of actions within the trace takes their precedence into account, e.g. an object must be created before being linked to another object.

4.2 Expressing the Extended Trace

An *extended trace* is a model which is an instance of the ExtendedTraceMM metamodel. Such a metamodel defines the notion of an ExtendedTrace as an aggregation of the different pieces of information required to derive the object interaction:

Parameters. Input parameters are used for setting attributes and for finding objects. Output parameters are used for returning values.

Search values. A search value relates a class and the input parameter used for finding specific objects of that class.

Domain Model. A reference to the Domain Model is preserved for typing instance specifications within the trace. It conforms to the Classes diagram of the Kernel package of the UML metamodel [9].

Snapshots. A reference to the pair of snapshots representing the source and target states is preserved for declaring instance specifications within the trace. They conform to the Instances diagram of the Kernel package of the UML metamodel.

Actions. The sequence of actions encoding responsibilities. Actions' metamodel is based on the IntermediateActions package of UML. Particularly, **createAction** is extended in order to contain nested actions for expressing object initialization.

GRASP. The application of GRASP encoding responsibility assignments. This part of the metamodel is discussed next.

Figure 7 details the part of the ExtendedTraceMM metamodel concerning the application of GRASP. This metamodel reuses a number of metaclasses from

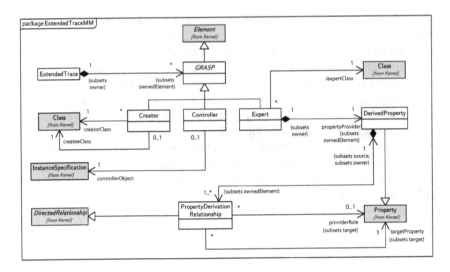

Fig. 7. The GRASP diagram of the ExtendedTraceMM package

the Kernel package of UML, colored in grey in the figure. Metaclass Controller represents an application of *Controller*, and the InstanceSpecification responsible of controlling the system operation is associated. Creator represents an application of *Creator*, and the involved classes are related by two separate associations. Finally, Expert represents an application of *Expert* that assigns the responsibility of knowing how a property is derived; straightforward applications of *Expert* are handled on the fly during the third stage. Expert has associated the DerivedProperty and the expert class. A derived property is a specialization of a standard Property, and is related to the properties that are required for its calculation (targetProperty role). Since there may be more than one association from the expert class to the owner class of a required property, that relation (metaclass PropertyDerivationRelationship) also specifies which opposite association end (providerRole role) needs to be used. For the POS example, instances of these classes can be used for expressing that the total of a sale is calculated using the subtotals of its sale line items, and so forth.

In Fig. 8 the extended trace for enterItem() is shown. Input parameter id is used as a search value for finding specific instances of ProductSpecification (e.g. message 1.1 in Fig. 4). Actions nested in the creation of sli specify the responsibilities involved in its initialization. Finally, Sale is the creator of SalesLineItem, and object r from sourceState is the controller of the system operation.

4.3   Synthesizing the Interaction

The third and last part of our technique consists of a model transformation called XTrace2CD that produces the object interaction. The source model of this transformation is the extended trace produced during the second stage, and the

```
 1  xtrace enterItem(id : Integer, qty : Integer) {
 2
 3       domain model POSDomainModel;
 4       snapshots sourceState, targetState;
 5
 6       search value id of ProductSpecification;
 7
 8       createAction sli : SalesLineItem {
 9            linkAction s, sli, contained-in;
10            setAction sli, quantity, qty;
11            linkAction sli, ps, described-by;
12       }
13
14       creator Sale of SalesLineItem;
15       controller r;
16  }
```

Fig. 8. Extended trace for `enterItem()`

target model is a UML communication diagram whose metamodel [23] restricts UML's to our practical needs.

The target model can be understood as a directed multigraph of objects, where a particular edge, called the *entry point* of the diagram, represents the message which starts the interaction. Such a message corresponds to the system operation, and by convention it has no source object and it is handled by the controller. The first step of the transformation consists of generating the entry point. In the second step, the sequence of actions included in the extended trace is iteratively processed in order. For each action a set of messages is produced for resolving the corresponding sub-interaction. This set involves one or more messages for the action itself, and since the controller is ultimately the source of every action in the interaction, the set also involves a path of messages from the controller to the object performing the action. Arguments required for performing the action, such as input parameters or objects, are collected along such a path. In what follows we briefly discuss the processing of each kind of action; a detailed example on a concrete extended trace can be found in [24].

Except for objects modeling collections, the structure of the target state is similar to that of the communication diagram (see objects and links of targetState in Fig. 3, and in the interaction in Fig. 4). In general, a merge of the source and target state is therefore used as the basis for the structure of the interaction. A [**createAction** c : C] induces a create message from an instance of the creator of C to object c. Nested actions are used for selecting the specific source of the message, its arguments, and possible nested sub-interactions. A [**linkAction** a, b, r] induces a message from an object which has visibility on a and b. The target of such a message is a which receives b as an argument, or viceversa, depending on the existing applications of GRASP *Expert*. Depending on the upper bound of multiplicity in the proper end of r, the insertion of the argument into a collection may be required as a sub-interaction. An [**unlinkAction** a, b, r] is treated similarly, but the possible sub-interaction could involve the removal of the argument from the collection instead. Finally, when not occurring as a nested action, a [**setAction** o, a, v] induces a message to o from an object which has visibility to it and has access to value v.

4.4   Tool Support

As a proof of concept for our technique we developed a prototype of the two tools shown as light greyed boxes in Fig. 1. The first tool named Engine is a reduced relational model transformation engine developed in Prolog. Its execution semantics is based on QVT Relations [8]. The engine processes relational model transformations as discussed in Sect. 4.1 and is also capable of producing the proper trace. The second tool named XTrace2CD is an imperative model transformation implemented in Kermeta [15] which synthesizes interactions as explained in Sect. 4.3. The details of both implementations are reported in [24].

We applied our technique to the complete *Process Sale* use case of the POS case study described in Sect. 2 using these tools. We defined the required contracts in our variant of QVT Relations for every system operation, and used the first tool for producing the corresponding traces. All traces are correct with respect to their associated contract. These traces matched those reported in [21] where their correctness was formally proved. In turn, we applied the second tool to the extended version of the traces for deriving the object interactions. Such a result matched that reported in [11]. The implementation of the prototype as well as all artifacts involved in the complete case study are available at http://mate.dcc.uchile.cl/research/tools/eoisc_mt/.

5   Related Work

The generation of design artifacts from analysis specifications has been extensively addressed, with varying levels of automation and involving different source and target artifacts. For example, [20] fully automates the generation of statecharts from scenarios and properties, [25] assists the generation of a class model from a formal requirements specification, and [17] automates the generation of pseudocode from a set of sequence diagrams. We use software contracts which are a common technique for specifying behavior, and we produce object interactions which are an abstraction of the runtime view of object-oriented systems.

The activity of generating object interactions from software contracts, as described in Sect. 2, is presented in [11]. This is a manual process where the developer must deduce responsibilities from software contracts, assign every single responsibility to objects using GRASP, and finally manually build the communication diagram. Our technique automates most of this process.

In [18], design is also based on RDD and conceived as a sequence of transformations performed in two separate phases. First, from an informal text-based problem description, a generative phase produces an initial design similar to a Domain Model, and identifies a set of responsibilities. Although they propose some techniques for automating this task, a great deal of manual intervention is required. Second, a transformational phase successively reconfigures the design. Such transformations are aimed at balancing the cohesion of participating classes, and based on design patterns applications. This approach uses one single design artifact called *collaboration graph* which can be regarded as a Design Class Diagram [11] but with no attributes or operations. The output of our technique is more detailed as it focuses on the dynamic aspects of the design, from which a Design Class Diagram can be automatically generated [23].

Visual contracts [13] are an alternative approach to software contracts à la Meyer. The behavior of an operation is specified by providing a pair of snapshots exemplifying its effect on a particular state, which conforms to a particular class diagram. Such a class diagram is transformed to structural Java code, while visual contracts are transformed to JML specifications that annotate operations within the Java code. The developer then manually implements methods for such operations. Although our technique uses snapshots that resemble a visual contract, its main input are traditional software contracts as they are more expressive. While their approach relies on manual method implementation, we generate method realizations in the form of a trace and object interactions.

In [3], a mechanism for generating a set of operations for a given class diagram is presented. Such a set embodies basic command operations which describe how the system state can evolve. State modifications are also expressed in terms of actions, and similarly to our technique, operations on specific classes need to be derived for supporting them. Furthermore, operations derived using this approach are intended to be executable, and the notion of dependency among actions is thus introduced. In our technique, such dependencies are represented by the ordering of actions within the trace. Finally, although the proposed mechanism could be automated, no tool support is reported.

6   Conclusions and Further Work

In this paper we presented a technique which automates most of the process for extracting object interactions out of software contracts using model transformations. For exploring the feasibility of our technique we developed a prototype tool which was successfully applied to a well-known case study from the literature.

This technique embodies the practical application of several aspects of Model Driven Engineering (MDE). We consider software contracts as relational model transformations, a relational engine is used in a non-standard fashion, a DSL was defined, and different approaches to model transformations (i.e., relational and imperative) were applied. As a whole, our technique can be regarded as a composition of model transformations. In scenarios where a complex transformation is divided into sub-transformations, defining their scope is not straightforward and the form of intermediate models (e.g. the extended trace) varies significantly. Applying our technique, software contracts can become cost-effective since important information can be extracted from them, and also such information can be used for producing other artifacts. The technique also provides a direct mechanism for testing software contracts, as the snapshot generated by the engine can be examined for checking if the transformation produced the expected result. Finally, an engine executing contracts on the actual system state, rather than on a model of it, can be understood as a functional prototype of the system at an early stage of development.

The technique we have developed currently lacks two desirable features. First, given the sequential form of the actions within a trace, it is not possible to perform case analysis. There are a number of situations where disjunctions could be required: (a) cases based on the values of input parameters, (b) cases based on the values returned by messages within the interaction, mainly for (i) alternative paths of execution imposed by business rules, and (ii) error handling. Case (b.ii) is generally ignored when specifying interactions since only typical behavior is usually shown. On the other hand, cases (a) and (b.i) may be addressed in a similar fashion. In this scenario, a different source state should be used for each case. Using several relations in the contract for expressing cases as discussed in Sect. 4.1 simplifies the identification of such canonical states. From them, different traces are generated as before, and may be merged afterwards; [17] proposes a technique aiming a similar purpose. Second, a common practice in object-oriented design is to introduce classes not present in the problem domain. This usually occurs as a consequence of applying GRASP *High Cohesion* and *Pure Fabrication* [11] or design patterns. Our technique restricts interactions to instances of classes in the Domain Model. Simons et al. [18] propose a technique based on model transformations that detects cases of low cohesive classes and suggest to restructure the design by applying design patterns. This technique can be applied after generating the interactions, hence improving the object design.

As further work we plan to enhance our technique for including the features just discussed, and also for achieving some degree of automation within the second stage. We also plan to evolve the existing prototype towards an integrated tool that fully realizes our technique.

References

1. Akehurst, D.H., Kent, S., Patrascoiu, O.: A Relational Approach to Defining and Implementing Transformations between Metamodels. Software and System Modeling 2(4), 215–239 (2003)
2. Alanen, M., Lundkvist, T., Porres, I.: Creating and Reconciling Diagrams after Executing Model Transformations. Science of Computer Programming 68(3), 155–178 (2007)
3. Cabot, J., Gómez, C.: Deriving Operation Contracts from UML Class Diagrams. In: Engels, G., Opdyke, B., Schmidt, D.C., Weil, F. (eds.) MODELS 2007. LNCS, vol. 4735, pp. 196–210. Springer, Heidelberg (2007)
4. Cariou, E., Marvie, R., Seinturier, L., Duchien, L.: OCL for the Specification of Model Transformation Contracts. In: OCL and Model-Driven Engineering UML 2004 Workshop, Lisbon, Portugal (2004)
5. Coleman, D., Arnold, P., Bodoff, S., Dollin, C., Gilchrist, H., Hayes, F., Jeremaes, P.: Object-Oriented Development: The Fusion Method. Prentice-Hall, Inc., Upper Saddle River (1994)
6. Czarnecki, K., Helsen, S.: Feature-based Survey of Model Transformation Approaches. IBM Systems Journal 45(3), 621–645 (2006)

7. France, R., Rumpe, B.: Model-driven Development of Complex Software: A Research Roadmap. In: FOSE 2007: Future of Software Engineering 2007, pp. 37–54. IEEE Computer Society, Los Alamitos (2007)
8. O. M. G. Inc. Meta Object Facility (MOF) 2.0. Query/View/Transformation Specification. OMG Document ptc/05-11-01 (November 2005)
9. O. M. G. Inc. UML Superstructure, v2.1.1. OMG Document formal/07-02-05 (February 2007)
10. Kaldewaij, A.: Programming: The Derivation of Algorithms. Prentice-Hall International Series in Computer Science (1990)
11. Larman, C.: Applying UML and Patterns: An Introduction to Object-Oriented Analysis and Design and Iterative Development, 3rd edn. Prentice Hall, Englewood Cliffs (2004)
12. Lawley, M., Raymond, K.: Implementing a Practical Declarative Logic-based Model Transformation Engine. In: SAC 2007, pp. 971–977 (2007)
13. Lohmann, M., Sauer, S., Engels, G.: Executable Visual Contracts. In: 2005 IEEE Symposium on Visual Languages and Human-Centric Computing (VL/HCC 2005), Dallas, TX, USA, pp. 63–70. IEEE Computer Society, Los Alamitos (2005)
14. Meyer, B.: Object-Oriented Software Construction. 2 edn. Prentice-Hall, Inc., Upper Saddle River, NJ, USA (1997)
15. Muller, P.-A., Fleurey, F., Jézéquel, J.-M.: Weaving Executability into Object-Oriented Meta-languages. In: Briand, L.C., Williams, C. (eds.) MoDELS 2005. LNCS, vol. 3713, pp. 264–278. Springer, Heidelberg (2005)
16. Rumbaugh, J., Jacobson, I., Booch, G.: Unified Modeling Language Reference Manual, 2nd edn. Pearson Higher Education (2004)
17. Selonen, P., Systä, T., Koskimies, K.: Generating Structured Implementation Schemes from UML Sequence Diagrams. In: TOOLS 2001, pp. 317–330 (2001)
18. Simons, A.J.H., Snoeck, M., Hung, K.S.Y.: Using Design Patterns to Reveal the Competence of Object-Oriented Methods in System-Level Design. International Journal of Computer Systems Science and Engineering 14(6), 343–352 (1999)
19. Stevens, P.: Bidirectional Model Transformations in QVT: Semantic Issues and Open Questions. In: Engels, G., Opdyke, B., Schmidt, D.C., Weil, F. (eds.) MODELS 2007. LNCS, vol. 4735, pp. 1–15. Springer, Heidelberg (2007)
20. Uchitel, S., Brunet, G., Chechik, M.: Behaviour model synthesis from properties and scenarios. In: ICSE 2007, pp. 34–43. IEEE Computer Society, Los Alamitos (2007)
21. Vignaga, A.: A Case Study in Formal Reasoning about the Use of State Modification Primitives. Technical Report 04-09, InCo/Pedeciba (2004)
22. Vignaga, A.: A Formal Semantics of State Modification Primitives of Object-Oriented Systems. Master's thesis, Pedeciba and Universidad de la República, Uruguay (February 2004)
23. Vignaga, A., Bastarrica, M.C.: Transforming System Operations' Interactions into a Design Class Diagram. In: SAC 2007, pp. 993–997 (2007)
24. Vignaga, A., Perovich, D., Bastarrica, M.C.: On Extracting a Design out of Software Contracts. Technical Report TR/DCC-2007-1, DCC, Universidad de Chile (2007)
25. Wahono, R.S., Far, B.H.: A Framework for Object Identification and Refinement Process in Object-Oriented Analysis and Design. In: IEEE ICCI, pp. 351–360. IEEE Computer Society, Los Alamitos (2002)
26. Wirfs-Brock, R., McKean, A.: Object Design: Roles, Responsibilities, and Collaborations. Pearson Education (2002)

Author Index

Lecture Notes in Computer Science

Sublibrary 2: Programming and Software Engineering

For information about Vols. 1– 4467
please contact your bookseller or Springer

Vol. 4799: A. Holzinger (Ed.), HCI and Usability for Medicine and Health Care. XVI, 458 pages. 2007.

Vol. 4789: M. Butler, M.G. Hinchey, M.M. Larrondo-Petrie (Eds.), Formal Methods and Software Engineering. VIII, 387 pages. 2007.

Vol. 4767: F. Arbab, M. Sirjani (Eds.), International Symposium on Fundamentals of Software Engineering. XIII, 450 pages. 2007.

Vol. 4765: A. Moreira, J. Grundy (Eds.), Early Aspects: Current Challenges and Future Directions. X, 199 pages. 2007.

Vol. 4764: P. Abrahamsson, N. Baddoo, T. Margaria, R. Messnarz (Eds.), Software Process Improvement. XI, 225 pages. 2007.

Vol. 4762: K.S. Namjoshi, T. Yoneda, T. Higashino, Y. Okamura (Eds.), Automated Technology for Verification and Analysis. XIV, 566 pages. 2007.

Vol. 4758: F. Oquendo (Ed.), Software Architecture. XVI, 340 pages. 2007.

Vol. 4757: F. Cappello, T. Herault, J. Dongarra (Eds.), Recent Advances in Parallel Virtual Machine and Message Passing Interface. XVI, 396 pages. 2007.

Vol. 4753: E. Duval, R. Klamma, M. Wolpers (Eds.), Creating New Learning Experiences on a Global Scale. XII, 518 pages. 2007.

Vol. 4749: B.J. Krämer, K.-J. Lin, P. Narasimhan (Eds.), Service-Oriented Computing – ICSOC 2007. XIX, 629 pages. 2007.

Vol. 4748: K. Wolter (Ed.), Formal Methods and Stochastic Models for Performance Evaluation. X, 301 pages. 2007.

Vol. 4741: C. Bessière (Ed.), Principles and Practice of Constraint Programming – CP 2007. XV, 890 pages. 2007.

Vol. 4735: G. Engels, B. Opdyke, D.C. Schmidt, F. Weil (Eds.), Model Driven Engineering Languages and Systems. XV, 698 pages. 2007.

Vol. 4716: B. Meyer, M. Joseph (Eds.), Software Engineering Approaches for Offshore and Outsourced Development. X, 201 pages. 2007.

Vol. 4709: F.S. de Boer, M.M. Bonsangue, S. Graf, W.-P. de Roever (Eds.), Formal Methods for Components and Objects. VIII, 297 pages. 2007.

Vol. 4680: F. Saglietti, N. Oster (Eds.), Computer Safety, Reliability, and Security. XV, 548 pages. 2007.

Vol. 4670: V. Dahl, I. Niemelä (Eds.), Logic Programming. XII, 470 pages. 2007.

Vol. 4652: D. Georgakopoulos, N. Ritter, B. Benatallah, C. Zirpins, G. Feuerlicht, M. Schoenherr, H.R. Motahari-Nezhad (Eds.), Service-Oriented Computing ICSOC 2006. XVI, 201 pages. 2007.

Vol. 4640: A. Rashid, M. Aksit (Eds.), Transactions on Aspect-Oriented Software Development IV. IX, 191 pages. 2007.

Vol. 4634: H. Riis Nielson, G. Filé (Eds.), Static Analysis. XI, 469 pages. 2007.

Vol. 4620: A. Rashid, M. Aksit (Eds.), Transactions on Aspect-Oriented Software Development III. IX, 201 pages. 2007.

Vol. 4615: R. de Lemos, C. Gacek, A. Romanovsky (Eds.), Architecting Dependable Systems IV. XIV, 435 pages. 2007.

Vol. 4610: B. Xiao, L.T. Yang, J. Ma, C. Muller-Schloer, Y. Hua (Eds.), Autonomic and Trusted Computing. XVIII, 571 pages. 2007.

Vol. 4609: E. Ernst (Ed.), ECOOP 2007 – Object-Oriented Programming. XIII, 625 pages. 2007.

Vol. 4608: H.W. Schmidt, I. Crnković, G.T. Heineman, J.A. Stafford (Eds.), Component-Based Software Engineering. XII, 283 pages. 2007.

Vol. 4591: J. Davies, J. Gibbons (Eds.), Integrated Formal Methods. IX, 660 pages. 2007.

Vol. 4589: J. Münch, P. Abrahamsson (Eds.), Product-Focused Software Process Improvement. XII, 414 pages. 2007.

Vol. 4574: J. Derrick, J. Vain (Eds.), Formal Techniques for Networked and Distributed Systems – FORTE 2007. XI, 375 pages. 2007.

Vol. 4556: C. Stephanidis (Ed.), Universal Access in Human-Computer Interaction, Part III. XXII, 1020 pages. 2007.

Vol. 4555: C. Stephanidis (Ed.), Universal Access in Human-Computer Interaction, Part II. XXII, 1066 pages. 2007.

Vol. 4554: C. Stephanidis (Ed.), Universal Acess in Human Computer Interaction, Part I. XXII, 1054 pages. 2007.

Vol. 4553: J.A. Jacko (Ed.), Human-Computer Interaction, Part IV. XXIV, 1225 pages. 2007.

Vol. 4552: J.A. Jacko (Ed.), Human-Computer Interaction, Part III. XXI, 1038 pages. 2007.

Vol. 4551: J.A. Jacko (Ed.), Human-Computer Interaction, Part II. XXIII, 1253 pages. 2007.

Vol. 4550: J.A. Jacko (Ed.), Human-Computer Interaction, Part I. XXIII, 1240 pages. 2007.

Vol. 4542: P. Sawyer, B. Paech, P. Heymans (Eds.), Requirements Engineering: Foundation for Software Quality. IX, 384 pages. 2007.

Vol. 4536: G. Concas, E. Damiani, M. Scotto, G. Succi (Eds.), Agile Processes in Software Engineering and Extreme Programming. XV, 276 pages. 2007.

Vol. 4530: D.H. Akehurst, R. Vogel, R.F. Paige (Eds.), Model Driven Architecture - Foundations and Applications. X, 219 pages. 2007.

Vol. 4523: Y.-H. Lee, H.-N. Kim, J. Kim, Y.W. Park, L.T. Yang, S.W. Kim (Eds.), Embedded Software and Systems. XIX, 829 pages. 2007.

Vol. 4498: N. Abdennadher, F. Kordon (Eds.), Reliable Software Technologies - Ada-Europe 2007. XII, 247 pages. 2007.

Vol. 4486: M. Bernardo, J. Hillston (Eds.), Formal Methods for Performance Evaluation. VII, 469 pages. 2007.

Vol. 4470: Q. Wang, D. Pfahl, D.M. Raffo (Eds.), Software Process Dynamics and Agility. XI, 346 pages. 2007.

Vol. 4468: M.M. Bonsangue, E.B. Johnsen (Eds.), Formal Methods for Open Object-Based Distributed Systems. X, 317 pages. 2007.